The Joy
of Being
Wrong

The Joy
of Being
Wrong

Original Sin
Through Easter Eyes

JAMES ALISON

Foreword by Sebastian Moore

A Crossroad Herder Book
The Crossroad Publishing Company
New York

The quotation from pp. 129–30 of Thomas A. Carlson's translation of Jean-Luc Marion's *God without Being* on pp. 205–6 appears by kind permission of The University of Chicago Press, Chicago, IL 60637, © 1991 by The University of Chicago. All rights reserved. Published 1991.

The translation of the first five canons of the Council of Trent on original sin, found on pp. 275–82, are taken from Norman Tanner, ed., *Decrees of the Ecumenical Councils*, 2:666–67, and appear by kind permission of Georgetown University Press, Washington DC 20057, © 1990 by Sheed and Ward Limited and Georgetown University Press.

The Crossroad Publishing Company
370 Lexington Avenue, New York, NY 10017

Printed in the United States of America

Library of Congress Cataloging-in-Publication Data
Alison, James, 1959-
    The joy of being wrong : Original Sin through Easter eyes / James Alison.
      p. cm.
    Originally presented as the author's thesis (doctoral) – Jesuit Theology Faculty in Belo Horizonte, Brazil.
    Includes bibliographical references and index.
    ISBN 0-8245-1676-1 (pbk.)
    1. Man (Christian theology) 2. Sin, Original. 3. Jesus Christ – Person and offices. 4. Paschal mystery. 5. Girard, René, 1923- . 6. Catholic Church – Doctrines. I. Title.
BT745.A55 1997
233'.14 – dc21   97-752
                                                CIP

3   4   5   6   7   8   9   10   02

Contents

Foreword

One should, one can, never say of a theological work that it is the definitive statement on its subject. But very occasionally one is tempted to do so, and this book represents that temptation in an acute form. On almost every page of the second part of the book where, having taken his time to establish his method, Alison proceeds to unlock the Christian Scriptures, I have found myself looking at long-familiar texts as if for the first time. Over and over again. One had forgotten that theology could do this — if "forgotten" is the word. Has it ever?

The method is the one that is implicit in the work of René Girard, who, like Schliemann with his shovel "knocking on the crowns of Troy," seems to have disclosed the ever-forgotten and myth-encased collective violence that lies somewhere at the dawn of human time and colors all we think and do. The "memory" of this violence, humanity's family secret, the real facts of life, is something the theologian either can or cannot summon as he or she pores over our texts; and on whether or not a theologian does so depends his or her capacity really to read the story of a man who, all theologians have to agree, is believed to have saved the world by shedding his blood, whatever that could possibly mean.

Salvation through the Blood has in fact been given almost every possible meaning, resulting in frightful cruelty and oppression under the Sign of the Cross. Who would have thought, wondered Urs von Balthasar, that it would fall to a nontheologian to uncover another, and a wholly nourishing meaning? The work of Alison is, on Girard's own avowal, the most profound and thorough theological elaboration of his anthropological insight. Rahner said long ago that what was needed was no longer a theology for man but an anthropology for God. Well, this is it. Taking as his theme a doctrine that much contemporary theology would regard as a nonstarter, that of original sin, Alison uses this doctrine to show us to ourselves in a way that reclaims, and makes once again resonant for us, the word "salvation."

That a work began as a doctoral dissertation is often a disincentive to buying it. In this case, it is an added recommendation. It means that a book filled with brilliant insights into the sacred text has got past the lynx eyes of a director and a doctoral board. All the neces-

sary homework underlies this act of sustained theological attention to
the Good News.

Here, in barest outline, is how I have understood Alison's ground-
work, the elaboration of a lived and generalized anthropology, work
deployed at the cusp between psychology and anthropology.

I naturally think that my desire is mine, is of me, that I am its subject and I know what I want. But so to think is not to see that desire
is *making* me. Desire is awakened in me by the sight of another desiring. This model-aroused desire feels the other as rival, and it is this
over-against-the-otherness that makes me feel *me*. Me is me against. I
discovered this mechanism in myself when I saw that my feeling of being passed over by a superior in the assignment of a job was taking on
a note of moral indignation. The radical *feeling* of being pushed aside,
a jostling, rivalry-shaped feeling, was putting on a high tone of moral
outrage. It was becoming a *duty* to stand up for my rights. Suddenly I
saw that this pseudo-duty was energy-consuming and that I could simply
stop the useless expenditure. I saw this as a newly possible dismantling
of a very old and rusty mechanism. The sense of moral outrage is rivalistic desire clothing itself in the trappings of a self over against another.
Desire now is no longer the mechanism behind the whole business; it
is *my* desire. "I" was there first. Then "I" wanted something, simply
wanted it, and had every reason to do so. But I have completely missed
the fact that the opposite is the real order of events: want becomes me-
against-another-wanting-something. I simply cannot see that the self I
oppose to the other is the creation of desire. The "self" is a cause into
which we pour our energy, and it takes some introspection to realize that
this energy is being spent on maintaining the illusion of an independent,
autonomous self — as opposed, we shall see when we come to the figure
of Jesus, to the self that is the gift to me of the Father of Lights.

Now this mechanism is operative in the familial, social, cultural inter-
connectedness of people. It is waiting to be kicked into operation by any
strong awakening of desire, what the human animal has largely in place
of instinct with its direct line to its object. Nevertheless its result can be
seen to be an illusion, a pseudo-selfhood, as I saw in that incident with
a superior. Now if the mechanism can be seen to be illusion-making,
it cannot be "of our nature." A mistake cannot be of the essence. The
essence is that about which the mistake is made. The fact that this mistake is world-wide and world-old, the very factory of history, does not
make it to be "of our nature."

This mistake, universal and seemingly synonymous with culture and
its institutions — primary among which is scapegoating and victimage,
the stabilizer of our violence — seems to be what is meant, or what could

or should be indicated, by "original sin." To understand this doctrine in
this way is to find for it a psychologically credible version, so that this
deep, world-old shadow on humanity is lifted up by a supernatural modeling for desire such as we have in Jesus, as exemplary living, cognate
teaching, psychic and physical healing, and final critical confrontation
with the whole power that holds in place the universal ego-illusion, a
confrontation that is a lonely act of love off the human scale that, in the
resurrection and explosion of the Spirit, raced through the world creating the new community based on the nonrivalistic modeling of the Son
of God.

The doctrine of original sin, once this basic fact about desire is understood, can be elucidated in a way that deals with all the confusions that
ordinarily beset the doctrine's exposition. Once I really understand, au-
tobiographically, that desire makes me feel *me*, a "me" so real to me that
it easily seems to be the subject of desire rather than desire's puppet,
I am in a position to handle the classic distinction in Catholic theology, blurred in a tragic Protestant theology, between original sin and
"concupiscence." If I may put this into didactic verse:

> The huge mistake about desire
> Is not itself our sin
> But it is living with a liar
> That's sure to do you in.

At last we get clarity around that notion for which vague words abound
because no one is quite clear about him- or herself. People who don't
know themselves are bound to come up with muddled notions where
theology is perforce psychological. "Proneness" to sin is typical — what
a miserably confused word! Its moralistic vagueness ducks the only serious moral question here: what is it, precisely, that original sin leaves
behind of itself in the baptized? In other words what are we up against
as we "work out our salvation"? Are we to think of ourselves as the
recovering alcoholic offered a martini at a party? My mentor Illtyd
Trethowan used to be scathing about the suggestion that our will was
somehow "wobbly" on account of original sin. Lonergan comes near a
specific answer when he describes the effect of original sin as "moral impotence." If he is evoking a sexual metaphor he comes close — though
then he is generalizing from the male form — for sexual impotence is
the unavailability of energy, of élan, of "oomph," for loving. But only
Girard's theory enables us to say *why* this energy is not easily available to us. It is because desire — which is what our primal energy is —
gets hugely diverted into the labyrinths of mimesis, into the pretentious
lie about itself. Thinking I am in love when I am not is a much better

example of it than the proffered martini. Desire has become a cuckoo in the nest of what I take to be my real self, but which is in fact the self-in-rivalry, the self over against.

Once this is deeply understood and identified-with, the tragic utterances of Paul about the almost perverse inefficacy of the law reveal new depths of meaning. The law tells me not to covet, but the "me" that hears this law is already the puppet of the coveting. Who indeed shall deliver me from this? No wonder Paul finds only one answer. With desire universally masquerading as the very self seen in its models, what remedy can there be but a radically innovative countermodeling for mimesis, one who was all that Jesus was and now is, did all that he did, taught as he taught, suffered what he suffered at our hands to be raised to glory in the heart of the believer? When I was able to say that what I take to be moral indignation is a sheer waste of energy that will happily flow another way, I was tuning in, in a small way, to the action of this countermodeling. Conversion is beginning when we become conscious of a redeployment of soul energies.

I'm sorry to be hogging space with this foreword. It is the best way I know to tell you that this is an incredibly good book. I have had to spell it out in my own way in order to commend the book wholeheartedly. What Alison succeeds in doing, miraculously in point of relentless thoroughness, is to show *both* the deep-rooted and all-pervasive character of original sin *and* its nonessential, its non-we character. These opposite emphases represent, for most theological minds, an either-or. Not for Alison — which means, not for someone who has discovered the meta-anthropology for our time, an anthropologically and psychologically credible version of original sin. The theologian who is prepared to explore our tradition with the aid of major literature, self-understanding, and contemplative praying has a key that opens door after door in our Jewish and Christian Scriptures. It is this approach of Alison's that creates the sense, time and again, of understanding the key texts for the first time.

A final point, crucial for Alison's exposition. The deep disorder in our desire is known only by contrast with the new modeling by Jesus crucified and risen. Still it must have started at some time. If it's a mistake, it happened at some time for the first time. But since the *possibility* for this mistake is present once the animal capacity for imitation is vastly enhanced by imagination and intelligence, so that we have culture, there does not seem to be any sense in imagining — as alas the new Catechism seems to be doing — a period, paradisal yet fully cultured, during which this mistake had not yet been made. The notion is unverifiable and unfalsifiable and pointless — unless we think that orthodox Christian belief compels us to posit a prelapsarian state which is recognizable in our own terms. One of the major contributions of this book is to show that it does not. On the contrary, the whole validity of the concept of original sin consists in a sense, most vivid and entirely new for the first Christian communities, of "what it was really like — although we could not realize this — without him and what he's done to us." To think that one is able to imagine a human life rather like ours, a cultural life, happy without Christ, because as yet unfallen, is fatally to trivialize the drama of Gethsemani, Calvary, and the Upper Room, the experience of the people who went through this trauma and tell us its story as the best news there ever was or could be.

Finally, a suggestion. After reading chapter 1, try jumping straight to part 2, cheating in other words; get a taste of the result of the homework done in part 1, as this will stimulate you to examine the foundations. Desire needs a bit of coaxing in order to engage in a rather gruelling bit of self-examination!

SEBASTIAN MOORE
Downside Abbey
July 1997

Introduction

Original sin is a very odd topic. A wide variety of people, irrespective of their profession of faith, their degree of theological training, or the absence of either of these, refer to it as to something obvious, whose meaning can be taken for granted. Yet, whether they want to affirm it or decry it, you'll be lucky indeed if you can get them to tell you what it means. This might put the doctrine on a par with certain items of the British coronation regalia — ancient baubles which process through Parliament year in, year out, but whose exact significance has perished. More than such baubles, however, original sin is capable of arousing a huge depth of feeling: some blame it, and the stage-villain Augustine, its senior brandisher, for the most spectacular crimes against humanity; others see it as a vital control on the self-defeating idealism of those who would restructure the world as though humans might one day be good. What for some is a self-evident truth about human nature is for others a leftover from the paleontology of yesteryear. Almost all would say that original sin has something to do with Adam and Eve, but it is by no means apparent why it should have anything to do with us.

I have, from my youth, been gnawed and chewed — indeed at some level imprisoned — by various of these currents of thought, lost references, opaque promises of some great truth. Yet I have found no work which began to offer satisfaction as to what original sin might mean. Histories of the doctrine exist and are valuable resources. However, a history of a doctrine does not tell you what the doctrine means, any more than form criticism, however polished, of a Bible text tells you what those verses mean. This is not because of a professional failure by historians or form critics, but because meaning is by nature alive to, and structuring of, the present, something we discover to have preceded us at the same time as we collaborate in its creation. There is no original meaning "out there," accessible to historical or archaeological objectivity. "Out there" are vestiges of vision cast in words and structures which serve no longer as a bridge to sight, except as they are synthesized anew.

I have sought then, from within the community of faith which gave birth to the words "original sin" and the concepts which surround them, to give life to the doctrine. This is a theological task, and I mean that in a rather particular sense: I take it that the theologian is one who is chivvied by the Holy Spirit into making available in words dimensions of a revealed vision by which God's people may live. This is done not simply by close adhesion to texts but by the constant work of rediscovery of the newness and freshness of the Gospel as we, compelled and repelled within the community of faith, try to live it out. For it is only that newness and freshness which enable the old formulae to rest snugly in their proper place, neither dominating the discussion nor being simply swept away. Thus, much more important than a proper verbal accuracy is the place of the doctrine within a whole scheme of vision. This is because a doctrine is not primarily something that we are supposed to know "about." Rather it is a constitutive part of the vision which empowers us to be children of God as Church, living grammar with which we learn to forge the intertwined life stories which we hope one day will surprise us as heaven. Where the vision is not available, then however correctly the formulae be cited, the Christian faith is not being taught, and the words have been pressed into the service of a different kingdom.

There have been some simple milestones in my search for the sense of original sin. Very young I learned of Jesus' saying that I should not try to remove the mote from my brother's eye while not taking the beam out of my own. Strange words, long mulled, with no obvious physical meaning, but which suggested a massive and as yet incomprehensible blindness with relation to my (very real) brother which was not something I might overcome by mental or emotional dexterity, but was just there. A blindness furthermore which was not mine alone, but everywhere. If someone had told me of "Jesus' anthropological vision," I wouldn't have known what that person was talking about, but the search to try to give content to this saying was inchoately underway before I understood that it was for the doctrine of original sin that I was searching.

Later I was told that my same-sex orientation was the fruit of original sin. The explanation was proffered as something which justified severe control and which seemed to call for drastic hatred of self in order to be good. But this too was puzzling: why was something which was held to have affected all people equally since Adam to be understood as justifying the massive "no" which Christian people spoke to the depths of my being, when it implied no comparable depth of "no" to the lives of my heterosexual contemporaries?

Later still I was made aware of the Thomistic teaching concerning the goodness of human desire — a striking contrast with the radical Evangelical view concerning the absolute corruption of fallen humanity with which I had been brought up and which I had believed and internalized. This coincided with my becoming aware of the Council of Trent and the way it saw the doctrines of Justification and of original sin as absolutely interdependent. In particular Trent's remarkable observation that concupiscence — *epithumía,* desire — in the baptized is not properly speaking sin, but comes from sin and inclines to sin, awoke in me a sense, not yet capable of being put into words, that here was something liberating if only I were able to give it an anthropological content, make of it something by which I might live.

At about this time I learned of a remark by Hegel to the effect that there is no Jewish doctrine of original sin. And so it turned out: the rabbis simply do not read the Adam and Eve story as Christians have done. This apparently banal observation opened up to me what I had not understood at all: that the doctrine of original sin is not prior to, but follows from and is utterly dependent on, Jesus' resurrection from the dead and thus cannot be understood at all except in the light of that event.

It was, then, with these lenses, questions, anxieties, and longings that I picked up René Girard's book *Things Hidden from the Foundation of the World,* and it was into these preoccupations that Girard's understanding of desire exploded like a depth charge. I felt as though I had been read like an open book — like the woman at the well of Samaria who went to tell her compatriots: "Come, see a man who has told me all that I ever did." For here was an understanding of desire that was both enormously simple and yet capable of yielding all the complexity which we need if we are to tell the truth about ourselves and others. Absolutely aware of the seriously corrupt and death-laden nature of human desire as it structures and moves us, it also shows how human desire as such is a good thing, fully capable of a slow and arduous transformation out of a death-based pattern of social relating into a pattern that is quite without stumbling blocks. I sensed, without knowing how these two were to be related, that Girard's understanding would be able to breathe spirit into the letter of the doctrine and offer a perspective, at once absolutely traditional and completely fresh, by which to live as a Catholic Christian in the late twentieth century.

The book on which you are embarking is my attempt to make the doctrine of original sin available as a constitutive element of any of our attempts to forge the Christian story. In chapter 1 I give a succinct account of mimetic theory — as Girard's understanding of desire is known — since this is to provide the key to all that follows. I then seek, in chapter 2, to sketch out the theological anthropology which flows from that understanding and which I discovered to be astoundingly in tune with the many hints of an implicit anthropology to be found in the texts of the apostolic witness. Chapter 3 is my attempt to work out a basic soteriology in the light of the reading of the New Testament made possible by application of the Girardian understanding. I follow this (somewhat heavy) path because the doctrine of original sin is an ancillary doctrine which is comprehensible only as part of the installation among us of Christ's salvation: indeed, it is my contention that the doctrine is really the explicitation of the critical anthropology which became available to us in the light of salvation. Easier reading begins with chapters 4 to 9, my exploration of this critical anthropological vision in the light of the resurrection. In chapter 10, finally, I attempt to confront the vision with the various signposts by which the magisterium of the Church and two significant theologians, Augustine and Aquinas, have sought to define what is, and what is not, part of the Catholic story.

This book was born as a doctoral dissertation presented at the Jesuit Theology Faculty in Belo Horizonte, Brazil. I am enormously indebted to the members of that faculty for their help and support at key moments of its gestation, and in particular to Ulpiano Vázquez, S.J., my supervisor. My friends Luis Stadelmann, S.J., Johan Konings, S.J., and Alvaro Barreiro, S.J., also made significant contributions, not least by the fraternal nature of the examination to which the latter two treated me. The bulk of the text was written while I was teaching in Cochabamba, Bolivia, where I was much helped by my colleague Antonio Menacho, S.J. I would like to thank Don Goergen, O.P., at that time my superior, whose belief in this work and consequent financial support, enabled me to bring it to completion. René Girard gave me unfailing backing at the time and much encouragement on the road to publication. Michael Leach and John Eagleson of Crossroad have been models of generosity and forbearance as they nudged the text into its final form.

Four people in particular have been the midwives of this work, keeping its author relatively sane, and indeed at times keeping him alive, in ways they can scarcely imagine: Jerry Cleator, O.P., with whom I lived the Gospel in Bolivia; Dr. Irene Adams, of Belo Horizonte, Brazil, with her constant friendship and hospitality to me in the midst of the emergency world of abandoned street-kids and people with AIDS which she embraces like a gratuitous mantle of hope; and Andrew and Kathleen McKenna, who provided me with books when I was in far lands, gave me a home when I had none, and have not ceased to put me together in my fallings-apart.

The names of these friends here are only the iceberg tips of their anonymous presence in the overall effort, and the book is dedicated to them with deep gratitude.

All biblical references are to the Revised Standard Version, except where I have altered the translation slightly to bring out a nuance. Translations from nonbiblical sources are mine except where otherwise indicated.

Part 1

Constructing a Theological Anthropology

Chapter 1

René Girard's Mimetic Theory

A Shift in the Story Line of Original Sin

The story line within which the doctrine of original sin is traditionally situated is very familiar. First God created the world as good. Then Adam and Eve, part of that good creation, fell from grace by committing a first sin, and so inaugurated the history of sin within which we live. God, wanting to save us, sent his son Jesus, who, by his death, atoned for that sin. The grace that was lost by Adam is restored in those of us who appropriate that saving death by baptism, and if we can but hold on to that grace by obeying the moral law and frequenting the sacraments, we will eventually inherit heaven. This immensely powerful schema, teaching us to inscribe our stories within a fall and a resurrection, seems to be the paradigm which underlies Christian orthodoxy.

I have come to understand that this view of original sin — whose crude version is "the world is in a mess, Christ is the solution" — is seriously inadequate. Let me suggest why. If the door of your house is wrecked, you remove the pieces, measure the frame, and buy or make a door to fit it. Your solution — the new door — depends on your prior assessment of the damage to be rectified. So, with our typical version of original sin, the sort of solution offered by Christ is rigorously dependent on the sort of mess he is thought to have come to sort out, a mess which we are supposed to know about independently of his coming because of the story of Adam and Eve. The controlling factor in the story of salvation is the sin, and what Christ did fits in with that, just as the controlling factor on your trip to the hardware store is the size of the frame, and the door fits in with that.

For the traditional story line to work we have to have an independent and prior assessment of the nature of the mess. But in the case of the Christian faith there is no such prior and independent access to the mess. What the mess consists in is not self-evident; it is not accessible to archaeological investigation; and there is no Jewish doctrine of original sin for Christians to inherit. Christian doctrines exist at all only because

of the resurrection, and it is only from the resurrection that it has become possible to look back at human origins and tell a story about them
as involving an original sin. Now look at what this means with relation
to your door: first you are given, and come to perceive the size of, a
door, and you are so delighted that you start to build a door frame and
a house around about it. The "solution" turns out to be the controlling
factor, while the "mess" (in this case, your gradual realization of what a
poor house you had prior to being given a door) is something of which
you become aware only as you take on board the novelty of what you
have been given. But this story, starting from the door and working back
to the construction of a more appropriate house, is a very different story
from the one which begins with the need for a new door to fit a previously measured frame. One is the story of Jesus filling a space left in an
old wineskin with just the right amount of new wine; the other is the
story of the gradual fabrication of a new wineskin able to hold the new
wine which is suddenly made available, a wine which dictates the terms
of the fabrication.

What I would like to suggest is that, while it is easy enough to point
out the inadequacy of the old story and to indicate the resurrection as
the proper starting point for a new one, the old story has in fact a very
much more powerful hold on us than might seem to be the case. It dictates the terms of reference within which we understand who God is:
someone who is first pleased with creation, then angry with sin, then
pleased with his Son's sacrifice; it dictates the understanding of the sort
of atonement offered by Christ, and thus of his life and ministry; and
it dictates the parameters of the sort of struggle with which we engage
in our moral lives. The new story offers a strikingly different perception
of the same realities, but a perception that has to be very slowly and
carefully elaborated as it gradually becomes available.

There is something both frightening and exhilarating about the collapse of an old and familiar story and the emergence of a new one.
Frightening, because the old provides a space which we know how to
negotiate, a story within which we can make sense of God, creation,
Church, sacraments, good and evil. Exhilarating, because in the new
story it is the discovery of the deathless and unambiguous nature of God
made available at the resurrection which leads to our being empowered
to move beyond an unfinished creation, one which we tend to snarl up.
At the same time we are permitted a parting glance at what we are in
the process of leaving behind as we come to construct a way of being
human that is to have no end. However, leaving the security of the old
story and embarking upon being swept up into the new leaves us vulnerable to a highly disconcerting perception of the violence and evil that

there is in the world, and of the depth of our complicity in that. This is the difference between a story which protects us from aspects of human reality, and one by which we lose our innocence and gradually learn to take our responsibility in the construction of a new reality.

It is because I am finding the change of the underlying story line to require so much more than it seems that, rather than set out the doctrinal consequences of understanding original sin from the perspective of Easter in a didactic manner, I have opted to introduce you to the understanding of desire which has made it possible for me to begin this journey. In other words, rather than simply sharing "results," I am attempting to share a process of discovery. This is because none of us can really learn *about* original sin except as we begin to become aware of our involvement in it. For this reason I begin my exploration of the doctrine of original sin with an account of René Girard's understanding of desire, for it was this which opened up for me the perspective I am seeking to offer to you.

Mimetic Theory

René Girard's understanding of desire is known by the name *mimetic theory*. It is the coherent theorization of what seemed like a small insight but turned out to be an objective discovery about human relations. Girard realized early on in his research[1] that this insight was not something he had invented; rather he had hit upon something of which many other thinkers had become aware, usually as the result of an arduous process of creative conversion while writing. Cervantes, Shakespeare, Stendhal, Proust, and Dostoevsky can all be shown to have reached a more or less conscious grasp of the mimetic nature of desire, along with an awareness of the anthropological significance of this desire as structuring, and structured by, human violence.

In a nutshell, Girard has discovered that human beings desire not lineally, as most thought presupposes (i.e., a subject desires an object — Tarzan, he love Jane), nor even, as Hegel, interpreted by Kojève, thought, by desiring the desire *of* another (i.e., what I really want is that you should want me — Tarzan, he want Jane to love Tarzan). Rather we desire *according* to the desire of the other (Visiting Hollywood Director fancies Jane, and Tarzan, suddenly, he find Jane fascinating). All desire is triangular, and is suggested by a mediator or model. This imitative desire leads to conflicts, which are resolved by a group's spontaneous formation of unanimity over against some arbitrarily indicated other

---

1. For a chronologically ordered bibliography of Girard's principal works see p. 311.

who is expelled or excluded, thereby producing a return to peace. In this way we humans create and sustain social order. The mechanism of the creation and maintenance of social order by means of the expulsion of the arbitrarily chosen victim depends for its success on the blindness of its participants as to what is *really* going on: they have to believe in the guilt or dangerous nature of the one expelled. What has made it possible to discover this mechanism has been the presence in human culture of certain divinely inspired happenings and texts which make clear what really *has* been going on: the victim is hated without cause. Humans thus begin to be enabled to break with the dominant forms of social structuring and to move instead toward forms which un-cover (dis-cover) victims and make possible a real peace, not one based on sacrifice and murder.

So mimetic theory has three "moments," each of which can be understood from this "lite" version. *The first moment is that of imitative desire:* I want a leather bomber jacket because I saw Tom Cruise wearing one in *Top Gun*. So far, so good. Tom Cruise is a long way away, I've never met him, and am not going to fight with him over his jacket. Anyhow, clever manufacturers have risen to the occasion by swamping the market with leather bomber jackets, so I needn't fight with the mediator of my desire. Closer to home, however, after seeing *Top Gun* a friend and I go shopping for a leather jacket; he wants me to go with him to say if his choice suits him. He spots a "Top Gun"–type jacket with a fancy design which he likes, but he doesn't have the cash. Mysteriously, none of the 378 other jackets in the store will do for me. I have to have *that* one. I sneak back later with my credit card and buy it. When I meet my friend later for a drink, he is not amused. We quarrel violently: "You pinched my jacket," he says. "I saw it first." "That's nonsense," I say. "I always wanted it," hiding from myself and from him the fact that it's really because I like him and want to be like him that I had to get it. And anyhow why was the idiot so keen that I admire it with him if he didn't want me to go for it? (If my friend were very clever, he would feign losing interest in the jacket, instead beginning to admire another one, in the far corner of the bar. It would be a sure way to get me to lose interest in the one I've bought. For the sake of the story, he's not so clever: our quarrel and mutual suspicion deepen.)

Now we are on the frontier between the first "moment" of mimetic desire and *the second, the moment of the unifying expulsion*. Neither of us can afford a really serious quarrel, because the sports team on which we play depends on our working together. We have to find a way of getting our act together. If either of us were at all humble we could each go to the other and admit that our desires were modeled on each other: my friend needed my approval in order really to want the jacket; I couldn't resist fixing on the jacket which he suggested to me. I'm sorry, he's sorry, we're friends again. However, we aren't models of humility. If, despite our lack of humility, we were really quite lucid we could sit down and say, "Why are we fighting? It's all the fault of that b*****d Tom Cruise. If he hadn't been showing off in *Top Gun,* none of this would have happened." Over a drink we can then excoriate Tom Cruise and movie stars in general. We would in fact be treating Tom Cruise as our scapegoat, and he would quickly have undergone all the permutations of sacrificial religion, from Icon to Victim to Evil Deity, in one afternoon. Luckily, he's not going to be much hurt by this sacrifice (laughing all the way to the bank, in fact), because he's far away. However, let's suppose that we aren't that lucid, and that the violence of our mutual envy remains, as it so often does, half-buried. We still have to make peace and are scarcely aware of how violent our antagonism is. Without our realizing it, over the next few days, the Mexican guy on the team, who had seemed harmless, if a bit of an outsider — little guy, funny accent — seems to us to become unbearable (a bit of gossip can fuel this nicely), and a wave of opinion rises up among team members to get him dropped from the side. We suddenly feel really passionately about what a disaster he is and campaign until he is dropped. My friend and I were shoulder to shoulder in that vital campaign. The bomber jacket forgotten and the Mexican gone, we're friends again.

So much for the unifying expulsion. *The third moment,* if we're ever lucky enough to get there, *is that of revealed discovery,* arduously acquired insight into what we have been doing all along: the discovery of our complicity in scapegoating violence and of the roots of that violence in our envious desire. It's when, years later, I begin to look at the incident not from the point of view of leather jackets, or of my friendship skills, or of the camaraderie of the team, but start to realize that maybe the person whose story it really was, apparently the least important person, was the Mexican. It is the story of how the Mexican got dropped and how I allowed myself to get swept up into the mechanism which led to that. Maybe I start learning sensitivity to the sort of mechanism in which I was involved, trying out alternative dynamics in my family or place of work. Maybe I start becoming wary of the currents behind my sudden enthusiasms for whatever (or whoever) has replaced Tom Cruise's bomber jacket in my affections. The point behind this third moment is Girard's understanding that it has in fact been the work of biblical texts, culminating in those produced around the death and resurrection of Jesus, that have opened up "what we're really doing" in our social and cultural lives, made it possible for us to detect the innocence of our victims, and nudged us into trying alternative forms of creating human togetherness.

Notes on the Words "Mimesis" and "Desire"

I hope that you found my example banal. It was meant to be. Heaven and hell open out from the banality of the locker room. Before looking at how Girard understands the coming into being of the human race ("hominization") and of the human self of each one of us, I would like to offer a note on the words "mimesis" and "desire," words which will occur too frequently not to demand some explanation. Girard uses the word "mimesis" because the word "imitation" is normally used to refer to an exterior and conscious type of imitation, by which someone does, or buys, or wears, something like someone else. This is only part of what is meant by "mimesis." Mimesis also involves the less recognizable ways in which we are constituted as human beings by receiving physical being, a sense of being, gestures, memory, language, and consciousness through being drawn into imitation of others. Mimesis is therefore interior to the constitution of humans and not merely something external added on to an already independent being. This, as will be seen, is immensely important for the theology of original sin: Pelagius thought imitation important for doing good (or ill), while for Augustine our very will is corrupted and needs saving by grace.[2] As will be shown, a theological anthropology building from Girard will rescue Augustine's insight within an interpersonal vision of what it is to be human: Girard's mimesis is emphatically not the same as Pelagius's imitation. There is a further reason why "mimesis" is used in preference to "imitation": Girard will make it carry a weight of conflictivity that the normal use of the word "imitation" cannot easily bear.

There are various modalities of mimesis to which Girard refers. By modalities I mean different valencies of one and the same functioning of desire, whereby we desire not lineally, from subject to object, but according to the desire of the other, in a triangular fashion. The modality which occupies most space in Girard's treatment is *acquisitive mimesis*.

2. Pelagius was a British monk active in teaching around the beginning of the fifth century. He preached a reformation of morals, to which end he insisted on the free human capacity to do good, and thus the importance of good works for salvation. For Pelagius humans do not have an inherent and binding tendency to sin but can exercise themselves in doing good in imitation of others, especially Christ, if they want to. What is referred to as "Pelagianism," a term largely derived from the debates between Pelagius's pupil, Julian of Eclanum, and St. Augustine, is more of a perennial temptation, surfacing in different forms in every generation, than a specific heresy. Commonly, Pelagianism is used as a convenient label for the attitude of mind by which some people think that they can save themselves rather than being utterly dependent on a gracious Other who saves them.

This is the desire whereby I imitate the desire of someone else for an object and so enter into rivalry with that person for the object. Elsewhere in Girard's oeuvre this desire is referred to as *possessive mimesis*. It is important to indicate at this point that it is but one modality of human desire as understood by Girard, because some interpreters have treated mimetic theory as though Girard postulated an ontological acquisitive mimesis as human desire.[3] Girard's thought is much more subtle than that — as is the Church's doctrine of original sin.

"Acquisitive desire divides by leading two or more individuals to converge on one and the same object, with a view to appropriating it."[4] There follows *conflictual mimesis* (elsewhere referred to as *antagonistic mimesis*). This is the moment of desire when, as the frenzy of desire causes the original object of rivalry to lose importance, while the mutual imitation of all in conflict continues to grow, at last the same imitation unifies the rivals against some arbitrary other whose expulsion brings peace. In this way Girard shows the working of the great mystery of desire, which in how it works is both concord and discord, and changes from one to the other, and back, without any apparent reason. Girard's study of Shakespeare shows how the playwright understood and explored the working of exactly this mechanism of mimetic conflict, which functions identically at interpersonal, erotic, and political levels.

There is another modality of mimesis in Girard, vital to bring out, particularly in a theological study. This goes under a variety of names: *unobstacled desire,* the mimesis of the disciple for the model where there is no rivalry, desire *au delà du scandale, nonrivalistic desire.* I shall refer to it mostly as *pacific mimesis.* This occurs in a naïve form between a disciple who is far from being on the same level as the model, so that the model is what Girard calls an external mediator, not close enough to provoke rivalry (vital for healthy parenting!). However, in its naïve form pacific mimesis always threatens to degenerate into rivalistic mimesis as the disciple and the model grow closer together, and so the model becomes what Girard calls an "internal" mediator to the disciple, who is thus in rivalry with the model, and the model in rivalry with the disciple, the two having become obstacles to each other. More importantly, there is a nonnaïve form of pacific mimesis, which is arduously acquired. Girard shows the depth and difficulty of the kind of conversion necessary to step outside rivalistic mimesis by illustrating the

---

3. Notably J. Milbank in his misreading of Girard's thought on pp. 392–98 of his influential work *Theology and Social Theory: Beyond Secular Reason* (Oxford: Blackwell, 1990).

4. René Girard, *Things Hidden from the Foundation of the World* (London: Athlone, 1987), 26.

conversions, at the level of desire, of such believers as Cervantes, Dostoevsky, and Shakespeare, and such nonbelievers as Proust and Stendhal,
showing how the same phenomenon is at work in all these writers (all
of whom were personally particularly sensitive to mimetic phenomena).
Girard sees the Gospels as teaching exactly this pacific mimesis. Humans
cannot renounce desire as such, for it is what constitutes us, but we can
learn to desire anew, without obstacles, which is to have our very being
re-created. For Girard even the darkest permutations of rivalistic desire
leading to pride and suicide (Kirillov, Nietzsche) testify in favor of an
original transcendence of pacific mimetic desire.[5]

"Desire" is, evidently, a key word within both Girardian, and the
whole of (post)modern, discourse, and its meaning will become more apparent through its use in what follows than by any initial definition. It is
defined by J.-M. Oughourlian as the movement by which mimesis gives
autonomy and individuality to humans.[6] This means that desire is a
specifically human phenomenon, but only relatively specific to humans.
That is, mimetic interplay can be observed in some animals, without
leading to the crisis which gave birth to specifically human desire (and
which will be described below). All human desire is mimetic, that is, it is
desire in imitation of the desire of someone (or some group) else. And all
mimesis is desirous: that is, all imitation is part of a movement between
people relating to the very constitution of their being.

Girard considers desire to be especially present in the modern world,
for we live in the midst of the collapse of social prohibitions and are
comparatively bereft of public sacrificial resolutions. The social institutions, rites, and prohibitions which protected us from each other's
violence no longer do so effectively. We are left bearing in our own desire vis-à-vis each other — meaning in all our relationships both intimate
and public — all the complications of violence, rejection, and competition which now have no public resolution. Desire is the "interdividual"
living out of a sacrificial crisis without public resolution. Some find this
lack of public resolution too hard to bear and come to crystallize in their
own lives a visible sacrificial resolution to this desire: addiction, obses-
sion, madness, and psychotic behavior are different in degree, not kind,
from what drives us all.

A further term used by Girard is *metaphysical desire*. This refers to
desire that has ceased to relate to a physical or fleshly object, having

5. René Girard, *Deceit, Desire and the Novel: Self and Other in Literary Structure*
(Baltimore: Johns Hopkins University Press, 1965), 189.

6. "En psychosociologie, ce mouvement de la mimésis qui autonomise, et qui, de façon
relative, individualise, s'appelle *désir*" (J.-M. Oughourlian, *Un mime nommé désir* [Paris:
Grasset, 1982], 24).

become so involved with the mediator or rival that we would use words like "prestige," "snobbery," and so on, to describe the desire — what in other circumstances would be called pride.

Hominization, the Social Formation of the Self, and Revelatory Texts

Now we are ready to look at some of the consequences of mimetic theory, starting with the process of hominization, moving to the formation of the individual, and then to the social group. Girard postulates an approach to the very long process of hominization, one necessarily dependent on his understanding of desire (which he reached long before he tackled this question). Acquisitive mimesis is present in higher apes and linked to the dominance patterns and relations of subordination found among them. The presence among them of "prestige" shows that mimetic rivalry without an object is already present. Mimicry applies to all their behavior except acquisitive behavior: this enables group cohesion under attack. It then becomes possible to show how mimetic rivalry intensifies among the higher primates, which is the process necessary for hominization. The intensification destroys dominance patterns and eventually mimetic conflict among animals becomes so intense that there are no longer available any simply instinctual or direct solutions allowing animal sociality to function.

The key moment is when acquisitive mimesis, setting community or group members against each other, gives way to antagonistic mimesis, which unites members of the group at the expense of a victim. This corresponds to the threshold beyond which animal societies are impossible: the victimage mechanism is the threshold of hominization. The increasingly human primate was able to transform the increasing violence in the crucial phases of its biological and cultural evolution into a force for cultural development. As mimetic violence grew, so it forged the ever more rigorous prohibitions within the group and ritual channeling outside the group. More and more elaborate cultural proto-institutions enabled the greater length of time needed for the immensely vulnerable and increasingly prolonged period of human infancy, and thus for brain growth. Thus it can be shown that the confluence of mimesis and the victimage mechanism enables Girard to account both for the continuity of the process of evolution and for the rupture between animal and human life. The true rupture is the collective murder based on a mimetic crisis, not one proto-murder as Freud thought, but a whole series over (maybe) millions of years. Each stage in prehuman sociality collapsed in a mimetic crisis resulting in a murder, leading to the possibility of the generation of ever more complex cultural forms of organization, based on prohibition and ritual to protect the group from mimetic violence.

This process also gave birth to the "sign." Just as mimetic desire gradually transformed instinct (as periodic sexuality became permanent), so the victimage mechanism produces the first form of noninstinctual attention. The peace or silence that follows the frenzy of victimage is the condition necessary for the emergence of this attention, fixed on the victim who (whose death) has wrought this wonder. Beyond the sexual object, the alimentary object, or the dominant individual, there is the cadaver, which is the first object of (specifically) human attention. This may have taken very many stages to produce properly human consciousness, but the constitution of that consciousness is linked to the victim and to the creation of the sacred that is strictly simultaneous with the development of human culture.

This genetic model of the emergence of human culture is the basis of what Girard calls "the genetic model of the exception that is in the process of emerging."[7] It is this, the victimage mechanism, and not some binary series of oppositions, which creates the possibility for human meaning, and the development of human language is the result of the meaning which develops around the victim. The victim appears to be good and evil, peaceable and violent, life that brings death and death that brings life. It is from this that language itself develops.

Here, before we approach the constitution of any given human being up until the present day, we have the genetic model which enables us to see how the very constitution of human culture is shot through with violent mimesis. All human sociality is born thanks to the victim, and particularly, to ignorance of the victim(s) that gave it birth. Human language and thought are already utterly inflected by this ur-violence from their conception.

Now we are in a position to begin the description of the constitution of the person. By reproduction, which is a form of imitation of the species, an infant is conceived. Mimesis in space and time, imitation of gestures and sounds, constitutes in the infant first memory, and then language. The imitation is (obviously) of someone else, prior to the infant — its parents or guardians or siblings. This means that the "I" or "me" which we all develop is constituted by imitation of the desires of others, which are therefore previous to it. The "me" is a highly mutable construct, radically dependent on the desires of others, a fact which each "me" does not usually recognize except to a very limited extent; rather each "me" insists on the originality of its own desires, seen as proper

---

7. Girard, *Things Hidden,* 100.

to and springing from "me." This failure to recognize (*méconnaissance*) has often been enshrined philosophically in traditions with myths of a transcendent or even preexistent ego, taken to be radically free from dependence on what is other than itself. What is important here is that the failure to recognize is not a mistake about something of which the "me" might be conscious, but is a failure to rest peaceably on what made it possible for there to be a conscious "me" at all.

The various mimetically formed, and forming, "me's" can live peacefully so long as they relate as models, not rivals. So, for instance, where there is good parenting, the child is enabled to receive a firm sense of being by the loving way in which the parent suggests the child into being, meeting its needs, showing it patterns of imitation that do not get it into trouble and that do not produce rivalry with the time and needs of the parent. (However, many young fathers go into a deep rivalry with their children as they see themselves displaced from the center of their wives' attention; likewise, many elder siblings when displaced from the center of the universe by new arrivals). In practice even infants with really fine, nonrivalistic parenting are different from others in degree, not kind. All infants are born into a world where the very desire that constitutes what comes to be their consciousness is already rivalistic, formed by the process of the constitution of human culture described above.

Parental and ambiental human suggestion is always itself previously inflected by traces of the acquisitive mimesis and the victimage mechanism by which every group's identity and every stable human personality are enabled to exist. The parental suggestion "imitate me," "be like me" always already includes the suggestion "do not be like me," "do not imitate me," which introduces the infant into the world of the double bind: the simultaneous suggestion "do" and "do not," which affects us all in the very constitution of our being. A trivial example, taken from a stage where a child is already fairly grown, illustrates graphically what in fact happens much earlier, before physical objects come into play: a cuddly toy is put into the hands of the child by a mother who has first showed the child how to play with it. The mother then goes to the oven and puts on the kettle. When she comes back three minutes later and finds the child stretching for the kettle, she screams with panic at the thought of the thing tipping over and scalding the child. How is the child to know that the kettle is not just another version of the cuddly toy? The child receives the message "imitate me" / "do not imitate me." Eager to please by imitating, it has been plunged into the world of rejection and failure to please, and its desire will always be inflected by the double bind. To learn that certain things are prohibited us because we lack the physical capability to deal with them or because touching them would do us harm is a highly complex apprenticeship involving being able to begin to sort out the double bind: "imitate me here, because to do so does you good" / "do not imitate me here, because imitating me will get you into trouble."

The result of the infant's double bind is that each "me" finds itself already mysteriously in rivalry with others — at first a feeble rivalry, owing to the hugeness of the model and the impotence of the disciple, but ever less feeble as the curious mixture of our sense of being as received and as struggled-for develops along with our bodies. (The degree of the mixture of being as received and as struggled-for is what depends on the excellence of parental love.) From its very inception, desire is competitive: wanting to have what the other has *instead of* the other; wanting to be what the other is *instead of* the other. This pattern is confirmed (and encouraged) during childhood and adolescence. Where desire is competitive, any object of rivalry quickly becomes irrelevant (one cuddly toy between two children quickly ceases to be important in the quarrel: what is important is having what the other has — the *other* is more important than *what* the other *has*). This would never happen were desire linear, based on an object, rather than triangular, based on imitation of the desire of the other. Violence obviously ensues from this acquisitive mimesis, and it is how desire works in every human, from tenderest childhood onward.

The violence of acquisitive mimesis makes all human social life fragile, and has done so throughout the long process of hominization. Here we have a cross-section of that process in its already early human stage. We can imagine a group which, because of the presence of acquisitive mimesis among its members — people wanting what the other has, or is, and fighting for it — suffers a crisis which attacks its very fabric. Violence rages among the members of the group until the group settles, thanks to the working of conflictual mimesis, spontaneously and arbitrarily upon a surrogate victim, who, because unable to retaliate, offers no threat of continuing the violence. The victim is often liminal, an outsider, someone with a physical disability or thought to be too prominent in the group. This victim is expelled — lynched or sacrificed — it matters not how, because the underlying mechanism is the same. Since the group spontaneously and unanimously settled upon the victim, blaming it in all sincerity for the group's woes and conflicts (often mythically represented as plagues, famines, and so on), the expulsion of the victim produces a moment of peaceful unanimity, which is the foundation of a new social order.

This moment of peace, of social order, following the lynching, is hugely important. The expelled victim is seen as having brought about the peace precisely because it is genuinely blamed for the disturbance which culminated in its expulsion. The group cannot accept that the victim was in fact arbitrarily chosen and not really responsible for the disorder, for that would leave open the question of who really caused the disturbance, and the conflict would not be resolved. It is, however, resolved by the convinced all-against-one of the act of victimization. Because the expelled victim has brought about the peace, after its expulsion it becomes sacralized: it becomes the god whose visitation has brought first chaos, then order, a being to be worshiped with gratitude and to be feared. The group henceforward maintains its social unity by repeating, in as exact as possible a form, the process which led to the production of peace, the reenactment by ritual of the original murder — that is, sacrifice (to the victim divinity), whether of humans or, in attenuated forms, of other levels of life. At the same time the group forms prohibitions of the sort of mimetic behavior that led to the violent crisis, while carefully organizing transgressions of these in the heart of the ritual reenactment of the crisis. What is important is that social unanimity be re-created and order maintained. The group begins to tell the story of its own foundation by myths, which always involve telling about the foundational murder, while disguising the truth about that murder. The story is told from the perspective of the lynchers, while real responsibility for the murder is displaced onto the god or gods who appear in the tale.

For a time the mechanism is effective in maintaining order, through the elaborate series of prohibitions and rituals. However, after a time, of course, its efficacy begins to wear down, since it is merely a highly elaborate patch over the real problems of the working of acquisitive mimesis within the community. As it wears down, there begin to appear signs of disorder and chaos once again, ritual seems to lose its effect, there does not seem to be the same devotion to the gods. This is the period called the "sacrificial crisis" by Girard. Eventually the system of order wears down so far that another outbreak of violence occurs, leading to another blood-letting, culminating in another expulsion and the establishment of a new altar to a new god.

All this happened over many thousands of years without losing its effect. What is remarkable is our ability to perceive from our own (Western) history that the sacrificial mechanism as a whole is increasingly ineffective. It is more and more difficult to be convinced of the guilt of the victim and easier to see the lie — not that this has made our social practice any less "sacrificial." Girard attributes the fact that social blindness is increasingly fragile to the Judaeo-Christian revelatory texts, which point out the lie on which social groupings base themselves. These texts have exercised a powerful demystifying force throughout history, even when their partisans have used them in ways exactly opposed to their revelatory power: that is, to make and hide victims rather than to reveal them and give them voice. Girard came comparatively late in the day to the Judaeo-Christian texts, and found in them, considered from a structuralist angle, just the same stories of violent foundation as in all myths. What amazed him was that the texts contain a reading of that same structure that is the reverse of all other myths: God is progressively revealed as on the side of the victim, not of the sacrificers. The old lie is undone from within.

There are hints of this in some of the Greek tragedians, but nothing as definitive and persistent as the revelation of the mechanism of the surrogate victim carried out in the Jewish Scriptures. Even in these there is a fair mix of texts, some which reveal the victim, others which show an understanding of a violent deity similar to other cultures. Girard highlights the story of Cain and Abel, the story of Joseph, many of the Psalms, the book of Job, and the songs of the suffering servant in Isaiah. The full revelation of the mechanism of the surrogate victim, and thus the introduction of definitive incredulity as regards its efficacy into the human community, is realized in the Gospels, and in particular in the passion of Christ. Finally Girard sees it as having been this event, and its being held up before humanity by means of the texts written in the light of the resurrection, which makes possible the hermeneutic of human desire leading to the mechanism of the surrogate victim that he thought (at first) that he had arrived at independently.

The Status of a "Theory"

Having given a tour of mimetic theory, I had better clear up what is meant by a "theory." One reason for this is that many readers are put off by what they take to be another "great theory" which seeks to explain everything. Particularly for people suffering from the withdrawal symptoms that result from disillusion with their own seduction by the *idées générales* of the nineteenth century — Hegel, Marx, Nietzsche, and Freud, and the various totalitarianisms (intellectual, political, and emotional) that these have produced — any idea that suggests other than the petit-point nihilism of the late twentieth century is a priori unacceptable.

Mimetic theory is a genetic understanding of human relations that takes into account both the constitution of the person and social structure. It can be entered into starting from very different places. From the individual or from the social group, from the process of hominization or from the conditions that have made the understanding itself possible, from a hypothetical starting point beyond historical investigation or from within the development of a history made possible by the working out of mimetic relations and their subversion from within. It is possible as well to start from other thinkers who have discovered mimetic theory for themselves and show this in a variety of different ways. In different works Girard starts from just such different points, and the understanding is accessible from any of them. Girard does not think of mimetic theory as "his" theory. He thinks rather that he has made more rigorous a basic truth about human relations discovered before him and independently of each other by many others.

In the light of this, I would suggest that rather than being one of the *idées générales* or *systèmes,* which Grasset erroneously imputes to Girard on the back cover of the livre de poche edition of *Des choses cachées,* mimetic theory is first of all a very small understanding or insight, a little glimpse of a *sagesse* that is of almost infinite application; such is its flexibility. It is both a very simple and a very difficult idea, precisely because it is only insofar as one allows it to illuminate one's own relationships that it yields anything. It is thus very different from systems of thought which impose a straight-jacket on thinkers who become involved in them and which can be grasped intellectually without involving the subject in some sort of conversion at the level of desire.

It will be apparent that such an idea — involving an insight into human desire, a hypothesis about hominization and the founding of human social life, and an awareness of our being structured by violence and death — cries out to be questioned regarding whether it can yield an enrichment of the doctrine of original sin. To this task we will now turn.

Chapter 2

The Search for a Theological Anthropology

A Two-Way Anthropology

In a programmatic essay entitled "Christology and Anthropology" W. Kasper outlines three theses concerning christology's need for a relatively independent anthropology.[1] First, such thought should have a positive attitude toward the modern turn to anthropology, should be critical of any particular modern anthropology, and should outbid anthropology by showing that humanization is truly realized only as divinization. Secondly, it should link the way in which Jesus' life is understood to be *for* us with an understanding of his preexistence, as inseparable parts of the same movement. Thirdly, it should provide a relational metaphysics based on the person (rather than substance), which can accept the modern shift toward anthropology and yet go beyond it. This should yield a new total view of reality, from the standpoint of the Christian faith.[2]

Independently of Kasper's search, J. Milbank, in his seminal work *Theology and Social Theory* has undertaken to demonstrate that any notions of the independence of modern social theory from theology are illusory.[3] It is his view that modern social theory was in historical fact deliberately constructed *against* Catholic theology and that it always contains an implicit theology, one that is always of a heretical nature. The key root of the difference between modern social theory and the social theory that is already present in Catholic theology is that the former is based on the assumption of the ontological anteriority of conflict, while the latter depends on the ontological metanarrative of anterior peace.[4] Milbank moves on to conclude that (Catholic) theology

---

1. In W. Kasper, *Theology and Church* (London: SCM, 1989), 73–93.
2. Kasper, *Theology and Church*, 92.
3. J. Milbank, *Theology and Social Theory: Beyond Secular Reason* (Oxford: Blackwell, 1990).
4. See especially chaps. 10 and 12.

is in fact already a social theory, a revealed social theory. It is a completely coherent perspective on human social life, but one from a divine starting point.

Of course, Milbank's treatment is a good deal more subtle and less triumphalist than I can suggest in a short space: his principal polemical adversaries are theologians who bow the knee before the supposed scientific autonomy of social science, affirming the need to borrow such a social science as mediator for their own theology. However, it is clear that what he is saying is, in some ways, very similar to what Kasper is saying: there is a revealed perspective on human social life (Milbank) or on the human being (Kasper), which Catholic theology needs to recover. The two would differ in that Kasper still feels the need to pay lip-service to "the modern turn to anthropology and the modern notion of autonomy," where Milbank would have no difficulty in doing for such notions what he did for social theory: demonstrate that these principles are themselves the bastard children (and deliberately bastard children) of Catholic theology, and that they cannot be assumed into that theology without debasing it. Milbank would have a positive attitude to anthropology as the necessary consequence of faith in the Incarnation, but a critical attitude to the modern turn to anthropology and modern notions of autonomy.

There is a real (but implicit) difference between the two as to how one should go about the task of constructing the "new total view of reality, from the standpoint of the Christian faith." From Kasper's starting point within a dialectical tradition it is not clear — theoretically — what real autonomous content christology has to enable it to act as a critical instance over against modern anthropology. Of course, in fact, it has the dogmas of faith; these, however, are not part of dialectical thought but simply given (though dialectical thought is obviously necessary in their elucidation). Maybe Kasper thinks that without such a dialectical turn to modern anthropology, theology becomes fideist and falls foul of the strictures of *Dei Filius*.[5] Milbank feels no such need. He is aware that

> Christianity does not claim that the Good and the True are self-evident to objective reason, or dialectical argument. On the contrary, it from the first took the side of rhetoric against philosophy and contended that the Good and the True are those things of which we "have a persuasion," *pistis*, or "faith."[6]

---

5. The First Vatican Council's constitution on revelation and reason.
6. Milbank, *Theology and Social Theory*, 398.

In line with this, he begins to set out what a revealed social theory would look like, something similar to Augustine's *City of God,* a theological metanarrative of ontological peace.

In fact, there is a missing element in both these accounts, in the way they mediate between the revealed overview and the human patterns of thought which they discuss. Of course Kasper is right: human thought as we know it is dialectical, but is not that part of the postlapsarian world that his christological anthropology seeks to overcome? How do you get from Kasper's dogmatics to a critical elaboration of a Christian anthropology? How do we get from a dialectical thought process (a conflictual consciousness) to a gracious and a given thought process (the ontological anteriority of peaceful truth)? Of course Milbank is right: God does not speak dialectically, but truth is self-giving in and from peace. Yet is not that truth unhelpful unless we know how to change from conflictual creatures to creatures capable of gracious reception of the given? How do you get from Milbank's ontological analysis to practical Christian living (as opposed to his entirely plausible theological construct)? How do we get from the understanding that peaceful truth is anterior to dialectical understanding to the practical discovery of the way out of the dialectical entrapment?

The answer I propose is a wisdom anthropology. This will, I hope, show how, in practice, we move from a dialectical to a given perception of human life, as well as showing how this properly human perception is simultaneously a divinely revealed one. This is because we are not talking about some special private insight into what humankind is like, but rather an arduous discovery made public by certain key persons as they moved from one sort of understanding of the human condition to another: an anthropology, then, of conversion. I want to use the word "wisdom" simultaneously in both its ordinary human sense and in the biblical sense which was to yield so much fruit in St. John's Gospel. There Jesus is seen as the presence of God's wisdom on earth and is shown to have perceived and spoken and acted from out of a particular perspective on human beings, and promised the presence of this perspective to his disciples after his death. There we are talking about a revealed perspective; yet it is a perspective that needed to be discovered (by the disciples) in an authentic human labor, or struggle, to understand and to perceive.

It is in the context of an anthropology of wisdom, or conversion, as revealed discovery mediating between a revealed perspective and a dialectical anthropology that I would like to situate the mimetic understanding theorized by René Girard. I am suggesting that as an anthropological understanding mimetic theory is peculiarly suited to revelation, indeed is concentric with it, and that this can be shown by the way it illuminates the major doctrines of the Christian faith without any sort of reduction. That is to say, it will be possible to make theological use of this anthropology while remaining theological, thus satisfying Kasper's concern that as Catholic theology takes on board the anthropological approach of modern thought it can "only match up to this task *if it remains theology and does not turn into anthropology.*"[7]

Let us look at this anthropological vision from the two ways of access on which Girard bases his understanding: first, that of revelation. Girard detects the presence in the Gospel texts of a rationality which he shows to be the same as the mimetic theory he had reached by other means. He also posits that this rationality was not entirely understood by the disciples and those who wrote the Gospels:

> The rationality I am disclosing, the mimeticism of human relations, is too systematic in principle, too complex in its effects, and too visibly present, both in the theoretical passages on scandal and in the accounts entirely controlled by it, to be there by accident. Nevertheless this rationality was not completely devised or created by those who put it there. . . .
>
> Under these circumstances the Gospels cannot be the product of a work that was purely within the effervescent milieu of early Christians. At the text's origin there must have been someone outside the group, a higher intelligence that controlled[8] the disciples and inspired their writings. As we succeed in reconstituting the mimetic theory in a kind of coming and going between the narratives and the theoretical passages, the words attributed to Jesus, we are disclosing the traces of that intelligence, not the reflections of the disciples.[9]

This matches Girard's view expressed in *La route antique:*

> There is an anthropological dimension to the Gospel text. I have never claimed that it constitutes the whole of the Christian revelation, but I do think that, without it, Christianity cannot truly be itself.[10]

There is a revelatory anthropology present in the Gospel texts, and it is an anthropology of mimetic desire. Its very origin in Christ can be seen by the way in which it is sometimes muddled in transmission, by, for instance, the use of demonic imagery, which can be shown to be the same *au fond* as the imagery of *scandal* which is to be found in the mouth of Christ and which is straightforwardly mimetic. So here it is suggested that the historical figure Jesus of Nazareth possessed an anthropological understanding that is at least remarkably similar to Girard's own

---

7. Kasper, *Theology and Church,* 93.
8. In French *qui domine,* so: "a higher intelligence which is master of . . ."
9. René Girard, *The Scapegoat* (London: Athlone, 1986), 163.
10. René Girard, *La route antique des hommes pervers* (Paris: Grasset, 1985), 239.

mimetic understanding and acted out of just such an understanding. It is also suggested that this understanding was not entirely grasped by the disciples, who yet transmitted it with occasional signs of their own incomprehension. In their case, it was an understanding that came by a certain sort of conversion, produced among them by what they understood to be the coming among them of the Spirit that had been in Christ, the intelligence and internal dynamic that had been at work in his life. So, on the one hand we have the given, the revelatory vision of how humans are, in purely human terms, with no indication of any conversion. There is never any suggestion of Christ having undergone a conversion experience. All the Gospels affirm his presence and his understanding as something that just *was*. On the other hand, we have a group of people who were enabled to accede to that vision, but arduously, by conversion. These are the two poles of the theological anthropology I am trying to set out: the given and the struggled for.

The first way in to the anthropological dimension of the Gospel text illustrated by Girard is by revelation, something purely given. The second (and in his own case, this way came first) is that of arduous discovery as revealed in the lives of certain authors — and of course there is no revelation unless there is a simultaneous process of discovery which enables the given to be made incarnate in human lives. Thus, in different works Girard traces the growth in mimetic understanding of certain authors. Particular attention is dedicated to Dostoevsky,[11] to Proust,[12] and to Shakespeare.[13] In all three cases a pattern of conversion is traced whereby a certain *sagesse* is acquired. This conversion is independent of formal religious belief, but seems unable to do without its imagery at a certain point. The conversion could be described as that from having a view of humanity marked by the scapegoating structure of the hero/victim, to having a view that can best be inscribed (and perhaps can only be inscribed) within the pattern of fall and redemption.[14] What Girard shows, particularly in the case of Dostoevsky and Shakespeare, is that this new anthropological vision acquired by the author is not a piece of eisegesis on Girard's part, but corresponds to something of which the authors in question were aware. Girard shows how Shakespeare's

---

11. In *Deceit, Desire and the Novel* (Baltimore: Johns Hopkins University Press, 1965), and *Dostoievski: du double à l'unité* (Paris: Plon, 1963).

12. In *Deceit, Desire and the Novel* and part 3 of *Things Hidden from the Foundation of the World* (London: Athlone, 1987).

13. In *A Theater of Envy — William Shakespeare* (New York: Oxford University Press, 1991).

14. See *A Theater of Envy*, 320: "Before he could embrace the fall-and-redemption pattern of *The Winter's Tale*, Shakespeare had to discard the old scapegoat structure completely."

understanding of mimetic desire broadens into a complete anthropological vision, especially in *A Midsummer Night's Dream* and *Julius Caesar*. What Girard elucidates is not his own idea, forced onto Shakespeare, but "Even though it has only recently been theorized, mimetic desire is not a modern idea which I am seeking to force, in an arbitrary and anachronistic way, on an author who wouldn't have recognized it. The idea is Shakespeare's own."[15] Girard is aware of Shakespeare deploying his mimetic anthropology quite deliberately: "The Shakespearean mimetic theory unfolds almost didactically in *A Midsummer Night's Dream*."[16]

So the same anthropological understanding is found to be present both in the teaching and activity of Christ, as witnessed to by the writers of the Gospel, and in certain authors, where the understanding does not have to be present as part of an explicitly religious outlook (as it is not in the case of Proust). This anthropological understanding links an understanding of the mimetic nature of desire with an understanding of the violent nature of desire, the resolution of that violence in a form of victimage, and, eventually, the overcoming of the pattern of desire in question by a pattern of desire that is a rupture from, and yet in continuity with, the old pattern. It is this understanding that I will now try to set out as clearly as possible.

The Constitution of the "Self"

In his work *Un mime nommé désir* J.-M. Oughourlian (coauthor with Girard and Lefort of *Things Hidden*) works out in depth the consequences of mimetic understanding for psychology.[17] Here I borrow from him in order to establish the basis for the theological anthropology which I am developing.

Oughourlian begins by asking why it is that the newly born infant is moved toward the adult. Why is there this movement such that the infant's attention can be captured by an adult? He is, of course, asking about something which involves, but is not on the same plane as, the purely biological. Why does the baby struggle to repeat the word which is pronounced by the adult? We all take such a draw, such a movement,

---

15. This sentence does not appear as such in the English text, which in this case is the original (*A Theater of Envy*, 9), but only in the French translation *Shakespeare — les feux de l'envie* (Paris: Grasset, 1990), 18. The above quotation is my translation from the French.

16. Girard, *A Theater of Envy*, 46.

17. J.-M. Oughourlian, *Un mime nommé désir* (Paris: Grasset, 1982); Eng. trans.: *The Puppet of Desire: The Psychology of Hysteria, Possession, and Hypnosis* (Stanford: Stanford University Press, 1991).

for granted, though of course it isn't automatic, as is evidenced by autistic children, who lack precisely the attraction, the draw, the movement toward an adult.[18]

This draw, which is what enabled all of us to have access to language and human society, has the same relationship to humans as gravity does to planets. It is the mysterious movement which is nevertheless evidently there (evidently as soon, that is, as it has occurred to someone to ask why things are as they are) and without which there would be chaos. This movement, Oughourlian, following Girard, calls mimesis. It is to psychology what gravity is to physics. It is made concrete in the imitation, learning, and repetition which is what enables an infant to become a socialized human being.

Mimesis is then the absolute condition for the existence of humanity (as opposed to quasi-mimetic or pre-mimetic animals). Human beings are social animals. It is our relationality to others that introduces us into being human, and that being-related-to-others works mimetically. Of course, like gravity, it is a principle of both attraction and repulsion. At first we are drawn toward and imitate a model and learn from it, but soon we imitate gestures that lead to rivalry, taking the same object as the model.[19] Our model becomes our rival, and we define ourselves "over against" another. So mimesis is both the condition for our attraction toward others and our separation from them, leading to the construction of our individuality and identity.

The fundamental draw, mimesis, has three dimensions to it in our lives: it is imitation in space, repetition in time, and reproduction in the species. In all of these, as must be obvious, the *other* is massively anterior to, and the condition of possibility of, any given self. Although rarely reflected on in treatises of anthropology, it is clear that any given human, prior to any decision, control, or self-consciousness(!), was entirely dependent on others and their propensity to reproduce the species, to be able to come into existence at all. Next, imitation in space is evidently fundamental to hominization: without it any form of social adequacy would be impossible. Repetition in time enables the memory to be born, thus making possible language and enabling the human to be kept together as one person throughout his or her life history. Language enables the separations to be made which permit the human to develop

---

18. Here Oughourlian refers to his own observation of autistic children. For a major study of autism that is compatible with this view, see F. Tustin, *The Protective Shell in Children and Adults* (London: Karnac, 1990).

19. I do not wish to suggest that the "self" is not something received. Of course it is, and the better the parenting, the more securely it is received. Here I am talking about the normal framework of movement within which and by which we each receive our "self."

an "I," or identity. It is thus mimesis in its spatial dimension which keeps humans together, constituting them as social animals (which *do* more or less the same thing); that is, it leads to sociogenesis, or the birth of society. It is also mimesis, in its temporal dimension, which keeps each human together and constitutes each psychologically; that is, it leads to psychogenesis, or the birth of the human psyche.

These two dimensions, which are, of course, inseparable in real life, lead to ontogenesis, which we might describe as the birth of the human being as a being with a consciousness. "Consciousness" is not, of course, a word describing a "thing" inside a person, but a way of talking about the relational (including, but not exhausted by, the linguistic) framework of human awareness and perception. So we have a psychosocial being who is not only genetically the fruit of reproduction, but is, in the make-up of his or her consciousness as well, utterly *other*-dependent. It is the draw, mimesis, which precedes consciousness and makes it possible. It is the force by which each of us is drawn into the relational systems of the human race.

Mimesis thus assures both the cohesion of the social tissue and the relative autonomy of the members who compose it. Desire is what we call the movement by which mimesis gives autonomy and individuality to humans. Desire works as follows:

An infant begins to imitate an adult, reproducing exactly what the adult does, insofar as physical difference permits. There is no "me" in the infant independent of the force which models it. The infant is imitating the form, or appearance of the model. Soon, however, the infant is drawn to the look, or the hand, of the model indicating objects outside itself (any object). The same draw that drew the infant to the form of the adult now draws the infant to the object which the model has designated: for instance, a toy is "played with" by an adult, put into the child's hand; the child learns to play with it — a rattle on a crib. We imitate not only what other people look like, but what they have. It is this movement toward an object that is exterior to the model which we call desire, and it is this which pulls us away from the model and begins to make us autonomous.

However, neither imitation of the form of the other nor imitation of what the other has is sufficient to constitute a "me." The third sort of imitation, which depends on the functioning of the other two (which precede it), bears on the *being* of the model — and is close to what Freud called identification: wanting to *be* who the other is. Imitating what a model has leads to rivalry, an impossible rivalry in the case of the infant, who is too weak to fight for things, which it can only receive by being given them. Rivalry is resolved at all levels of human life by the expulsion of a victim. Here, and in purely psychological terms, such an expulsion takes the form of an assertion of the incipient self over against the model, in order to take the model's place, or be him or her. It is the many "victories" in this struggle which constitute the process of imitating the being of the model, or identification, which permit the constitution of the "me."[20]

This may sound like a description of all of us as little ontological murderers, or would-be murderers, as though that were what is natural and proper for humans (as in the famous "Oedipus complex"). However, that would be a misreading: there is nothing ontological in this description, as can be seen by the way in which Girard's analysis of the Oedipus complex precisely undercuts the necessarily murderous element of infantile rivalry postulated by Freud.[21] It seems important, against any tendency to see infantile murderousness as ontologically necessary for hominization, to uphold that the sense of the self, the être of Oughourlian, is always received as a given, even when that preceding givenness, or the reception, is seriously marred by violence of circumstance, or parental incompetence or ill will. The relationship between the être as received and as acquired by more or less violent appropriation is at the heart of the theology of original sin.

The description I have given leads to an understanding of the human self, the "me" of each one of us, as being an unstable structure, one that is changeable, malleable, and other-dependent, whether it likes it or not. The other is always anterior to "me." It also means, and these are two fundamental theses of Oughourlian, first, that it is desire which engenders the "me" and which brings it, by its movement, into existence; and, second, that desire is mimetic, that is, it moves in imitation of the desire of another.

Since the "me" of each one of us is founded by desire, we cannot

---

20. It would take an infant psychologist to be able to unpack a little more clearly the element of identification in the mimetic formation of the "me." Here I choose to give Oughourlian's text because of the conceptual density of the description and the many consequences (theological not least) which flow from it: "On the sociological level, René Girard has admirably demonstrated that the mechanism capable of bringing undifferentiated violence, the product of appropriative mimesis, to an end, is the victimary mechanism. On the psychological and individual level the mimetic conflict unleashed by the mimesis of appropriation has a history which is intimately involved with psychogenesis: since the resolution cannot be that of the death of the model, owing on the one hand to the weakness of the child and on the other hand to the social structures, that is, the culture, produced by the victimary mechanism, there remains only one possible victory in this struggle for the life of the psyche, and this consists in the psychological 'death' of the model, that is to say, in the appropriation by the child of the very being of the model by the game of identification" (Oughourlian, Un mime, 25).

21. See René Girard, Violence and the Sacred (Baltimore: Johns Hopkins University Press, 1977), chap. 7, and Things Hidden, part 3, chap. 4.

say that desire is our own, as though it belongs to some preexistent "me." It is the other way around. The "me" is radically dependent on the desires whose imitation formed it. This means that there is no "real me" at the bottom of it all, when I've scraped away all the things I've learned, all the influences I've undergone. Psychology is what goes on *between* people, not, in the first place, *in* any particular individual. Having grasped this is what permits Girard and Oughourlian to talk of an *interdividual* psychology. In more accessible terminology this means that psychological facts have to do with relationships. Psychological problems have to do with broken or disturbed relationships, and psychological wholeness has to do with restoring and mending broken relationships.

When we talk about a person, or a subject, or an individual, we use words to indicate, well, the person, or the subject, or the individual in question. Normally we use those words loosely and wouldn't want to be tied to some of the consequences of our use of them. Few of us would think it legitimate if someone drew conclusions of a philosophical sort from our use of the word "person" or "individual" regarding our deepest-held beliefs or attitudes toward the way people develop and are. And, talking loosely, that's no problem. Except of course that we often are fooled by our usage into consequences and feelings which may not square with what we really know to be the case.

I bring this up because the words "person," "subject," and "individual" militate against the sort of understanding — outlined above — of how, let us say, Pedro, is constituted. They suggest a firmness of identity, a fixity, and an independence that I hope to have shown to be illusory. It was for this reason that Oughourlian invented the word "holon," or borrowed it from Koestler, to apply to *the purely psychological being, the structure which is permanently becoming in the midst of continuous exchanges with similar structures*. It is the basic unit of interdividual psychology and can refer to individuals, families, tribes, nations, and so on. It is a whole which is coherent with regard to its constituent parts, but at the same time is part of a larger social whole.

Thus psychology has to do with the way holons interact, holons which are generated mimetically. The true psychological fact, the center of interest, is the relation between two holons.

The "I," then (Pedro's life story), whose constitution we have followed, is a holon constituted by desire which is the desire of another holon mimetically transposed. It maintains its existence thanks to two pieces of "forgetfulness." First, it "forgets" what it owes to the desire which produces and animates it, calling that desire its own. Second, the desire could not produce an autonomous "me" in the holon if it did not "forget" what it owes to the desire of the model holon which it has imitated.

This is, so far, healthy and normal. Without it, the "me" formed by desire could not come into existence. It involves a sort of "unknowing," a nonrecognition of the other's rôle in my genesis, but which does "me" no harm for as long as the other is taken as a model and not as a rival. However, if the other is taken as a rival, not a model, this "unknowing" becomes a self-deception, something pathogenic. It becomes an insistence on the radicality of the "me" as being the origin of its desire and an insistence of the desire on its being prior to the desire of the other (who thus becomes the rival rather than the model). That is to say, the "me" tries to identify itself over against others, in reaction to whom it is constituted. It is this insistence that is at the root of human psychoses and neuroses.

The "unknowing," whether in its benign forgetful or its harmful denial form, is not something of which any given "I" is conscious. This is not to say that it is unconscious, but that it is what permits consciousness. It is not a mysterious, subjective inner reality, but an unknowing of the real state of affairs that have constituted the consciousness, a state of affairs which always works the same way — mimetically in relation to the desires of another holon.

Thus every "me," at any given moment during its life, is in movement with relation to the other which precedes and enables it to come into being. On the one hand, it is stretching toward a recognition, an acknowledgment of the other which constitutes it, which is therapeutic, enables it to come together, form a strong healthy "me," which lives in peace since it treats the other as a model. It is a "being with." Or, on the other hand, the "me" is exacerbating its unknowing into a denial of its alterity, which means that, as it takes the other as rival, so it becomes splintered, dissociated, and subject to pathological repetitive mechanisms. Of course, none of us has immediate access to his or her "I" to inspect it and see which way it is going. None of us can be conscious of what constitutes our consciousness. It is only relationally that we can detect and modify our lives — but to be aware of that is already therapeutic, since it involves an awareness that we are moved from without.

This is the sort of world into which we emerge. Even without the sort of traumas many people undergo in early infancy, which have marked effects on their lives, our "I" is formed in imitation of the desires of those around and, in earliest life, those who parent us. This means that built into our "I's" are all the desires which they have, and, as we come to appreciate when we grow up a bit, many of those desires and patterns of behavior are themselves wounded, inadequate, violent. However, we've already been formed by that before there was a "me" to know about it.

We start, then, as a radically needy little *anthropos,* that is, a human for whom the satisfaction of immediate bodily necessities is never enough. Simultaneously to those bodily necessities, for whose satisfaction we are marvelously programmed, there is what might (with great care) be called an ontological need, a radical need to *be,* a need which draws us to others and to imitate them in order to acquire a sense of being, something felt as a lack. The better we are parented, the more that need is met by the "sense of being" being given. Yet, however well we are parented that need is never fully met. We grow up, in short, conflictual little animals, with a built-in mechanism for shoring up our fragile identity, for producing security and order, both as individuals and in groups. We learned this while we were building our "I," and as we continue to build it. We try to expel the "other" who is our rival. Our "I" is in fact built on that expulsion. It means that we often build up *over against,* rather than by serenely allowing the other to be a beneficent influence on our lives. As if by magic we know, as small children, how to strengthen our group: by finding someone weak to cast out, someone against whom we can all be. In later years we may pass most or all of our adult lives locked into conflict with some other — whether a person, an idea, a nation, or whatever — without whom we cannot easily do. There are innumerable permutations — as innumerable as people — of the way that mimetic desire moves us throughout our lives, many of them violent, both emotionally and physically. It is strange that even when there is a great deal of love around for us to receive, we are often hurt in our ability to receive, and so reject it. This is our condition. This is what we start with, living on the brink between a wisdom which enables us to recognize where we have come from, and a self-deception, an exacerbated unknowing, which binds us further into violence toward ourselves and others, a violence in which we are all ineluctably constituted.

Long before the Self

So far we have a description of the constitution of the self that seeks to lay the proper stress on the anteriority of the "other" and of the mimetic nature of the relationship with the other, a relationship of suggestion and attraction by the other, leading to a humanizing and socializing imitation, which culminates in the constitution of the self. However, this anteriority and alterity have a history. It is worthwhile, following both Girard[22] and Oughourlian,[23] to spend some time in postulating the mimetic working of the long road that led from higher ape to human. At the outset it must be said that we have no mode of access to the phenomena in question, which are necessarily prehistorical. The hypothesis explaining the mimetic road to hominization, however, has the great advantage over other theories that it inscribes the genesis of human culture in nature and relates it to a natural mechanism without depriving culture of what is specifically or exclusively human.[24]

The idea, borrowing from J. Monod's realization that the mimetic power of the brain increased prior to hominization, starts with a group, or groups, of increasingly mimetic apes. As mimetic rivalry increases, so the forms of animal sociality, based on dominance patterns, begin to collapse. Intragroup violence based on acquisitive mimesis (already adumbrated in apes) leads to a victim, and very slowly and gradually to the fencing around of (no doubt innumerable) victims with certain prohibitions to prevent the violence happening in the group. Hominization would therefore be the long, slow process of the domestication of mimetic effects, following crises which both produced victims and the need for prohibitions. As mimetic effects are domesticated, so periods of peace become available permitting the very long period of human infancy: the brain, on its way to becoming human, is able to cope with a degree of mimetic functioning that would simply have been catastrophic in a group that had not begun to develop the prohibitions and rituals that hedge around the victim. Thus, simultaneously, the emergence of culture, of human forms of socialization, and of the enormous increase in the capacity for mimesis which characterizes the human brain were brought about by collective murder, which alone provides for the genesis of human culture in nature.

It is of course the moment that death ceases to become something simply biological and starts to become an object of fascination that life too becomes something that is in itself fascinating, beyond the instinct for survival. This vision of hominization posits the growth of a certain quality of group attention fixed on the victim, precisely because this fixing of attention corresponds to the (apparently miraculous) lull after the mimetic storm. The attention begins to be fixed on the cadaver of the unanimous victim and links the cadaver with the extraordinary effect it has had in producing peace out of violent chaos. The mechanism of an awakening of attention is the first beginnings of

---

22. In part 1 of *Things Hidden*.
23. In *Un mime*, 57–58.
24. See *Things Hidden*, 97.

human consciousness. The victim is seen as having produced this, and the (unimaginably) slow awakening of the human consciousness develops exactly as the mechanisms for controlling mimesis develop. In this way, the birth of the sacred and the beginnings of human culture are simultaneous, both flowing from the cadaver which is in the process of acquiring significance.

In this way, too, there begins to come into existence a *sign,* and thus the beginning of meaning and language. This sign is the exception that is in the process of emerging[25] — the victim in fact — and all the binary systems of signs that have been noted by structuralist anthropologists flow from this exception. Every possible signifying element has its starting point in the victim. That which has functioned as transcendental signifier in the formation of the human race is the victim. The signified is all the meaning which the community confers on the victim, and the sign is the same victim as reconciliatory[26] — that is, as gradually becoming part of ritual and language by being substituted for, in order to keep alive the marvelous peace for which it was first seen as responsible.

It should be pointed out (insistently) that when describing the emergence of cultural forms of prohibition, the lengthening period of infancy permitting brain growth, the gradual development of the attention fixed on an object beyond instinct (and thus the awakening of consciousness), as well as the emergence of the sign and of the beginning of language and ritual, what is being described took place simultaneously, and over a hugely long period of years (only empirical study can begin to verify how many) and, even so, only with an enormous amount of difficulty.

The anthropological evidence for this begins to exist with the myths which show the invisibility of the founding murder. The murder can always be shown to be there, but it is tucked out of the way, a representation of some form of collectivity excluding some sort of divinity, for instance. What Girard shows is that the murder is there, in some form or other, but is always represented from a certain perspective, the perspective of what has been a positive action.[27] The consciousness which was engendered by the progressive working of the victimage mechanism involves a failure to recognize what really happened: it is a mis-remembering. The human memory is distorted from the outset in its representation of what happened and why, thus covering up the transference of which the victim was the object. The failure to recognize and thus the distorted perspective of the lynchers is connatural to,

25. Girard, *Things Hidden,* 100.
26. See Girard, *Things Hidden,* 103.
27. Girard, *Things Hidden,* 115.

consubstantial with, the development of human consciousness. Human thought, as well as human memory, were born of the founding murder, of which they are always a distorted interpretation.

Continuing in this line, Girard suggests the way in which the progress of mimetic desire, involving the reprocessing of symbols, led to two fundamental "moments."[28] As imitative rivalry, in itself sterile, began to become fruitful thanks to the gradual invention of ritual and prohibition, so there was born "the ability to look at the other person, the mimetic double, as an *alter ego* and the matching capacity to establish a double inside oneself, through processes like reflection and consciousness."[29]

Here we have reached in the understanding of hominization the same key moment we reached in our description of the coming-into-being of the "self." We have, by now, a definitely human self, a self formed by the social other which precedes it, an other which is consubstantial with it, and an other to which the self is related in an already skewed form. This is fundamental from both a philosophical and a theological point of view. From the philosophical viewpoint, it tends to support Wittgenstein and those thinkers who have sought to demonstrate the implausibility of the mentalist picture of the human as bequeathed us by Descartes, Kant, and the epigones of Enlightenment. Rather than being the irreducible fundament, beyond which no questioning can go, human self-awareness, self-consciousness, the capacity to reflect, is shown to be a highly developed construct, constituted by mechanisms of desire long anterior to it, of which it is not itself aware: how can one be spontaneously aware of what constitutes the background possibility of awareness? Furthermore, the other, and the violent other, is constitutive of human reason, for which, therefore, any sort of ethical objectivity is entirely illusory, except insofar as that reason does in fact become capable of awareness of its formation through, and therefore complicity with, whatever is being talked about.

We can talk about an inherent link in every human life between the distortion of the founding murder — the perspective of the lynchers, which is consubstantial with and anterior to our consciousness — and our nonacceptance of our utter dependence on the other who forms us, the element of pathogenic denial of our alterity shown by Oughourlian (above). We are simultaneously formed by the founding murder and unable to accept complicity in the violence implied by that.

From the theological point of view, it is of no small interest that we

---

28. Not, evidently, chronological flashes, but rather thresholds attained in time.
29. Girard, *Things Hidden*, 284.

have here an anthropology that suggests that awareness of the other and awareness of the self come about simultaneously, and as part of the same process of (controlledly) violent desire. That is to say that both awarenesses and the attitudes that flow from them are simultaneously distorted. Not only that, but the only way of access into the formation of the distorted "self" is via the distorted other, and thus the only access to any sort of transformation of the malleable construct which the "self" has been shown to be passes through a change in the structure of the relationality with the other. This has two implications: first, there is no change in "me" except insofar as there is a change in the relationality with the other; and second, this change can be initiated only by the other. We have here the beginnings of an outline of what an anthropology of grace might look like: any form of Pelagianism is, in the first place, an anthropological mistake, a mistake about the simple conditions necessary for this sort of animal to be able to begin a change at the level of the formation of the "self."

Unpacking the Picture

There are various consequences of the above picture of what it is to be human that I would like to spell out. The first is the way in which the longstanding dichotomy between the individual and the social is dissolved — and with it, maybe, the old philosophical saw of the One and the Many. The primacy of the victim-in-the-process-of-forging-sacrality in the constitution of properly human culture (and thus sociality and order) suggests that the dichotomy between individual and collective is dependent on a misreading of the victimization. Meaning was given to all by the emerging exception of the victim (who was in reality no different from the others). However, that meaning could only be read as a differentiation, whereby the sense of the collective, the many, was forged over against the one. For many centuries, of course, the "many" was assumed to be the good, the stable thing, and the "one," the different person, the odd one out, to be dangerous and threatening — because possessed (like the original victim) of both good and bad qualities to a marked degree (did not the original victim both "cause" the social upset and then "save" the group from the violence it had caused?). Such a view, that of the good many and the dangerous individual, relies on the distorted apprehension of the founding scenario.

In exactly the same way, the modern, "enlightened" equivalent relies on the same distortion, but from the reverse side: it is the individual who is the sacred good, imbued with inalienable rights and with an inalienable freedom and conscience. The "many," the social other, are

the threatening and dangerous element, who may at any moment fet-
ter "my" freedom or rights, which are always worked out over against
the social other. To be able to claim the high ground of victim status
is indispensable for furthering whatever cause "I" seek to sponsor. In
this case, as in the previous, there has been no escape from the founding
sacrality of the victim, as indeed there cannot be without a recognition
that the victim is exactly the same as the many, and that the difference
is produced by a collectively held delusion.

A further dichotomy is subverted, one which has long taxed the
human sciences, and that is the difference between the social sciences,
seen as dealing with objective matters "out there," and psychology,
taken to be related to an individual, without it being clear how these
matters were related. Because of this dichotomy it became possible to
have, simultaneously, a Marxist discourse about society and a Freudian
discourse about the individual, without the two ever marrying. In
theology this same dichotomy has been found (perhaps especially in progressive circles) with a neo-Marxist discourse about social reality and a
transcendentalist view of the individual that could scarcely be less critical of the foundational suppositions of the liberal capitalist order.[30]
This can of course have very deleterious consequences for the living
of a Christian life, where personal and affective elements of life are
deprecated (as bourgeois or alienating) in favor of a massively "objective" approach to the "real" problems of transforming society. It is
scarcely surprising that this approach is usually both highly *machista*
and more or less incapable of dialogue — other people are simply insufficiently converted to "my" objective understanding of reality. That is
their problem.

In the light of the anthropology I have been setting out, it becomes
possible to relate social structure and personal formation in a way that
permits both personal change and social change at the same time. If the
formation of human social order and economic reality are seen from the
point of view of the same paradigm as the constitution of the self by
the anterior working of victim-related mimetic desire, then economic,
political, psychological, and erotic reality can be seen to be part of exactly the same mechanism.[31] This means that transformation of the "out

---

30. See J. Milbank's comments in *Theology and Social Theory*, 228–52.
31. The mutual implications of these dimensions of mimetism are brought out in Girard's treatment of *Troilus and Cressida* in *Theater of Envy*, chap. 17, and also, more
specifically, in P. Dumouchel and J.-P. Dupuy *L'enfer des choses: René Girard et la logique
de l'économie* (Paris: Seuil, 1979), and M. Aglietta and A. Orléan, *La violence de la mon-
naie* (Paris: PUF, 1982). There are hints of thought in this direction in H. Assmann and
F. Hinkelammert, *A idolatria do mercado: Ensaio sobre Economia e Teologia* (Petrópolis:
Vozes, 1989).

there" passes through the recognition of the complicity in its structures of the person seeking transformation. The complicity in question is not only at the level of having voted a certain way, for example, or making a living from a "tainted" industry, but at the level of desiring according to the patterns that form the political system which produced that voting, or that form the economic system which leads to such industries. To put it crudely: the anthropology I am setting out makes it possible to understand that the structural catastrophe of a corrupt and inadequate health care system and the pattern of desires and behavior of a transvestite prostitute with AIDS who is seeking treatment somewhere within the belly of that leviathan are part of the same phenomenon. The transformation of the patterns of desire that have produced the one and the patterns of desire that have produced the other can only be simultaneous and can only start from the recognition of personal complicity.

This leads on naturally to a further consequence of the anthropological picture I have been attempting to set out. The collapse of the world of subject and object, and of subjective and objective. This can be illustrated by comparison with Hegel's notion of the subject and the formation of subjectivity. Like Girard, Hegel saw desire as constituting consciousness, but in his view it was the desire *for* the desire of the other which produces the confrontation with the other which leads to human self-consciousness, and thus subjectivity. However, in Girard's view, that model is just one possible (and a distorted) permutation of the way in which desire moves, in principle, according to the desire of the other. This means that the constitution of human self-consciousness is not *in principle* a conflictual reality, constituting self by means of an over-against, even though it is always so historically. In principle, the recognition of the alterity of the desire which forms the "self" is possible, and therefore the other is not an object over against "me," and my knowledge of the other is part of being consubstantial with it. This analysis tends to show that the subject/object dichotomy is part of the preconscious background to perception formed by the foundational murder and the separative distortion which gave rise to consciousness. The dichotomy is collapsed to the degree in which the self shifts from a pattern of rivalistic *méconnaissance* of the other which is anterior to it to the beginnings of a pacific *reconnaissance*.

It is exactly this which Oughourlian shows in his discussion of the formation of what he calls the *moi-du-désir* (the self constituted by desire):

> The self, founded on *méconnaissance,* could not be conscious of it [i.e., of the *méconnaissance*]. Nor could the desire that engenders that self. But this *méconnaissance* is a failure to understand factual reality,

things as they really are, a reality which is *constant* and *objective*. The *méconnaissance* should not under any circumstances be confused with the psychoanalytic unconscious, which is fundamentally *subjective*.[32]

Thus knowledge of the other is objective insofar as it is relational, based on the real appreciation of the rapport between the other and the self. This perception is very nearly reached by X. Pikaza, who discusses the Hegelian model of the constitution of the self in comparison with the Girardian model,[33] but mysteriously does not apply his insight to the trinitarian models he has been discussing, where he indicates how much Rahner and Barth remain Hegelians in their conception of God as absolute and foundational subject.[34] Were he to have done so he would have seen how the Girardian model permits a trinitarian ontology in which the incipient sabellianism of "God as absolute subject" and the persons as *seinsweisen* is overcome.

Further consequences flow from the model under examination, owing to the way in which desire is shown to be anterior to language (and thus reason), to will (and thus freedom), and to memory (and thus history). In the first place, language is shown to be part of a distorted construction of a worldview. The key binary opposites (good/evil, life/death) are shown to flow from the lynchers' perspective on the victim. Thus the whole human system of signification, rather than being in any sense independent of the sense world and not deceived by it, is already utterly shot through with a certain betrayal of truth. Human reason is a tradition-borne phenomenon, but that human tradition, which is utterly constitutive of the possibility of human culture, is already a form of treason of the truth and can reach truth only with very great difficulty after a long time. In this sense Girard demonstrates that it was not, as is often suggested, that reasonable people proposed scientific theories of causality, and thus showed up the silly superstition of burning witches for the offense against reason that it was. Rather, it was the gradual collapse of belief in the real guilt of such mythical victims which led to the possibility of the proposal of scientific theories of causality.[35]

The human will, and thus "freedom," is also shown to be a highly ambiguous construct. At any given moment in which a human wills or desires, that will or desire is utterly shot through with the other which is anterior to the formation of the will. That is to say, we are constitu-

---

32. I have adapted slightly E. Webb's translation of p. 35 of *Un mime*, p. 19 of *The Puppet of Desire*.

33. In X. Pikaza, *Dios como Espíritu y Persona* (Salamanca: Secretariado Trinitario, 1989), 329–37.

34. Pikaza, *Dios como Espíritu y Persona*, 125–31.

35. See Girard, *The Scapegoat*, 95–99.

tionally heteronomous. The insistence on the autonomy of the human will is part of the self-deception of the "self" that is acting out of denial of the alterity which forms it. The more strongly that alterity, the heteronomous nature of desire, is denied, the more completely we fool ourselves as to our independence in what we want and how we choose. In these circumstances, it becomes possible to talk about freedom only to the extent to which we move toward a recognition and acceptance of our heteronomy. So much can be recognized by an atheist, and indeed by any critic of the liberal world order, where the concept of freedom has been reduced to that of choice. However, ultimately it means that the only real concept of freedom is theological, made possible by the irruption of a different sort of Other into the other-which-forms-us and the setting free of our freedom. But more of that anon.

The third of the three traditional "powers of the soul," memory, is shown also to be constructed in ambiguity. In the case of the human race, the construction of memory, and thus of time and history, is part of the very slow process of the constitution of mimetic controls around the victim. It is the beginnings of ritual, and thus of repetition of acts tied to the founding violence as well as the introduction of prohibitions linked to that violence which enables there to begin to be the human dimension of time and the human capacity to tell the story of a self over time. It is just so in the case of each infant, where it is the repetition of sound and gesture over time which lead to the possibility of the infant acquiring memory and language, and thus the ability to tell the story of the self. Here, too, it can be seen that the human memory, both *qua* race and simultaneously *qua* member of it, is forged in inaccuracy. Thus, any human history or telling of the human story is likely to miss the point of the story. This is not because the memory is inaccurate in the sense of our having severe problems remembering whether Christopher Columbus did in fact cross the Atlantic in 1492. It is because the whole constitution of memory was born by the workings of mimetic desire from a distorted relationship with a certain sort of violence. If that violence had been instantly seen for what it was, then there would not have entered into operation the mimetic constructs which led to the coming into existence of the memory as we know it, and therefore of history.

It becomes possible thus to recover the sense in which memory is a cover-up, a certain sort of forgetting that other things may be remembered. This ties in with the very ancient perception that truth, far from having to do in the first place with simple objective facts, as we are inclined to think, needs a certain sort of un-forgetting. That is what *aletheia* means. Something of the same is contained in our words "discovery" and "revelation." Rather than things being clear, and our just meeting them, the truth is covered and must be dis-covered, or veiled and must be re-vealed.

The final consequence that I would like to bring out of this anthropological model is related to its bodiliness. The mimetic exchanges we have been discussing, which led to the process of hominization, were not something tacked on to bodies. The corporality of our condition is the *sine qua non* of the development of desire, and from it language, freedom, and memory. It is only as bodies that we have language, freedom, consciousness, memory, and so on. Because of this, it means that the human being is a completely historical being. That is, each of us is "thrown into"[36] a world where it is precisely the concrete, historical, contingent acts and occurrences which constitute and form each person. The other which forms us is a social, historical, and physical other. This has the consequence for any theology of salvation that that salvation works precisely at the level of producing a different social other, through contingent historical acts and texts, with physical relations, signs, and so on.

This, of course, places us on a somewhat different course from any transcendental anthropology, which sees, as a matter of philosophical truth, the human being as imbued with a somehow experienced orientation toward grace and glory[37] and therefore the concrete, contingent, historical acts of salvation (the prophets, the coming of Christ, the existence of the Church, the sacraments) as merely making explicit the universal availability of grace. In such a view, "the historical events, the human acts and images which can alone be the site of supernatural difference, are here reduced to mere signs of a perfect inward self-transcendence, always humanly available."[38]

At this point it seems important to try to indicate why the transcendental element seems unnecessary in a fundamental anthropology. This will also help situate the anthropology I have been trying to set out with relation to its theological status, prior to hinting at its potential in other fields.

I do not want to deny (indeed I want heavily to affirm) that all Christian anthropology must posit that all humans are, just by the fact of being humans, called to participate in the divine life. However, it seems to me that this *theological* doctrine is an important human discovery made in the light of the death and resurrection of Jesus of Nazareth and is part of a discovery that we are, in fact, quite different from what we

---

36. G. Vass's phrase in *The Mystery of Man and the Foundations of a Theological System* (London: Sheed and Ward, 1985), 81.
37. Vass, *The Mystery of Man*, 75.
38. Milbank, *Theology and Social Theory*, 222–23.

normally think we are. That is to say, the doctrine of the universal vo-cation to *theiosis* is itself part of the discovery of salvation as a difficult process worked out in hope, in which we hope to become something which we are not, or are scarcely, now.

If we detach the doctrine of the universal vocation to *theiosis* from the element of discovery in hope of something which contradicts our daily lived experience and turn it into a quasi-philosophical description of what we all are, inescapably, then we merely transform the doctrine of the security of salvation — which is applied in Catholic theology only to the Church, that visible, historical, contingent body (and not to each member, who works out salvation with fear and trembling) — into a universal philosophical principle. This means, in theological terms, that the anthropology in question becomes an anthropology of presumption, a subtle form of anonymous semi-Pelagianism,[39] and thus shortcuts the way in which discovery of the universality of the call to *theiosis* is, for each of its participants, a radical conversion and part of the revelation of salvation.

Let me therefore try to set out the way in which the anthropology I have been trying to set out differs from this (and the answer is, only very, very slightly). The human being is constituted by what is other than himself or herself, and is always utterly related to this other which is an-terior to himself or herself. The other I'm talking about is, of course, the human, social, cultural, material, environmental other proper to our planet. It is this other that has forged language, memory, will, and the capacity to relate to the other. So much might reasonably be recognized by anyone, independent of religious conviction. However, that is not to say that the anthropology I have been setting out could have been set out *except* from a theological perspective. In fact, it was a very partic-ular set of contingent historical actions, lives, and circumstances that made it possible to perceive the rôle of the victim as foundational to human being,[40] contingent actions involving a reversal of perspective on the relation of any one of us to that victim. That is to say, it was a par-ticular set of historical events which made it possible fully to recognize the *other* which forms us. And it made it possible to recognize this pre-

---

39. Some monastic theologians in fifth-century Gaul reacted against Augustine's insis-tence on the absolute primacy of grace, teaching that we are capable of the first step toward salvation, which is thus independent of the grace which comes to work after this. This teaching is called semi-Pelagianism. Like Pelagianism, it reappears in different guises in each generation.

40. This is not to say that other anthropologists have not come to the conclusion that the human being is, *ab initio*, a killer, and formed by killing: see, for instance, W. Burkert, *Homo Necans: The Anthropology of Ancient Greek Sacrificial Ritual and Myth* (Berkeley: University of California Press, 1983).

cisely in the simultaneous act of revealing that there was a different sort of other that could form us in a different sort of way: that is to say, there is a different perspective on the founding murder than that which is connatural to us.

In this way, we can say that every human being is, in fact, constituted by and with an in-built relationality to the other which formed him or her. This other constituted the very possibility of human desire. We can also say that owing to the way in which we are in fact constituted, that desire is rivalistic and builds identity, to a greater or lesser extent, by denial of the alterity, and the anteriority, of the other desire. That is to say, human desire, as we know it, works by grasping and appropriating being rather than receiving it. In this sense, we are all always already locked into the other which forms us in a relationship of acquisitive mimesis, that is, in a relationship of violence which springs from, and leads to, death.

It became possible to understand this (in fact) not from natural rational deduction (though there is nothing inherently incomprehensible about it), but precisely because of the irruption of a *novum* into the midst of the social other which forms us, a *novum* which is a revelation of a different sort of Other, an Other that is completely outside any form of rivalistic desire and that made itself historically present as a self-giving and forgiving victim. This self-giving victim, from outside human mimetic rivalry, revealed precisely that the death-locked lie of mimetic rivalry flowing from culture's hidden victims is not the original mode of desire, but a distortion of it. That which was chronologically original (and seemed to us to be simply natural) is *discovered* to be logically secondary to an anterior self-giving and creative desire.

It is, then, this constantly self-giving other, discovered to be logically anterior to the social other which formed each of us chronologically, which makes possible a transformation of each of us by producing an alteration of our alterity, such that we come to have our "self" formed by this other Other. The transformation of our "self" via our constitutive alterity happens not through some universal transcendence, but exactly through the givenness of certain particular historical actions and signs, moving us to produce and reproduce just such historical acts and signs.

If we discover, then, at the culmination of a series of historical incidents God as constantly giving himself to us gratuitously, with no appropriation, it is but a small thing to understand God's gratuitous self-giving to have been always already present. And here is the rub: not as always already present *in history,* because history itself is a production of memory built on distortion, but as the *historical subversion from within* of history, as the way out of the distorted human construct of time, and thus always already present as a form of history which tends to eternal life. The history of salvation is in fact always a critical counterhistory, a historical undoing of the dynamic of human time and the making present in the here and now of lived signs of an unending being-together.

We have, then, in any given human being, a self formed by the desire of another. That desire is lived in rivalistic inflection, what I have called desire of grasping or appropriation. We also have the discovery that the possibility of the existence of any desire at all was an anterior desire that is in no sense rivalistic, which we call the creative love of God. The gratuity of God's love works precisely and only as self-giving; working to produce in each human a capacity to accept — as purely gratuitous — the self-giving other. The permanent self-giving is more than an offer of self-giving, it is self-giving itself, but it can never be lived as self-giving by humans who grasp and appropriate the other. Grace can be lived only as something permanently gratuitously received. The great anthropological transformation, therefore, is of the way in which we move from being constituted by an anterior desire which moves us into deadlock, by grasping and appropriating our sense of being, to being constituted by a self-giving other that can be received only as constantly and perpetually self-giving, as gratuitous, and therefore never grasped, never appropriated, but only received and shared. If it is true to say that it is more blessed to give than to receive, this is because we are the sort of creatures who can only properly (gratuitously) give as part of an imitation of a gratuitous reception. Real giving and real receiving are a mutually structuring reality. We are talking of the person who is beginning to be empowered to move from feeling that society, the others, owe *him* something, toward being able to be toward other people — to act out for them — what *they* think is owed to *them*.

What this means is that the gratuitous self-giving of God is always present contiguous to, and subversive of, any given now, and it is the gratuitous presence which has made itself explicit in concrete human historical circumstances. It is not universal human self-transcendence which makes itself explicit in the events and narrations of salvation, but the universally present self-giving of God, enabling us to become receivers, rather than graspers, of the other which forms us, revealed as purely gratuitous. The problem between intrinsicist and extrinsicist accounts of grace is not a problem, in the first place, of the theology of grace, but one of the anthropology of reception. The dilemma between grace as somehow "owed" to a human and grace as somehow "already imbued in the human" shows that the discussion is taking place entirely within an anthropology of grasping and appropriating and is not focusing on the necessary gratuity of the transformation into gratuitous receivers of what remains lived in gratuity. One of the things revealed by the doctrine of original sin is that it is our capacity to receive gratuitously that was damaged in the fall: not our capacity to *receive,* because we have to receive in order to exist, but our capacity to receive *gratuitously,* which is the only way in which we can share in divine life, because that life can never be other than gratuitous.

Can we then talk of a universal *desiderium naturale,* natural desire, for God? Well, once again, only as a result of the acceptance of the revelation that the real source of the anteriority which forms us is a purely nonrivalistic, self-giving desire (love). What we have without that faith is a construction of desire that never breaks out of circles of appropriation and exclusion. It would be wrong to call that desire a natural desire for God. We might properly call it a natural desire for being, but an idolatrous desire for being, since we are incapable of merely receiving being. So we go to idolatrous lengths to shore up our fragile sense of being, being prepared to sacrifice the other to save our "self." What we can observe is that, in any given historical instance, our desire is for things which have become obstacles to God precisely because they are desired appropriatively, by grasping. It is in the transformation of our receptivity that our desire becomes a desire from and for God and is discovered to be such not as something plastered over our distorted desires, but as the real sense behind even those distorted desires, as something anterior to them. It is in this sense that we become sons and daughters of God as we discover that our belonging to, our being held in being by, the other is more secure and original a way of being in the world than our grasping and appropriating things. The tourist grasps and appropriates on his way through, because he knows that these things, these sights, will not be his tomorrow. The dweller in the land does not need to hold on to them, because she knows that they will be there tomorrow, and it is they that have formed her, not she who possesses them. The *desiderium naturale* is "there" as something that can be recovered.

In this sense I am completely in agreement with J. L. Segundo when he insists that it is quite wrong to see any human construction of values as implicitly pointing toward God simply because they are a human construction of values.[41] Human desire is a good thing because it can in principle be drawn into the desire of God, precisely as human desire, and indeed we know from faith that it was for this that it was created. That does not stop the very condition of possibility of our desire of God (the

---

41. See J. L. Segundo, *La historia perdida y recuperada de Jesús de Nazaret* (Santander: Sal Terrae, 1991), 55.

human structure of desire) being lived without even an implicit reference to the pacific gratuitous other which can transform us into receivers of our being. It is possible for human desire to be lived as idolatry, a complete missing of the point (a "falling short of the glory of God"), an exacerbated desire for metaphysical autonomy, and thus a seeking to appropriate (rather than receive) life for the self, a living from death to death — running from our own death and causing that of others. In this way I hope it is possible to see that the theological anthropology which I have been setting out is in fact well suited to the basic insight of the liberation theologians that the choice is not between theism and atheism, but between the true God (the God of life) and idolatry. This is rather better suited, I would suggest, than a transcendental anthropology, which effectively pre-pardons idolatry without transforming the idolator, without giving him or her the chance of a real restructuring of heart.

I would conclude this section with a brief consideration of the rôle and status of theological anthropology. As far as I can see, there is no Catholic theological anthropology that is not simultaneously part of Catholic theology, and thus part of the human attempt to maintain alive and spread the divine revelation. So all theological anthropology is or should be part of a grace-filled persuasion of revelation. It is indeed (if one can dare to say such a thing) a concrete historical part of the concrete historical way in which God calls us to be reconciled to Him in Christ. There seems to be an underlying problem with the discussions relating to nature and grace which became focused around the era of the *nouvelle théologie,* which might be described as a residual rationalism. This is shown in the way in which the creation of an anthropology is attempted as if it were a neutral intellectual feat. I do not mean by this that the humans described are presented as neutral — they are clearly not (they are presented in rather too rosy a light by my standards). Rather, the act of presenting the rosy human is treated as a neutral intellectual feat, rather in the line of the rationalist apologetics which sought to present, as a supposedly neutral intellectual feat, the *praeambula fidei,* an intellectual scaffolding permitting access to the reality of God prior to the material proper to revelation, which would be presented once that threshold was reached.

Now, in fact, rational apologetics and transcendental anthropologies are no less part of the rhetoric of faith than dogmatic explanations. What I have attempted to do is provide a shamelessly dogmatic anthropology in my search for a greater intelligence of faith. If an earlier generation of Catholic theologians was seeking a relatively autonomous presentation of anthropology, it was in part to avoid the accusation of Protestantism or fideism. This was in obedience to the chapter on revelation of *Dei Filius,* and in particular to the first canon to that chapter, which reads: "If anyone says that the one true God, our Creator and Lord, cannot be known with certainty from the things that have been made, by the natural light of human reason: let him be anathema."[42]

Here it should be pointed out that it is not an article of faith that anyone ever *has* in fact known God with certainty by the natural light of reason; still less is it a moral obligation on Catholic theologians to prove by the natural light of human reason that God *can* be known in this way. It is a declaration that all Catholics must *believe* as an article of faith, following St. Paul at Romans 1:20, that it is in principle *possible* for human reason to know God, that is to say, that human language is capable of telling the truth about God.

What is at stake is the principle of analogy, by which some truth value is possible even to fallen human speech. I hope that it is apparent from the anthropology that I have set out that it does exactly show why we *believe* that it is possible to know God by human reason, precisely because we believe in the real analogy between human language even in the distorted form in which we build with and are built by it, and the un-forgetting, dis-covering, truth-bearing form to which we aspire by an arduous conversion. In this way, there is nothing a priori implicitly fideistic about an unashamedly dogmatic anthropology, such as the one I have been setting out, so long as, within its understanding of conversion, it can be shown to respect the (theological) principle of analogy. I rather suspect, indeed, that it is only a dogmatic anthropology, unbothered by any residual apologetic neutrality, that is *able* to present, without shame, a rather less than rosy picture of the human condition, because the very presentation of the human condition is part of the divine story of what we are becoming.

Testing the Anthropology for Dogma

We began with a reference to W. Kasper, who was setting out the necessary criteria for an anthropology suitable for christology. Even though the present work is not, in the first place, about christology, I think it important to demonstrate at least the compatibility of this anthropology with, and at most hint at its fecundity for, some major dogmatic concerns of Catholic theology.

---

42. Denzinger-Schönmetzer, 3026; Eng. trans. from N. Tanner, ed., *Decrees of the Ecumenical Councils* (London: Sheed & Ward, Washington: Georgetown University Press, 1990), 2:810.

Trinitarian Theology

The major concern of a theological anthropology with relation to the theology of the Holy Trinity is to produce a more adequate (strictly, a less *in*adequate) analogate for the understanding of what the Church has traditionally taught with relation to the "persons" which constitute the One God in whom we live and move and have our being. Traditionally, the analogate has made use of the concept of "person" more or less available within human discourse, and has in fact modified that discourse in order both to enrich the human notion of person and to permit us to discuss Christian monotheism while avoiding elementary forms of reductionism or tritheism. J. Zizioulas has shown how the invention of the notion of person was the work of the great Greek patristic theologians working with the material bequeathed to them by classical thought, which of itself did not know of such a concept.[43] The traditional perspective on the person within trinitarian theology has been to start with an understanding of an individual person and move from that to an understanding of divine persons, who are held to be different from human persons in that, in their case alone, relationality is not an accident of a preexisting substance, but their relationality is their substance: a divine person is a subsistent relation.

Perhaps the most influential analogate for the persons in the Trinity is that elaborated by St. Augustine, whose model saw the relations within the Trinity as best compared to what goes on within one human person: the key elements in the human soul of memory, intellect, and will. This is sometimes called the "psychological" model of the Trinity. St. Thomas, even though he was not seeking a psychological analogate, but a metaphysical one, to answer the question "what is it for an immaterial being to have immanent acts?" also used for his account of immanent action a model drawn from the working of intellect and will within one person.[44] In both these highly influential models, it is one human person who is the (admittedly inadequate) analogate for God.[45]

More recently, following on Hegel's description of human self-consciousness as being produced by confrontation with the other, his notion of subject and object (and, in particular, subjectivity), his awareness that desire precedes consciousness, and his understanding of human

---

43. See his greatly rewarding work J. Zizioulas, *Being as Communion* (Crestwood, N.Y.: St. Vladimir's Seminary Press, 1985), especially 27–65.

44. Thomas Aquinas, *Summa Theologiae*, I, q. 27, a. 1 resp.

45. See J. Ratzinger, "Zum Personenverständnis in der Theologie," in *Dogma und Verkündigung* (Munich: Erich Wewel Verlag, 1973), 205–23, consulted by me in English translation in "Retrieving the Tradition: Concerning the Notion of Person in Theology," *Communio* 17 (Fall 1990): 439–54.

desire as desire for the desire of the other, K. Rahner and K. Barth gave
descriptions of the Trinity starting from the perception of God as absolute and foundational subject. X. Pikaza has pointed out that both
theologians are inclined to attribute the dialogical element in God to
a single subject:

> Both interpret Hegel in a partial (individualist) way, and conceive the
> person of God (and of humans) as absolute subject. Logically, in this per-
> spective, the person of God comes to be understood as the sole subject
> who reveals (him)self, or communicates (him)self in (his) three forms of
> being, or modes of subsistence.[46]

This model is therefore no less "psychological" than previous models,
but has a different psychology, with a different understanding of desire
and the constitution of the desiring individual. As a model it presents
the difficulty that it is stuck within the subject/object dichotomy: either
God is the subject, and we run the risk of Sabellianism, in persons who
are really modes of the single subject, or God is three subjects, and we
run the risk of tritheism.

The anthropology I have been outlining offers, of course, an analogate that is no less psychological than its predecessors. However, it
differs in treating, in effect, any given human as a created subsistent
relation. This means that it can never conceive of God from the analogate of one human person, but rather it conceives the human person
as being brought into, and maintained in, being by another anterior to
it, to whom it is constantly related. J. Oughourlian forged his use of
the word "holon"[47] in the course of his explanation of his new interdividual understanding of psychology. It might be useful to use this word
instead of "person," because of the unavoidable polysemy surrounding
the modern use of "person." The holon refers, in Oughourlian's usage,
to human beings, either as individuals or groups. It is a relational entity
within a movement of interaction. There is no such thing as a holon-
by-itself. Oughourlian calls it "a purely psychological entity, a structure
in permanent becoming at the heart of continuous exchanges with other
similar structures."[48]

Oughourlian's interdividual psychology is then "the study of the
modes of interaction of the holons between themselves, interactions
which, by their very exercise, constitute the existence of each one of the
holons."[49] It is this which leads him to say that the psychological fact is
not situated within any particular body "or in the reassuring totality of

46. Pikaza, *Dios como Espíritu y Persona,* 130.
47. See above p. 31.
48. Oughourlian, *Un mime,* 32, my translation (here and in the following citations).
49. Oughourlian, *Un mime,* 33.

any 'me,' but rather in the mysterious transparency of the interdividual rapport."[50] Thus he presents us with a description of the mimetic constitution of the self that is simultaneously psychological and sociological. The basic unit for understanding what it is to be human is not an introspection, but a mimetic "rapport" between two holons. The holon A is the other (or them) as constituting by mimetic desire the holon B (which is me, or us). In no holon is desire original. There is a constant interchange of desire between the self and the other, and the other is of course a self in constant movement by what is other than it, and so on. It is this model which, *mutatis mutandis,* offers a new analogate for the Trinity. The Trinity can then be described as a *rapport interdividuel entre deux holons,* an interdividual *rapport* between two holons.

In the psychological sphere, from which the interdividual description was adduced, there is of course no origin to desire. No holon can appropriate to itself the originality of a desire without becoming locked in a pathological relationship with the other whose desires it imitates. This is a key difference between a human holon and the divine holon we call the Father. The Father is unoriginated love, pure giving. There is no other that is anterior to Him. All desire originates in the Father, all love. Beyond all competition. There is no other source of human or angelic desire than the Father as unoriginated love.

The holon Father loves his image, his likeness, one who is exactly like Him in all things except being unoriginated. The Son is not unoriginated, because that would give two origins, and unoriginated giving can only be one, beyond number. He is not exactly originated either, because he shares completely in the pure gratuitous givenness (itself unoriginated) of the Father. He is distinct in his sharing in unoriginatedness by receiving unoriginated giving. He receives it completely, because he is the exact image and likeness of the Father, able therefore to receive the Father and, as a perfect likeness, completely reciprocate the giving. That is, as a perfect image, he is a perfect imitator of the Father, with no sort of rivalry; there is no sense in which he wants to appropriate the originality of his love for the Father as his own. Thus, he is without any over-against in his relationship with the Father. So perfect is the imitation that the two holons are the same unoriginated givenness, different inflections of love within that givenness.

The holon Father and the holon Son are therefore constituted by a *rapport interdividuel,* called the Holy Spirit. This is the unoriginated love giving and imitating that giving (reciprocating the love) fully and perfectly and simultaneously. Thus the Father and the Son are consti-

---

50. Oughourlian, *Un mime,* 33.

tuted by a simultaneous giving and imitating. It is this imitative love whereby the Father gives his likeness and the Son, who is that given likeness, imitates the Father, and the Father imitates the Son, and the Son the Father, and so on ad infinitum — which is traditionally called perichoresis.

The Holy Spirit is therefore, as *rapport interdividuel,* the giving of the Son by the Father, and the imitation of the Father by the Son, which are the same thing. In the perfect imitation there is no distinction between what the Father gives the Son and what the Son gives the Father. Son and Spirit are the same sharing in unoriginated giving except for their sharing in unoriginatedness by being given and being the giving of the given, respectively, rather than being its unoriginated origin. Thus one might say in traditional language that the Spirit proceeds from the Father through and from[51] the Son, and that the Son proceeds from the Father in the Spirit. The novelty here is in the greater clarity offered by the application of the imitative understanding of desire to the unoriginated giving in love that is God.

The *rapport interdividuel* in the case of God alone is also a holon, since it is the same unoriginated love as the holon Father and holon Son, and is their perfect imitation. It thus could not be any less than a holon like them, since it is exactly as the imitative likeness of pure giving and His identical given image that the Spirit is. In this way, we can make sense of the description of God as in three persons, substituting person by the marginally less inadequate term "holon," which will bear the full weight of the Church's doctrine on the Trinity at least as well as "person" and, I would say, with fewer misleading connotations.

Sense is also made in this purely relational account of the giving in God of how it is possible to talk about three "subsistent relations" (which is what a holon is) in one God. The key to this is imitation so perfect that the Other is the same. There is no difference between the holons, which would imply an over-against, an envious mimesis, but

---

51. In this model of thought there is no rivalry between the Father and the Son, so the Filioque cannot be understood as either diminishing the fullness of origination in the Father, nor subordinating the Holy Spirit to the Son. Rather, the Filioque can be seen as a useful reminder of the way in which — because there is, in principle, no rivalry between the Father and the Son — something can be wholly and authentically from a *human* without in any way being less wholly and completely divine. Something very similar is affirmed in the way in which, in the original *Ekthésis paterôn* (The fathers' exposition of the faith) at Constantinople (as opposed to the version we now recite on Sundays as the Creed), of Jesus it is said that he "sarkôthenta ek pneumatos hagiou kai Marías tés parthénou" (became enfleshed from the Holy Spirit and Mary the Virgin — shared agency) rather than "incarnatus est *de* Spiritu Sancto *ex* Maria Virgine" (became enfleshed *by* the Holy Spirit *out of* Mary the Virgin — principal agent and vessel). See N. Tanner, ed., *Decrees of the Ecumenical Councils,* 1:24

merely the distinctness of the acceptance of the giving, or the enjoyment
of being given. We cannot at all imagine what a purely given distinctness, without any over-against, might be, what a relationship entirely
outside the sphere of envy might mean. For in God difference does not
mean separation, but mutual enjoyment of the same by the same, so that
the holons constantly foster and cherish each other in ever more joy-
ous imitation rather than appropriate the given over against each other.
What I call the distinction, then, as opposed to "difference," between
the holons, is something which we can only describe in via, as we move
toward purely given identities; these distinctions can only be described
negatively, as utterly unlike difference. Where difference would be an
obstacle to sharing in the fulness of unoriginated giving, distinction is
what makes it possible.

I hope that this is sufficient to suggest the possible fecundity of the
anthropology I have discussed for trinitarian theology. In the following
chapters I will offer further hints of the way in which such an anthropology can illuminate the human process of the discovery of God as
Trinity, the process which is the working out of the revelation made in
the crucifixion and resurrection of Jesus.

Christology

By positing an anthropological understanding that is remarkably similar
to the one I have outlined, as part of the understanding of humanity
present in the teaching and action of Christ, it is possible to engage in
a rich hermeneutic of the Gospels, as Girard does in the second half of
The Scapegoat. It is also possible to carry out a rereading of St. Paul's
theology of the sort carried out by R. Hamerton-Kelly.[52] I have myself
tried to indicate the directions which might be followed in a "Girardian"
christology in *Knowing Jesus.*[53] Here very briefly I will set out some
considerations arising from the application of the model I have been
developing.

In the first place, by positing in Jesus an anthropological understanding founded on an intelligence of the working of mimetic desire and its
victimary consequences, it becomes possible to understand a key feature
of the Gospels, which is the simultaneous presence of this understanding
in the words and actions of Jesus and of the misunderstanding of these
same words and actions by the disciples. It makes absolute sense to see
the possibility of the simultaneous presence of the two as owing to what

---

52. R. Hamerton-Kelly, *Sacred Violence: Paul's Hermeneutic of the Cross* (Minneapolis:
Fortress, 1992).

53. J. Alison, *Knowing Jesus* (London: SPCK, 1993).

the Gospels themselves indicate as having taken place, that is, a teaching by Christ which the disciples were unable to understand while he was alive, and the beginnings of their being able to understand after the resurrection. What is suggested (exactly as the Gospels themselves suggest) is that after the resurrection the victimary intelligence which had provided the inner dynamic of Jesus' life came to possess the disciples, so that they were able to see what had been going on all along from Jesus' point of view. The Gospels themselves would be the written form of the apostolic witness to the working of that intelligence in the life, death, and resurrection of Jesus. In the light of that intelligence it can be seen both how Jesus understood himself to be the self-giving victim in the process of founding the new Israel of God (the people living from, and not by exclusion of, the self-giving victim), and how that presence of the self-giving victim automatically implied the bringing into being of a new unity of humans with no barriers or frontiers of race, purity, and so on — the first authentically universal community, in fact. The mimetic anthropology yields an understanding, then, of the inner dynamic at work in the creation of the Church and of the New Testament, as well as positing an account of Jesus' self-understanding that owes nothing to a Cartesian or mentalist description of Jesus' "self-consciousness."

Here, however, I would like to suggest the richness of the anthropology for a different christological question: that of the human "person" of Jesus and a new account of what is implied in the "hypostatic union." Oughourlian's account of a holon-based interdividual psychology is able to find a test-case in the working of hypnosis.[54] He is able to show how a holon A (hypnotizer) produces in a holon B (the person under hypnosis) a new *moi-du-désir* — self formed by desire. This is, of course, a short-lived "self," which can remember the life of the previous "self," but, when the "spell" is broken, the previous "self" has no access to the life of the self that was formed under hypnosis. The point of this is to indicate that the relative success of hypnosis in producing a "self" is precisely because the method follows the mimetic working of desire: the "self" is called into being by the suggestion of the "other" at the level of desire.

This can be tied in exactly with the way in which Jesus was related to his Father. It becomes possible to see Jesus' human self as being "suggested" (or called, or loved) into being by the Father, exactly through the normal human physical means. It is to just such an intelligence of who Jesus was that John gives witness in the way in which he portrays Jesus as being utterly dependent on the Other who called him into being

---

54. Oughourlian, *Un mime*, 239–303.

(John 5:19ff.), and yet utterly one with his Father. A completely non-rivalistic imitation is at work ("I do everything which I see my Father do"). There is no sense in which Jesus tries to forge his own identity over against that of his Father; there is no grasping in Jesus' mimetically formed self (see Phil. 2:5–9). Thus the purely gratuitous self-giving of the Father is completely imitated in the life story of the Son. This enables us to affirm the hypostatic union as being the "hypnotizing" into historical being of the person of the Son, and makes sense of the insistence of theology after the Third Council of Constantinople that Jesus is not a human "person" but a divine person in a human nature.

The consequence of this approach to the question of the hypostatic union is that it enables us to see Jesus as having a human desire, human will, human intelligence, and so on, so that it is not necessary to postulate anything humanly "special" about Jesus, in whose case all these are formed by a nonrivalistic mimesis, which is *in principle* a possibility for us. Thus it becomes possible to see Jesus not as *a* god, with the implications of a special sort of difference in his humanity, but as God, precisely as a fully human being. The reason why this is important is that the imputation to Jesus of something "special" in his humanity, something which we could never be, is to present Jesus as urging upon us a particular form of human imitation of the sort "imitate me / do not imitate me." That is to say, Jesus would, for us, remain stuck within the double bind of distorted mimetic desire, from which he would thus not be able to release us. However, part of the point of the doctrine of the Incarnation is exactly that it shows that here is a human we can imitate fully, have our relationality completely transformed in his following, such that we too are able to become sons of the Father in a dependent, but not in a limited way. It is not true that, "yes, you can become sons, but no, not in the way that I am the Son." Christology undergirded by an anthropology of pacific mimesis is able to yield the sense in which humans are called out of the double bind. In Christ there is no "yes" and "no." Only "yes" (2 Cor. 1:19).

Further hints of the fecundity of mimetic anthropology for christology will be found in the discussion of creation in Christ in chapter 3 below.

Faith

J. Ratzinger has pointed out that it is a typically Christian mistake to assume that when we talk of "religion" and of "faith" we are essentially talking about the same thing: it would be quite wrong to describe every religion as a "belief."

The Old Testament as a whole classified itself not as "belief" but as "law."
It is primarily a way of life, in which, to be sure, the act of belief ac-
quires by degrees more and more importance. Again, by *religio* Roman
religious feeling understood in practice mainly the observance of certain
ritual forms and customs. It was not crucial that there should be an act of
faith in the supernatural. . . . It is by no means self-evident that the central
expression of Christianity should be the word *Credo,* that the Christian
should describe this attitude to reality as being that of "belief."[55]

It is my suggestion that the anthropology I have been outlining enables us to make much more sense of faith as the underlying structural
reality of the concrete historical presence of Christianity. It can do this
and at the same time show the relationship between the faith of the
Church and the gift of faith in any given member of the Church, avoiding the residually Cartesian and mentalist pictures of the invisibility and
individuality of faith which so color modern approaches, both in those
accepting and in those experiencing difficulty with faith.

Following the approach I have outlined above, it would be perfectly
correct to talk about faith as, in the first place, an ordinary human form
of relationality, not only that, but as an indispensable one, by which we
are all constituted. For we are suggested into being by others on whom
we are dependent, and our being is constituted by all that alterity, on
which we rely. Wittgenstein has magisterially exposed the implausibility of the Cartesian picture of methodological doubt.[56] Doubt is itself
shown to be a very highly developed form of behavior, utterly dependent on a bedrock of given, that is, unexamined, certainty. We would
consider mad the person who, on opening every door, carefully checked
that there was a floor on the other side of it so that she did not fall into
a hole. So we are in fact formed as humans by a certain form of faith.
We have allowed ourselves (before there was a "self" to do the "allowing") to be suggested into a pattern of relationality which we take for
granted. For instance, as a twentieth-century English schoolboy I was
fed from an early age a certain view of English history and of the Reformation in England. Such views have been formative of the historical,
political, religious, and national attitudes of a whole series of similar
English people. Even though, as I acquired some critical faculties,[57] I
have come in large part to disbelieve the views and distrust the emotions associated with them, it is still from within a whole seedbed of
acceptance, formed by such things as the English language (and what

---

55. In J. Ratzinger, *Introduction to Christianity* (San Francisco: Ignatius Press, 1990),
22–23.
56. See especially L. Wittgenstein, *On Certainty* (Oxford: Blackwell, 1969).
57. Not enough, do I hear the reader cry?

it owes, for instance, to the King James Bible), the English education system (and what it owes to the existence of a state religion and the comparative absence of a *laïque* and anticlerical spirit), and of course a family, who have taken a certain part in and been formed in certain attitudes toward these and other formative events. Luckily it is not possible completely to sever oneself from formative human faith, from one's being suggested into being. To achieve that would be to reduce oneself to gibbering silence.

What the mimetic anthropology suggests, then, is that in every case we are suggested into being and to a greater or lesser extent accept and are nurtured by that anterior other. Of course, that anterior other is always already violent and deceptive, as well as nurturing and educative, as is, therefore, in degrees varying according to circumstance the "self" that is called into being through the workings of human faith. What I would like to suggest is that what we call supernatural faith works in exactly the same way, by the mimetic calling into being of new "selves." That is, what makes such faith possible is the irruption of an "Other" into our lives of a different sort than the somewhat nurturing, somewhat violent other which has formed our "self."

What we have, then, is the anthropological precondition for the real transformation of being that Catholic theology has always defended as being proper to supernatural faith. However, it is important not to leave the matter there, since in fact the irruption of the new "Other" might be understood to be a sort of divine lightning bolt, in which case the transformation of the "self" would be something entirely invisible to, and not part of a change in, human relationality. It would simply be an abstention from human relationality.

However, the new "Other" has always, in fact, worked by producing a human subversion of human relationality, such that there are real human patterns of behavior to be learned as part of the suggestion of our new "self" into being. It becomes possible then to talk of supernatural faith as the long process by which a particular Middle Eastern people were brought into having a certain sort of different "self." This process enabled them both to come to a certain understanding of the new "other" that was calling them into being and to develop new patterns of relationality, understood by comparison with the patterns of relationality evidenced among their territorial neighbors (and often invaders, conquerors, and colonizers). Over a very long period of time, this people did become aware of the importance of the utter otherness of this new other as a precondition to a real difference being made to themselves. Hence the ferocity in defense of the monotheism and the insistence on keeping the Other free from images. The trouble with images of God is not that they are images of God, but that they tend to reduce God to a function of the human-formed "self."

Within the context of this process of the human discovery of the complete alterity of the Other, and therefore of the possibility of human difference, and taking for granted all its real achievements which had formed him, Jesus led a group of disciples through a highly condensed historical reworking of the process by which Israel had reached its understanding of the Other. In this he presupposed the structure of Jewish belief present in his disciples. What he did with them, both by his teaching and in particular by his life, lived out toward his death, and through his resurrection, was gradually open up a further and richer perspective onto who the God whom Israel had discovered really is. That is to say, Jesus' life and death, especially as illuminated retrospectively by the Holy Spirit after the resurrection, served in a concrete, visible, practical way to add a further and definitive perspective onto who the "Other" really is. What Jesus can be said to have done is gradually, painstakingly, but visibly and historically, to have stretched and shaped anew the perception of the other "Other" in the lives of certain particular, historical individuals, whom he chose *for that purpose* — to be his witnesses.

This means that he produced in them a certain sort of faith in God, going a step beyond the Jewish faith in the image-lessness of God by permitting the discovery of a particular image of God. This image of God is the human victim. This image alone is shown to free the perception of God from any sort of human appropriation and manipulation, because it means that for any human God is the inconvenient other who threatens the stability and security of the human "self." No one can appropriate this "other" to himself, because this "Other" can be known only on its way out of (as it is expelled from) the other which forms us anyhow. Furthermore, if God is the human victim, this means that access to God is available not only within the particular racial or cultural group that made the discovery possible, but is universally true wherever the human "self" is formed by victimization, at individual and group level. That means everywhere.

So supernatural faith, the suggestion into being of a new other, becomes possible precisely through a certain historical enactment, kept alive by certain historical persons, who maintained alive for others the possibility of encounter with this suggestion by the construction and transmission of certain repeatable, historical actions (like baptism and the celebration of the Lord's Supper), and certain historically repeatable words and texts. Simultaneously they also maintained alive, as part of the contingent historical mechanism of keeping available the access to

the new "Other," a certain watching over the practice and interpretation of these actions and texts, certain institutional forms (what we call
Church order). Historically it was this Church order that permitted the
structuring and transmission of Word and Sacrament. All this occurred
within the context of the keeping alive of the discovery of God as victim
as the basis of a completely new sort of unity of all humans, regardless
of race, tongue, etc. The new "Other" is therefore available universally
precisely through the presence of the particular historical persons, acts,
and institutions which bear witness to it. That concrete historical set of
practices, texts, and institutions is in fact the beginning of the calling
into being of the new human "self," as subversive of the ways in which
normal human identity is formed.

The consequences of this picture are, I hope, evident. Faith is, in the
first place, the faith of the Church, and is structured *as* Church, *as* the
unfulfilled but nevertheless real sign of the coming into being of the new
unity of humanity formed by and around a totally new "other": God
as self-giving victim. Supernatural faith is, then, in the first place the
faith of the Church, and it is, by its nature, Catholic, because universal.
So there is in principle no properly speaking supernatural Christian faith
that is not a certain sort of concrete (and therefore visible) human participation in the concrete historical body whose perception of the "other"
was first stretched open by the actions and words of Jesus, and whose
actions, texts, and institutions continue to stretch to keep alive fidelity
to that perception.

Thus, for any person in history, whose "self" is formed by the
"other" which is the "world," supernatural faith is the induction into
the historical body and its practices whose underlying structure is faith.
(Of course, this induction may happen in varying degrees of ecclesiality, owing to the scandals of human schism and fissiparousness, which,
of their nature, are irruptions of the separative self formed by the
"worldly" other.) However, it is not just his or her induction; rather it is
his or her induction into these actions and practices *as* stretching him or
her out of the worldly self and into the beginnings of a new (collective
and individual) self, whose full ramifications are not yet known. Each of
us can be suggested into new being only through and with the human,
historical signs of that new being which are given us in the Church
(which is given us as the Church). The Church is then the human sign
of the new "other" making possible our access to our possession by that
"Other."

This faith is, of course, necessarily operative in the lives of real
persons if it is to be real. That is to say, for each person something
distinctive must be known, and relaxed into. What we are called to

know is that there is a different "other" and that this "Other" is different in a certain way (that is, is self-giving love, quite outside the reciprocity of human relationality, as made visible in Jesus' self-giving on the Cross). Furthermore, this self-giving love creating the possibility of a new human relationality (a new unity of the human race) does in fact seek to include me, as one such human, in this transformation. Both elements, traditionally called *fides qua* and *fides quae,* are simultaneously indispensable for the proper relaxation into the hypnosis of the other "Other." The process of faith in the life of the person is therefore precisely the learning to relax into the suggestion of this other "Other," a process that is arduous because what is being undone is the way in which our selves are formed and constituted by the "worldly" other, which is at many points in denial of the peaceful mimesis, which is the new "Other's" way into us.

An example of this process might be someone who is being disbelieved or falsely accused by the people with whom she lives, to such an extent that she is tempted to believe, and accept as true, their attitude toward her. In the midst of this, she can remember that she is, in fact, loved exactly as she is, regardless of the ambiguities of her behavior, by God, the other "Other," and that her real "self" is in fact held in being by that Other rather than the human other which is harassing her. By remembering the real love of this other "Other," she is able to act toward the harassing other by forgiving them (an action in imitation of the concrete pattern taught and lived by the historical person who permitted the recasting of the understanding of God as outside human mimetic double binds), that is, by acting toward them in a way that is gratuitous, from outside the realm of violent mimetic desire which would entrap her if she allowed herself to be defined by it. In this way a real step is taken, with her active participation, toward the formation of the new "self" that is being called into being by God, and this step is taken precisely within a human network of meaning, memory, and patterns of relation made available by a contingent human story, kept alive by a contingent human set of practices and institutions.

The element of supernatural faith is, therefore, present, as leading us out of our formation by the harassment of the old "other." This means that it is a form of learning relaxation in the midst of struggle. It is a reality present while there is still a worldly other forming and pulling us. It is for this reason that there is no faith in heaven. For there we will be pacifically possessed by the new "Other" without any tension from the old other, which will have passed away.

The mimetic anthropology also permits us to see how the "new self" is in fact both a new creation, but also the recovery of what we were

originally supposed to be, such that the self formed by the desire of the
world, although original in time, is not original in logic: for there to
have been such a self, there was necessary the mimetic structuring of
desire which was created in order to permit us to share divine life by
possession. Our chronologically original state is a distortion of our ontologically originary state. The new self through faith is not just a rescue
job (saving us *from* the world) because the first try was a botched job.
Rather it is the rescue *of* the first job (saving us *in* the world).

In this model, then, faith is intrinsically linked to contingent historical factors and is thus dependent on visible historical practices. Faith is
shown to be a gift that is collective, related to the calling into being of a
"we" and of the "I" as part of that we. In brief it shows faith as a historical process of discovery and of the maintaining alive of that discovery
by its continuing to be a discovery, that is, by the continuing work of
un-covering the presence of the Other as victim, and of creating signs
of that discovery, celebrating that presence both in repetitive ritual ways
and, simultaneously, in stretching toward and serving the victims which
the old other, in ourselves and in others, constantly creates and covers.

Now, if this sounds too much like a simple assertion of Catholicism
then it should be pointed out that it is a two-edged assertion. For those
of us who have been summoned into the re-creation of our "selves" in
and as the Catholic Church run the terrible risk of not being signs of the
new "Other" but rather of giving other people no grounds for believing
that there *is* a new "Other." This is what happens when we have the title
of signs and witnesses to the new "Other," but our patterns of behavior
are formed entirely or predominantly by the old other. This is when we
give scandal instead of giving witness: we make it appear that God is
part of the human double bind of mimetic desire rather than being a
pointer to an "Other" entirely outside and subversive of that double
bind. We become doubly obstacles to God's pacific summoning of the
human race into a new unity, in the first place in the ordinary way in
which we are all obstacles to each other, and in the second place by
misrepresenting God so that God is believed to be part of the same. We
are, as it were, interrupting the hypnosis rather than being the human
vehicles of that hypnosis.

This consideration also suggests the function of the theologian in the
Church, which is to help in the work of maintaining the discovery alive
by helping in the detachment of human thought processes from their
bases in the rivalistic understanding proper to the old other. The ecclesial intelligence of the faith is, then, a divine impulse toward a constant
purifying of language and practice so as to allow God an ever less ob-
stacled possession of us, precisely because it is through human words

and practices that God wishes to have access to us. The theologian seeks to make words formed in and through the old "other" become capable of transmitting, or at least not betraying too grotesquely, the new "Other" — the vertiginous belief that words themselves need not be stumbling blocks, but can also be vessels of God.

Conversion

It will not be necessary to spend much time, in the light of the above, suggesting that mimetic anthropology is par excellence an anthropology of conversion. The transformation of a *moi-du-désir* via a transformation of alterity has to do precisely with the changing of heart implied in the word *cor-vertere*. What can be shown is the way in which faith, because it is what permits us to live on the interface between the old other which formed us and the new other which seeks to form us anew, is intrinsically related to conversion. Nor is it difficult to show how this conversion is intrinsically ecclesial. The new heart is created in us by the old heart — which is too small and rigid and bound with the consequences of the double bind — being broken. The new heart is ecclesioform in that it is summoned into being as we are summoned into living as a sign of the new unity of humanity. The conversion works as we recognize our complicity in creating victims, cease to regard ourselves as a victim, and begin to see ourselves as covictimizers. This is a first step toward the learning how to create concrete acts of solidarity with our own and other's victims, even though, as we will discover, this increases the likelihood of ourselves being victimized. In the concrete circumstances of humanity, what the new unity of humanity looks like is the beginnings of the gathering of penitent persecutors around the body of the self-giving victim, whose forgiveness made their new perception possible, and the creating of acts of worship of the victim, both in celebration and in acts of fraternal service.

Conclusion

With the above, I hope I have justified my pretension of setting out an anthropology of wisdom, that is, an anthropology which functions as revealed discovery mediating between a revealed perspective and a dialectical anthropology. In this way I hope to have helped forge a tool that can be applied in differing fields of Catholic theology without reducing theology to anthropology. I have sought to call it a wisdom anthropology because it is no use as a merely intellectual device. Positing, as it does, the formation of the intellect through the workings of distorted desire, it suggests that there is no access to anthropological vision except through a certain sort of conversion. That is to say, it is only in the degree to which a person comes to recognize the extent to which he or she lives in denial of alterity and is constituted by mimetic desire leading to and flowing from victimage that he or she will begin to acquire some sort of clarity of understanding of who any of us really are. The understanding which we are on the way to acquiring is, of course, a properly human understanding, but it is acquired through something like an initiation, a discipleship, and the theology resulting from it would not be true to its anthropological bases were it not also an experience of conversion.

Chapter 3

The Search for
a Soteriology

The doctrine of original sin is a derivative doctrine. Like many of the key doctrines of the Catholic faith, it does not spring straight out of the text of the New Testament. The New Testament is, rather, the written form of the apostolic witness concerning the salvation wrought by the life, death, and resurrection of Jesus of Nazareth. It was later controversies that led to the elaboration of what we now call the doctrine of original sin, which was then understood to be a necessary part of the new perception on God and on humankind brought about by the events and interpretations that constitute the apostolic witness. What we have in the first place is a teaching concerning salvation. As part of the developing understanding of that salvation and of the universal necessity of the death and resurrection of Jesus for that salvation, the doctrine of original sin was slowly forged. Thus, in any attempt to approach the doctrine, it is necessary not to consider it in the first place in itself, but rather to look at the sort of salvation the Catholic faith holds to have been offered to us. From this starting point, it should become possible to see what the doctrine of original sin might mean and how it is related to the Church's understanding of salvation. This latter point (how it is related) is as important as the former (what it might mean). Too often, the doctrine of original sin is treated as a starting point relatively independent of revelation, as though it were simple human common sense that there is something terribly wrong with the human race. This "something terribly wrong" then becomes a foundational reality, from which we can understand salvation. Such an approach leads to theological presentations of the sort "the world is a mess — Christ is the solution," and an understanding of salvation as essentially salvation *from* the world rather than *of* the world, as Catholic teaching would hold.

This chapter, then, sets out a theology of salvation to enable us to rediscover the doctrine of original sin as an integral part of the revelation of salvation.

64

Revelation as Discovery

It is one of the advantages of the anthropology that I have been trying to set out that, by insisting on human alterity rather than some supposed imbued transcendental relation to God as constitutive of what it is to be human, it permits us to consider divine revelation as a process of human discovery. That is to say, it is not frightened of the utterly contingent, human, historical process by which cultures arose and declined, events occurred, peoples were formed, events were reenacted, texts were brought into existence, previous events were reinterpreted, the texts themselves were edited and reedited. It is not as though divine revelation needs somehow to be protected from all such happenings, in order really to be divine revelation. Rather it is precisely in the midst of such manifestly human happenings that divine revelation has occurred as a process of the self-manifestation of God that is simultaneously the coming into being of a certain intelligence regarding who human beings are.

In his remarkable book *Science and Faith: The Anthropology of Revelation,* E. Gans indicates that there is an unresolved dilemma between positive anthropology, which sees no break between prehuman forms of life, and generative anthropology, which proposes a scene of origin.[1] It is Gans's suggestion that religious thought has always held on much more firmly to the need for a scene of origin than positive anthropology, because it is aware that there is a rupture of some sort between *almost* being a human and *being* a human. The possibility of representation, or the origin of language, is what is brought about by and in the scene of origin, and in this sense, as Gans points out, we are talking about a foundational event that is unique, that occurred only once.

> Human monogenesis can only occur at the extreme limit of biological monogenesis: its concentration in a unique event.... Man is defined by his possession of systems of representation that permit him to transmit to other members of his species large quantities of context-sensitive information that could not be borne by the slow and limited process of genetic mutation and transmission. Nonhuman species have no scene of origin; specific experiences may modify or "condition" their behavior, but can effect no irreversible change in their relation to the objects of their appetite. Man is the only animal for whom collectively remembered scenes, or events, exist.[2]

This means that there is no possibility of approximation to any originary scene from the standpoint of positive anthropology. Positive

---

1. E. Gans, *Science and Faith: The Anthropology of Revelation* (Lanham, Md.: Rowman & Littlefield, 1990).

2. Gans, *Science and Faith,* 6–7.

anthropology, by definition, can only have access to empirical evidence of what is already human: rites, myths, archaeological remains. There is, by definition, no human evidence of what was prehuman. The only access to an originary, foundational event is by a purely hypothetical construct of an event. Such a construct would need to show the way in which an event, which was led up to and constituted by purely animal behavior, was able to yield, from within those animal mechanisms, human representational behavior. This construct is not a piece of original knowledge about what happened, which has somehow mysteriously been maintained alive by some form of traditional transmission, for, by definition, that which constitutes and structures consciousness and which was not, at the time, part of a human representational order is not something of which the newly conscious humans can be conscious. Rather, the construct is an a posteriori approach in the light of what we know now.

In this I differ somewhat from Gans. Gans posits the moment of the constitution of human monogenesis as, in itself, a moment of revelation. By this he means the birth, through a particular event, of an entirely new form of awareness. It seems to me that he is right about the birth of the new form of awareness, but wrong to call that a revelation. A revelation implies that something that had been covered, hidden, is now dis-covered, unhidden. However, in the moment of the constitution of a properly human consciousness there was nothing previously human to be uncovered. By definition, what led up to and permitted the forming of the human representational awareness was not itself human. The constitutive event itself is not dis-covered, or revealed, in the birth of the new human awareness. Rather, it is precisely this event that is hidden, or covered, in the structure of the awareness which it has made possible.

Gans rightly argues that the thesis of the necessity of an original event is independent of how any given theorist chooses to reconstruct that scene.[3] He then gives his own reconstruction, in which a group of prehumans, engaged in a hunt, surround a large edible animal. Each notices the appropriative movements of all present toward the animal (reaching out to grab their bit), which has just died from violent blows. Sensing the violent nature of the scene and the potential for conflict, each aborts his gesture toward the beast. The aborted gesture toward the beast in the center functions as a designation of it, and so, communally, the highly desirable beast in the center becomes untouchable, and the gesture a *sign*. Thus we have the first act of representation, linked to collective performance and ethical restraint. We have the birth of

---

3. Gans, *Science and Faith*, 3.

human awareness.[4] This birth of human awareness immediately has a locus with a center (the edible animal), and a periphery (the gesturing proto-humans). All human awareness is then related to a center outside itself which is what has constituted it as human awareness. Thus there is a constant necessity to keep alive, to recover, the relationality forged in this originating scene in all human culture.

In the light of what I said above about the necessarily a posteriori nature of the hypothesis of the original event, Gans's reconstruction can be linked to where he thinks humans have *now* got to. His position is what might be described as liberal Jewish. History is the story of how this original scene was enabled to be understood first by the Mosaic revelation at the burning bush (with God occupying the center and Moses the periphery), then by the Pauline revelation on the road to Damascus (with the persecuted Jesus — a man — at the center, and Paul on the periphery). By thus effecting the shift from God to man in the center, and so removing the sacrality of the prohibitions on imitative rivalry from the center, the Jewish-Christian tradition would have laid open the bases for the possibility of a competitive market economy, the dynamo of progress, which is seen as that toward which the process of human revelation has been heading. There is then, at the base of Gans's view, a certain confidence in human progress as working toward the best and a certain lack of ambiguity about the foundation of human culture in something as apparently trivial as the killing of a piece of big game.

It seems to me, along with Girard, that the foundational event is far more likely to have been one of intraspecies violence culminating in a death of one of the members of the group. In the Girardian version of the rôle that the original scene plays in the structuring of the possibility of human awareness, the relation between the center and the periphery, and thus the way that the sacred other appears to have made all the difference, is no less vital than in Gans's model. It means that all human awareness thereafter is structured by its relation to what has just become a human cadaver, which has not been perceived as a victim but rather as a fascinatingly causative element. But this too is a piece of a posteriori hypothesizing. I think this *because* I think that human origins were revealed in the death and resurrection of Christ. Because that is the paradigm of where I understand humanity to be, I understand the foundational event to have been a profoundly ambiguous one, in which the birth of human awareness is simultaneous not with the *revelation* of something, but with its occultation.

Where Gans moves from talking about his primary revelation — the

---

4. Gans, *Science and Faith*, 5.

scene of origin — to discussing secondary revelations, such as the Mosaic revelation and the Pauline revelation, both of which permitted access to the human originary scene, I think it important to see revelation as a process of human dis-covery, implying that there is something to be uncovered. This means seeing revelation not as a particularly important form of human progress, by which we came to be the sort of people we now are, but rather as a constant counterforce, a constant un-covering of something which we tend to cover up as a result of being human beings as we are.

Gans reckons that, for his view of an anthropology of revelation to work, there is no need to posit any form of supernatural intervention in human history. He is, however, convinced of the need and importance of the rôle played by the human language of divine intervention in the past. It was this which permitted the discovery of the relationship of each one of us to the center of the original scene (the large edible animal). It is only the use of the language of the divine that permitted Moses and Paul to empty out the confusion of other human representations that rushed in to occupy and manipulate the center of the original scene. In fact, Gans goes so far as to show how the doctrine of the Trinity is really the culmination of the human process of revelation, because it is this doctrine which shows the real structure of the center of the originary scene.[5] It is now possible to do without such language and shed the myth of celestial intervention.

Clearly, my own approach, and Girard's, does not seek to do without celestial intervention. Indeed, it is one of the primary tenets of the approach that I have been outlining that it becomes possible to develop the sort of anthropology I have set forth only *because* there has been a divine revelation. There is no reason to think that human awareness could contain within itself the radical critique of the possibility and manner of its own coming into being, as an immanent development of itself. So, in talking about revelation I am talking about something no less anthropological than what Gans is describing. I am talking about a human process of discovery, and one which tends to re-create the original scene in which human awareness was born. However, I am talking about a human process of discovery that is made possible by the irruption, into contingent, historical, human life, of a difference, a difference of perspective and regard on exactly the same human events, accessible by exactly the same human means. It is exactly this divine revelation *as* a

---

5. Gans, *Science and Faith*, 107–12. It is not the least of the extraordinary intellectual strengths of Gans's book that an avowed atheist is able to give both an orthodox and a highly illuminating treatment of the doctrine of the Trinity as applied anthropology.

human process of discovery that has made it possible for us to understand that there is no necessary conflict between divine revelation and
anthropological discovery. This understanding is itself a very peculiar
historical and cultural construct, one that is by no means self-evident,
and indeed has not been arrived at by most human cultures.

If I may build, then, on my understanding of, and disagreement with,
Gans, it would be to say that a hypothesis of an original event is necessary to describe human being. Such a hypothesis is necessarily an
a posteriori construction in the light of a current understanding of how
humans are. The great moments of discovery in Judaeo-Christian history
are anthropologically structured around, and do indeed open up an ever
sharper perspective on, what such an original event might have looked
like. The opening up of the perspective on the originary scene is what
permits human freedom. However, the process of dis-covery has, in fact,
happened not as the unaided outworking of a human dynamic, but as
a divine revelation.

This means positing that the slow development of the understanding
of who human beings are and the slow development of the understanding of who God is are a simultaneous process, and impossible the one
without the other. Revelation is the process of the discovery of who God
really is that is subversive of the culturally developed understanding of
who humans are, and in turn is constitutive of a new identity of what
humans are on the way to becoming. However, it is these things as an
apprenticeship which involves learning to see the same reality from a
different perspective: specifically the hugely culturally complex (and apparently very rare) process of learning to look at the act of victimization
from the point of view of the victim, which subverts identity (in order
to rebuild it), rather than from that of the lynchers, whose viewpoint
constitutes an identity that is also a cover-up.

A divine revelation cannot be argued for from neutral premises, for
there are no neutral premises. According to what you think has been
revealed, that is the measure of your revelation. If what you think has
been revealed is something which humans can, with their awareness constituted as it is, look squarely in the face without any prompting or help,
then you can dispense with divine revelation (as Gans does), though
not, of course, with its anthropological correlate. I do not think that
anything human could have revealed the constitution of the human consciousness in human victimization, because I do not think that we can
accede to that sort of awareness of who we are without simultaneously
being absolved of our complicity in that violence. I know of no neutral
description of our complicity in founding violence that is not either part
of an accusation (in which case, who is accusing us and why? Are not

they too constituted by the same violent relation to the center of our scene of origin?) or part of a forgiveness (which is possible only from someone who is either totally outside the scene of origin, or inside it as victim and not participant, or both). Constituted in alterity as we are, we cannot absolve ourselves. For us to accede to that sort of revelation we needed to be able to be absolved by some other, and by some other intimately related to the center of our scene of origin, which was the other that first constituted us. This too is, of course, all a posteriori. I think all that because I believe in the forgiveness of sin. I would then refine my understanding of divine revelation to say that the discovery of who God really is has happened through the human process of discovery that human beings can forgive sin: that a divine prerogative has become human without ceasing to be divine. This is not to limit, for instance, the discovery of God as gratuitous Creator to being a subsection of the forgiveness of sin; rather it is to insist that, in our case, it has taken the making present of the forgiveness of sin for us to be able to see with sufficient clarity, to understand creation as something gratuitous, and not, for instance, part of the establishment of divine order out of preexistent chaos.

With this in mind, I will attempt to set out some of the principal moments of that human discovery in the midst of its contingent historical process.

The Resurrection[6]

Eric Gans, in the book I have cited above, when dealing with the revelatory moments that have led to our gaining access to our scene of origin, posits two key revelations: the Mosaic and the Pauline. He says, almost *en passant,* that no special revelatory experiences undergone by Jesus are transmitted to us.[7] Rather it was Paul's perception of him as Christ-as-human-victim in his revelation on the road to Damascus that was important for constructing the theological mystery of Christianity and the Trinity. Now, here I think that Gans is just plain wrong, not about Paul's perception of Jesus as Christ-as-human-victim, but about that experience being the central moment of the Christian revelation. The Christian revelation was not, as Gans rightly suggests, a revelatory experience undergone by Jesus. However, neither was it a single, Pauline

---

6. A considerably less compressed account of some of the material dealt with here is to be found in my *Knowing Jesus* (London: SPCK, 1993).

7. Gans, *Science and Faith,* 85.

moment of insight.[8] Rather it was the resurrection of Jesus from the dead made available to a large number of people, including, finally, Paul (1 Cor. 15:3–9).

What we have then is a public revelatory experience, made available to a number of people, and especially to a small group who had been prepared for that experience by the life, leading up to the death, of the one who appeared after the resurrection. Now it seems important to note that all the texts we have with relation to Jesus either formally insist that he was raised from the dead or are clearly structured by an awareness that he was. That is to say that the texts themselves are the witness, put into writing, of the irruption into the midst of a group of humans of a completely new phenomenon: a man whom they had known before, whom they knew to have died, who came back into their midst. It is equally clear that, if Jesus had *not* been raised from the dead, then there would have been no such texts. Those who had accompanied Jesus during his adult life would have suffered a loss at his death and might have meditated on what he had meant to them as one does when one loses a friend. However, eventually they would have got over it. He would be just another dead man, even an especially just dead man, but still like all those other dead people whom the circumstances of human tyranny and confusion put to death.

So, in the New Testament texts, we have a witness to a life and a death, a witness that is structured by the revelatory presence of the resurrection. If there had been no resurrection there would have been no texts and no guiding understanding of what the life and death of Jesus had been about. Prior to the texts, therefore, is a revelatory experience of a group of people, an event. It is this event that I would like to explore, attempting to find out something of the density of this event as evidenced by the witness that has been put into writing.

In the first place, the resurrection was something that happened to Jesus. It is quite clear from the New Testament accounts that the apostolic group is claiming this. The same Jesus who had been put to death also rose from the dead. His resurrection was as objectively related to him as his death. No one thinks of someone else's death as, in the first place, a subjective experience that happens to the onlooker. Everyone knows that it is something that happens to the person concerned. It is quite plain from the New Testament texts that the resurrection of Jesus was seen as having done something extraordinary and indescribable to

---

8. In taking the line he does, I'm not sure if Gans is aware of how close he comes to the liberal Protestant view of Paul as the founder of the Church. Elsewhere (p. 12) he shows little respect for Protestantism!

that death, which happened to a real person. All the talk of death having been overcome would have been nonsense if the resurrection had not undone the real death undergone by a real person. Any attempt to make out that the death was real enough but that the resurrection was essentially a subjective experience in the lives of the disciples is but an example of modern eisegesis, and an eisegesis based on one of two possible starting points.

The first starting point is that the apostolic witness is not trustworthy (a perfectly intellectually coherent position). In that case we should not believe what the apostolic witness says: they were making things up for reasons of their own. Furthermore it is not only the resurrection of Jesus that becomes dubious; by exactly the same criterion the very historical existence of Jesus can be called into question. This is a plausible position given that our relationship to the events described, and the interpretation put on them in the New Testament texts, is that they are accessible to us only by our trusting the apostolic witness. Either we accept on trust the apostolic witness or we do not.

The second starting point is that the disciples *thought* that the resurrection was something objective that really happened to Jesus, and so described it in the way they did. However, from the vantage point of "modernity" or some such position of supposed superiority, we know better than they, and in the light of our more sophisticated philosophical techniques we are able to reread the texts and see that *in fact* what is being described is a subjective experience. Now this does not seem to be an intellectually coherent position. This is saying "we accept the apostolic witness, but we do not accept this bit of it, because we understand this bit better than the apostolic group." It is quite clear that whatever the apostolic witnesses are describing, it was something which broke the categories of easily available speech, something entirely new and unexpected, and furthermore something which they saw as definitive and unsurpassable. For us to claim that we understand it better than they is effectively to claim that it was not definitive and unsurpassable, because we, in our understanding, have surpassed it and are able to understand it. That is to say, the approach I am describing is somewhat contradictory. It is a way of not accepting the apostolic witness while pretending to. Considered as an intellectual approach to a text from a different culture it also shows an incapacity for alterity, for being able to imagine that something might be being described in the text which in fact blows open all approaches to reality, including our own. It is as though that can only be accepted which can be digested within our frame of reference; that whose acceptance alters our frame of reference cannot be accepted. But then human thought is inescapably either tentatively open to alterity or else totalitarian, but never detached or neutral.

Accepting, then, the reality of Jesus' resurrection, we can begin to inquire as to the witnesses' perceptions of that event and, in particular, to the appearances which were the signs that the event had taken place and which, as signs, were events in themselves. It would be proper to start by looking at the circumstances of the disciples after the crucifixion and before the resurrection. From their point of view, their relationship with Jesus had suddenly ended. They had all the memories and loose ends of the way Jesus had influenced their lives, but the possibility of reciprocity from Jesus had ended. So their emotions were held in a vacuum. It was not merely a neutral vacuum, as if they had had nothing to do with Jesus' death; it was a tragic vacuum because of the way they had abandoned and (in Peter's case) denied Jesus. That is to say that along with the beginnings of mourning, there was present the guilt of betrayal, or at least abandonment, of their friend when the going got tough.

The disciples were not only mourning and feeling guilty, but were also severely disappointed. After all, Jesus was not for them just a friend or a relation who had been killed, but a leader who had promised them much and whom they had trusted to lead them to some sort of radical upheaval in Israel (quite what sort was not clear). They had trusted him, and embarked upon an extraordinary adventure with him, and it had come to nothing. Furthermore, these reactions were held within a generalized fear of what might become of them in the wake of their leader's execution. They were, after all, identifiable, probably by both accent and dress, as foreigners, and many were from the region from which Jesus himself had come. As foreigners in the capital of a police state, ones linked with a major criminal who had just been executed, it is fully understandable that they met behind locked doors. They may indeed have been more frightened than they need have been: it is quite possible that they thought of themselves as to some degree part of a politico-messianic movement,[9] in a way which Jesus did not. This will have led them to feel the danger of their position maybe more acutely than they need have.

What we have then, in the apostolic circle, is a group of disillusioned, frightened, guilty, mournful, semi-traitors. It was into their midst exactly as they were that Jesus began to appear starting on Easter Sunday. The whole Christian understanding of revelation hangs from these appearances: without them there would have been no Christianity.

---

9. Witness their question to Jesus even after the resurrection: "Lord, is this the time when you will restore the kingdom of Israel?" (Acts 1:6).

The first category by which we can approach the density of the witnesses' experience is that of gratuity. The irruption into their midst of Jesus after his death was totally gratuitous. That is to say it was not part of any ordinary human mechanism of reciprocity. Someone who is attacked may attack back, but someone who is killed does not come back to kill. By killing someone we are in fact terminating the possibility of reciprocity on their part. So the resurrection was completely gratuitous for the disciples: unexpected, it was not part of any human story that any of them knew how to tell (or could know how to tell). It was indeed the beginning of the possibility of a totally new human story. Nothing in popular Jewish belief in a resurrection on the Last Day had prepared them for this. Furthermore, the resurrection of Jesus was for them something utterly "other": their first reactions were ones of consternation and difficulty in identifying what was going on. This irruption of what is utterly other is by no means simply a delightful experience. Where the "customary" other (the people and places who surround us) is often experienced as constraining, this "customary" other at least gives us a certain sense of security. The "removed" other, like experiences in foreign lands or in the midst of unforeseen upheavals, is both exciting and frightening — exciting as we see new things and frightening as we appear to be at the mercy of forces we do not know how to control or deal with (how does one cope with an angry foreign policeman whose language one can scarcely understand? Is one not more likely to get a rough deal at his hands than back home?).

The "utterly" other is then even more exhilarating and terrifying, because it completely throws our frame of reference. In the case of the risen Jesus, the disciples experienced this disturbing sense of the utterly other (it was necessary for the risen Lord to say, "Why are you troubled?" [Luke 24:38] or, "Do not be afraid" [Matt. 28:10] or, "Peace be with you" [John 20:19, 21, 26] when he first appeared) before they were able to glimpse something familiar — and say "It is the Lord" (John 21:7). But even so, this was not a collapsing of something strange into something familiar after all. The experience seems to have been that the utterly other had a familiar center without ceasing to be utterly other. That means that it could not be approached as simple *presence* which could so easily be turned into part of what we dominate and control, but was presence always as other — leading the disciples on and out of themselves. So we find the conviction that it is the same Jesus who is present, and present physically, but at the same time a frank recognition that he could not be instantly recognized. He is announced (in Mark 16:7) as the one who "is going before you to Galilee." He is recognized in Luke only at the culmination of leading the disciples through a reinterpretation of Scriptures — and he vanishes as soon as recognized. As an irruption of the "utterly" other, Jesus' presence is not one that can be held on to or reduced to part of our world, but is itself a disturbing presence as "other," as leading on.

This presence that is utterly other is also physical (as Luke and John attest). In this way the gratuity is emphasized: a ghostly presence could have been part of the "other" which haunts one — a projection of a guilty conscience (as Herod imagined John the Baptist into rising from the dead, Mark 6:14–16). A physical presence underlines both the continuity of person (the presence of the marks of the crucifixion also attest to this) and the way in which that person is quite outside any scheme of reciprocity, any sort of posthumous vengeance from beyond the grave.

It may seem unnecessary to say so, but this presence is also a *human* presence. It is not as though, after his death, Jesus gave up his pretense of being human and resurrected as God. Rather, the apostolic witness underlines that he was resurrected as a human being. This is evident from the way in which a clear distinction is made between the risen Jesus, who is a human being and at a certain moment ascends to heaven, and the Holy Spirit, which is not a human being.

So we have a certain density of presence to the disciples that is radically other, and yet familiar without ever losing its otherness: what one might call a presence which leads out rather than a presence which comes home. But this is not all. For this presence appeared in the midst of the frightened, ashamed, disappointed abandoners. And there is no sense in which the presence was a ticking-off, a form of rebuke for having abandoned Jesus. That is to say, part of the nature of the gratuitous presence is that it is forgiving. The risen Jesus did not need to say to those who had run away, "I forgive you": his presence to them was a forgiving presence, was forgiveness as a person. So in Luke and John he gives them power and commands them to forgive others as the way of spreading this presence dynamically in human form. To the disciples themselves the very fact of his gratuitous presence was forgiveness. This enabled their confusion and sorrow to be loosed within them because the focus of their sorrow and guilt and confusion had come back from right outside it and was not affected by it. The risen Jesus was not reciprocating anything done to him, but was a presence of love without condition. Now it is worth noting that this gratuitous presence as forgiveness was only forgiving because there was something to forgive. The forgiveness was not a change of attitude on the part of Jesus or God, but a change in their relationship to the "other" on the part of the disciples. If there had been nothing to forgive, it would still have been possible to perceive the gratuity of the other as simply loving.

Because there was something to forgive, this gratuitous loving is experienced as forgiveness. Gratuity is experienced as the lack of retaliation where some sort of retaliation is to be expected, and then as the giving of something unexpected. This surprising nonreciprocation is what pulls the person experiencing it out of the reciprocating mode-of-being and enables that person to begin to receive and then transmit love as something simply given.

So we have a presence that is gratuitous, human, physical, elusive because leading on, and experienced as forgiving. There is a further dimension which must be brought out in order to describe less inadequately the presence of the resurrected one to his disciples. This is the way in which Luke and John both attest that the risen Jesus still bore the marks of his death. This insight is difficult to express clearly, but it means that when Jesus rose, it was not a simple continuation of his life (as if he were simply a few days older), with his wounds cured by God, but rather that he was given back to the disciples as simultaneously dead and alive. In the risen Lord there is no chronological distance between the death and the life; rather the complete "otherness" of the resurrection life is that it is not on the same level as either human life or human death, and is thus able to give back both simultaneously. The risen Lord is thus always the crucified and risen Lord. This difficult concept is attested to famously in the visions of the slaughtered lamb in Revelation (5:6), where the triumphant lamb is triumphant *as* slain, not because, having once been slain, it is now fully recovered. I suspect that this is what lies behind the difficult Semitic idea that Jesus was unable to be held by the pangs of death (Acts 2:24): for Jesus merely to have been cured of death would mean that the resurrection life was on the same level as death, merely its contrary and stronger than it. However, more is shown: the resurrection life has emptied death of its power by showing the *form* of death (the marks of crucifixion) without its content. What is given back is not only the particular act of God in the case of Jesus, of loving him through and beyond the barrier of death, but the permanent way in which God has made of death an empty threat: his gratuitous, loving presence is always present as overcoming death at any given moment. So the risen presence is of the dead-and-risen one as gratuitous forgiveness revealing love beyond death.

This brings us to a final point about the density of the dynamic of the risen presence to the disciples, one which once mentioned is too obvious to need much illustration. This is the way in which the experience of the risen Lord was understood to be in some sense definitive, or originary. The risen Lord was the irruption of something utterly new that was understood to relate to the beginning of creation, or a new creation. St. John's description of the Garden harks back to the Genesis account of creation; Paul talks of a new creation. John and Matthew in different ways imply that that final judgment is already realized in the presence of the crucified Lord. The irruption of something originary into history is also the irruption of what is final and definitive. Now this, it seems to me, brings us back to our discussion of an originary scene. For what we have been describing is a revelatory presence that has a quite specific structure: the other as gratuitously forgiving human victim irrupting into the midst of those who were unable to avoid some sort of contamination with complicity in the victimization.

Here is something quite clear: we have a foundational scene of origin in reverse, in which the victim is uncovered and given back in order to permit a new sort of foundation that does not depend on a cover-up. This permits us to see the resurrection not in the first place as the next step in the chronological continuation of the life of Jesus, as though everybody knew that Jesus prophesied his death and resurrection, he interpreted his death beforehand in the Last Supper, he died, and then he was resurrected, the next part of the story. The resurrection is the possibility of a completely new and previously unimaginable human story, a rereading of all human stories from a radical perspective that had previously been hidden. It had previously been hidden by the reality of death. So the resurrection brings the completely new perception of what Jesus' life and death had been about: the Father's interpretation of Jesus' life as hated without cause. By giving him back, the Father permitted a fresh rereading of the death of Jesus, and of his life and self-interpretation leading up to it, and thus affords a completely new perspective on human victims. Thus, when Paul has his vision on the road to Damascus, he is perceiving exactly the same new regard on human life as previously had been experienced in a public way by the disciples: this is the revelation of God as human victim.

The Intelligence of the Victim

A revelatory presence would have had no significance unless it provoked simultaneously a certain shift in human understanding. It is exactly this shift in human understanding that the texts of the apostolic witnesses reveal. That is to say that the presence of the crucified and risen Lord to the disciples did not so much "reveal" a piece of information that had previously been unknown; rather it permitted a manner of looking upon reality that had previously been impossible, a human perception of reality that was not available while death was still a definitive reality for all humans.

To explain this more fully it is perhaps worth indicating that what was revealed was not in the first place that there is a resurrection of the dead. It is clear that by the time of the Maccabees elements of popular and pharisaic Judaism did believe in the resurrection from the dead. That the Pharisees believed in the resurrection from the dead is shown by their support of Paul in Acts 23. Martha believed that her brother Lazarus would be raised on the last day (John 11:25). In this sense Jesus' resurrection recast an existing belief in the resurrection so that resurrection was from now on linked to his person: it is not just because of the fact of being human that one rises from the dead, as if it were just the next stage of some journey. Rather one rises from the dead if in one's life one has been associated with the life and death of Jesus. The "fact" of the resurrection from the dead, as news of the existence of a hereafter, is of secondary importance compared to the whole new kind of perception that it made possible.[10]

However, the shift in human understanding to which I am referring was not the addition of information about the afterlife to what was previously known; it was the possibility of a radically new regard on human life and relationships. The Gospels are clear on this: before the resurrection there was a great deal that the disciples were unable to understand about what Jesus was saying, toward what he was leading them, and so on. From the resurrection onward they were able to understand something quite new about Jesus, about God, and about human beings. This is shown by the simultaneous presence in the Gospels of two sorts of understanding: the incomprehension, or miscomprehension, of the disciples, and at the same time the clear comprehension of Jesus of what was to come to pass. This presence of two understandings in the same texts was made possible by the texts themselves having been written *after* the resurrection, when the apostolic group was able to understand, for the first time, what Jesus had really been about and at the same time to understand that, unlike themselves, *he* had understood what was going on all along.

This new understanding, or intelligence, of the life of Jesus permitted the disciples to go back in their memories and reinterpret what they had witnessed, recalling and making a unified sense out of what had not seemed to possess a unified sense before. This rereading included, of course, an honest appraisal of their lack of understanding, and indeed of their abandonment and betrayal of their master, and how even *that*

---

10. It is interesting that St. Paul spends the first fourteen chapters of 1 Corinthians working out the consequences of the shift of perception and dedicates only one chapter to the question of the fact of the resurrection.

was part of what had to happen. The evidence for this is the way they were able to make a unitary sense out of the texts of the Old Testament pointing to the death of the Messiah.[11] In the appearance of Jesus on the road to Emmaus (Luke 24:25–27) it is exactly this that is indicated:

> "O foolish men, and slow of heart to believe all that the prophets have spoken! Was it not necessary that the Christ should suffer these things and enter into his glory?" And beginning with Moses and all the prophets he interpreted to them in all the Scriptures the things concerning himself.

The risen Lord permitted a completely new rereading not only of his own life and death, but of the way that life and death reinterpreted the Scriptures. It was not that the apostolic group was able to find a whole series of proof texts in the Scriptures to bolster their belief in the risen Lord, but rather the presence of the crucified and risen Lord was suddenly the hermeneutic key permitting a reading of the Hebrew Scriptures that was able to show God's self-revelation as a process leading to a point of culmination of which they were, through no merit of their own, the witnesses.

The apostolic group was perfectly aware that this change was being produced in them in the aftermath of the resurrection, and they give witness to this awareness in their description of the Holy Spirit. In the first place, a clear distinction is made between the presence of the risen Lord, who is a human being, and the Holy Spirit, who is not a human being. This distinction is clearest in Luke/Acts where the Ascension is accomplished before the coming of the Holy Spirit. However, it is implicit in John, where Jesus breathes the Holy Spirit into the disciples on the first evening of Easter. That is to say, it is not merely the fact that the risen Lord is present that is the Holy Spirit, but he actually gives them something that is his, but not totally identical with himself. John brings out the difference when he has Jesus tell the disciples that it is to their advantage that he should go so that another advocate may come (John 16:7), and indicates that the other advocate will bring about an understanding that was not possible before the death of Jesus (John 16:12–13). John also brings out the identity by insisting that it is the things *of Jesus* that the Holy Spirit will bring to mind and reveal (John 16:14–15). This shows that the disciples understood themselves to have received a profound new intelligence into what Jesus had been about, who God is, and who human beings are that had not been available before Jesus' death and became available shortly after his death. This intelligence, which they understood to be the inner dynamic of the whole life and death of

---

11. Including their abandonment of him; see Zech. 13:7, quoted at Matt. 26:31, Mark 14:27, and John 16:32.

Jesus and what had formed his relationship with his Father, I choose to call the intelligence of the victim.

By this term I do not mean a peculiar sort of intellectual brilliance, some sort of an increase in intelligence quotient. I mean the exploratory and creative human understanding concerning God and humanity which Jesus showed in his life leading to his death and which was made manifest to the apostolic group by his resurrection. As they became possessed of this intelligence the disciples began to reread the process leading up to Jesus' death as the story of the self-giving and self-revealing victim, who alone had known what was going on. They were able to understand that Jesus' death was not an accidental interruption of a career that was heading in another direction, but rather that his whole life had been lived in a peculiar sort of way *toward* that death and that he had been aware of this. It is because of this that all the Gospel accounts are focused around the passion, toward which they build. The disciples, then, were aware that the intelligence of the victim which they now possessed was not only a postresurrection intelligence, but had been a preresurrection intelligence in the person of Jesus alone. It was an intelligence that had, all along, been guiding the life and death that they had accompanied and witnessed. What was unique was the way in which after Jesus' death they began to be able to tell the story of this life and death not from their own viewpoint, as muddled hangers-on, but from the viewpoint of the dead man, of the one who had become the victim. It is not as though they had invented a profound new insight into Judaism to honor the memory of a dead teacher. Rather they were now able to see clearly the inner unity of the interpretation of Judaism which their teacher had been explaining to them as with reference to himself. They were able to see his life through his own eyes: that is, tell the story of the lynching from the viewpoint of the victim's own understanding of what was going on, before the lynching, leading up to, and during it.

This intelligence of the victim is not, however, a piece of arcane knowledge passed by a teacher to a group of initiates, a secret to be divulged only to other initiates. Jesus taught perfectly publicly, though the Gospels do show that he gave privileged teaching to a few (the twelve), and even among them he was particularly careful in his preparation of Peter, James, and John. The difficulty of Jesus' teaching had something to do not in the first place with its own content, but with the constitution of the consciousness of those he was teaching. It was as if they had a veil over their eyes until after the resurrection. That is to say, what Jesus was revealing was something about which human knowledge is shrouded in self-deception. The disciples' understanding was (as ours is)

formed by what Jesus was trying to change: that is, the constitution of
our consciousness in rivalry and the techniques of survival by exclusion
of the other. What the disciples became aware of after the resurrection
was that the person whose consciousness is constituted in rivalry and
survival by victimization does not possess the intelligence of the victim.
The beginning of the perception of the intelligence of the victim is already an alteration in what constitutes human consciousness, permitting
us to see things from the viewpoint of the victim and from the point
of gratuitous self-donation. This, they saw, was already fully present in
Jesus' life: his human awareness was simply not constituted by the same
"other" as their own. It would of course take some time to move from
the perception that the other who formed and moved Jesus was simply
the Father, to the awareness that this meant that the Son was in fact a
perfect imitation (or *eikôn*) of the Father, to the awareness that this implied an equality of substance with the Father, and the beginnings of the
doctrine of the Trinity.

After the resurrection, then, Jesus' moral teaching and his teaching
concerning discipleship were able to be understood not as extra features
of his life, unrelated to his passion, but structured by exactly the same
intelligence of the victim that led to his passion. Exactly the same is true
of Jesus' understanding of the coming of the kingdom of God which he
preached, which was also the foundation of the new Israel in his victimary death, which he prepared. So, for instance, the Sermon on the
Mount paints a picture of blessedness as being related to the choosing
of a life that is not part of the violence and power of the world, going
so far as to show solidarity with those who are of no account in this
world, even if this means suffering victimization because of the option
taken. The parallel passage to the beatitudes, the parable of the sheep
and goats, shows the same intelligence at work: divine judgment is recast
entirely in terms of practical human relationship to victims, independent
of formal creeds or group belongings. The only relationship that matters in the judgment is that with the victim. This intelligence is not only
present in those passages which obviously and explicitly have to do with
victims and persecution (which are not a few), but is present at one remove in all the moral teaching: in the rest of the Sermon on the Mount
Jesus teaches about the way in which we are constituted in violence —
so anger is the equivalent of murder, lust of adultery, and so on. The law
cannot reach this, the constitution of our consciousness (as Paul was to
demonstrate forcefully in Galatians and Romans),[12] so Jesus gives a se-

---

12. See my "Justification and the Constitution of Consciousness: A New Look at
Romans and Galatians," in *New Blackfriars* 71 (1990): 17–26.

ries of teachings about how to break out of violent reciprocity, learning not to be run by the violence of the other (going the second mile and so on). This freedom, when lived, permits us to live gratuitously with relation to others, even if they then victimize us.

Lest this sound too like a strategy for coping with an evil world or some sort of paranoia, it is important to insist that the disciples' perception, after the resurrection, was that Jesus possessed this intelligence from the beginning, and that the self-giving, the gratuity, was prior to the intelligence. To put this in a different way: Jesus was able to teach about the intelligence of the victim because his human consciousness was not formed in violence but was pacifically given and received. Thus he was able to live his life in self-giving, and it was his self-giving that enabled him to understand the intelligence of the victim and interpret the Jewish Scriptures around this central perception. From the point of view of the disciples, the process was the other way around: as they became possessed of the intelligence of the victim, so they were able to perceive the gratuity which made it possible. But they also perceived that in Jesus the gratuity was always there and had made the intelligence of the victim connatural to him: in this world, what a purely gratuitous human presence perceives *is* the intelligence of the victim.

In this way, the evangelists are careful to indicate that there was no "death wish" in Jesus. It was not as though he wanted to die and thus become a posthumous martyr and hero. The person who seeks to be martyred in this way is still very much formed by the violent desires of the world: needing a peculiar form of victory over your enemies. John stresses in particular Jesus' freedom with relation to his "hour" and the way in which he was laying down his life of his own accord (John 10:18): Jesus' self-giving out of freedom was what gave him his intelligence of himself as fulfilling the promises of the Messiah of Israel as victim.

The disciples were able to perceive in this gratuity the element of the given in the whole of Jesus' life, and read this back into the telling of his story even before his ministry and passion. It was this element of gratuity, from which welled the intelligence of the victim, that enabled them to begin to understand that Jesus was a man who was connatural with God. Matthew and Luke both read elements of the gratuitously given nature of Jesus into his birth and infancy and show the presence of threat and lynching not far from him even then (with Luke emphasizing the gratuity, and Matthew the threatening lynching). John takes the final step of tracing back explicitly the gratuitous self-giving of this man into God. In his prologue John shows the self-giving as prior to the rejection, and in the passion narrative he shows God giving a victim into human hands that is far more than any of the cultic victims which the figures of the Old Testament sought to offer to God.[13]

The first of the two key shifts permitted by the intelligence of the victim was a new perception on humans as formed in violence, with victimization as the constitutional base of human awareness. The second is the shift in perception that this affords with relation to who God is. As it becomes possible to perceive humans as constitutionally violent, so it becomes possible to understand God as entirely without violence. What allows the intelligence of the victim to be applied to human culture is the completely gratuitous self-giving of God that is anterior to it. Thus we are able to accede to the way in which, for it to be possible to understand God as love (1 John 4:7–11), it was necessary that the human victim be revealed. Only the revolution wrought by the intelligence of the victim made this understanding possible. That God is completely without violence, that God is love, was a discovery made possible only by the self-giving of Jesus to death, and therefore the discovery that our awareness of God had, up till then, been distorted by our own complicity in violence, unrecognized and transferred or projected onto God. That distortion is undone. So the intelligence of the victim works two ways: revealing the human being, and revealing God, simultaneously. The intelligence of the victim is simultaneously the definitive demystification of God and the final undeceiving of the human being. We can express that simultaneity only dialectically, but of course as a revelation the simultaneity was not dialectical, but gratuitously given: the two discoveries were simultaneous and part of the same discovery. God is entirely purely gratuitous self-giving, and what that looks like in the midst of humanity is like a dead human victim, and what that says about our relationship to God is that we are related to God as to a dead human victim, either in ignorant complicity in the victimization or, from now on, in the beginnings of a penitent solidarity.

The Founding of the New Israel of God

So far I have been presenting the intelligence of the victim as the shift in intelligence made possible by the presence of the crucified and risen victim to the apostolic group. That is to say, I have been emphasizing the way in which the divine revelation of the self-giving victim and the human discovery of the intelligence of the victim were simultaneously made available to the disciples. This may sound uncomfortably as

---

13. See J. D. M. Derrett's brilliant *The Victim: The Johannine Passion Narrative Reexamined* (Shipston-on-Stour: Drinkwater, 1993).

though what the Christian faith is really about is some sort of revelation, or knowledge, or intelligence, and that everything else is secondary. This would lead to some sort of gnostic interpretation of Christianity. Here I think it important to indicate that the revelation and the discovery of the intelligence of the victim is not only some intellectual matter, but is in fact identical with salvation, or redemption. This is not because I wish to reduce salvation to a form of knowledge, but because I wish to indicate how this form of knowledge is, and was intended by Jesus to be, constitutive and creative of a new human reality. That is to say, as humans come to perceive the reality of God as victim and of humans as victimizers (which can only be a practical intelligence of *my* complicity in the structures of violence which form me and which I pass on), so we are impelled to the construction of a different form of social other, one built *from* the self-giving victim, rather than one built *by exclusion of* the victim.

This leads us to examine the way in which Jesus' intelligence of the victim proportioned a certain sort of critique of the Israel of which he was part. It would be possible to imagine what I might call a dialectical critique of Israel in the light of the intelligence of the victim. This would be one where a prophetic figure, like Jesus, comes along, with a certain sort of intelligence and makes a critique of Israel in the light of this intelligence. He would be saying: Israel has got it all wrong; we must start again by founding something new. So he founded something new called Christianity in the light of the intelligence of the victim. Some interpretations of the origins of Christianity (particularly those influenced by Luther's transference of his hatred of the Catholic faith onto Judaism) do indeed follow this dialectical pattern. However, this would not be faithful to the presentation of the sort of intelligence of the victim to which the apostolic texts give witness. In that witness, it is quite clear that Jesus preached the coming of the kingdom of God, or of heaven, as a fulfillment of God's promises to Israel, and yet the beginnings of the fulfillment of the coming about of that kingdom happened as the recasting of the people of God around the same person of Jesus as self-giving victim. The operation of this shift, from the preaching of the kingdom to the foundation in Jesus' victimary person of a new people of God, is what I am examining here.

In the previous section I tried to make it clear that the witnesses perceived a difference between their accession to the intelligence of the victim, a necessarily dialectical process involving their own conversion, and their awareness that this intelligence was pacifically held by Jesus (or that it was what pacifically possessed Jesus) from the beginning. They also demonstrate that Jesus applied this intelligence *to Israel* from the beginning. This is clear from the way in which he replied to the question about divorce: "from the beginning it was not so" (Matt. 19:8; Mark 10:6). That is to say, his attitude toward Israel was not based on a dialectical critique, but on what one might call a foundational, or gratuitous, critique, which is only a critique at all by accident, because in the first place it is an understanding of what was in the beginning.[14] So when he criticizes the scribes and Pharisees, it is not part of a new proposal that he is making in the light of which they look foolish. His concern about them is that in them Israel is falling short of what it should have been from the beginning. Hence, in places it is suggested that they are Egyptians, who are holding up the real Exodus of God's people. This is done with particular subtlety in Mark 3:1–6. There the way in which Moses placed before the people of Israel the choice between good and evil (Deut. 30:15), the way in which God took Israel out of Egypt with mighty arm and outstretched hand, and Pharaoh's hardness of heart are all recalled in the incident of the cure of the man with a withered hand (which becomes outstretched) despite the hardness of the heart of the Pharisees, who did not understand the choice on the Sabbath between doing good or evil, and went out to seek to destroy Jesus.

Here the problem is not with the nature of Judaism, but with the way in which its current spokesmen are falling short of what they should have known and been *ab initio*. Exactly the same intelligence underlies the famous "woes to the Pharisees" in Matthew and Luke.[15] The critique, which is obviously made out of a huge sadness concerning the fate of Jerusalem (O Jerusalem, Jerusalem, etc.), is precisely that the whole point of the foundation of Judaism, the calling of Israel out of Egypt, was to build a nation that was not like other nations, a nation that did not victimize, that cared for the widow and the orphan, treated well the sojourner (for remember that you were strangers in Egypt), that did not enslave (for remember that you were slaves in Egypt). That is to say: the calling of Israel was God's project for being authentically human, for the rescuing of Abel from beneath Cain's stones, and this vocation as universal model for humanity is being betrayed by the current representatives of Israel, who are fully complicit in the construction

---

14. By a "dialectical critique" I mean one that is provoked into being by an opposition to what is found present, a critique that is inseparable from an attitude of "over against" and is thus intrinsically violent.

15. Girard's essay on this, largely reproduced in *Things Hidden,* 158–67, has been considered one of his most original contributions to biblical understanding ever since its first publication in the *Bulletin du Centre Protestant d'Études* of Geneva (1975), though elements of it had appeared in a discussion in *Esprit* 429 (1973): 528–63.

of the identity of Israel by exclusion of the victim, in the tradition of their forefathers who killed the prophets. Again, what makes this critique possible is Jesus' given understanding of the plan of God from the beginning.

This is once again shown in the way in which in Mark (implicitly in Jesus' approach to Jerusalem and to the Temple, and in his parable of the murderous tenants of the vineyard) and in Luke (more explicitly, in a number of parables), Jesus is represented as conducting, and in fact being, the visitation of God to inspect his project. However, this whole critique of the situation of Israel is incidental to what Jesus is really about, which is the fulfillment of God's promises in the bringing about of his project. What God wanted from the beginning, Jesus is here to do: to establish the universal possibility of a new sort of humanity, which must pass first through Israel. It is in this light that we can begin to understand the way in which Jesus set about the foundation of the new Israel of God.

He did this by the calling of twelve disciples to be his witnesses and to be the eschatological fulfillment of the twelve tribes of Israel and by preparing them insofar as possible for the way in which the new gathering together of Israel would have to pass through the rejection of the Messiah. Again, what comes first is the fulfillment of God's promise to create a new sort of humanity starting with Israel — the purely given. What becomes apparent — the intelligence of the victim — is that in the concrete, contingent circumstances of this sort of humanity, and even, sadly of the people of Israel, who had been prepared all along by the law and the prophets, this promise would have to be fulfilled through the victimary exclusion of the Messiah, to enable it to become clear once and for all who God is, what humankind is, and what sort of project God has for humankind.

It is in the light of this that Jesus produced his most remarkable piece of teaching and prophetic acting out of a mime: the Last Supper. This was the fulfillment of the Passover as the foundational act of Israel. The Passover was the feast which instituted Israel. In it God called Israel out of Egypt, and at the same time there was celebrated the foundation of the victim people who were expelled from Egypt by their oppressors. It was this feast that was established as the foundational act by which the people of Israel received their identity as chosen. They were summoned out of Egypt as a victim people so that God might establish a covenant with them at Sinai, in which his choice of them to be a light to all nations was ratified. God's project was the establishment of a saving element among the nations who might live as no other nation did, keeping in mind their having been slaves in Egypt, and so constructing their own life in such a way as to give witness to the God who hears the cry of the oppressed, who saved his people from oppression.

In celebrating the Last Supper with his disciples, Jesus was calling to mind God's foundational project for Israel. However, he was recasting this foundational project in his own person. He was to be both the gratuitously self-giving one and the expelled one simultaneously: this was how he interpreted his own death the night before it happened. Jesus also combined this understanding of the foundational feast of Israel with an understanding of himself as the beast slaughtered for the making of the covenant at Sinai, whose blood was scattered over the people and the altar. He was also the Passover lamb whose blood was to protect the members of the new Israel. Furthermore, he combined all these with an interpretation of himself as the suffering servant of Isaiah 53. He understood his self-giving to be the victim as a salvific act by which a new people would be ransomed. He gave in the Last Supper a brilliant new nexus of teaching and interpretation of Scripture to indicate clearly the nature of the new people he was founding, a new people founded from the self-giving victim. He commanded his disciples to repeat this, since his presence after the resurrection was always to take the form of the self-giving victim risen as the foundational forgiveness of the new Israel.

It is clear, then, that the intelligence of the victim is not a simple illumination, but a creative and constitutive revelation, creative and constitutive of a new way of being human: as reconciled with each other around the body of the self-giving victim. Furthermore, this creative and constitutive revelation is not seen as something entirely new, but as bringing to light what God had always intended human society to be. The sense in which this bringing to light of God's plan for reconciling humanity implied a critique of Israel is understood to be incidental and accidental to the purely gratuitous self-giving of God made visible in the self-giving of Jesus as victim in the midst of the people of Israel. Luke in particular (in Acts) brings out the way in which the rejection by Israel of the self-giving of God was really possible only *after* it had been preached to them that the Messiah had come, been crucified, and in his resurrection was offering the possibility of forgiveness and the reunification of the whole house of Israel. First it was presented to them, in the wake of Pentecost, that all God's promises to them had been fulfilled in the self-giving and forgiving victim, and so the fulfillment of Israel as the first-fruits of the reconciliation of the whole of humanity was still an open possibility. Acts is, in one sense, the sad story of how the possibility was missed and how the offer of the reconciliation of humanity with God was launched anyhow and Israel began to become a theologically neutral concept.[16] The center of God's project moves with Paul from Jerusalem to Rome, and thus to the ends of the earth.

So the intelligence of the victim, possessed after the resurrection by the disciples, illumined the way in which Jesus' intelligence of the victim, the consequence of his being formed in gratuitous self-giving, had led him deliberately to engage in a foundational act. This was not, however, a totally new (and therefore dialectically critical) foundation, but a revelation of what God had projected to found from the beginning, and at the same time the fulfillment of that project. This is a concrete new way of being human, made possible by the forgiving victim permitting humans formed in violence to undergo a change in relationality, a change in the constitution of their consciousness, or their heart, and so to begin to form a humanity reconciled among themselves and with God, who has given himself to them as victim. What was being established was Abel coming back from the dead and inviting Cain back from his restless wandering in the land of Nod to partake in a banquet which would be the reestablishment of lost fraternity, perhaps the creation of a fraternity beyond even what had been lost.

So we have seen the way in which the intelligence of the victim, made possible in the disciples by the presence to them of the crucified and risen Lord, permitted the simultaneous discovery of who God is and who humans are. At the same time it permitted the disciples to understand that Jesus, moved by this same intelligence of the victim, had been enacting a concrete, historical, foundational way of bringing to light the full depth and dimensions of a concrete historical project on the part of God, a historical act that was made available through the institution of a sign of extraordinary subtlety and complexity. In this way we see something specific to the Christian understanding of what a religion might be: that it is a salvific revelation or a revelatory salvation. The revelation bringing about the intelligence of the victim is creative of and constitutive of a new historical, linguistic, representational community, which is simultaneously seen to have been originary: what humans were always meant to be.

The Universality of the New Israel

The disciples, once they began themselves to be possessed by the intelligence of the victim, slowly began to be able to understand not only that Jesus had made a concrete historical foundation of a new Israel, but that this new Israel was universal. This was not a simple change

---

16. Paul's treatment of Israel after the rejection follows a somewhat different path.

of understanding, but a huge revolution in cultural comprehension that was not at all easy to bring about, and its consequences were not arrived at smoothly. The first evidence of this change is in Luke's account of Pentecost in Acts. There we have the arrival of the Holy Spirit, the spirit of the crucified and risen Lord, and with it, of course, the same intelligence of the victim that had been manifested on the road to Emmaus, described in terms of the undoing of the separation of humanity which came about as the result of the collapse of the tower of Babel.[17] That story, told in Genesis 11, is about humanity prior to the call of Abraham, and so is about the parlous state of humanity as revealed in its solution in the founding of Israel. The arrival of the Holy Spirit at Pentecost was the fulfillment of the way in which Israel was the beginning of the creation of a new humanity that was not based on the murder of Cain and on the arrogance of Babel, the attempt of humans to build a unity over against God rather than from God.

This same spirit, the spirit of the self-giving crucified and risen victim, soon impelled the apostolic group to recognize that the new unity of humanity that was being offered was not one that could be tied to the social and cultural limits even of the people who had alone been chosen to make it possible to understand that God was present as self-giving victim. It was with considerable difficulty that Peter was pushed into carrying out the first gentile baptism. The Ethiopian eunuch was able to be baptized when Philip had explained to him the fulfillment of the Isaian passage of the suffering servant in the light of the intelligence of the victim (Acts 8:32–33 quoting Isa. 53:7–8). Slowly, and not without some conflict, resolved only at the Council of Jerusalem, the apostolic group realized that the presence of the crucified and risen Lord had started the process of the breaking down of all cultural, racial, and national barriers. It was not as though they were simply witnesses to an important piece of information: that a man had died and risen from the dead. Rather they were witnesses to the culmination of a dynamic whereby the basis of the possibility of the reconciliation of all humanity with each other and with God had been made available, thanks to a history of quite specifically Jewish discoveries concerning who God is and who the human being is, which had finally reached a definitive focus in the presence of the crucified and risen victim.

This can be expressed in another way: the Jewish people, through their history, had discovered (there had been revealed to them) some-

---

17. Is it fanciful to imagine that the tower of Babel was a Babylonian Ziqqurat, on whose summit human sacrifice was performed as a way of producing social and cultural unity?

thing of the relationship of God and victim — understanding themselves as victim people loved by God. This discovery had always served as a critique of the way other nations were ordered, on the basis of human sacrifice and victimization of one sort or another. In the case of the prophets, this critique was often applied to Israel itself, as it had been tempted to become like the other nations. Now, in the final, definitive prophetic revelation, the complicity of Israel itself in building its community barriers and shoring up its identity at the expense of victim, was revealed by the presence to Israel of the forgiving victim. However, this presence, at the same time as being something that could only have come about through and in Israel, which alone had discovered the categories which made the revelation possible, also served as a radical critique of any sort of sacred *difference* to which Israel might pretend. The moment Israel had yielded its final and definitive discovery about who God is and who humans are, it instantly became liable to exactly the same critique as all the other nations, and in no sense the proprietor of the critique. No one can be proprietor of a critique that applies equally to everybody, even if it was only in their terms of reference that the critique came to light.

What was revealed, then, in the light of the intelligence of the victim is that *all* human societies, and not merely all *gentile* societies, base themselves on victims and are blind to their complicity in victimage. Therefore the possibility of the beginnings of the new unity of humanity, based around the self-giving victim, is not essentially linked to any geographical, racial, cultural, or linguistic group, but rather can begin absolutely anywhere where two or more people come together, forming their unity as something received from the self-giving victim rather than forming a fake unity at the expense of some victim — a unity based on penitence at complicity in violence rather than the much stronger-seeming sort of unity that comes from shared hatred.

This means, of course, that the new Israel, the new people of God, has a single, unique, and unrepeatable foundation: the self-giving victim. That self-giving victim was a real historical person who was made available through real historical acts and circumstances. In principle, therefore, the universality of this self-giving victim is as absolute as the universality of the presence of humans basing themselves on exclusion. The foundation is universally available as creative critique, wherever there are people who base their social and personal unity and identity on exclusion. However, for the potential universality of the single foundation to become reality, it needed concrete historical people to make available the news that this foundation was available, and how it had become available, by telling and transmitting the contingent historical

story of the events in Jerusalem.[18] It is this contingent historical transmission of the universality of the self-giving of the victim that is also,
itself, the creative sign of the new unity that was given by the self-giving
victim.

To put this in somewhat less complicated language, the intelligence
of the victim makes it apparent that belief in the resurrection automatically implies belief in Jesus' founding of one unique Church and of
the Church as something necessarily universal. It also implies simultaneously that the making available of the self-giving of the victim as the
basis for the new humanity is not something unconscious, but something which happens as part of a contingent, historical construction of
a sign of the new humanity and the contingent historical transmission
of a story. The universality of grace (the self-giving of the victim) is not
accidentally but essentially linked to the historical institution which it
brought into being, not because grace is entrapped within the institution, but because it is this contingent historical body which grace brings
into being.

Here it is worth making a small excursus on the problem of the so-
called anonymous Christian. The importance of this term lies in the way
it stresses (as the Church teaches) that there are people outside the visible transmission of signs and texts which constitute the Church who,
in ways unknown to us, are positively related to the mystery of Christ,
and therefore are able to inherit eternal life. The problem with the term
"anonymous Christian" seems to me its link with a certain sort of anthropology, one insisting that a certain sort of universally saving grace
is already present in people just by the fact of being human, one which
therefore makes of the visible contingent Church simply the explicitation of what is essentially an anthropological universal. I would suggest,
as a consequence of the theology of grace that I have been developing
above (for that is what it is), that a more useful approach to this problem might be to talk of the universal christoformity of grace, whether
present in sign or present anonymously.

When Jesus taught the parable of the Good Samaritan (Luke 10:25–
37) he was not teaching that the Samaritan was in fact an anonymous
Jew. He was identifying the concrete way in which divine grace is made
humanly present: as a turning toward the victim. The intelligence of the
victim is proposed as the criterion of the presence of grace. We can say,
then, that grace is always christoform: the gratuitous presence of the
self-giving victim is simultaneously a critique of the way humans are
and a constructive forgiveness of humans permitting the construction of

---

18. "Faith comes by hearing" (Rom. 10:17).

a creative sign of a new human reconciliation. Now the creative sign of the self-giving victim bringing about a new humanity par excellence is the Eucharist-based Church. And this is a visible reality. Indeed, the only way we have come to know that God and the self-giving human victim are essentially linked is through the contingent historical events, signs, and texts discussed above. However, this very fact obliges us to recognize that the self-giving of the victim, a divine self-giving, is constantly pushing wider the human limitations of the contingent historical sign and is perfectly capable of creating anonymous proto-signs of the reconciliation of humanity with God wherever there are humans to be reconciled — the field of opportunity is universal.

Let the parable of the Good Samaritan pose some critical questions to two stories. There was a small town in the interior of Brazil whose hairdresser, at an early stage of the AIDS crisis, was discovered to be HIV positive. The vast majority of the population of the town were Catholics, and thus fully integrated into the sign of the reconciliation of humanity. Yet, confronted with the hairdresser with the virus, they reacted by expelling him unanimously from the town (as it were, leaving him by the side of the road to die). The sign of the reconciliation of humanity around the victim was dead, because no one had the intelligence of the victim, no one perceived and lived the universal christoformity of grace.

On the other hand, in his film *The Last Emperor*, Bertolucci shows an incident in which the former emperor, now a municipal gardener, sees his sometime ideological mentor, who had reeducated him into life in the new communist China, being carried off for execution as part of the Cultural Revolution. The gardener instantly tries to intervene, exclaiming that he knows this man, a good man, and a good communist, who should not be carried off to death. He persists until he is beaten off by the guards using the butts of their guns. Whether this incident is factual or not, it is certainly illustrative. Here is someone entirely outside the visible sign of the self-giving victim. Yet he perceives that an unjustifiable lynching is taking place and shows solidarity with the victim, intervening even at the risk of his own life, though in fact the superior power of the soldiers merely brushes him aside.

This action of the gardener did not make of him an anonymous Christian, but we can talk of him having been touched by what I have called the universal christoformity of grace. To be a Christian is to live out the universal christoformity of grace visibly, in order to create the sign, which is itself contagious to others, all of whom live in a world whose social order is based on victimization. The important thing is not whether people are Christians or not, anonymously or explicitly, but whether the universal christoformity of grace is being lived out as genuinely constructive of the new unity of humanity. The importance of this approach is that by talking of the universal christoformity of grace, rather than the anonymous Christian, I am saying there is no grace available to human beings that does not involve a turning toward the victim, that is, a certain form of conversion. If saving grace is automatically imbued in human beings just as we are, though capable of being explicitated in ecclesial signs, then there is little reason in principle why the hairdresser's co-citizens might not simply carry on being baptized and married and making their first communions in ignorance of what they had done and inherit eternal life just so. Likewise, the guards leading the mentor to his death might inherit eternal life just through being good communist soldiers. However, in fact, the question Jesus was answering when he told the parable of the Good Samaritan was that of the criterion for inheriting eternal life (Luke 10:25). And the answer was given in terms of the intelligence of the victim. Any anthropology that does not include that criterion seems to fall short of adequacy as an aid to theological interpretation.

A further consideration about the nature of the universality of the foundation of the new Israel is brought to light by consideration of Paul's teaching on justification being made available by grace through faith. What Paul preached was the intelligence of the victim; or, in his words, the Messiah as crucified, the power of God and the wisdom of God. The power is the creative construction of the new humanity made possible by the victim, the wisdom is the intelligence of the victim, which, had the powers of the world possessed it, they would never have crucified Jesus (1 Cor. 1:17–25; 2:6–8). The grace in question in any discussion of justification by grace is the grace of the self-giving victim. What this grace has brought about is a new way of being human which knocks down the wall that separated Jew from gentile. That is to say, the grace which justifies does so by bringing into existence a new unity of humanity which does not justify itself over against any other group. Any group which justifies itself over against any other group is still tributary of the mechanism of the formation of identity by victimization. The making just that comes from grace is precisely the construction of a new unity that is not based over against any other, but receives its identity as given from the self-giving victim. That is to say, the foundation of the new Israel, a collective identity, is the making present of this justification by grace through faith. Those who through faith in the presence of the self-giving victim come to form part of and construct this new Israel are, insofar as they form part of and create this new unity, being justified by grace through faith.

This of course takes us completely outside the Lutheran controversy, with its individualization of the key concepts. What is shown is that grace, making present the self-giving of the victim, brings into being a new people whose active construction of this new unity (their good works) is not part of some self-justification, or some comparison with other people or other groups. Rather it is the only way any of us can receive the grace of the self-giving and forgiving victim: it is precisely as we learn *not* to separate ourselves from others, compare ourselves with others, modes of behavior and attitudes of heart which are dependent on our formation in victimization, that we are enabled to take part in the construction of the new people, which is based on the self-giving of the victim. The central Pauline category for the explanation of salvation is the intelligence of the victim, understood in its full ecclesial and universal sense: the making present of the grace which justifies is identical with the making present of the Church as universal.

Thus far, then, I have sought to show how the intelligence of the victim, which was made available to the apostolic group at and after the resurrection, is the discovery of the internal dynamic in the life of Jesus which illuminated what he was doing in founding the new Israel and the way in which this new Israel was, by the dynamic of its foundation, the universal sign of the reconciliation of humanity with God, a universal sign of a reality that has not yet been fulfilled, but is being fulfilled in embryo wherever the new Israel is concretely realized. That is, however, not all that was understood in the rereading of the presence among them of the crucified and risen Lord by the apostolic group. The recasting of the human perception of God, of Israel, and of humankind that was brought about by the intelligence of the victim also led to the recasting of the understanding of the perception of creation.

Creation in Christ

It is often noted by scholars that the various indications to be found in the Pauline corpus,[19] and elsewhere,[20] of the preexistence of Christ, and his involvement in some mysterious way with the creation of all that is must be part of a very early understanding on the part of the "primitive Christian community."[21] The hymns are regarded as pre-Pauline, inserted by Paul (perhaps with alterations) into his epistles. However,

---

19. 1 Cor. 8:6; Col. 1:15–20; Eph. 1:3–14; I do not include Phil. 2:5–11, because I consider this very early hymn to be concerned with the way in which Christ is the un-falling of Adam rather than being centered on his preexistence. It contains no reference to his mediation of creation.

20. John 1:1–2; Heb. 1:2–3.

21. See, for example, M. Hengel, *Jésus, fils de Dieu* (Paris, 1977), 13ff.

there is a great resistance to regarding as plausible the affirmations of the same reality put into the mouth of Jesus himself by John: "Truly, truly I say to you, before Abraham was, I am" (John 8:58), and "Father, glorify thou me in thy own presence with the glory which I had with thee before the world was made" (John 17:5). Here it must be noted that it is not the exactitude of the words that is being doubted, for I know of no scholar who considers the Johannine speeches of Jesus to be verbatim accounts; rather it is notorious that it would in no way be considered strange for authors of antiquity to put speeches into the mouths of their protagonists. What is considered highly implausible is whether Jesus could have held the opinions that are imputed to him.

That is to say, we have a strange disjunction: on the one hand agreement as to the extreme antiquity of the understanding of Christ's preexistence and mediation of creation in the Christian community, and on the other the denial that this understanding could have been that of Jesus himself before the Crucifixion. The apostolic group is held to have been able to understand something that Jesus was not himself able to understand, and this despite the insistence of the Gospels, and particularly John, that Jesus understood things before the apostles, and they were able to understand *what he had already understood* only after his resurrection and the coming of the Paraclete. The teaching of Christ's preexistence can therefore be presented as an overflowing of the primitive Christian community, which is to suggest that it is, in a certain sense, "mythical" — an exercise in the posthumous sacralization of Jesus, but not something literally true. At the same time, I am aware of no scholar[22] who can indicate positive reasons *why* this sort of understanding or this particular type of posthumous florilegium should have flowed from the resurrection.

It seems to me that in the light of the elaboration of the intelligence of the victim which I have been attempting, it does become possible to see why the presence to the apostolic group of the crucified and risen victim should have recast their understanding of creation. I will attempt, in a highly tentative and experimental way, to set out what seems to me to be an internal coherence between the intelligence of the victim and the recasting of creation.

The reader will remember the Girardian generative scene: the scene which gives birth to representation. For Girard this is probably a scene repeated very frequently over many centuries or millennia as the conditions of hominization (the development of mimetic desire and the

22. Other than F. Dreyfus, who attributes the understanding to a teaching of Jesus himself, probably to the select three disciples — Peter, James, and John (*Jésus savait-il qu'il était Dieu?* [Paris: Cerf, 1984], 57–71).

forging of cultural controls) are brought about, before the actual time of hominization and the birth of properly human culture. The scene involves a group in which growing mimetic rivalry leads to the collapse of differences and the resolution of the resulting violent chaos in an aleatory and unanimous act of victimization. This victim, having been expelled, is held to have produced the resulting peace, whereas in fact it is the unanimity against the arbitrary victim that is the reestablishment of peace. Thus a certain sort of misunderstanding, the illusion of the persecutors, of what has been going on is vital for the production and maintenance of the peace: the victim must be held to be truly guilty but also, because it has produced the peace, to enjoy a divine quality. Where before there was violence and chaos, now, thanks to the departing divinity, peace and order have been established. So in the development of the myth and the rituals that flow from this, we have a two-faced divinity, both disturbing and pacifying, who produces order out of chaos.

It is this that is important for the understanding of the recasting of the perception of creation that followed the resurrection. We start, in pre-Jewish (and abundantly in extra-Jewish) mythology, with an understanding of creation that is intrinsically related to the divine production of order out of chaos. It is this same extra-Jewish material that is reworked, in the light of the covenant, in the first chapter of Genesis. It is interesting that the reworking is not complete: the account of creation is not entirely recast in the light of the covenant, and there are signs of the remains of a creation-out-of-chaos myth in the description, as the words *tohu wabohu* (Gen. 1:2) attest. Particularly the Jahwist editor(s) have undertaken a rereading of the origins of the world in the light of Israel's experience of salvation: the true "direction" of everything is known from its finality, the revelation of God at Sinai and the election of Israel. It is this rereading in the light of an experience of salvation which led to a subversion of pagan world views, and permits an understanding of creation which accords with a single and benevolent God.

However, this subversion in the light of the experience of salvation is still only partial in Genesis: we still have elements of a story of creation by the suppression of preexistent chaos. What I would like to suggest is that the partiality of the subversion is related to the still partial subversion of the mythology which covers over the founding victimization at the basis of human culture. Very close to the story of the creation we have the story of the expulsion of Adam and Eve by God from paradise, a story in which God is still involved in victimizing, on the way toward the understanding that expulsion is a purely human mechanism and that God is its victim rather than its instigator (John 1:1–18). Then we have the story of the foundational assassination, where it is revealed that what we have is simply a sordid murder, in which God is not an accomplice. Yet, in his posterior treatment of Cain, God is seen as involved in the setting up of the (ultimately fatally flawed) cultural mechanisms by which humans protect themselves from the spiral of internecine violence: the beginnings of the link between God and the law whose caducity will be so forcibly argued by St. Paul.

We have, then, a partial intelligence of the victim at work: the founding murder is revealed as a sordid crime, and creation is the beneficent work of a single God, but there remain some elements proper to the vision produced by the founding murder, the persecutory illusion. My suggestion is that these two work in tandem: the re-vealing of the real sense of creation and the complete setting free from the illusion produced by the founding murder are part of the same process. The Old Testament itself seems to point to this. To the degree in which the arbitrary nature of victimization or persecution becomes apparent in the Old Testament, so it becomes possible to tell the story of a foundation or creation which does not involve a god in the suppression of chaos. It became possible to give a nonmythological account of creation, because it became possible to see that God is anterior to any human violence, and thus anterior to chaos. Thus it becomes possible to understand creation as *ex nihilo*. It seems to me to be enormously important to indicate the huge cultural process of discovery, of the overcoming of the victimary illusion, which made possible what appears to be an abstract piece of philosophical reasoning.

The signposts for this process are relatively late documents of the Old Testament period: These are Daniel 12:2:

> And many of those who sleep in the dust of the earth shall awake, some to everlasting life, and some to shame and everlasting contempt.

and 2 Maccabees 7:23:

> Therefore the Creator of the world, who shaped the beginning of man and devised the origin of all things, will in his mercy give life and breath back to you again, since you now forget yourselves for the sake of his laws.

These documents are from the Hellenistic period where, for the first time, the faith in the resurrection of the dead is clearly taught.[23] Faith in the resurrection is derived here from an understanding of God as vindicating his persecuted faithful ones, either the persecuted Maccabees or those who remain faithful in the midst of persecution in Daniel. That is

---

23. There are more than mere hints both of a resurrection of the dead, maybe even in the flesh (thus indicating a new understanding of the Creator), and of a noninvolvement of God in human victimization in the book of Job, 19:25–27; however, textual difficulties make the reading less than completely clear.

to say a perception of God has been developed as vindicating persecuted victims by raising them from the dead: belief in the resurrection is intrinsically linked with God as not allowing his persecuted ones to be forever silenced. This is simultaneous with the perception that the violent means by which social order is being maintained (by the persecutors) is just that, and no more: God is not involved. Now it is no accident that the understanding of the noncomplicity of God in this victimary violence, even though it be colored by the way in which God is seen as partial to his own (chosen) people, permits the Jewish thinkers to see through the victimary illusion with sufficient clarity to be able to affirm *in the same period* the doctrine of creation *ex nihilo*. That is to say, even though the vision of God in Maccabees is evidently partisan and God is vindicating his own over against wicked persecutors, the intelligence of the victim has advanced sufficiently for it to be possible to separate the perception of God as Creator from any complicity with the suppression of chaos.

I am suggesting that the development of the understanding of the resurrection of the dead and that of creation *ex nihilo* is a simultaneous development, and that it is the intelligence of the victim that makes it possible. This is a vital part of the *praeparatio evangelica,* for it provides the clue to the way in which the resurrection of Christ, by completely revealing the mechanism of foundational victimage, also completely revealed the understanding of creation. I am speaking of a simultaneous recasting of the two understandings: that of the resurrection of the dead and that of creation, in the light of the same understanding: the intelligence of the victim. Thus, in the resurrection accounts of Jesus there has disappeared the element of a divine vindication of Jesus over against his enemies. Jesus' resurrection is not revealed as an eschatological revenge, but as an eschatological pardon. It happens not to confound the persecutors, but to bring about a reconciliation. God is revealed not as partisan, interested in vindicating a particular group over against its enemies, but rather as the self-giving victim of the remaining victimizing tendency of even the chosen people. This permits the definitive demythologization of God. God, completely outside human reciprocity, is the human victim. The Father is the origin of the self-giving of the human victim. Thus, far from creation having anything to do with the establishment of an order, what is revealed is that the gratuitous self-giving of the victim is identical with, and the heretofore hidden center and culmination of, the gratuitous giving that is the creation. There is no Christian perception of creation which is not forged through the intelligence of the victim, and principally by the gratuitous self-giving which underlies and makes possible that intelligence.

This means, of course, that when we speak of creation we are not speaking in the first place of the process by which things came, or come, to be. That description is proper to scientists, especially those not limited in their empirical observation by the hidden filters of pagan theological notions (normally held implicitly and unconsciously).[24] It means that when we speak of creation we are speaking of a relationship, a relationship of purely gratuitous giving, without motive, with no second intentions, with no desire for control or domination, but rather a gratuity which permits creatures to share gratuitously in the life of the Creator. The relation of gratuity is anterior to what is and has ever been. This perception, the perception that the giving in gratuity is anterior to what is, was made possible by the presence to the disciples of the crucified and risen victim, whose self-giving was thus seen to be the way in which creation is a reflection of God: it was the intelligence of the victim that opened up for them the structure of the universe.

Seen in this light, the New Testament evidence makes abundant sense. It is already clear that John alludes to creation in his account of the first day of the resurrection. This becomes even clearer in his prologue, which can be seen, as can the whole of the Johannine recasting of God, as the consequence of the shift in perception permitted by the intelligence of the victim. The resurrection of Jesus made it possible to see that the same self-giving toward victimization present in the life of Jesus was the perfect image and imitation of the Father, revealing the Father as he really is, fount of all self-giving. The self-giving of Jesus was then the Word, the Logos, the full self-revelation of the Father. Furthermore, the self-giving of Jesus exactly reflects (but does not exhaust) the self-giving of the Father, and this means that the relation of gratuity, anterior to all that is, is common to both of them, Father and Son.

From this it follows that the gratuitous self-giving of God into the hands of humans (the Johannine "handing over") as far as to become a human victim, so that humans can learn to cease killing each other and come to be participants in the imitation of God, *is the true perspective on creation, revealed by the intelligence of the victim.* Just as in the case of the editors of the pre-Genesis myths, it is from an understanding of the end, or purpose, of the act that its beginnings are understood. So

---

24. For an example of the way in which pagan theological notions underpin the attempts of a theologian and scientist to talk about creation in modern idiom see A. Peacocke, *Creation and the World of Science* (Oxford: Oxford University Press, 1979). In chap. 3, "Chance and the Life Game" (especially 106–10), Peacocke speaks with approval of the way in which the scientific notion of creation he is advocating is compatible with that shown in Hindu myth by Shiva "the Creator-Destroyer" and the dance of Sakti. He seems entirely unaware of the regression he is making, in the name of "science," to a notion of creation that involves the divinity in violence: his notion is incompatible with the degree of demythologization present in Genesis, let alone that present in John or Paul!

here the resurrected victim, by revealing the purpose, or finality, of the whole act, also simultaneously reveals the dynamic behind its beginning.

This is affirmed also in the pre-Pauline hymns of the New Testament. In 1 Corinthians 8:6, the origin of all things is the Father, who has given all things. However, all things are made in imitation of, through, the Son, who is the perfect imitation of the Father. If the Son is the perfect and uncreated imitation of the Father, then everything which is a created imitation is made in the image of, through, the Son. The presence of the Son and his victimary death made accessible as forgiveness reveal the whole "why" of creation. We find the same thing in Hebrews 1:2–3:

> ... but in these last days [God] has spoken to us by a Son, whom he appointed the heir of all things, through whom he also created the world. He reflects the glory of God and bears the very stamp of his nature, upholding the universe by his word of power. When he had made purification for sins he sat down at the right hand of the Majesty on high.

So the intelligence of the victim, by purifying the perception of God as involved in the establishment of order and revealing at the same time the God who gives himself as victim to make possible a totally different order, at the same time reveals the whole drift, direction, and purpose of creation.

The same message is to be found in Colossians 1:15–20. The hymn proceeds from the new comprehension of the Creator to the reconciliatory death. That is to say, it proceeds in the order of logic, not in that of discovery. The order of discovery is the inverse: it begins with the blood of the Cross, and moves backward until it comes to be understood that the crucified and risen Lord reveals the full sense of creation. The same, finally, can be found in Ephesians 1:3–14, where the structure of the hymn begins and ends in heaven, passing, in the middle of the hymn, through the victimization on the Cross, which has revealed the plenitude of the project.

What I have tentatively explored, then, is the way in which I take the intelligence of the victim, made present to the disciples after the resurrection, to have been part of the same intelligence that was at work in the Jewish people permitting the overcoming of the victimary illusion and the understanding of God as Creator. I hope to have shown that there is an internal coherence between this intelligence, the resurrection of Christ, and the way in which the apostolic community came to understand that creation was in Christ and that Christ preexisted creation. That is to say, the doctrines of the preexistence of Christ, and his mediation of creation, are not sacralizing "extras," tacked on to a doctrine of salvation that doesn't really need them. They are internally coherent with and the necessary premises of the understanding of salvation that was made available by the intelligence of the victim.[25]

There is an important consequence to this approach. This is that the Christian doctrine of creation, that creation happened in Christ, is not a piece of abstract information which can removed from the story of how it was discovered and used to found an abstract anthropology about our *ur-Christlichkeit*. It is a discovery that is part of the intelligence of the victim, that is to say, that it came into our hands as part of our understanding of salvation. I bother to labor this rather obvious point because, if we proceed forward from the creation in Christ as from an abstract metaphysical definition toward an understanding of who we humans are (the order of logic, of the Greek Logos, rather than the order of discovery), rather than moving backward, from the intelligence of the victim which illuminates a violent and bloody murder, we more or less fatally underestimate the drastic nature of the human violence which produced the circumstances which made possible the revelation of God. The tendency is to banalize the human condition and end up with a theory about God, creation, and humanity which has no space for all our experience of treachery, envy, lies, violence, exclusion, and so forth. Yet it is this experience which has to be recognized if we are going to share in the life of forgiveness which is the life of the risen human victim.

I would suggest that it is particularly important to see the doctrine of creation in Christ as the *end* of a long process of discovery rather than a metaphysical starting point from which abstract deductions about human nature can be made. For only if it is remembered that it is the *end* of a process of discovery can it be seen that the discovery of creation in Christ was made as part, as a necessary part, of the discovery of our salvation. Furthermore it can be seen that this discovery was *simultaneous*

---

25. A small excursus. It is possible to take a further, rather obvious, step in this line of thought. The apostolic group was able to understand, in the light of the change of their understanding wrought by the intelligence of the victim, the internal coherence between the self-giving of the victim they had known historically and his preexistence and mediation of creation. If we can accept that Jesus possessed the intelligence of the victim *before* his death, as the apostolic witness unanimously indicates, then there is no reason in principle why Jesus *before* his death should not have known (and maybe taught), *as part of the human intelligence of the victim* (and not as part of some divine illumination utterly unconnected with a human process of knowing), that he was preexistent and the mediator of creation. I am not here seeking to prove that he did know or teach such a thing. However, once one has understood the full implications of the understanding that I have called the intelligence of the victim, it does, fascinatingly, become possible to imagine how such human knowledge might have been held. Simply to refuse this option is really to say that Jesus just wasn't as bright as the apostolic group; they managed to draw the conclusions from the intelligence of the victim which Jesus himself hadn't managed to get to. Now all the apostolic evidence is that Jesus had a human intelligence and a dense teaching that was markedly more profound than what his disciples could grasp. The grounds for a new approach to this age-old question are now available.

with the discovery not of our *ur-Christlichkeit* but of our complicity in violence, our *ur-Kainlichkeit*. If there is an abstract metaphysical step to be made, it is to be made backward from the historical reality of our being revealed as murderers to the conviction that the humanity of Christ shows that this state as we live it out is not our ontological state. To detach the doctrine of creation in Christ from its discovery as part of the intelligence of the victim and then to build a theological anthropology from it seems to me to be a sure recipe for semi-Pelagianism.[26] Against this, it is a matter of historical fact that the discovery of the Christian sense of creation was made as part of the discovery of the forgiveness of sin.

Trinity: The Monotheism of the Victim

There is at least one further dimension to the revelatory discovery that occurred in the light of the intelligence of the victim, though its formulation took somewhat longer than that of the founding of the Church, the universality of the Church, and the perception of creation as mediated in the preexistent Son. This is the discovery of the peculiar density of monotheism that we call the Trinity.

There seems little doubt that Jesus before and up to his death was teaching his disciples a new perception of God, the God whom he called his Father in a unique sense. This is attested to in a number of ways in the Gospels. In Mark, where all is so subtle and implicit, there is curiously little teaching by Jesus about God. The emphasis is much more on the way that Jesus himself is — in a way that is narrated rather than defined — somehow identified with God. The christological concentration of this Gospel is after all announced at the beginning, confirmed at the baptism, made humanly accessible at Caesarea Philippi, underlined at the transfiguration, and given its definitive contour by the centurion beside the Cross. Thus, the sabbath incidents, rather than breaking new ground about God, show Jesus as acting with the liberty of the one who founded the sabbath for human beings. The calming of the storm (in Mark 4) shows that the mariners who called on the Lord to calm the sea in Psalm 107 and the disciples who call on Jesus to do the same were both calling on the same person. The parallel stories of the woman with a hemorrhage for twelve years (and thus unable to be married) and

---

26. This seems to me exactly what has been reached by J. L. Segundo in his treatment of grace and sin, following on his borrowing from K. Rahner, P. Teilhard de Chardin, and G. Bateson, in his *Evolución y culpa*, vol. 5 of his *Teología abierta para el laico adulto* (Buenos Aires: Carlos Lohlé, 1972); in English see *Jesus of Nazareth, Yesterday and Today*, 5 vols. (Maryknoll, N.Y.: Orbis Books, 1984–88).

the twelve-year-old girl who died (before she was able to be married) show Jesus as being the promised bridegroom of Israel (thus *Talitha cumi* — the bridegroom's words in the Song of Songs). The implicit (and, of course, as yet undefinable) divinity of the Son in Mark's Gospel has its only parallel in the Gospel of John, where a later generation and different cultural world needed to bring out and explicitate the transformation of monotheism that would be betrayed if the apparent simplicity of Mark was taken (as it was being taken by some — for instance, the Ebionites) to imply a "low" christology.

In Matthew, both in his use of Marcan material and in his own discourses, we have more directly theological teaching: teaching bearing on the nature of God. The Sermon on the Mount is littered with references to the Father: Father who is in Heaven, Father who sees in secret, or is in secret; Father who knows what you need; Father who is perfect. What is properly theological about the teaching is the function these definitions have within Jesus' discourse. Jesus is indicating a certain sort of moral teaching, one which could be described as breaking people out of human reciprocity, based on violence, and showing them a purely gratuitous form of relationality that is quite beyond any sort of human violence: so the Father sends rain on just and unjust alike; he is quite outside any human form of distinction between good and bad, insider and outsider, pure and impure. It is by becoming capable of a purely gratuitous relationality with the human other that one is able to become perfect as the heavenly Father is perfect. Even the apparently vengeful aspects of the Father in some parables serve exactly the same purpose: the figure of the Father functions as a criterion for current human relationality. So the leaving of the separation of the wheat and the tares to a divine judgment is not a teaching about a divine judgment, but one about the fallibility of human criteria for separation and how divisions of the world into good and bad, insider and out, must not be the way of followers of Jesus. Likewise, the parable of the sheep and goats is the revelation of a separation of themselves from forgiveness made by those who did not notice the victim, while those who did notice the victim have passed beyond any sort of separation. The apparently violent language about God has as its function the introduction of people into a relationality that is beyond the violent reciprocity that seems to be implied in the language.[27] It is this gratuitous relationality beyond violence that is the Father.

Luke brings this out even more explicitly, presenting Jesus as conducting God's visitation of his people, and this visitation as being one which

---

27. I deal more fully with the shift in the discourse about God from language of violence to language of love below when examining the Pauline and Johannine witness.

brings life to the dead, health to the sick, forgiveness to sinners, and in other ways fulfilling the promise of Isaiah 61:1–2. In his development of the Sermon on the Mount, Luke goes beyond Matthew's removal of the Father from any sort of violent reciprocity. Where the Father in Matthew's sermon is described apophatically, in Luke he is described kataphatically. The Father is not just evenhanded in his goodness: he is actively kind to the ungrateful and the selfish. Matthew's injunction to imitate the perfection of the Father becomes "Be merciful, even as your Father is merciful" in Luke. In the parables proper to himself, Luke emphasizes the gratuity of the Father who seeks and finds and is quite beyond considerations of merit in his generosity. A theme which comes up again and again in Luke is the gratuity of grace. So the elders of the Jews who are friends of the centurion of Capernaeum (Luke 7:1–11) come to ask Jesus to cure the man's slave because the centurion "is worthy." They consider Jesus' miraculous cures within the frames of reference and the give and take of the piety of which they are part. The centurion himself, being outside the framework of that piety, is able to see that divine grace is not part of any system of rewards and punishments but simply grace, and so tells Jesus, "I am not worthy." Luke's ironic parallel brings out the nature of the novelty and gratuity of God that Jesus made present.

Luke's teaching on the disciple as an unworthy servant goes further: the true disciple is one who has broken out of considerations of who deserves what. Luke emphasizes this by his two contradictory and parallel accounts of the eschatological banquet: one where the one coming in (which one of *you*, rather than the Master) is served by his servants, whose job it is (17:7–10), and the other (12:37) where the *master* comes in and sits the servants down and serves them. The disjunction caused by the parallelism serves to shake out any notion of desert or expectation of service, for that is what "one of you" would expect. However, the coming of the "master" is not to be understood within the expectations of "one of you," but is a purely gratuitous irruption,[28] beyond any possible worthiness. There is a further passage, unique to Luke, in which God is removed by Jesus from any sort of human *quid pro quo:* in 13:1–5, the perception of God is removed from any link with a current disaster being seen as a punishment for sin:

> There were some present at that very time who told him of the Galileans whose blood Pilate had mingled with their sacrifices. And he answered them, "Do you think that these Galileans were worse sinners than all the

---

28. And quite probably a reference to the self-giving of the Master in the midst of his servants, as victim, that is represented in the eucharistic banquet.

other Galileans because they suffered thus? I tell you, No; but unless you repent you will all likewise perish."

In this Luke is giving voice to what Matthew had in his verses on the sun rising on good and evil (5:45) and what John, with more development, has in his account of the man born blind (John 9).[29]

All three synoptic accounts are, of course, entirely postresurrection accounts. That is to say, in all three cases the deep structure of the work is the intelligence of the victim permitting a rereading and an ordering of their understanding of the life of Jesus toward the passion and, in the case of Luke, toward the foundation of the universal new Israel in Acts. So the understanding of God which they show has undergone the vital change *to* which Matthew and Mark scarcely give formal evidence, but *of* which they are very solid evidence. This is the change in the image of God brought about by the resurrection of Jesus. That is to say, whatever Jesus may have actually taught about God, as witnessed to in the synoptics, is of comparatively little importance beside the change in the perception of God that he wrought by his whole living out of his life and death, which was given back in the resurrection. It was as a result of this event that the real change of perception was operated. God was revealed as "the God who raised Jesus from the dead" (Acts 5:30; Rom. 8:11), a new sharpening of the perception of Israel that God was "the God who brought our fathers out of Egypt" (Exod. 13:8, 9, 14, 16; 18:1; Num. 20:16; 23:22; Deut. 4:20, 37; 6:21; 9:26; 26:8; 1 Kings 8:51–53; 1 Sam. 10:18; Josh. 24:6).

This change of perception of God brought about by the resurrection of Jesus was not a content-less change, but a radical redefinition. Paul illustrates this perhaps most clearly in his reflection on Deuteronomy 21:23 ("his body shall not remain all night upon the tree, but you shall bury him the same day, for a hanged man is accursed by God") in Galatians 3:10–14: "For all who rely on works of the law are under a curse.... Christ redeemed us from the curse of the law having become a curse for us — for it is written, 'cursed be everyone who hangs on a tree.'"

Paul had been converted by the presence of the Lord as "he whom you are persecuting" on the road to Damascus. He then had to confront the evidence of Jesus' death on the Cross, a sure sign that Jesus had

---

29. In this brief overview, I have left out consideration of those verses in Matthew and Luke where the special nature of the relationship between Jesus and his Father is indicated (for example, Matt. 11:27, Luke 10:21–22). I take it for granted that part of Jesus' specifically theological teaching was his indication that his Father was to be understood starting from himself, a teaching whose full meaning became clear after the resurrection, permitting the christological rereading of his life to which the Gospels bear witness.

been cursed by God, with his new knowledge that God had raised this Jesus up. Does not the resurrection give the lie to the curse? Paul was able to see that his zeal for the law, in persecuting, and the law itself, in indicating that the result of a human violence was God's curse, were not, after all, faithful representations of God. In his zeal for the law, he had been persecuting God; and the law itself, rather than revealing God, justified human violence against God's chosen one. The conclusions Paul drew from this concerning the caducity of the law are well known.

What this example illustrates is the huge change of perception of God that occurred owing to the resurrection, permitting God to be talked of now with purely gratuitous categories, without elements of punishment or curse. It is worth indicating that this was not an immediate change of perception: for Paul, as for any learned Jew, the Scriptures were, and remained, normative in understanding God. So rather than telling of the recasting of God as a modern person would do — in comparatively abstract terms, indicating that before the resurrection God had been simply misunderstood as involved in violence, threatening, punishing, cursing, and so on, as well as blessing and creating — Paul (and, as we shall see, John) told the story in a different way. They took literally the threats and the promises of God in the Old Testament: threats of the punishment of God's people and promises of a savior, of a Messiah, of a new covenant. For them, Jesus' life was lived as the person who both took on himself God's punishment for Israel and was God's promise for Israel. That is to say, the way they received the intelligence of the victim at first was perceiving that God had sent Jesus to fulfil his promises by simultaneously fulfilling the punishments. In the death of Jesus, God exhausted his threats toward and punishment of his people, and by raising Jesus up he fulfilled his promises, making possible a new people living from the self-giving of the forgiving victim. It is to this that Paul gives witness when he tells the Corinthians that "the Son of God, Jesus Christ, whom we preached among you . . . was not Yes and No; but in him it is always Yes. For all the promises of God find their Yes in him" (2 Cor. 1:19–20).

The subtlety of this approach is very difficult indeed for modern non-Semites to understand: it is not for nothing that some Old Testament scholars view most modern Catholics (including the Vatican Congregation which excised some of the more "scandalous" chunks of the psalms from the Liturgia Horarum after the Second Vatican Council) as crypto-Marcionites.[30] We cannot easily cope with the notion of a vi-

---

30. For example, N. Füglister, cited by N. Lohfink in *Violencia y pacifismo en el Antiguo Testamento* (Bilbao: Desclée de Brouwer, 1990), 29. Marcion was a Christian teacher in the mid-second century who found the God of the Old Testament so repulsive that he jettisoned the Hebrew Scriptures, keeping only the New Testament, especially the Pauline

olent God who cajoled, bullied, threatened, punished, ordered prophets to slay people and so on, let alone imagine how this God is somehow related to the New Testament perception of God as Love. However, it seems important not to run away from the narrative discourse within which Jesus forged his understanding of what he was about and which was used by the apostolic group to explain their understanding of the salvation he had brought about. Without such a discourse it becomes almost impossible to understand what, for instance, Paul might have meant when he said (or quoted) that God "made him to be sin who knew no sin, that in him we might become the righteousness of God" (2 Cor. 5:21). It also becomes impossible to understand the depth of the joy of the preaching of the Good News: that a new age had dawned in which God's grace was freely available, God's punishments having been exhausted and the promised salvation given.

Now this discourse, largely inaccessible to modern minds and, where accessible, often understood in a way that is frankly blasphemous (so that even after the resurrection God continues to punish, cursing people with AIDS and so forth) has, it seems to me, its exact abstract theological and anthropological counterpart in the development of the doctrine of the Trinity. In the Pauline writings we have what one might call trinitarian elements — an understanding of the way salvation has in fact been carried out in Jewish history — within a discourse of God dependent on Old Testament imagery. An example of this might be Galatians 4:4–6:

> But when the time had fully come, God sent forth his Son, born of woman, born under the law, to redeem those who were under the law, so that we might receive adoption as sons. And because you are sons, God has sent the Spirit of his Son into our hearts, crying, "Abba! Father!"

Here we have the dynamic presentation of trinitarian elements (God sending his Son, giving the Spirit of his Son, so that we might become sons) within the language of law and redemption. By the time we get to the Johannine writings, and particularly the epistles, the shift out of the Old Testament discourse and toward the abstract anthropological understanding of salvation is further advanced. We get a simple definition presented as being the absolute kernel of the Gospel:

> This is the message we have heard from him and proclaim to you, that God is light and in him is no darkness at all. (1 John 1:5)

---

and Lucan texts. While few nowadays have heard of him, the temptation of Marcionism, or the arbitrary chopping out of the "nasty bits" of the Old Testament, is very much present in modern Christianity, as is its opposite error, fundamentalism, or the equal treatment of what the Old Testament says of God with the New Testament revelation. In place of these a progressive understanding of revelation is neither ashamed of the nasty bits, through which God has revealed himself, nor unable to distinguish between God and human violence.

That is to say, the Gospel *is* the revelation of the monotheism that is utterly purified of violence;[31] and then, further on:

> ... for God is love. In this the love of God was made manifest among us, that God sent his only Son into the world, so that we might live through him. In this is love, not that we loved God but that he loved us and sent his Son to be the expiation for our sins. (1 John 4:8b–10)

Here God is shown as the love that was made manifest through the intelligence of the victim.

What we have then is a gradual process of the recasting of God in the light of the resurrection of Jesus, so that it is seen that the previous discourse, within which Jesus had operated and within which his victimary self-understanding was forged, was in fact a provisional discourse. In the light of the resurrection it gradually becomes possible to see that it was not that God was previously violent, now blessing now cursing (see Deut. 32:39), but had now brought all that ambivalence to an end. Rather, it became possible to see that that was all a human violence, with various degrees of projection onto God. God had been from the beginning always, immutably, love, and this love was made manifest in sending God's Son into the midst of violent humans, even into the midst of their persecutory projections of God, so that they might treat him as a human victim and thus reveal the depth of the love of God, who was prepared to be a human victim simultaneously to show the depth of his love for humanity and to reveal humanity as having been locked into the realm of the Father of lies.

The process we have seen in the Pauline writings and in the Johannine epistles is then the definitive demystification of God and human beings, so that it becomes possible to look again at the crucifixion and the resurrection and develop a perception of God only as derived from *that* event. So it becomes possible to see the crucifixion as the meeting point between, on the one hand, a human act of violence and, on the other hand, the love of the Father, who sends his Son into humanity as an act of love, the Son who gives himself freely to being victimized by human beings as part of his imitative love of the Father, and the Holy Spirit, who is the inner dynamic of the relationship between the two of them. Jesus on the Cross gives up his Spirit to the Father. The Father at the resurrection gives back the Spirit to the Son, and the two of them are then

---

31. It is worth noting J. Ratzinger's insight, borrowing from I. Frank, that for St. Irenaeus the authentic objective of the preaching of Jesus and the apostles was the announcement of the one true God and his proper service, and that this announcement constitutes the essential nucleus of both the Old and the New Testaments. See J. Ratzinger, *Teoría de los principios teológicos* (Barcelona: Herder, 1985), 19–20. This becomes entirely plausible in the light of the understanding I am developing of the Trinity as the monotheism of the victim.

able to give this same Spirit, the Spirit of the crucified and risen victim, to humans as induction into a new way of being human — becoming children of God,[32] quite outside the violence of the "world."

The understanding of God as Trinity then is the understanding that the Cross of Christ, made alive in the resurrection, was in fact a relational reality — a reality of giving and of self-giving that was saving as revealing and revealing as saving. The Trinity is revealed as the salvific density of the Cross. It is the understanding of God made available by the intelligence of the victim, which can thus be seen as the dynamic which produced a huge change in the discourse about God. What I have attempted to do, then, in a few pages when a long book would be more adequate, is show that the intelligence of the victim gradually led out of the ambiguous discourse about God within which the salvific act had in fact occurred and permitted a new discourse about God that I have called "abstract anthropological" (as distinguished, perhaps, from the "narrational anthropomorphic" discourse of the Jewish Scriptures), because it permitted the final revelation of God as love and of violence as human, as part of a salvific forging of forgiveness in historical human terms.[33]

From this recasting of God in the light of the resurrection of the forgiving victim it then becomes possible to understand both who humans really are and who God really is — understanding both in relational terms. This is particularly clear in John's Gospel, where the relationship of Jesus to God — as a son in utter dependence and yet equality without any rivalry, yet imitating perfectly — is simultaneously the adumbration of the relationship of Father and Son in God *and* the revelation of a definitive anthropology. Humans are called to live in a relationship of dependence and yet equality, of pacific imitation without rivalry, and this is shown as something humanly possible. This serves, even within John's Gospel, as a critique of current human practice: the Pharisees are shown as living within a mimetic dependence on the reputation gained from other people, and therefore unable to believe in Jesus.[34]

---

32. See John 1:11–12, the chiastic center of the prologue: "He came to his own home and his own received him not. But to all who received him, who believed in his name, he gave power to become children of God."

33. A full demonstration of this would, of course, require a rereading of the Apocalypse, with its apparent recrudescence of the ambiguous discourse about God. Such a rereading would have to take into account the peculiarities of the apocalyptic genre, a genre by no means unique to Christian discourse, and possible ways in which the book of the Apocalypse is a subversion of that genre from within.

34. John 5:43–44: "I have come in my Father's name, and you do not receive me....How can you believe, who receive glory from one another and do not seek the glory that comes from the only God?"

Then again, in chapter 8 John gives an extraordinary dialogue between Jesus and some Jews who had formerly believed in him. The
question in anthropological terms is: "Who is the other who moves
you?" Jesus gives witness to himself being moved by the Father, the
same Father who chose Abraham. There is another "other" who moves
his interlocutors, the father of lies who was a murderer from the beginning. The criterion for perceiving by which "other" they are moved is
that they seek to kill Jesus. That is to say, humans are always moved
by another. Either it is the other of pacific self-donation, or the other
which maintains order by expulsion and killing. Knowing the Father is
being a human who tends toward the victim; not knowing the Father is
being a human who lives by creating victims. Simultaneously in John's
Gospel we have the manifestation of God and the manifestation of an
anthropology based on murder.[35] It was thus that the intelligence of the
victim made possible a radically anthropological rereading of the Old
Testament, showing the gradual revelation of God as not complicit in
violence and humans as complicit in violence. The discovery of the Trinity is also the discovery of a radically anthropological hermeneutic of
the Scriptures: the hermeneutic of God as human victim. This is the final
working out of the hermeneutic key proposed by Jesus to the disciples
on the road to Emmaus:

> "O foolish men, and slow of heart to believe all that the prophets have
> spoken! Was it not necessary that the Messiah should suffer these things
> and enter into his glory?" And beginning with Moses and all the prophets
> he interpreted to them in all the Scriptures the things concerning himself.
> (Luke 24:25–27)

Conclusion: An Understanding of Salvation

In this chapter I have attempted to set out a theology of redemption
that is also simultaneously a theology of revelation as human discovery.
I have tried to show how this theology flows entirely from the resurrection, that is, from the presence to the apostolic witnesses of the crucified

---

35. It seems proper to indicate that in John's Gospel the adumbration of what I have
called the abstract anthropological view of Trinity and humanity is set within a highly sophisticated Semitic narrational account of how Jesus is the promised victim of Israel and
fulfils in his person the rôles of King, Shepherd, Scapegoat, Prophet, Messiah, and persecuted just one. I am grateful to J. D. M. Derrett's *The Victim* for the massive evidence
of John's use of Old Testament material in his construction of his Gospel and in particular his passion narrative. In the light of Derrett's account and what I have set out here
(the simultaneous presence of the two sorts of discourse) it perhaps becomes possible to
understand why John's Jesus is both a profusion of Semitic fulfillments and a curiously
abstract character, not completely "engaging" with the world through which he moves to
his death.

and risen one. This risen presence has permitted a reading of the apostolic witness which shows the inner coherence of the coming of the kingdom of God as the foundation of the Church and the Church as the universal new people of God that is the sign of the reconciliation of humanity with God around the person of the self-giving victim. I have shown that exactly this same understanding made possible the recasting of the understanding of creation in terms of the self-giving gratuity of the victim and simultaneously permitted the discovery of the true density of the one God as a relational God in three "persons." This whole process, permitting the definitive demystification of God, also permitted the definitive demystification of humanity and made possible a radically anthropological perspective on the world, the anthropology of the other as victim. What I have tried to show, in short, is that Catholic orthodoxy is the living out and making present as sign of this revelatory soteriology flowing from the resurrection. It is this whole process, a process which might be described as the creative bringing to light of the forgiveness of sin, which permits us now to take a more detailed look at what the Church might mean by its teaching on original sin.

Part 2

Stretching the Shape of Forgiveness

Chapter 4

The Resurrection and Original Sin

The Joy of Being Wrong

In order to show what the doctrine of original sin might mean, it is necessary to return to first principles and examine the apostolic witness to try to identify the roots of what was later to develop into a formal doctrine. It goes without saying that the formal doctrine is not to be found explicitly set forth in the apostolic witness, any more than is the doctrine of the Trinity. Part of my contention indeed will be that the development of these two doctrines is not only legitimate as a proper working out of the shape of salvation produced by the death and resurrection of Jesus, but that these doctrines are, in some sense, parallel and mutually dependent outworkings of the presence of that salvation in the midst of humanity.

I have argued above that the epistemological starting point for any understanding of Christianity is the presence to the disciples of the crucified and risen Lord. That is to say: the only reason there is any Christianity at all is because of the resurrection. Any doctrine that does not, therefore, ultimately flow from the resurrection, as a development of its content and consequences, must properly be questioned as to its starting point and as to its validity. If such a doctrine cannot be shown ultimately to flow from the resurrection, then, heeding Paul's monition in Galatians 1:8, it should be discarded.

The New Testament is concerned in the first place with an announcement about God. This is made absolutely clear in 1 John 1:5:

> This is the message we [i.e., "John" representing the apostolic witness] have heard from him [i.e., Jesus] and proclaim to you [i.e., the Church, actual or yet to be], that God is light and in him is no darkness at all.

The resurrection of Jesus was not a miraculous event within a preexisting framework of understanding of God, but the event by which God recast the possibility of human understanding of God. For this to happen God simultaneously made use of and blew apart the understanding of God that had developed over the centuries among the Jewish people.

115

God did this in the person of Jesus, through his life and teaching, leading up to and including his death.

There is a first step to this recasting of God through the resurrection of the crucified Jesus, and this is the demonstration that death itself is a matter of indifference to God. Jesus had already taught exactly this in his answer to the Sadducees in Mark 12:18–27,[1] a teaching which must have seemed mysterious at the time because it showed that in Jesus' perception of God, as opposed to that of his interlocutors, there was already, before Jesus' death, a clear awareness that an understanding structured by death cannot begin to speak adequately about God. The content of the teaching was made available when Jesus himself was raised, and it became possible to see that God's love for this man was such that that love was unaffected by death, and that for that love death was no necessary separation, for love could carry on being reciprocal even through death. For God, death is as if it were not, which is why Abraham, Isaac, and Jacob live in God.

This marks a decisive change in the understanding of God, one which had been a long time in the making, since if God has nothing to do with death, if God is indifferent to death, then our representations of God, all of which are marked by a human culture in which death appears as, at the very least, inevitable, are wrong, as Jesus remarked to the Sadducees: "You are greatly mistaken." The resurrection of Jesus, at the same time as it showed the unimagined strength of divine love for a particular human being and therefore revealed the loving proximity of God, also marked a final and definitive sundering of God from any human representational capacity. Whereas before it could be understood that God did not die, nor change, nor have an end, this was always within a dialectical understanding of what does happen to humans. With the resurrection of Jesus from the dead there is suddenly no dialectical understanding of God available, because God has chosen his own terms on which to make himself known quite outside the possibility of human knowledge marked by death. The complete freedom and gratuity of God is learned only from the resurrection, not because it did not exist before, but because we could not know about or understand it while our understanding was shaped by the inevitability of death.

So we have a first step in the recasting of God by the demonstration of the impossibility of perceiving God within the frame of reference structured by death. This, if you like, is a step made by the "fact" of the resurrection: that, in the midst of history, this man who was *dead* is

---

1. For a fuller treatment of this passage in this vein see my *Raising Abel: The Recovery of the Eschatological Imagination* (New York: Crossroad, 1996), 35–41.

now *alive*. The second step is made by the "content" of the resurrection: that *this* man who was dead is now alive. God loved *this* man, who was killed in such and such a way as a result of such and such human motivations, thus confirming his teaching and revealing the iniquity of what put him to death.

Here we have an apparent paradox: it was the extraordinary proximity of God to the human story — such that God was actually involved in it as one of us — that permitted us the possibility of understanding for the first time the degree of the distance of God from any of our representational possibilities. In more traditional terms, it was only the complete immanence of God in our history as raising a concretely dead man from the dead that revealed the complete transcendence of God. What I would like to suggest is that it is exactly this paradox that is also present in the recasting of sin. The two steps by which the understanding of God was recast are also, simultaneously, steps in the recasting of the understanding of sin. In the first step it is exactly in the degree to which the understanding of God is separated from death that the fulness of the human nature of death becomes apparent. This is so because there is no longer any divine necessity or fatality about death: whatever death is, God has nothing to do with it. That is to say, it becomes apparent not only that death is simply present as something which just is, but, precisely because of the resurrection of Jesus, it becomes present as something which need not be.

The second step shows that death is not merely something which has nothing to do with God and which need not be, but that as a human reality it is opposed to God. It is not only that our representation of God is inaccurate, needing refocusing, but our representation of God is actively contrary to the understanding of God which God wishes to make known. That is to say that the death of *this* man Jesus showed that death is not merely a biological reality, but is also a sinful reality. To put it in another way: it is not just that death is a human reality and not a divine one, but as a human reality it is a sinful reality. God, in raising Jesus, was not merely showing that death has no power over him, but also revealing that the putting to death of Jesus showed humans as actively involved in death. In human reality, death and sin are intertwined: the necessity of human death is itself a necessity born of sin. In us, death is not merely a passive reality but an active one, not something we merely receive but one we deal out.

However, God did not raise Jesus from the dead merely to demonstrate his own deathlessness, or rescue Jesus from the middle of the human reality of death as a bodyguard may rescue a beleaguered pop star from the midst of a pressing crowd of fans, to get her away from it all as quickly as possible. The third step in the recasting of God and the recasting of sin is that God raised up this man who had been killed in this way *for us*. The victim of human iniquity was raised up as forgiveness; in fact the resurrection was the raising up of the victim as forgiveness. This it was which permitted the recasting of God as love. It was not just that God loved his son and so raised him up, but that the giving of the son and his raising up revealed God as love for us. This is the witness of the remarkably similar passages found in John 3:16–17[2] and Rom. 3:21–26,[3] as well as of course 1 John 4:9–10.[4] If the third step reveals God as forgiving us (and the presence of the crucified and risen victim was exactly this revelation), then it also simultaneously reveals that death is not only a human reality, and one inflected by sin, but that the human reality of death itself is capable of being forgiven.

Furthermore, as it became clear that the whole purpose of raising Jesus from the dead was to make forgiveness possible (i.e., none of this happened for the benefit of God, and all of it for the benefit of humanity), so it becomes clear that that forgiveness stretches into our human death. That is to say, the forgiveness which flows from the resurrection affects not only such acts as we may have carried out, but, much more importantly, what we had hitherto imagined to be our very natures. If death is something that can be forgiven us, we were not only wrong about God, but we were fundamentally wrong about ourselves.

Let me try to unpack this difficult notion a little. If God can raise someone from the dead in the middle of human history, the very fact reveals that death, which up till this point had marked human history as simply something inevitable, part of what it is to be a human being, is not inevitable. That is, death is itself not simply a biological reality, but a human cultural reality marking all perception and a human cultural reality that is capable of being altered. This it seems to me is the decisive point at which any pre-Christian notion of sin and the Christian understanding must differ. The drastic nature of sin is revealed as something which has so inflected human culture that death is a human reality, and not simply a biological one, one which decisively marks all human culture. This nature of sin as related to death is simultaneously revealed as

2. "For God so loved the world that he gave his only Son, that whoever believes in him should not perish but have eternal life."

3. "For there is no distinction; since all have sinned and fall short of the glory of God, they are justified by his grace as a gift, through the redemption which is in Christ Jesus, whom God put forward as an expiation by his blood, to be received by faith. This was to show God's righteousness."

4. "In this the love of God was made manifest among us, that God sent his only Son into the world, so that we might live through him. In this is love, not that we loved God but that he loved us and sent his Son to be the expiation for our sins."

something which need not be. It is not that God can, of course, forgive all our sins, but then there is also death which is just there. It becomes clear that God is not only capable of forgiving us for such things as we might have done, but the shape of his forgiveness stretches further than that, into what we *are:* we are humans tied into the human reality of death. We need no longer be.

This is an anthropological discovery of unimaginable proportions. At exactly the same moment as God is revealed as quite beyond any human understanding marked by death, entirely gratuitous love, so also it is revealed that the human understanding marked by death is something accidental to being human, not something essential. Here we have the linchpin of any understanding of original sin: that what we are as beings-toward-death is itself something capable of forgiveness. Furthermore we can see that the only way we are able to appreciate our true condition as humans-marked-by-death is precisely as it is revealed to us that that condition is unnecessary. It is in this way that the doctrine of original sin is the culmination of the revealed understanding of being human: the shape of divine forgiveness revealed in the resurrection of Jesus shows itself to stretch into our congenital involvement with death. The doctrine of original sin is the doctrine of the un-necessity of death. Its epistemological possibility is the discovery that the forgiveness of sins reaches further than the forgiveness of actions or intentions: it reaches into who we are as constituted in and by death. What is particularly vital is that if there had been no resurrection-as-forgiveness, there could have been no understanding of death itself as a reality of sin and therefore no anthropological discovery of the nonnecessity of death.

We might put this more simply by saying that the presence of the crucified and risen Lord to the disciples revealed that humans are wrong about God and about humanity, not simply wrong as mistaken, but wrong as actively involved in death. And this being wrong does not matter any longer, because we can now receive the truth, and thus life, from the forgiving victim. This then might be said to be a first approximation to original sin: that the doctrine of original sin is the doctrine according to which divine forgiveness makes known the accidental nature of human mortality, thus permitting an entirely new anthropological understanding.

The Johannine Witness

The logic of the above development of thought can be seen for itself. But was this in fact the way that the apostolic witnesses, whose understanding is normative, perceived the effects of the resurrection? A look

at both the Johannine and the Pauline witness suggests that it is exactly
so. Let us look first at the Johannine witness.

In John chapter 9 we have, according to Raymond Brown, "Johannine dramatic skill at its best."[5] We also have an extraordinary
meditation on the redefinition of sin as worked by Jesus. At the beginning of the tale, we find the disciples questioning Jesus as to the cause
of the blindness of a man blind from birth in terms of sin. Is he blind
because of his sin, or that of his parents? At the end of the chapter,
Jesus indicates the change in the understanding of blindness that has
come about thanks to his presence: "For judgment I have come into this
world, that those who do not see may see, and that those who see may
become blind" (John 9:39). What has happened in between?

The structure of what has happened is twofold: it is simultaneously
that of an inclusion and an exclusion. In the first place, the story is of an
inclusion. The man was blind from birth and thus cut off not only from
a certain participation in a human good, but also from full integration
into the community of Israel. His blindness was considered part of a
moral defect that meant he was ipso facto impure and unable to participate fully in the cultic life of Israel.[6] His sight is easily given him on a
sabbath, and he is integrated into the life of the people by the process of
his healing. The healing has various elements: clay[7] is used, mixed with
Jesus' spittle, thus showing Jesus as fulfilling the original creation and
bringing it to perfection.[8] The man is sent to a pool outside the city and
comes back seeing. Most commentators see in this detail, as in the whole
story, reference to the baptismal process of illumination, thus indicating
that a historical incident is being retold in the light of the resurrection,
which had made of baptism the way in to the Church. It is by this washing in a pool, considered by rabbinic sources a place of purification,[9]
that sight was given. The man was now able, at least in theory, to be
integrated fully into the life of Israel.

Then there is the story of the exclusion: the former blind man is
taken to the Pharisees, and, as they investigate the nature of his cure,
it becomes more and more apparent that Jesus was involved in the cure.
Since such a cure would suggest the messianic nature of Jesus, the Phar-

---

5. In Raymond Brown, *The Gospel according to John,* Anchor Bible (New York:
Doubleday, 1966), 1:376.

6. Leviticus 21:18 prohibits blind descendants of Aaron from exercising the priest-
hood, but the disciples' question about sin indicates a popular appreciation of blindness as
going further than mere cultic disqualification.

7. Heb.: *adamah/adam* — the obvious pun.

8. This is also the sense of Jesus' sabbath miracles: showing God not as resting but as
continuing and fulfilling creation.

9. See Brown, *The Gospel according to John,* 372.

isees at first doubt the cure and then become increasingly abusive in their questioning. Finally they throw the former blind man out. During this process of increasing violence, there is simultaneously a process by which the blind man (who had never seen Jesus, because he actually received his sight at the pool of Siloam) becomes increasingly aware of who Jesus is: first he is just a man, then a prophet, and finally he is a man from God who is superior to Moses (having done a work after all, that had never been known since the world began). At this point he is cast out. Jesus then comes to him, and he is able to recognize his benefactor as Lord and worship him. It is interesting that it is during the process of his exclusion that he comes to perceive with increasing clarity the nature of his benefactor, at the same time as the Pharisees become increasingly hardened in their attitude toward Jesus.

Jesus' final comment, "For judgment I came into the world, that those who do not see may see, and that those who see may become blind," is his assessment of the whole story. In the first place Jesus has carried out no active judgment at all. The only judgment related in the story has been that of the Pharisees, casting the man out. This is part of the ironic Johannine recasting of judgment: it is by being crucified that Jesus is the real judge of his judges. So because Jesus is the cause of the former blind man's expulsion, the former blind man shares Jesus' rôle as judge of those who have expelled him. It is not that Jesus simply abolishes the notion of judgment or is merely much more of a judge than the other judges: the sense in which Jesus is a judge is a subversion from within of the notion of judgment. The judgment that excluded the former blind man is revealed as the judgment (also discernment) that the expellers are really blind.

In this story then we watch a revolution in the understanding of sin, a revolution that takes place around the person of Jesus but is actually worked out in the life of someone else. The structure of the story is the same as is to be found time and time again in John: that of an expulsion, or proto-lynching, one of the many that lead up to the definitive expulsion of the crucifixion, which is also the definitive remedy for all human order based on expulsion. The revolution in the concept of sin consists in the following: at the beginning of the tale, sin was considered in terms of some sort of defect that excludes the one bearing the defect. At the end of the tale sin is considered as the act of exclusion: the real blindness is the blindness which is not only present in those who exclude, but actually grows and intensifies during the act of exclusion.

This change of perception is precisely the change that was wrought by the resurrection of the crucified Christ. That is to say that what John has done is apply to one of Jesus' no doubt historical healings of a blind man on the sabbath the revolution in the understanding of sin that came about as a result of the resurrection. The sin of the world is understood quite specifically as being involved in the work of "your father the devil," who "was a murderer from the beginning."[10] Sin is recast entirely in the light of the casting out of Jesus. Jesus is quite specifically shown as having no problem with the sort of "sin" that is taken to exclude the "sinner" from the community: he cures the blind man with no problem at all (just as, in the previous chapter, he held nothing against the woman caught in adultery, but everything against those who would stone her). Sin is revealed as the mechanism of expulsion which is murderous, and those are blind sinners who are involved in that mechanism without being aware of what they are doing. The problem is not with those who are only blindly part of the mechanism of exclusion: they at least do not know what they are doing, and thus have no guilt. The problem is with those (like the Pharisees who question Jesus in John 9:40) who form part of such mechanisms of exclusion, but think that "they see" — that is, think that they have moral insight, know good from evil, are capable of discernment and judgment. Such people not only take part in mechanisms of exclusion, but justify them as good and from God. Their guilt remains.

We have here, then, a further subversion from within. Just as Jesus subverts the notion of judgment from within, so also the notion of sin is subverted from within. Jesus doesn't abolish the concept of sin or simply define it much more strongly than before.[11] The notion of sin is subverted from within, in the light of the resurrection of the crucified one, in such a way that what sin is is shown to be much more drastic than previous interpretations, but from quite a different direction. Sin is not what excludes in the person of the excluded one, but the dynamic act of excluding in the persons of the excluders.

We can go further with this Johannine approach to sin. There are indications present in chapter 9 that more is intended in this story than a merely casual description of a particular incident regarding sin. The question of the sin as being related to the origins of humankind is hinted at in Jesus' use of clay in his restoration, or fulfillment, of creation, as

---

10. John 8:44. This is part of the proto-lynching that immediately precedes the story of the man blind from birth.

11. Exactly the same notion of subversion from within can be applied to Matthew's handling of the relationship between Jesus and the law: he came not to abolish but to fulfil the law. However, this fulfillment is not a mere tightening up of the law, but a recasting of the law around the persons of victims, who therefore become the criteria by which the law is to be understood. Thus the fulfillment of the law is a subversion from within of the current understanding of the law and was rightly seen as subversive by those who regarded themselves as the guardians of the law.

well as in the insistence that the man was blind from birth. The relation of this story to something original is understood by the former blind man himself, who reckons that never (*ek tou aiônos*) has such a healing taken place. In the light of John's irony this means much more than that a particularly spectacular miracle has taken place, such as has never taken place before. It also suggests that there has been present a blindness from the beginning of the world that only now is being cured for the first time. Furthermore, when Jesus speaks, at the end, about judgment it is clear that he is not concerned with a particular local incident, but about a discernment relating to the whole world (*kosmos*). Here we have a highly subtle teaching about the whole world being blind from birth, from the beginning, and about Jesus, the light of the world coming to bring sight to the world, being rejected precisely by those who, though blind, claimed to be able to see. All humans are blind, but where this blindness is compounded by active participation in the mechanisms of exclusion pretending to sight, this blindness is culpable.

What we have then in chapter 9 alone is a worldview of the sin of the world and the way Jesus comes to remove that sin, on his way subverting the understanding of sin completely. When this worldview is linked to other Johannine passages, we begin to get something close to what one might call a theology of original sin. In the first place consider the passage already alluded to in chapter 8, where Jesus discusses with the Jews who had believed in him their paternity and his. This passage is the Johannine equivalent of the woes to the scribes and Pharisees which appear in Matthew and Luke, where the ultimate criterion is the same: participation or not in a religion based on murder. Matthew and Luke specifically indicate that the history of murder of which this generation is accomplice goes back to Cain. When John refers to "your father the devil [who] was a murderer from the beginning" this is also a reference back to the primordial murder which Genesis places at the beginning of human culture. Related to this primordial murder is a culture of lies, lies related to murder, as well as a blindness that cannot see the truth. Abraham was part of the way out of this culture based on the murderous lie, and if Jesus' interlocutors had been sons of Abraham as they claimed, they would not be trying to kill him, but they are trying to kill him, and therefore are sons of Cain, whose desires were produced by the devil. Where Paul talks of sons of wrath, John talks of sons of the devil, who was a murderer from the beginning. The idea is the same: from the beginning human culture is radically mendacious and murderous. This can be understood only in the light of the Son who reveals the true Father, and thus true sonship.

This subversion of the original order of the world is brought out

again in John 16, where Jesus tells the disciples, in the context of warning them about persecution and being killed, that he will send them the
Defense Counsellor.

> And when he comes, he will convince the world concerning sin and right-
> eousness and judgment: concerning sin, because they do not believe in me;
> concerning righteousness, because I go to the Father, and you will see me
> no more; concerning judgment because the ruler of this world is judged.
> (John 16:8–11)

It is exactly this of which we have been talking. The understanding made
available after the resurrection of Jesus enables sin, righteousness, and
judgment to be seen in an entirely different light. Sin is now recast in
terms of Jesus. To believe in Jesus is to believe in the forgiveness of
sins made available by the victim risen as forgiveness. Those who do
not believe in Jesus remain in sin, because they remain in the mode of
casters-out. It is those who receive the cast-out one who are enabled
to live without sin. Righteousness is defined in terms of Jesus, because
he goes to the Father, therefore goodness is seen in terms of the loving
obedience by which Jesus gave witness to his Father even to death: righteousness is the mutual self-giving of the Father and the Son which we
call love, love lived out under the circumstances of victimage. Judgment
is redefined in terms of Jesus because in what appeared to be the judgment and expulsion of Jesus, it was really the ruler, or *Archôn,* which
can equally well be Satan or the governing principle of the world, who
was revealed for what he is, and thus judged.

Thus, when John shows the subversion from within of the understanding of sin that is operated by Jesus' death and resurrection, he is
quite specifically doing two things. The first is to depict sin as, in fact,
the condition of blindness within which all humans live, unless enlightened by the Light of the World. This blindness is related to a governing
principle that has been present from the beginning of the world, and this
governing principle is directly linked to an initial murder which has determined the content of the sort of blindness that is being described. This
murder-related blindness is able to be perceived for the first time thanks
to a different murder (that of Jesus), and the resurrection that enabled
the victim to be received as forgiveness. The first beginnings of "sight"
about sin consist in the recognition of one's complicity in the murderous
order of the world, and therefore of the degree of one's blindness. All
other understandings of sin are understandings that are blind to the real
order of the world, and are thus all the more blind when they claim to
have some insight into what is good or bad without being aware of the
dynamism of expulsion that in fact structures their "vision."

The second thing John is doing in his subversion of sin is linking directly the subversion of the understanding of sin with the subversion of the understanding of the Father. This is what is meant by the Holy Spirit convicting the world with regard to the understanding of righteousness (vv. 8–11).[12] The new understanding of righteousness was made available by the resurrection opening up the free flow of love between Father and Son. For John, as can be seen from these passages, the change in the perception of God that is brought about by the resurrection is also, simultaneously, a change in the perception of sin. I will return to this crucial point later, since, as I hope will become apparent, the doctrine of original sin is the anthropology that is uncovered by the resurrection as the necessary counterpart to the discovery that God is Trinity.

It is quite wrong to say that John knows only of the "sin of the world" or structures of sin, but not of original sin. It is clear from his texts that there is a distinct understanding that the sin of the world has origins, and origins of a quite specific sort. The passages I have indicated bear clear witness to John having understood as one of the first fruits of the resurrection the making available of the understanding that we are all wrong (blind), and that this does not matter. Being wrong can be forgiven: it is insisting on being right that confirms our being bound in original murderous sin.

The Pauline Witness

If it can be accepted that one of the first fruits of the resurrection in terms of human understanding is a new understanding of God (deathless, loving his son, and thus showing righteousness) and simultaneously a new understanding of humankind (constituted in death, killing the son, and thus showing sinfulness, within a context of forgiveness), then we can imagine two stages (at least) to the preaching of this new insight. The first is an early stage in which this insight is preached as such, within the terms of reference of the linguistic-religious matrix within which the insight was born. The second stage is the gradual development from this insight of a new language about God and about humankind, where, consonant with the insight itself, there begins to develop a theology based on the new understanding of God and a dependent anthropology based on the new understanding of humanity. It seems to me that we have evidence of exactly this process in the juxtaposition of the Pauline and the Johannine witnesses.

---

12. It is no accident that John uses the same term here as Paul when Paul is making exactly the same intellectual shift in Romans 1:16–18. We have here a nexus of ideas very close to the original kerygma.

In the Johannine witness, set out above, we have a later stage in the development where the anthropological working out of the insight is clearer, as is the clarification of the understanding of God from elements of discourse formed within human violence.[13] Thus John is able both to offer a theology worked out from the new understanding of God and reveal the anthropological mechanism that led to the revelation more clearly as an anthropological mechanism. In the Pauline witness we have a somewhat earlier stage in the working out of the same insight, where the place of the Johannine anthropological mechanism is taken by Paul's meditation on the function of the law. It seems to me that by reading the Pauline version of the same basic insight in the light of the Johannine development it becomes possible to achieve a certain clarity as to what Paul is about that is entirely faithful to his thought. The evidence is to be found in the first eight chapters of Romans.[14]

In the first place we can see that for Paul the Gospel is the Gospel of the righteousness of God. This is what the death and resurrection of Jesus has revealed for him. That is shown in Romans 1:17 and again in Romans 3:25. What has happened in between these two references is that Paul, because of the necessity of clarifying the question of the exact theological nature of the law, has gone in for a long explanation of the inverse consequence of the same revelation of the righteousness of God: the revelation of what he calls the wrath of God. The content of this revelation is exactly the same as what I suggested above: that all humans are constitutionally wrong (we all have a "debased mind," 1:28) and constitutionally idolaters, as is demonstrated by our not knowing the righteousness of God. It would be well to examine this notion of the wrath of God because of the easy misunderstanding to which it is prone.

The word wrath (orgé) appears ten times in Romans. Only once does it appear as the wrath of God (Rom. 1:18). On the one occasion where it appears to be something inflicted by God on people as a result of our wickedness (Rom. 3:5) Paul expressly indicates the mythical nature of the terminology ("I speak in a human way"). On all the other occasions where the term appears (2:5, 8; 4:15; 5:9; 9:22; 12:19; 13:4, 5) it is impersonal. Even in the first case, where the orgé is linked to theou, the content of the wrath of God is itself a demystification of a vindictive account of God (whose righteousness has just been declared). For the

---

13. But see John 3:36! It is clear from the context, however, that this is an anthropological reality, not a theological one. It is less immediately clear that the same is true of the Pauline uses of wrath (though it is no less true).

14. I am much indebted for the treatment that follows to R. Hamerton-Kelly, *Sacred Violence: Paul's Hermeneutic of the Cross* (Minneapolis: Fortress, 1992), especially chap. 4, "Sacred Violence and Original Sin," 88–119.

content of the wrath is the handing over by God of us to ourselves. Three times in the following verses the content of the wrath is described in terms of handing over: 1:24; 1:26; and 1:28. That is to say, the wrath, rather than being an act of divine vengeance, is a divine nonresistance to human evil.[15] However, I would suggest that it is more than that. The word "handed over" (*paredôken*) has in primitive Christian sources a particularly subtle set of resonances.[16] For God is described as handing over (*paredôken*) his own son to us in a text no further from our own than Romans 8:32. The handing over of the son to us and the handing over of ourselves to sin appear to be at the very least parallel. The same verb (*paredothé*) is used in 4:25, where Jesus was handed over for our trespasses and raised for our justification. I would suggest that it is the handing over of the son to our killing him that is in fact the same thing as handing us over to our own sins. Thus wrath is life in the sort of world which kills the son of God.

It would seem that here (and especially in 4:25) we have a remnant of a very early transference of terminology, or word play. The same process can be observed in the only other (and earlier) Pauline use of the word "wrath," 1 Thessalonians 2:16. There wrath (described impersonally, simply "the wrath") has come upon the Jews "unto the end." The content of the wrath is the persecution by the Jews, killing Jesus and the prophets. The problem is not merely that they have killed Jesus, but they have not received the word of God, and therefore remain in wrath — which would seem to be the delusions of religion based on persecution from which the Thessalonians have been set free by receiving God's word and learning to imitate Christ's suffering of persecution. Again, the defining factor in wrath is the death of Christ.

It becomes possible to suggest then a series of stages in the transformation of the sense of the word "wrath." There is abundant evidence that in a very early representation of Jesus' death, following Isaiah 53, the crucifixion was represented as Jesus bearing the iniquity of us all.[17] The divine wrath that should have fallen on Israel fell on him. The next stage is the realization that the language of the divine wrath itself, in the light of the resurrection, must be reconsidered. However, within a highly conservative (i.e., non-proto-Marcionite) cultural matrix we have, prior to the elaboration of a completely new theological language, the ironic

---

15. As Hamerton-Kelly indicates, *Sacred Violence,* 101.

16. This word is vital and recurrent in all the Gospels, where much is made of the irony of God handing over Jesus, Judas handing over Jesus, and Jesus handing over himself.

17. In his detailed study of the use of Isaiah 53 in the New Testament, *Le Christ est mort pour tous* (Paris: Cerf, 1993), P. Ternant shows that the texts we have in the New Testament admit of no interpretation of the death of Jesus in terms of satisfactory substitution.

turning upside down of the old. It is to exactly this stage that Paul bears witness, even going so far as to introduce an explicit note as to the ambiguity of the language of wrath (3:5). So we have a gradual ironic subversion of the language of wrath, whereby that which is initially seen as something active (God being angry) is recast to show God being right-eous in the midst of human anger, but without losing the word "wrath." Something of the same process can be seen (but more obviously) in the Johannine reworking of the theme of God's judgment whereby God's judgment of humanity consists not in any judgment actively exercised by God, but in the judgment undergone by Jesus at the hands of human beings. We are judged by our relationship to that judgment. We see then how God "handing over" Jesus to us can be described as God's wrath, when the content of that wrath is the human violence exercised against Jesus, or the simultaneous handing over of ourselves to idolatry typified in the killing of Jesus. The Pauline use of the word "wrath" demon-strates what I tried to indicate above in terms of the slow process of the separation of the properly theological and the properly (but depen-dently) anthropological discourses that are the necessary outworkings of the double revelation flowing from the resurrection: that of who God really is and of what humanity really is. Paul is at an earlier stage than John in the same process.

The next factor in the Pauline testimony is not only the revelation of human idolatry, but its universal quality. This is abundantly illustrated in the first three chapters of Romans, where Paul is keen to illustrate precisely that all, both Jews and Greeks, are under the power of sin (Rom. 3:9).

It is not only sin that is universal, but for anyone who believes in the goodness of God that has been made manifest in the handing over of Jesus followed by his raising up, then righteousness is universally avail-able. It is of course the same insight that has brought the understanding of wrath to its sharpest definition — the killing of the son of God — that has made it possible to be set free from wrath. This is the import of 5:9: "Since therefore we are now justified by his blood, much more shall we be saved by him from the wrath." The true understanding of wrath came about exactly at the same moment as there emerged the possibil-ity of being freed from it: it is the forgiveness of the resurrection which defines the nature of sin.

This leads Paul into a highly complex series of arguments about the law, which I will not follow here. However, it seems important to indi-cate that it is precisely from his understanding of the universal nature of the sinfulness of humanity that he understands that law, which is in itself holy (7:12), has become a function of that sinfulness. In the first place, the law brings about knowledge of sin (3:20) just as it also bears witness to the righteousness of God, along with the prophets (3:21). However, it not only serves as an epistemological instrument, in the good sense of letting people know what sin is. It is an instrument of wrath (4:15). That is to say, the knowledge of sin that it brings about, rather than being salvific, becomes part of the sinful human world of mutual judgment and recrimination. At least where there is no law, there is no transgression.

Paul indicates however that the law actually increases sin (5:20). It is hard not to read 5:21 as indicating that the increase of sin produced by the law was made manifest in the death of Jesus ("sin reigned in death"), while the resurrection brought about that "grace might reign through righteousness." Paul goes even further with this line of thought in 7:5, where the law again has an active rôle in arousing sin. I would suggest that this verse is wrongly interpreted if "flesh" is taken in the modern debased sense (i.e., basically sexual). It seems far more probable (and in line with Pauline usage)[18] that "flesh" means "within the persecutory religious framework" which Paul associated with Judaism, and that the sinful passions in question, rather than lust, etc., mean the persecutory zeal which led Paul to persecute Christians — that is, the zeal which was at work in his members to bear fruit for death.

We can therefore see something very similar to the (much clearer) Johannine analysis above: sin is universal and easily forgiven through faith in the God who raised Jesus from the dead. So the blind man (and thus blindness from the beginning) was easily cured. However, there is the complicating factor of the law, which appears to enable people to be just by knowing good and evil (the Pharisees in John 9 who "could see"). In fact, not only does the law not permit people to become just, but it locks them further into wrath, which is the judgmental attitude of those who think they have a superior knowledge, leading them to involvement in persecution and death, just as it had led Paul himself. That is to say, rather than sin being overcome by the law, it is compounded by it, making sin even more lethal. So the Johannine Pharisees are driven deeper into blindness by their pretensions of sight. And of course, as in John,[19] the paradigm for the law being wrong is the death of Christ. Where for John the death of Christ revealed the structuring mechanism of sin at work in the authorities, in Paul it reveals the complicity of the law with sin and thus, finally, the caducity of the law. Paul explicitly says that "Christ is the end of the law that every one who has faith may be justified" (Rom. 10:4). He is the "end" of course in multiple senses, one of

---

18. See Hamerton-Kelly, *Sacred Violence*, 120–29, 146–50.
19. See the ironic juxtaposition of John 18:31 and 19:7.

which for Paul is that the law achieved its purpose in leading to Christ's death, thus revealing definitively the true nature of sin whose accomplice it had been. That is exactly what is said by 7:13. Having fulfilled its ambiguous purpose, the law is at an end, now that righteousness is made available by faith in Christ.

At a later stage I will examine the complex Pauline understanding of the relationship between desire, law, and sin. Here it is sufficient to indicate that he, like John, considers that the law makes righteousness (sight) more rather than less difficult.

Finally, of course, Paul is famously aware that the universal sinfulness that he is describing is historically original and related to death (5:12). Sin and death are ascribed to Adam. Death was not invented by the law, because sin-related death reigned from Adam to Moses, even though between the two people were ignorant of the law. Furthermore, the consequence of the universal failed mind that is at the center of our idolatric state is the complexes of envious desire that lead to murder. That is to say, the same elements appear in the Pauline argument as in the Johannine story. The anthropological elements are rather less developed in Paul than in John. Paul uses complex rabbinical arguments instead, and this accounts for much of our difficulty in understanding him. He uses Adam's transgression rather than the original murder to illustrate his theme, because it enables him to relate the primary prohibition (Gen. 2:15–17) with the Mosaic law, and therefore fits in with his discussion of the caducity of the law. The Adam story also enables him to relate sinful desire with the law (7:7–11), which is vital if he is to maintain the goodness of the law and yet show how it has become part of a perverted world order.

Having seen therefore that the apostolic witness bears witness to the double revelation that I have described, of the new vision of God and a new clarity concerning the universality of sin, now capable of forgiveness, it would be interesting to see the way in which this redefinition of sin in terms of that which can be forgiven is the culmination of an anthropological development from the Old Testament.

The Culmination of the Discovery of Sin

If the paradigm of original sin has become, thanks to the resurrection, the sphere of human violence, often sacralized, culminating in the putting to death of Jesus, it becomes important to see that this anthropological discovery is not only a one-shot job, made possible by a particular miraculous intervention (the resurrection), even though it could not, of course, have been understood without the resurrection.

There is a whole history of the development of the understanding of sin in the Old Testament which can be shown, following the hermeneutic pattern indicated in Luke 24:26–27, to culminate in the vision made possible after the resurrection. What is interesting, therefore, following Girard's analysis, is the way that we can see two contrary tendencies at work in mythology on the one hand and the Old Testament on the other: in the former the movement of an ever greater occlusion of the collective violence against the victim and, in the latter, the inverse road toward an ever greater understanding of the human nature of violence and of the innocence of the victim, as well, therefore, as an understanding of the human being as related to violence.

In *Violence and the Sacred* Girard shows how the three pillars of "primitive" religion, myth, ritual, and prohibition, are interlinked and how all three flow from the misunderstood mechanism of the surrogate victim. That is to say, an original murder brings peace; myth is the telling of the story of the foundation of the peace, or order, from the perspective of those involved in the lynching as persecutors; ritual is the reenactment of the circumstances of the murder in a slightly distorted form to reproduce the benefits that the murder brought about in terms of social harmony; and the prohibitions (often scrupulously disobeyed for ritual purposes alone) are directed against the supposed causes or forms of acquisitive and conflictual mimesis which led to the crisis culminating in the murder. Typically the prohibitions are against the crimes of which the original victim was held to have been guilty. Often the prohibitions appear arbitrary: there is no clear reason for their existence, since their link with the original murder has gradually been lost.[20]

Given this, it enables us to see why in so many "primitive" religions "offenses" scarcely seem to have any ethical content, but are related to transgressions against apparently mythical prohibitions. Expiation for the offenses is made either by group sanctions against the offender or, in the case of those groups that have elaborated a sacrificial system related to some gods, by means of expiatory sacrifices which restore the lost order. The relation of offenses to an ethical "conscience" is a huge development present in very few cultural groups.[21]

Girard's reading of mythology enables us to see something of the development of an ethical conscience, of a perception of good and evil

---

20. This analysis is, of course, retrospective. We could not expect any of those involved in the establishment of the myths, rituals, and prohibitions to understand what they are doing, let alone in these terms. That is exactly the point!

21. See L. Scheffzyck, "Pecado," in *Conceptos fundamentales de la teología* (Madrid: Cristiandad, 1967), 3:387–98.

and the way this is related to an original murder. In chapter 6 of *The Scapegoat* we are presented with three myths, the similarity of whose relation to an original collective murder Girard demonstrates. The myth of Zeus, Dionysius, and the Titans is very close to an original murder: the child Dionysius is lured by the Titans (who wave noisy rattles) into their power, murdered, cooked, and eaten. Zeus, the child's father, resurrects his son and fulminates the Titans.

In a myth that is structurally very similar, the child Zeus is being protected from being murdered at the hands of his father, Chronos, by a group of Curetes. The child gives away his hiding place by crying, and there is a danger that Chronos will find him. The Curetes therefore protect him by surrounding him and making a great din with their weapons. The noise frightens the child, who cries, and, to cover the sound, the Curetes make even more noise around the child with their weapons. So the element of collective murder has been removed, and the lynch mob has become a group of protective warriors.

In a third myth, from a quite different culture, a further change has taken place. Baldr is a perfect god, who is protected from being murdered by his mother having exacted from all things, animate and inanimate, an oath that they will not harm him. All the other gods therefore are able to play at casting every kind of missile at him without his being harmed. Loki, the trickster god, doesn't take part in this game, but seeks out the mother, who reveals that she didn't exact the oath from the mistletoe, since it seemed so tender. Loki gets a piece of mistletoe and puts it into the hand of Baldr's blind brother, Höhr, who hasn't been able to throw missiles owing to his blindness. Loki then guides Höhr's hands with the mistletoe to Baldr, who is thus killed by the mistletoe. Again the central structure is identical: a group of gods surrounding a god who is killed. However, here there has been some sort of development of the myth. The responsibility has been displaced from the collective, who actually hurled projectiles, onto the blind brother, who is treated as having done the killing. However, this brother is declared really innocent of the murder: he was blind, the weapon was farcically impotent, and his hands were guided. The whole murder is blamed on a god who did not in fact take part in the collective murder, Loki. He manipulated, found the weak point, found the weapon, and tricked Höhr into killing his brother.

What we have then is a comparative study showing the way in which the violence that originally was shared by many (even if those "many" were gods or demigods) is gradually displaced onto the few, or even onto one figure alone (Chronos or Loki), while the real responsibility for the violence is shirked. Girard's suggestion is that in the development there is "a certain sharing of *good* and *evil:* moral dualism appears as *collective* violence is eliminated."[22]

We can go a long way with this. It suggests that the understanding of good and evil arises from a series of displacements of responsibility arising from an original collective murder. In the first place the groups in question blame the victim, or the god, who are interchangeable, and so the whole founding violence is transferred into the divine sphere while maintaining its collective element. Then it is the collective element that is displaced in favor of a single murderer, maybe a brother (and myths where the founding murder is fratricidal abound), and then that is itself displaced in favor of a trickster, a figure who is half divine but is well on its way to becoming that familiar figure in depictions of good and evil: a devil. This last displacement is of course perfectly compatible with an ever more "spiritual" set of deities, or even a single deity. Here too is the place where "fate," necessity, or *anangké,* comes to play a rôle in Greek tragedy. Under a semi-philosophical guise, a further displacement of responsibility has taken place.

The important thing is to notice the mechanism that is present behind these displacements. In every case, fault is being transferred, responsibility is being avoided, and someone else is being indicated as the author of evil. The group transfers to the victim, the gods transfer to the god, the collective displaces to the brother, the brother to the trickster, and so on. That is to say, the motor force behind the representation of good and evil that emerges is the same accusatory mechanism that produced the original murder. The perspective is always the same, a collective exculpation at the expense of a victim and consequently a vision of good and evil that is blind to its own origin.

In the light of this it becomes possible to see the variety of extraordinary conquests which Israel made in its understanding of sin, without ever developing a unitary vision of sin. The process of subversion from within is at work in the Old Testament. This can be seen in the way in which in Genesis the acquisition by Adam and Eve of "the knowledge of good and evil" is seen as highly ambiguous. So much so that it is this acquisition that effectively expels them from the garden so that they may not eat of the tree of life, as well, and live. The knowledge of good and evil is linked to an expulsion and linked to the human condition taking place in the realm of death. Secondly, one of the first signs of the presence of sin is the presence of the mechanism of displacing responsibility: Adam to Eve, Eve to the serpent. This in itself means, thirdly, that the rôle of any demonic figure as decisively causative of evil is subverted: it

---

22. René Girard, *The Scapegoat* (London: Athlone, 1986), 72.

is limited to a rôle of a suggester of evil. The involvement of God in the Genesis story is that of having implanted an initial law concerning the tree of good and evil, an involvement which springs from the theology of the law in whose light the Genesis story was retold: there is no divine responsibility for human sin. The beginnings of the possibility of human responsibility for sin, and thus of human freedom, emerge.

In the story of Cain and Abel once again the murder is not justified, and responsibility is laid where it belongs. There is still a hint of mythical arbitrariness in the acceptance by God of one sort of sacrifice and not the other. However, Cain is clearly shown as (unsuccessfully) fighting a desire which he is told he can master (Gen. 4:7): he need not have murdered Abel. There is no room for any fatalism or necessity in the murder. In the gap created between mythical necessity and the murder are born both sin and freedom.

The major source of the understanding of sin in the Old Testament is, of course, the law. It is worthwhile considering what an extraordinary event the law constituted from two interrelated vantage points: looking at it as a project for a people and, perhaps more surprisingly, looking at it as an instrument of epistemological discovery. In the first place, the law is given as part of a founding of a people in the wake of an expulsion. So here already there is a major subversion of the usual relation between original expulsion and prohibition which Girard has identified. The law is not a series of prohibitions among the persecutors to prevent the violence, attributed to the victim, which led to the social chaos resolved in the victimization. The law institutes a social project for the victim people so that it not engage in the sort of victimary practices in which the former persecutors of Israel had engaged. It is for this reason that exiles and sojourners are to be particularly well treated, that slaves may not be made. Furthermore, this social project is linked to divine benevolence: it is understood that Israel is a people that is on the way to something, is a becoming in history. The law is given as part of a covenant of love: because God has loved Israel, God has chosen Israel, and for no other reason (Deut. 7:7–8). From this it becomes possible to understand sin in terms of infidelity to the covenant, which is a failing to become in history what God willed Israel to become, for its own good. Here it is quite clear that sin is defined in terms not of some maintenance of a social order, or magico-ritual abuses, but in terms of a positive theological reality: a divine plan, from which sin is a form of defection.

Of course, in the Old Testament itself there are many remains of other, more mythical understandings of sin and punishment, where a theological rereading seems scarcely to have made an impact: for instance, forty-two boys are shredded by two she-bears for having jeered at Elisha's baldness (2 Kings 2:23–24). The extraordinary parallels between the story of Lot and the destruction of Sodom in Genesis 19 and that of the destruction of the Benjaminites because of an almost identical incident at Gibeah in Judges 19–21 suggest an ancient myth in the background of both of them of divine punishment amid scenes of collective violence, only lightly retouched with the emergence from the fray of possibly formerly victimary figures. It is not the existence of such stories in the Old Testament that is remarkable, but the simultaneous presence of elements bearing witness to a process of demythologization of the same sorts of stories.

If the law was born as part of a social project of nationhood subversive of victimary practice, remarkable in itself, then even more remarkable, and comparatively little commented on, is its rôle as an epistemological instrument.[23] By this I mean that, over a long period of time, the attempt to live by the law and to be faithful to it permitted two quite different sorts of discoveries. In the first place it is highly probable that it was fidelity to the law that permitted the discovery of monotheism (as opposed to monolatry). Exegetes agree that the period of the Babylonian exile and immediately thereafter was a crucially rich period for the development of Israelite theological understanding. It was the crisis provoked by seeking to be faithful to the law and God's promises in the circumstances of the apparent powerlessness of God in the face of the greatly superior Babylonian culture and pantheon, and perhaps especially by the fact that the return from exile was owing to Cyrus's benevolence, that led to the awareness that there is only one God. The monolatry enshrined in the law (thou shalt have no other gods before me) became the instrument for the discovery of monotheism under the circumstances of the exile. It is not only that the God of Israel punishes Israel's enemies (dealing blows at Assyrian armies, for instance), but the one, universal God can even use a gentile emperor to further his plan of love for Israel. Faithfulness to the law under the circumstances of complete defeat opened the possibility of a reconceptualization of God. Were it not for the possibly fanatical and at least "imprudent" adherence to legal monolatry by the Jews, the great discovery of universal monotheism would not have been made.

In the same way, the law was an epistemological instrument in the discovery of sin. As the prophets (especially) sought to call Israel back to faithfulness to the covenant (and therefore to the law), so there devel-

---

23. This is to do nothing other than emphasize the positive side of the same reality of which Paul emphasizes the negative side in Romans 3:20–21.

oped an anthropological understanding of sin. Thus there is a shift from representations of God hardening the heart (for instance, of Pharaoh, Exod. 4:21, etc.) to the notion of God testing and tempting human beings (Gen. 22:1), and finally this too is put to question and denied in the Wisdom literature (for instance, Sir. 15:11–17).[24] The book of Job can be read as a struggle with this set of ideas, where Job wrestles with the much more primitive theologies of his "friends," even though there are only hints at a decisive break with an understanding of God as torturer. A similar development occurs in which a tribal notion of sin, and therefore of diffused punishment of sin, is gradually broken down in favor of a view that God does not punish the children for the iniquities of the fathers (Ezek. 18), but seeks individual responsibility and turning aside from sin.

At the same time as these shifts were occurring, we have a fundamental discovery in ethical terms: the discovery of the human heart. Here I do not mean merely a discovery of emotions or passions,[25] but a properly theological discovery: that of the relationship between the seat of human attitudinal patterns and God. If there is such difficulty in keeping the law, if Israel has so much difficulty in keeping faith with the covenant, is this not because of the human heart? The human heart is understood to be something "desperately corrupt" (Jer. 17:9). Of particular importance in the understanding of the heart is the relationship between envy and violence. This is clear in the account of the murder of Abel. It is clear again in the reaction of Joseph's brothers to Joseph. Ahab has Naboth killed for no less. The formidable violence exercised by the "friends" in their discourses against Job is shot through with envy. Some 100 of the 150 psalms indicate or hint at a situation where a group of enemies, filled with envious violence, are arrayed around a single just man.[26] This discovery of the human heart as a theological reality, possible only within the growing cultural frame provided by the law and the discovery of monotheism, is intrinsically linked with the development of a concept of subjective guilt, of which the evidence is to be found in the psalms (for instance, 32, 38, 51). The depth of sin and the awareness of God's capacity for forgiveness grow together, as can be shown by the penitential exhortations of the prophets (for instance, Isa. 1:16ff.; Jer. 18:11; 25:5; Ezek. 18:21, 31; Hos. 6:1ff.; Joel 2:12ff.). This theological development culminates in the awareness that for Israel to

---

24. "Do not say, 'It was he who led me astray,' " . . . , etc.
25. There is no shortage of these in, for instance, *The Iliad!*
26. See the analysis of R. Schwager in *Must There Be Scapegoats? Violence and Redemption in the Bible* (San Francisco: Harper & Row, 1987), 91–109.

be able to live the covenant, it will actually be necessary for God to give the people a new heart, as Ezekiel prophesies in 36:26.

If envy is its motive force (see Wis. 2:23–24), far more time is spent in the Old Testament pointing out that violence is what is really abominable. The flood came in Genesis 6 because God could tolerate no longer the violence that abounded on the face of the earth. The priestly codex clearly interprets the sin of humankind as violence.[27] Many of the prophets rail against violence and bloodshed (e.g., Hos. 4:2; Mic. 7:2, 5–6; Isa. 59:2–7; Ezek. 7:10–11; 22:1–27). And it is important that in these quotations they are not railing against the violence of other nations (which they also do abundantly), but are pointing the finger at the presence of violence in Israel. It is not any sort of violence, but what is usually described as an escalating ladder of violence building up from swearing and lying to murder. The particular horror of this is that murder is fratricidal. The Jewish commentator Pinchas Lapide has pointed out that for the Jewish tradition, taking as its starting point Genesis 9:5ff., all sins of murder are fratricide.[28]

It is from this perception that the same process of inspiration is able to understand sin as essentially a relational matter. Rather than being a matter of failure of observance of prescriptions (though there is no exaggerating the importance these play in the Old Testament), sin has to do with relational disturbances which lead to violence among the whole community. Hence the arrival at simple universal ethical prescriptions such as Leviticus 19:17–18: if the problem is fratricide, then the solution is love of neighbor as self.

Some of the prophetic critique goes further, in understanding that the presence of fratricidal violence, the reign of death, is a universal phenomenon, which is a veil of blindness that is over all peoples (Isa. 25:7–8). When, therefore, Isaiah talks of the darkness (9:2; 42:16; 59:9; 60:2; etc.) out of which God will lead his people, it is a particular form of darkness to which he is referring, a darkness related to the reign of death, to the boot of the tramping warrior and the garment rolled in blood (Isa. 9:5). This theme is not greatly developed, but there is enough of it present to suggest that prophetic insight went as far as to see sin as related to the reign of death precisely in the measure in which God is increasingly perceived as entirely foreign to death.

None of this is to suggest that there is a theology of original sin in the Old Testament. There is in fact no unitary understanding of sin in the Old Testament, nor a unified hermeneutic key by which to interpret

---

27. See Schwager, *Must There Be Scapegoats?* 48–49.
28. P. Lapide, *The Sermon on the Mount* (Maryknoll N.Y.: Orbis Books, 1986), 49.

the many different understandings of sin which are to be found. It is to suggest, however, that the law and the covenant played a rôle in Israel's self-understanding such that real conquests were made in the subversion of myth, and thus real insight gained simultaneously into the understanding of God and an ever less mythical anthropology. This permitted an ever greater separation of divine and human violence, an ever sharpening view of the latter, and an ever less easy admission of the former. A perception was able to be developed of the human heart as involved in violence and as needing to be trained away from that. There are hints of an etiology of sin in the Genesis account (though the Adam story scarcely reappears at all in the rest of the Old Testament)[29] and a reference to Eve's sin in Sirach 25:24. However, Jewish tradition considers Sirach apocryphal, not part of the canon of Scripture.

The subversive process of the discovery of sin, which is the same as the discovery of freedom, reached a certain point in the Jewish tradition: moral life involves the struggle between an evil impulse (*yetzer ha-ra*) and a good impulse (*yetzer ha-tov*). The former is active from birth; the latter comes with the age of discretion and can control the former if the person feeds himself on the law.[30] Once again, it is the positive framework of knowledge, the law, which permits us to understand in what sin consists. The understanding of sin as original required a further sharpening of perspective, which was also simultaneously a further deepening of the drastic character of the human condition and a heightened awareness of God. We are back to the double insight into God's deathlessness and human deathfulness provided by Jesus' resurrection. It is now clear not only that human beings must struggle against evil to avoid death, but a step further has been reached. The resurrection reveals that human beings are already shot through with death in a way that no amount of struggle can avoid. It is not that we are sick, but that we are dead. Life is not something fought for, but something given. There is no real freedom that does not pass through a recognition of complicity in death.

The increasingly drastic character of the human condition obliges us to a closer look at the relationship between human desire and victimage, and it is to this that we now turn.

---

29. B. Pottier has indicated that contemporary exegesis has found allusions to the story of the fall in Exodus 28:11–19; Isaiah 7:14–16; Wisdom 2:23–24; 10:1–2; see *Le péché originel selon Hegel: Commentaire et synthèse* (Namur: Culture et Vérité, 1990), 159.

30. See R. Hamerton-Kelly, *Sacred Violence*, 89.

Chapter 5

The Intelligence of the Victim
and the Distortion of Desire

A Shift in Perception

The resurrection made possible an understanding of being human as in some way, yet to be discussed, unnecessarily involved in death. It is, as it were, the fact of the resurrection which revealed the fact of unnecessary human involvement in death, the possibility of forgiveness reaching even into human death. However, there is more than this. The resurrection made possible a shift of perception on the part of the apostolic group as to the content of human involvement with death. This is related to what the disciples had not understood while Jesus was teaching them before his death and to what they did understand after his resurrection. This nonunderstanding is clearly presented in all the Gospels as related to Jesus' death in a rather particular sense. It was not that they merely did not understand, and after the resurrection, with the coming of the Holy Spirit, they did understand. The nonunderstanding itself was related to death. Their understanding of what Jesus was about was marked by the normal human limit of understanding which is that death is a definitive reality, and therefore that their relationship to Jesus and what he was teaching was something circumscribed by the normal parameters of human life and death. Jesus' understanding was not marked by that understanding: he was thus able creatively to imagine the possibility of a self-giving into the hands of violent men as not only a salvific revelation of the sort of love the Father is, trusting himself into his Father's hands, but also as an educational exercise for those as yet unable to understand the nondefinitive nature of death.

After the resurrection and because of the presence to the disciples of the victim raised as forgiveness, the disciples were able to understand the nature of the educational process by which they had been brought, before Jesus' death, to the very brink of an understanding, but how it was in fact only Jesus' death, made alive by the resurrection, which was the final step in the educational (or revelatory) process which enabled

139

them to leave the understanding formed by the parameters of death. In line with what I have tried to show above, the educational process and the shift in perception resulting from that was itself an understanding of that which the disciples were themselves on their way out of. That is to say that, once again, the content of original sin is known only in the process of its forgiveness.

Perhaps the most fruitful way to show the human content of the involvement with death is to show the insight available after Jesus' death which enabled the apostolic witnesses to go back in their memory and reread their past involvement with Jesus in its light. This is the understanding of Jesus' life and death as a *skandalon,* or stumbling block.

The *Skandalon* Revealed

There are a series of texts in the apostolic witness which give evidence of a particular theological understanding of Jesus' life and death and attribute this understanding to Jesus before his death. These are texts which show Jesus' life and death as related to a prophecy in Isaiah 8:14: "Behold I am laying in Zion a stone that will make men stumble, a rock that will make men fall."[1] This is juxtaposed with Isaiah 28:16: "Behold I am laying in Zion a stone, a cornerstone chosen and precious, and he who believes in him will not be put to shame."[2] The two quotations are related in the apostolic witness to Psalm 118:22: "The very stone which the builders rejected has become the head of the corner."

The *locus classicus* for the combination of these texts is 1 Peter 2:6–8, where all three texts appear as interrelated. However, the nexus of ideas is much more widespread than this and appears to have been fundamental very early on in Christian preaching as interpretative of the way in which Jesus had fulfilled the Scriptures. The way in which Paul refers to Christ crucified as a stumbling block in 1 Corinthians 1:23 is given more depth by his own explicitation of its sense in Romans 9:33. In Acts 4:11 Peter's preaching refers to Jesus in terms of Psalm 118:22. More important is the way the text of the psalm and that of Isaiah 8:14 appear in Jesus' own mouth in Luke 20:17–18 as his own interpretation of the parable of the murderous tenants.

The theology behind this nexus of ideas seems to be as follows: God has given Jesus into the midst of Israel, which has been scandalized by him and has killed him, fulfilling the Scriptures. However, for those who can overcome the scandal of his death, he is the foundation of a new

---

1. This is the version as given by Paul in Romans 9:33, where Isaiah 8:14 is already conflated with Isaiah 28:16.

2. This is as quoted in 1 Peter 2:7.

edifice. Where in the original Isaian passage the happening is related in terms of God tripping up Israel, with God himself causing the scandal, the apostolic witness (made especially evident in the Lucan parable of the tenants) shows the scandal to be purely the result of human violence and self-deceit, violence and self-deceit made visible in the persecution and murder of the prophets and finally in that of the Son. For those already locked in these attitudes leading to death, then, it appears scandalous that the rejected one should be the new foundation.

What we can see in the light of this is the way Jesus' teaching and practice leading up to his death had, already, as its object the setting free of his hearers and disciples from their being scandalized by him precisely so that they could become part of the new edifice that was to be founded in his rejection. There is ample evidence that the apostolic witnesses were able to reread Jesus' practice with them precisely in terms of his attempting to lead them out of scandal, to prevent them being caused to stumble by him. So he tells the disciples of John the Baptist, at the end of a list of signs that accredit him as the "one who is to come," "And blessed is he who is not scandalized at me" (Matt. 11:6; Luke 7:23). Those who are unable to accept his teaching are described as having been scandalized by him (Matt. 13:57; 15:12; Mark 6:3). In the parable of the sower some are scandalized by persecution (Matt. 13:21; Mark 4:17) and so do not bear fruit. The process of Jesus attempting to lead his hearers beyond scandal is shown in John 6. There Jesus attempts to bring his hearers on from their understanding of his miraculous feeding of the five thousand, an understanding rooted in food and a kingly messiah, toward his own subversion of the Passover and the manna in the desert as pointing to himself as the authentic bread from heaven. During the discourse, the eager listening of his audience is gradually turned into furious questioning, linked by allusion with the murmuring of Israel against Moses on its way to the Promised Land. Finally even many of his disciples find it hard to take, and Jesus asks them if this scandalizes them (John 6:61). The scandal is what prevents people from perceiving the unity of Jesus and the Father (v. 62), and for John the flesh is precisely the human condition locked in scandal, while the spirit is what leads people beyond scandal into a belief in Jesus as revealing the Father, and the Father as he who sent Jesus into the world (vv. 63–65). Many of the disciples are caused to stumble, but Peter and the other eleven stay, having perceived that Jesus has words of eternal life: that is, they have overcome the scandal, at least to some extent. Even so, Jesus knows that one of them is a *diabolos* who will betray him (v. 70). The word *diabolos* here is quite specifically not used to indicate a metaphysical entity, but a human person locked in scandal.

However, if Jesus' teaching is concerned with enabling his disciples not to be caused to stumble by him, he knows full well that in fact they will all be caused to stumble by his death. The Gospels illustrate this process with particular care. Once again the stumbling centers around a fulfillment of Scripture, and one evidently important in the earliest days of the Church, Zechariah 13:7: "I will strike the shepherd and the sheep will be scattered." This text appears in Mark 14:27 and Matthew 26:31, as well as by an obvious allusion in John 16:32. In all three contexts it appears linked with the notion of *skandalon*. This is most obvious in Matthew, where the text is quoted to justify Jesus' claim that all would be scandalized by him that night (26:31). Peter refutes this by claiming that he will not be scandalized and receives the prophecy of his denial. In Mark, Peter understands the quotation in terms of stumbling and promises not to be scandalized (14:29). In John, the allusion appears in an exchange where Jesus has said specifically that "I have said all this to keep you from being scandalized" (16:1). The disciples claim to have understood this, and Jesus, to show them that they haven't understood, then prophesies that they will all be scattered.

We thus have a very coherent body of witness to the ultimate stumbling block being Jesus' death. Jesus knows that he can lead his disciples up to a certain point, but finally they will be scandalized by him, and that only the resurrection, at the same time as it removes the stone from the mouth of Jesus' grave,[3] will remove the final stumbling block. The stumbling block that it will remove is the human impossibility of following and imitating another man in a path of self-donation that regards death as without substance. What we see then is the link between the notion of the stumbling block and the notion of discipleship. What we have in the Gospels is Jesus teaching the disciples to imitate him in all the things he does: in preaching, teaching, healing, and exorcisms. He would have them imitate him in his self-giving toward death, as all the warnings about the persecutions to which they will be prone indicate. However, he knows that, in fact, they will not be able to imitate him perfectly in this until after his death and resurrection, so he prepares them as far as possible for his death. In this way at least they can be his witnesses, and after his death they will be able to live out the imitation of his self-giving unto death, thus bearing witness to the Father, without fear of death.[4]

---

3. See René Girard, *Things Hidden from the Foundation of the World* (London: Athlone, 1987), 431.

4. Here we are very close indeed to the primitive understanding of the foundation of the Church, with Peter, the rock, having to be converted from being a stumbling block into

The Content of the *Skandalon*

Although the apostolic witness derives the main lines of force in its understanding of *skandalon* from the postresurrection understanding of the way in which Jesus had fulfilled the Scripture, it would be wrong to think that this exhausts the meaning of *skandalon*. The words *skandalizô* and *skandalon* appear too often in Jesus' mouth, with too coherent (as well as too rich and too dense) a set of meanings for it to be doubted that Jesus himself taught in terms of the stumbling block before his death. When Jesus was teaching the disciples how to avoid being scandalized by him, he was not only teaching them something about him, but something about them: what it is to live in a world of *skandala*. That is to say, he was not only preparing a particular group of people under particular circumstances to avoid being scandalized by a particular event; he was doing that as part of a general teaching about the human condition and the way out of it as involving a certain sort of imitation called discipleship, a sort of imitation which is a moving out of a being caught up in a desire which leads to victimizing, and a moving into a sort of imitation which, in the structure of this world, will lead the disciple to run grave risk of victimization. The *skandalon* defines the former desire (in John, the flesh), while the Spirit defines the latter.

This is the understanding behind the Matthean Sermon on the Mount. All those who are called *makarioi* are those who have been "scandalized" by the order of this world and live in a relation of dangerous proximity to being victimized by that order. Because they have been scandalized by the order of this world, precisely because of the precariousness of their belonging, they will not be scandalized by Jesus himself, and thus are able to identify with the "blessed one" of Matthew 11:6 who is not scandalized by Jesus. These will be able to form part of the new victim people whom the new Moses is projecting from the mount in fulfillment of the old, a victim people salted for sacrifice (5:13) that will be the new Zion, the city on the hill (5:14), which alone will accomplish the law and the prophets (5:17).

Jesus then goes on to show clearly that righteousness cannot be defined by the law, but the roots of righteousness must be found at the level of desire. He reveals the evil of human desire to be much more drastic than the law could fathom and righteousness as having to do with a transformation of that desire: so anger is the same as murder, a lustful look the same as adultery, being caught up in the stumbling

---

the foundation stone. If this is made most explicit by the conjunction of Matthew 16:18 and 16:23, the story of the conversion of Peter is a vital part of all the Gospel accounts.

blocks of desire much worse than any form of physical defect, not one of which can exclude from heaven. This world of drastically sinful desire is treated as a relational reality: Jesus is not talking about some sort of wicked desire locked into the solitude of an individual person which must somehow be exorcised. He is talking about a deformation of relationality such that we are scandalized by each other and give scandal to each other. This can be shown by the remedy: freedom is to be found by not allowing oneself to be caused to stumble by the evil done to one: one must not resist evil, one must go the second mile. There is only one way not to be locked into the scandals of this world, and that is by learning to forgive, which means not allowing oneself to be defined by the evil done. It is quite clear from Jesus' teaching that he considers humans to be locked into a certain sort of reciprocity, which it would be wholly consistent to identify with the *skandalon,* and that he teaches the way out of that sort of reciprocity into a wholly new sort of reciprocity. This new sort of reciprocity is made concrete in forgiveness and other acts of not being trapped by the *skandalon* and in this way is able to begin to imitate the perfect gratuity of the heavenly Father, in whom there is no *skandalon.*

This becomes particularly clear in Matthew 7. There we have the commandment not to judge, and it is explained that the reason for this is that all our judgment is scandalous, because we have already tripped over the log in our own eye. This is a rigorous revelation of the way we are tied into each other by the *skandalon,* and the way we must detach ourselves from it (one so important that it is taken up by Paul in Rom. 2:1). Our knowledge of each other is projective and in its mode already distorted. Only in the degree to which we allow our own distortion to be corrected will we be able to know the other with limpidity. In case it is not clear already that this reciprocal involvement in turning each other into stumbling blocks, which is at the heart of Jesus' moral teaching, has, at its roots, an understanding of desire, a few verses later Jesus' further teaching on prayer makes exactly this point. In Matthew 7:7–11 prayer is shown to be a learning to desire without stumbling blocks in imitation of the Father who is without stumbling blocks. We must not let our desire remain at the stage whereby we think that we will not get what we want but must learn to believe in one who gives gratuitously what we really want. Prayer is a constant reeducation of desire out of a mode of stumbling blocks and into a mode of desiring and receiving gratuitously. And this is then directly referred back to our human relationality (7:12): we must treat others in the same way, learning how to substitute a gratuitous reciprocity for a reciprocity formed by the *skandalon.*

Jesus is under no illusions but that this understanding of desire is in fact an extremely difficult thing to grasp, and those who find it are few, and they find it with difficulty. Yet it constitutes the narrow way that is the way to life, while the wide way, in which we mostly live, is the way to destruction. Life within the *skandalon* is the way of mutually assured death (7:13–14). All this demonstrates that there is a specific content to the notion of *skandalon,* and one which goes back to Jesus himself. It might be defined by saying that all humans are locked into a reciprocity, what Girard refers to as an interdividual psychology, which is rooted in a desire which is fatally headed toward death, our own and that of those we victimize. It is exactly at this level of our constitution in death-related desire that Jesus' ethical teaching seeks to set us free by teaching a new, but no less reciprocal, form of desire, which will enable us to fulfil the law and the prophets from the heart.

Lest it be thought that Jesus' interdividual psychological insight is to be found in Matthew alone, exactly the same understanding can be found in Mark.[5] It is not only that the (undoubtedly original) lines about it being preferable to be maimed than to be scandalized appear (Mark 9:43–47), but the whole psychological insight is demonstrated practically with relation to children. The antidote to the rivalistic desire present among the disciples in their desire for greatness is the learning to recast desire in terms of seeking out and receiving the unimportant, like children (9:36–37). It is the unimportant ones who must not be scandalized (9:42), for it is they, marginal and peripheral to the complex world of adult desires bound up in scandal, who are able to receive the gratuity of God (10:14–15). Rich people are particularly constituted in scandal. For the rich young man, his riches are a stumbling block to his following Jesus (10:17–22), and riches constitute a stumbling block to entry into the kingdom which it is impossible for human beings to overcome (10:24–27). This is to say that such people are so locked into the scandal-based order of the world that they have no access to the reformation of desire based on gratuity which constitutes entry into the kingdom of God. The same ideas are present here as in the Matthean Last Judgment scene: entry into the kingdom is the same as the recast-

---

5. The understanding is obviously present in Luke, with many of the same passages as those discussed above — the teaching on prayer amplified in exactly the same sense, the parable of the Good Samaritan and the parable of Lazarus pointing in exactly the same direction. Luke 17:1–4 contains in a nutshell the teaching on scandal as an inevitable part of the human condition, but one which must be avoided and from which the only way out is forgiveness. Luke clearly shows his understanding of Christ as a stumbling block very early on in his Gospel: see Simeon's prophecy to Mary in Luke 2:34–35. In this prophecy the sort of stumbling block that Jesus is to be works *both* at the level of the group (old Israel/new Israel) and at the level of human psychology (revelation of hearts)!

ing of desire from a scandalous involvement in the order of the world toward a reaching out to the victims of that order.

In John's Gospel the same basic dualism of constitutive desire has been developed to so much more marked an extent that I will treat it in chapter 7. For the moment, suffice it to say that when John portrays the world as in the power of Satan, dwelling in a darkness in which people stumble (*proskoptein,* John 11:10) and in which they tend to lynch in obedience to their father who was a murderer from the beginning, it is to the same understanding of which he gives evidence: human beings are constituted in a distorted reciprocity leading to victimization. The sheep — those who imitate without stumbling — hear Jesus' voice and follow him without being scandalized, even though the shepherd will be killed. They are not scandalized by that death, because they know that the shepherd gave himself freely to being killed and can take up his life again: that is what permits them to overcome the scandal of his death (John 10).

Thus we can see in the apostolic witness that the intelligence of the victim made available a quite specific understanding of the content of human desire. Humans are constituted by an interdividual desire that is a distorted reciprocity and leads to death. It is not only that humans die, but their involvement with death is of a quite specific sort: the very constitution of human desire is cast in the mode of *skandala* by which we receive death from each other and mete out death to each other by our involvement in mutual victimization. The same path that permitted us to see the recasting of divine wrath in terms of human involvement in death, typified in the handing over of Jesus by God to human beings, has also permitted us to see the recasting of a divinely placed stumbling block in terms of the divine revelation of humans constituted in mutual and reciprocal stumbling that leads them to death. The whole drift of this movement toward a purely anthropological understanding of these realities is most clearly seen in 1 John 2–3. There love is defined in terms of a reciprocal relationship between brothers, and the stumbling block is the relationship of hate between brothers (2:7–11). This stumbling block is then illustrated in terms of the hatred of Cain for Abel leading to murder (3:11–15). This is the real content of the sin of the devil from the beginning: hatred between brothers leading to murder, and this is the sign that eternal life is not in that person. The *skandalon* and the original murder are directly interrelated as that from which Christ has come to set us free.

The Pauline Understanding of Desire[6]

Where the other texts of the apostolic witness we have examined refer sinful origins preferentially to Cain and Abel, either explicitly or by implication, Paul works out his understanding of sinful origins with relation to Adam. The same basic idea is behind both: that Christ in his death and resurrection has overcome the human order based on whichever of the two "beginnings" is in question; so the beginnings are invoked only as a help to understanding what we are now on our way out of in Christ: the chronologically later is the determinative pole of the argument; the former is the illustrative pole.[7] In chapter 9 I conflate the Cain and Abel version of sinful origins and the Adam version — what one might call respectively the concentration on murder itself and the concentration on desire leading to murder. Here I merely hope to illustrate the Pauline analysis of the latter.

There is a quite specific reason behind Paul's option to discuss sin in terms of Adam. This is related to the polemic about the law that underlies and occupies so much of both Romans and Galatians. By rereading the Adam story, which contains an original prohibition (Gen. 2:15–17),[8] in the light of the Cross, Paul is able to show the relationship between desire and the (Mosaic) law, which is seen as an explicitation and elaboration of the original prohibition, in such a way as to demonstrate the caducity of the latter and the universally death-bound nature of the former.

I am not seeking to make an exegesis of the Pauline texts. Nor am I seeking to prove that Paul "already" has a doctrine of original sin. Rather I am trying to show that for Paul, starting from Adam rather than from Cain and Abel, it was no less apparent (and maybe even more apparent) than it was for the rest of the apostolic tradition that what we have been brought out of by Christ is a human condition (a) constituted by distorted desire (b) and lived out in a mimetic interdividuality in which it is the "other" who forms and moves the "I." This human condition (c) comes from and leads to death and (d) is from the begin-

---

6. For a more detailed look see P. Grelot, *Péché originel et rédemption à partir de l'épître aux romains* (Paris: Desclée, 1973), as well as R. Hamerton-Kelly, *Sacred Violence: Paul's Hermeneutic of the Cross* (Minneapolis: Fortress, 1992), chaps. 4 and 7. See also R. Hamerton-Kelly, "Sacred Violence and Sinful Desire: Paul's Interpretation of Adam's Sin in the Letter to the Romans," in R. Fortna and B. Gaventa, eds., *The Conversation Continues: Studies in Paul and John in Honour of J. L. Martyn* (Nashville: Abingdon, 1990), 35–54. See J. Alison, "Justification and the Constitution of Consciousness: A New Look at Romans and Galatians," in *New Blackfriars* 71 (1990): 17–26.

7. See specifically Romans 5:14, where Adam is *typos tou mellontos*.

8. "You may freely eat of every tree of the garden; but of the tree of the knowledge of good and evil you shall not eat, for in the day that you eat of it you shall die."

nings and affects the whole of the human race. That is to say, for Paul
as for the other witnesses a certain sort of anthropological understanding is a necessary consequence of and basis for the understanding of the
salvation that has been wrought in Christ.

Let us look at this claim point by point:

(a) *The human condition is constituted by distorted desire.* Adam appears explicitly in Romans only in 5:12–21, in lines that are infamously
central to the Augustinian interpretation of original sin. However, it is
not there alone that the early chapters of Genesis make their appearance. The early chapters of Genesis are the vital allusive framework of
the whole of Romans 1–8, and it is in the light of them that Paul argues with his interlocutors, for whom the text would have been not only
familiar but also an authority. In Romans 1:32 Paul shows that he considers that all humans know of the primal prohibition that is found in
Genesis 2:15–17. This law is to be found inscribed on the hearts of both
Jews and gentiles (Rom. 2:15). It is thus reasonable to read Paul's understanding of the fulfillment of the law as love of neighbor (Rom. 13:10)
as the positive command made necessary by and in direct contraposition
to the negative command of Genesis 2:15–17.[9] The primal prohibition
is being read in the light of Jesus' commandment.

The use Paul makes of the primal prohibition is to be found in Romans 7:7–20, which involves an implicit reading of the Adam story.[10]
It is necessary to fill in some steps which Paul jumps (presumably because of the familiarity of what is being described to his interlocutors).
The primary positive commandment is to love the neighbor as oneself.
The encapsulation of the Mosaic decalogue is in the commandment not
to desire (*ouk epithuméseis,* which we normally translate by "covet" or
"envy"). It is this prohibition which is read as being the content of the
prohibition not to eat of the tree of the knowledge of good and evil.
That is to say, it was an initial act of covetousness, or envy,[11] which
broke the original prohibition, cast God in the rôle of a vengeful rival,
and introduced humans into the world order in which envy governs
human relationships. It is in this world order that the commandment
to love the neighbor as oneself fulfils the original prohibition, by aiming
at restoring fractured human relationality. Behind this understanding is

---

9. See R. W. Thompson, "How Is the Law Fulfilled in Us?" in *Louvain Studies* (1986):
31–41, quoted in R. Hamerton-Kelly, *Sacred Violence,* 99.

10. See Grelot, *Péché originel,* 97–98: "Derrière le tableau qui en est fait, on devine
en surimpression la scène de l'Éden, comme si le genèse de la conscience humaine aux
origines et celle du Moi en chaque individu présentaient des traits interchangeables," with
references to the exegesis of Lyonnet and Feuillet.

11. The suggestion into being of envy is marvelously conveyed by the "eritis sicut dii"
of Genesis 3:5.

the reading (well attested within Jewish circles, see Wis. 2:23–24) of the Genesis story as the way in which envy came into the world, with its consequences for humanity.

The primary problem, according to this reading of Genesis, which Paul's shorthand enables us to intuit, was that God gave a prohibition for the benefit of human beings (not to eat of the fruit of the tree of good and evil). This same prohibition became for human desire, turned to envy (by imitating the suggestion of the serpent), a sign of God withholding something of his being from humans. Envy turned a prohibition given for our benefit into a sign of divine rivalry with us rather than divine love for us, and humans were thereafter constituted in rivalry, the fruit of envy. This reading of Genesis lies behind Romans 7:7–12. Paul explicitly says that the law itself is not sinful, but was meant to bring life, "but sin, finding opportunity in the commandment, wrought in me all kinds of covetousness" (7:8), where "me" is Adam, Paul, and everyone. He goes on: "I [Adam, Paul, *omnes*] was once alive apart from the law, but when the commandment came, sin sprang to life[12] and I died" (7:9). Paul interprets the serpent of Genesis in terms not of the devil but of sin: it was sin which found opportunity in the commandment to deceive humans. Human desire, in itself good, turned to envy. Making use of the commandment, it deceived itself and led to death.

Paul demonstrates this because his argument is that the law of Moses is the continuation and explicitation of the original prohibition. That is to say, the law, which in itself is good, was from the beginning the occasion of the distortion of desire, and since then is not only the occasion of the distortion of desire, but actually contributes to the further distortion of desire. The law has, as it were, become prisoner to, and works as a function of, the world of sacralized violence that has resulted from the breaking of the original prohibition. I say sacralized violence since the twin effects of the rupture of the original prohibition were to produce an envious and vengeful perception of God and a human race constituted in envy and rivalry leading to death: it is the conflation of these two elements which produce the "violent sacred" at the root of all idolatry, and thus of all human culture. The combination of a rivalistic notion of God and a rivalistic living of humanity constitutes the sphere of death from which God has sought to set us free in Christ. Paul argues that desire has turned the original prohibition into a stumbling block, such that all human beings live in the mode of stumbling through dis-

---

12. *Anazaô* here does not mean "revive," pace the RSV, since there was nothing to revive from. For the meaning with the force of the *ana* diminished see Bauer, Arndt, and Gingrich, *A Greek-English Lexicon of the New Testament* (Chicago: University of Chicago Press, 1979), 53.

torted desire. This same distorted desire affects even the law, which was meant to reveal and control the desire, and as such turns the law into an instrument of death. For this Paul's own experience as a law-inspired persecutor of Christ was paradigmatic.

This enables us to see the structure of Paul's analysis of universal sin in Romans 1:18–32. The first effect of human transgression following the Adamic model set out above was to provide a distorted image of God and simultaneously to divinize things that were not God (1:18–23). Envious desire turns what should have been a pacific model (God) into an obstacle, and then seeks out obstacles, turning them into models (gods). The next step is that, just as Adam and Eve noticed their naked-ness and human erotic life became complicated by distorted desire, so human bodies and passions become perverted and distorted (1:24–27). The final step, corresponding to the life of humanity once expelled from the Garden (and thus to Cain, Lamech, Babel, and so on), is that the whole of human life and culture is utterly infected with distorted de-sire leading to strife and murder, and all under the sentence of death resulting from the original prohibition (1:28–32).

Before turning to the interpretation of Romans 5:12–21 let us look at the underlying psychology by which this distorted desire is present among humans, that is, the claim above (b) that *the human condition is lived out in a mimetic interdividuality in which it is the "other" who forms and moves the "I."*

That it is the "other" who forms the human "I" is already implicit in the account of desire distorted to envy which we have seen above. From God pacifically forming the "I" by means of his righteous com-mandment, it is now the order of sin which forms a conflictual "I." That Paul understands human consciousness in this way is shown by the metaphors he uses for sin. He insists in 6:15–23 on the fundamental heteronomy of the human condition: we are slaves either to sin or to righteousness, which is to say that our "I" is formed by our relationality with that which masters us, be it God or the sinful order following on from Adam's sin (5:12). What Christ has made available, in revealing the righteousness of God, is human faith in that righteousness. Hence the rôle for Paul of faith: it enables us to recover the perception of God's goodness that distorted desire had destroyed by turning God into a jealous rival. Faith, whose importance for Paul can scarcely be under-estimated, is that form of knowing adhesion to the righteousness of God that has been revealed in Christ's self-giving. This divinely given ability to resist believing anything evil or rivalrous in God permits the complete reconstitution of the self which had been formed as a result of rivalistic desire. This enables "an obedience from the heart" (6:17) to this newly revealed other, and thus the reconstitution of the whole human "I" governed by the new other, in a "slavery" (6:19) whose end is eternal life rather than death.

It is the same understanding that underlies the metaphor of the indwelling of sin to be found in 7:13–25. Sin is a force which moves all persons so that they cannot obey the law they know to be true (the fundamental prohibition against envy and its positive counterpart, love of neighbor as self). Thus the existential condition of every person is that of a conflictual self moved from without. The "I" is not something which controls but which is controlled by sin which has reached within (7:20).[13] The only force capable of undoing this constitution of the self by the violent other of sin is God as revealed and made available by Jesus Christ (7:25). Exactly what this change might consist in can be shown by reference to Galatians 2:19–21, part of a passage dealing with many of the same themes as Romans. The other in question, God working through Jesus Christ, is able to re-form the "I" of Paul so completely that his "I" is actually replaced by Christ: "It is not I who live, but Christ who lives in me" (Gal. 2:20). There could be no clearer indication of a mimetic psychology than the de-possession of the "I" formed by the world and the constitution of an "I" that is possession by Christ.

We can therefore talk about Paul's understanding of the human subject in terms of triangular desire, whether a beneficent or a maleficent triangle. This can be seen in three steps: Initially the subject lived in a relationship of pacific imitation of (obedience toward) the model (God) and was able to love Eve and creation (the object designated by the model) in a nonrivalistic fashion. This constituted the first Adam. Then, when free desire distorted itself to envy, the model became a rival, and its will (the prohibition) an obstacle, the object became conflictual (nakedness, work, strife), and the subject was constituted by the sinful other. Now, with the coming of Christ, by producing an imitation of Christ, the Holy Spirit forms a new "I" that is at peace with God (Rom. 5:1).

R. Hamerton-Kelly illustrates the same Pauline understanding of the triangularity of the mimetic structuring of the self, centered around the

---

13. No less an authority than St. Thomas has this to say about this verse: "That the carnal man be sold to the power of sin as if he were in some way the slave of sin is shown by the fact that he does not move himself, but is moved by sin [*ex hoc aparet quod ipse non agit, sed agitur a peccato*]. In fact, one who is free moves of himself; he is not moved by another" (*Super Epistolam ad Romanos Lectura*). St. Thomas thinks, of course, that real freedom consists precisely in being moved from within by God, who is not "another" in any normal sense, precisely because there is no rivalry between the Creator and any of his creatures; thus they can occupy the same "space" (for instance, a human will) without displacing each other.

sort of desire that is at work in the sexual relations discussed in 1 Corinthians 6:13–20.[14] Using the terminology made popular by Nygren,[15] he shows that the relationship with the Lord is one of "agapaic" mimesis, while the relationship with the prostitute is one of "erotic" mimesis. In both cases desire forms the subject through the other: it is through the subject being formed in agapaic (nonrivalrous) love for the Lord that God is able to "raise us up" (reconstitute the subject); while the erotic mimesis (founded on rivalry, seeking to fulfil a felt lack in the subject) which binds a subject to a prostitute causes the subject to sin "against his own body." That is to say, acquisitive desire, by reducing the other to a function of my feeling of lack (*envie*, envy), reduces the "me" who is formed by my relationality with the reduced other.

In this way we begin to see how the various images and metaphors used by Paul to describe sin (indwelling, enslaving, deceiving) rather than being merely mythical descriptions of some abstract power are all relational metaphors working within an interdividual mimetic anthropology. This is for no other reason than that it is within this framework that Paul is able to account for the way in which the resurrection of Christ, opening up the goodness of God and the possibility of faith in that goodness, is able to reconstitute the human "I" in such a way that we are enabled to inherit eternal life. We are enabled to see once again that it is the structure of salvation that yields an anthropology of human involvement in sin. The same structure that gives us the proto-trinitarian formula of salvation in Galatians 4:4–6 accounts for the passage from sin to salvation within the terms of reference of a triangular mimetic and interdividual understanding of human desire.

This enables us to move on to look at my claim above (c) that in Paul's view *the human condition* constituted by distorted desire and lived out in mimetic interdividuality *comes from and leads to death*.

One of the many reasons for the complications in interpreting Romans 5:12–14 is that it is the place where Paul conflates two different accounts of the relationship between sin and death. These two accounts are present in different parts of Romans. The first account, which is the one which most suits his argument concerning the law, might be called an extrinsic account of the relationship between sin and death. Adam transgressed a prohibition; this transgression carried an explicit death penalty from God, so death came into the world, and everybody else ever since has lived in the realm of death. In this account, left to its

---

14. Hamerton-Kelly, *Sacred Violence*, 116–17.
15. Neither Hamerton-Kelly nor I, however, accept the "sharp Protestant edge to Nygren's argument, that cuts away the Catholic idea of grace perfecting rather than replacing nature" (Hamerton-Kelly, *Sacred Violence*, 162).

own devices, sin is a separate reality from death. Death is merely an extrinsic punishment for sin: because we all sin, so we all die. In Romans 5:12–21 this understanding is clearly present in the reference to the transgression of Adam (*parabaseôs,* v. 14) and the judgment following the one trespass bringing condemnation (vv. 16, 18). In Paul's shorthand the presence of this extrinsic account is important since it permits him a series of arguments from objective transgression to objective salvation and enables him to proceed with his argument about the law.

Simultaneously there is present an intrinsic account of the relationship between sin and death: death and sin are involved in each other without any necessary recourse to some divine sentence. From the moment envy distorted desire, desire has been toward death. Death is, as it were, the content of sin, and so is capable of reigning by the presence of sinful desire, and itself producing sinful desire. This understanding is clear in the use of the word "reign," where death is a dynamic reality which is the content of the sins of those between Adam and Moses, even where those sins were quite different from Adam's, with its formal sentence (v. 14). Death reigns again in v. 17, and in v. 21 sin reigns in death, again showing the interchangeability and thus the intrinsic co-implication of these two realities. This intrinsic understanding of the relationship between the two realities is important since it permits Paul to give the content of salvation. So in v. 15 the free gift and the trespass are compared: the content of the trespass consists in the exact opposite of a free gift, that is to say, desire distorted to envy, acquisitive grasping. In v. 17 it is the content and end of the trespass and the content and end of the free gift that are compared. The content of the acquisitive grasping is death, while the content of gratuitous self-giving is life.

This distinction between the extrinsic and the intrinsic understandings that are being conflated by Paul in Romans 5:14–21 enables us to make some observations concerning Paul's vocabulary in this passage. In Paul's usage the word *parabaseôs* (RSV: transgression) has the objective sense of a violation of a command or prohibition. The word *paraptôma* (RSV: trespass) combines the objective sense with the desirous involvement that leads to it and is its content. The word *hamartía/hamartanô* (RSV: sin) refers to a desire-and-death-formed state of affairs which is of course made actual in particular sins. Given this, we can now apply what we have learned from the rest of the passage to the understanding of the notorious 5:12–14 and see how it can be interpreted. I would suggest that it is fair to interpret the verses as follows:

> Therefore just as through one man the sinful state of affairs was brought about in the world, and through this sinful state of affairs, the reign of death, just so did the reign of death penetrate all men, involving them

all in the sinful state of affairs. The world indeed lived in a sinful state
of affairs before the Mosaic law; however, while there was no law no
sort of moral assessment was possible, but that did not stop the reign of
death dominating, in the period between Adam and Moses, over those
also whose active involvement in the sinful state of affairs was not in the
likeness of the transgression of Adam, who is the type of the one who was
to come.

J. I. González Faus, in his treatment of Romans 5:12, posits three
principle differences of interpretation of this verse, according to whether
the antecedent of the famous *eph'hôi* is Adam (following Augustine),
death (*thanatos,* following Photius), or nonexistent (i.e., *eph'hôi* is a
simple link clause).[16] Of these the first is the least plausible. I have used
the second, implying that death is causative of the sinful state of affairs,
but the third (which commands the widest reading particularly among
Greek fathers) would make very little difference to that. It would read
" ... just so did the reign of death penetrate all men, given that all were
involved in a sinful state of affairs." What is important is that in both
cases the reign of death and the sinful state of affairs are mutually implicatory, their counterparts being the mutually implicatory gratuitous
self-giving of Christ and the reign of life.

Thus we can see how Paul melds two understandings of the relation
between sin and death together: one I have described as extrinsic, but it
might also be described as mythical, relying as it does on an interpretation of Genesis involving God in active punishment (which goes against
the whole grain of Paul's thought), but having its use in Paul's polemic
about the law; the other I have described as intrinsic, but I might describe it as anthropological since it relies on a mimetic understanding of
distorted desire as constituting us all interdependently in death-oriented
patterns of desire.

In this context it is worth noting that Ephesians, which if not by
Paul is nevertheless a canonically valid interpretation of certain Pauline
themes, gives a similar picture of death being already present in our
lives. We are characterized as sons of disobedience and children of wrath
because, respectively, of the "prince of the power of the air" or the
"desires of body and mind," where the content of these two principles
is exactly the same: our being involved in death, were it not for God
making us alive with Christ.[17]

---

16. In J. I. González Faus, *Proyecto de hermano: Visión creyente del hombre* (Santander: Sal Terrae, 1987), 329–31.

17. The Epistle of James is unquestionably non-Pauline (!), yet even here we find a passage which alludes both to the Adam and Eve story and to that of Cain. In James 1:12–15
the temptation leading to sin is the work of a person's own desire (so the serpent and sin

This enables us to turn, finally and very briefly, to my claim (d) that in Paul's view, the human condition which I have been outlining above *has been from the beginnings and affects the whole of the human race.*

This in a sense is too obvious to discuss, since Adam clearly plays a double rôle in Paul's thought. He is the first human, and thus all other humans are necessarily affected by the condition of living in the reign of death which he bequeathed to us (Rom. 5:12: *pantes*, "all"; 5:18: *pantas...pantas*, "all...all"). He is also the archetypal human, such that his experience is paradigmatic of that of all humans (7:7–24). Paul is, in any case, apart from any reference to Adam, perfectly clear that he understands that "all men, both Jews and Greeks, are under the power of sin" (Rom. 3:9) and that "all have sinned and fall short of the glory of God" (Rom. 3:23).

The universality of sin is not in question. It is also quite clear that the understanding of the universality of sin proceeds directly from Paul's understanding of the uniqueness of Christ's resurrection in opening up the righteousness of God, not from his understanding of Adam. To put this another way: it is not that Paul starts with Adam and so deduces the universality of sin. He deduces the universality of sin from the particular contingent revelation of God's righteousness in Christ. Adam then becomes a convenient way of talking about this universality, particularly given that, by means of Adam, Paul can show that constitutive sinful desire goes deeper than the law and tends to manipulate the law toward its own death-ridden ends. That enables him to teach the universality of sin especially to those who might think themselves to have been exempted from the universality of sin owing to their keeping of the law. That is to say, Adam owes his place in Paul's thought to his relationship with desire, not to his being the originator of universality. We might say that because sin is universal, so it goes back to the beginnings of the human race. Adam is a useful way of illustrating this under the polemical circumstances in which Paul is writing because of the relationship between desire and prohibition which is so well illustrated in Genesis 2–3. It would be quite wrong however to imagine that Paul was making some historicist claim about Adam by using him in this way. Paul, like rabbinical exegesis in general, was perfectly capable of a highly subtle and knowing use of myth to demythologize, as witness his freedom in

---

couching at Cain's door seeking to master him are both interpreted as the subject's own desire, and no responsibility can be shifted onto anyone else). Desire gives birth to sin, and sin when it is full-grown brings forth death. Once again distorted desire is the motor of death, which is the child of desire. James's tendency to demystify, not permitting worldly values to influence theological understanding (for instance, 1:20: "the anger of man does not work the righteousness of God"), is at one with the tendency to an anthropological understanding of sin we have seen in the Pauline texts.

interpreting the serpent of Genesis 3 as sin. Paul's primary interest is in an anthropology illustrative of salvation.

The analysis of the way the apostolic witnesses work from the intelligence of the victim made available by the resurrection shows that, at root, the Pauline understanding and, for instance, the Matthaean, have a common insight into the human condition. Matthew 5 shows the way in which the human condition is more drastic than anything that can be protected by the law, and only a recasting of desire understood in terms of a radical reciprocity that is imitative of the Father will find reward. This is exactly the same insight into anthropology that Paul shows where he indicates that desire is anterior to and manipulative of the law, so that only a recasting of desire made possible by faith in the righteous, and not rivalistic, nature of God (as revealed by the self-giving and resurrection of Jesus) will enable us to inherit life.

This perception of a common anthropological insight, cast in very different language and examples, permits us a further approximation to the doctrine of original sin: that it describes the universal human distortion of desire toward death within an interdividual, or mimetic, understanding of human psychology.

Excursus on the Devil

In the popular mind, the image of the devil has always been linked with the question of original sin; this is due to the reading of the serpent of Genesis 3 as the devil or Satan, a reading authorized by Revelation 12:9.[18] Insofar as the devil is treated as a causative factor and one who can be blamed for the ills of humanity, such a reading remains within a mythical understanding. The apostolic witness makes abundant reference to the devil, Satan, and demons; what is curious, however, is that the tendency is to use the discourse to demythologize.

This can be seen with regard to the principles behind both "angles" on original sin that I have been discussing. In the "Cain and Abel angle," the devil is the murderer from the beginning. The same devil is also the prince (archôn) of this world, but even on the (rare) occasions when he appears as an independent entity (the temptation narratives), he is always present as a governing principle. As a governing principle the devil enters into specific people, or they become manifestations of the principle, but in all cases the content of what they do when moved by

---

18. "And the great dragon was thrown down, that ancient serpent, who is called the devil and Satan, the deceiver of the whole world." I will not here attempt to examine the theology of the devil in the book of Revelation, precisely because of the complexity of the way in which the apocalyptic genre uses mythological language for nonmythological ends.

the devil is purely human.[19] In the "Adam and Eve angle" the devil's envy is the source of distorted human desire. Once again, however, the New Testament accounts that allude to the birth of distorted desire treat it as in fact a purely human phenomenon: that is, they read the serpent as the self-deceit of human desire, rather than a culpable outside agent.

In fact, we can talk about the treatment which the apostolic witness makes of the devil/Satan within and as illustrative of the same fundamental anthropology that I have been setting out above. In the first place, the only rôle which the devil/Satan has in the New Testament is as one who is in the process of being defeated. Jesus has seen him fall like lightning from heaven (Luke 10:18) — which is to say that his transcendence is on its way out. In Colossians 2:15, Christ is described, in an image taken from a Roman military triumph, as having "disarmed the principalities and powers and made a public example of them, triumphing over them in it [i.e., the Cross]." That is to say: by revealing in the Cross the mechanism by which the devil was the princ(ipl)e of the world — that is, the mechanism of collective murder as the basis of human order — and making this knowledge available, the principal arm of the devil has been destroyed. Exactly the same understanding lies behind Hebrews 2:14–15:

> He himself likewise partook of the same nature, that through death he might destroy him who has the power of death, that is, the devil, and deliver all those who through fear of death were subject to lifelong bondage.

John indicates quite specifically that the ruler of this world is cast out by Jesus' death (12:31) and then illustrates the process by which this happens in purely human terms: Jesus offers a morsel to Judas, and with the morsel, Satan, having already put it into Judas' heart to betray Jesus (13:2) enters into Judas (13:27). Then, when Judas comes to betray Jesus, it is the ruler of the world in person who comes (14:30). But Jesus' freedom in self-giving has already overcome the "principle" which is even presented in this Gospel as tempted by Jesus into revealing itself by its action (thus the Johannine Last Supper).[20] The irony of the Crucifixion is that, precisely by killing Jesus, the princ(ipl)e of this world reveals its game, and thus loses its power forever.[21]

---

19. It is worth observing the distinction, clear in the New Testament, between the language of demonization (*daimonion/oi, daimonizomai*), referring to bizarre human upsets, and that referring to the devil (*diabolos, satanas*), where it is behaviorally "normal" wickedness that is at work.

20. See J. D. M. Derrett, *The Victim: The Johannine Passion Narrative Reexamined* (Shipston-on-Stour: Drinkwater, 1993), 97–109.

21. In the words of J. D. M. Derrett, "in order to free the convicts, the Great Accuser,

If the devil is revealed as something on its way out of existence, or at the very least out of exercising power, that is not its only point in common with original sin. Where the notion of *skandalon,* or distorted interrelational desire, is vital to the latter, the former's very name (*diabolos*) is "divisive obstacle." Thus when in John 6:70 Jesus announces that one of the disciples "is devil" (without an article), he is indicating that this disciple is an obstacle. The same appears in Matthew 16:23 even more clearly: Peter is called Satan, and this is interpreted to mean a stumbling block (*"skandalon ei emou,* you are a stumbling block for me"). However, rather than this referring to some bizarre possession, Jesus goes on to explain that this means that Peter is on the side of human beings, not of God — and this because he was opposed to Jesus' moving forward to his death. Here, once again, the satanic stumbling block is shown to work at the level of the relationship between two people, even though this particular stumbling block (preventing Jesus' self-giving to death) would have been far more than just a normal interdividual scandal: it would have prevented the revelation and thus the destruction of Satan's mechanism. Peter's conversion was to be of universal significance, turning him into the foundational rock of the Church; likewise, because of his very proximity to Jesus he might have prevented the whole of salvation, thus for a moment the universal principle of stumbling — the adversary — was applied to him.

The devil is also understood within the same mimetic understanding of psychology that we have seen to be vital for the anthropology of salvation. This scarcely needs saying, since it is precisely interdividual psychology based on mimetic desire which accounts for the constitution of the consciousness by means of the other and thus makes it possible to talk in a nonmythic way about possession by another and being moved by another. This is so whether we are talking about a pacific possession (as was the case with Jesus, often suspected of being possessed because he was apparently moved by another, the Holy Spirit) or a conflictual possession (as is the case with those of us who are "slaves to sin" and moved by sin against our better judgment, as in Romans 6–7). However, the mimetic nature of desire is illustrated graphically in the accounts of the devil's temptations of Christ in Matthew and Luke. First the devil tries to undermine Jesus' identity (*"if* you are the Son of God"), attempting to make him feel a lack and so prove himself out of a feeling of lack of being. Jesus' replies show that he receives his sense of be-

the Pieces-Eater, spontaneously collaborated, so that at the Resurrection the 'modified dualism' of the religion became a monism, and there is only one Power, in effect, since the wiles of Satan are now 'known'" (*The Victim,* 141). Exactly! An important testimony, since Derrett is no Girardian.

ing as Son from God and by a nonenvious obedience toward God. The final Matthaean temptation shows the devil explicitly as deviated transcendence: the devil offers to give Jesus power over everything if he will worship him. That is to say, distorted desire is the ruling principle of all the kingdoms of the world, and it was being offered to Jesus to incarnate that principle if only he would distort his desire from pacifically imitative of God to conflictually acquisitive. The devil here is represented not only as obstacle, but as mimetic distortion of desire, making gifts that should be received from God turn into obstacles that turn us away from God. The irony of this passage is that by his obedience to God, by his allowing God to constitute his consciousness pacifically and without obstacles, Jesus is in fact enabled, himself, to *become* the bread by which human beings can live because it is the same as the word which comes out of God's mouth. He is able to *become* the Temple from which he refused to cast himself down. Finally he *becomes,* in his death, the king of all the kingdoms of the world.[22] However, all this comes about as something he receives the hard way, through obedience to his Father, not something he grabs via a short-cut, through allowing his desire to be distorted to an acquisitive mimesis.

The devil is not only "on his way out," an obstacle, and one understood within the framework of the mimetic anthropology shown to be vital for understanding original sin. He is also a foundational principle. This we have seen in the way in which he has in his gift all the kingdoms of the world (Matt. 4:9; Luke 4:6–7), in which he is the prince of the world, founded in murder (John). However, it is seen most spectacularly in the synoptic account of the exchange in which Jesus asks whether Satan can cast out Satan (Matt. 12:22–39; Mark 3:22–27; Luke 11:14–22). Girard has dedicated one of his most difficult and profound essays to these passages.[23] He shows that Jesus is enunciating the foundational principle of all human communities (kingdoms, cities, houses) by indicating that all are based on violent expulsion: Satan expelling himself. And for this reason, the whole of human culture is ultimately self-destructive, since its foundations depend on its being divided against itself. It is in these circumstances that Jesus comes casting out demons by the Spirit (or finger) of God and announcing that the kingdom of God has come upon his interlocutors. That is to say, the whole self-giving life and death of Jesus, already present in his teaching and miracles, rather than being part of the world of mutual expulsions

---

22. Might not certain Johannine themes be elaborated workings-out of the synoptic temptations?

23. "Satan Divided against Himself," chap. 14 of *The Scapegoat* (London: Athlone, 1986), 184–97.

founded on being divided against itself (at the base of which Girard detects the hidden scapegoat mechanism), is founding and bringing about
a form of human community which is based on the self-giving victim
and not on the driving out of victims. His "casting out" is not so much
a casting out as a making redundant, by exposing it, the old lie, and
making an alternative form of community available.

Girard in fact sees the concept of the demonic, both in its single
principle (Satan, the devil) and in its multiple manifestations (demons,
possession), as a rigorous indication of the way conflictual mimetic desire and the scapegoat mechanism are linked: simultaneously a force of
division in chaos and of union in hatred:

> The demonic allows, on the one hand, for every tendency toward con-
> flict in human relations and for the centrifugal force at the heart of the
> community, and, on the other hand, for the centripetal force that brings
> men together, the mysterious glue of that same community. In order to
> transform this demonology into true knowledge we must follow the path
> indicated by the Gospels and complete the translation that they begin. It
> is obvious that the same force that divides people by mimetic rivalry also
> unites them by the mimetic unanimity of the scapegoat.
>
> Clearly this is what John is speaking of when he presents Satan as
> "liar and the father of lies" because he is "a murderer from the start"
> (John 8:44). This lie is discredited by the Passion which shows the victim's
> innocence.[24]

Once again, at the root of the language of Satan and the devil in the
apostolic witness, and particularly from the mouth of Jesus, we have
a consistently anthropological tendency, revelatory of human reality,
rather than a mythical tendency, displacing responsibility and manu-
facturing unnecessary entities. The language of Satan and the devil is
shown to contribute to our understanding of the way we are cast in
interrelational modes of stumbling, not only as individuals or in particular relationships, but also and simultaneously as part of (and thus
contributing to and being manipulated by) the whole human structure
of existence. It is this structure which is on its way out of existence,
thanks to the new creation which Christ has brought about.

Conclusion

The question about the intelligence of the victim is the question of
the understanding which Jesus had before his death and which was
concomitant with his free self-donation up to death. The freedom in
self-giving enabled him to perceive with clarity the working of the

---

24. Girard, *The Scapegoat*, 196.

human heart and teach that perception in ways which the apostolic witnesses, beginning after the resurrection to understand what he meant, bear out. At the root of this human understanding is a complex series of teachings about the *skandalon,* related respectively to distorted desire, interdividual relations, death, victims, murder, and the foundation of two human orders, one of which is the peaceful subversion from within of the other. It must from this be quite clear that Jesus himself had and taught an anthropology in the light of his theology, an eschatological and drastic anthropology, of which traditional accounts of original sin scarcely manage to capture the structure, but whose recapturing can enormously enrich our account of salvation. It is precisely as a tool which enables us to piece together so much of the extraordinary human intelligence that was at work in teaching and preparing the apostolic witness that Girard's mimetic theory recommends itself to Catholic theology. Previous theologies of original sin have tended to emphasize either the historical dimension of original sin seen in terms of Adam, to the detriment of the existential dimension which is reduced to some objective transmission of a *culpa* and its accompanying *poenae,* or on the other hand the existential dimension, seen in terms of anxiety and *déchirement intérieur,* rather despising the "mythical" relation of this to history. In the light of mimetic theory we begin to see how it might be possible to understand the way in which the existential and the historical structure each other, thus rescuing the existential from the purely subjective and the historical from the purely objective. The doctrine of original sin is at the midpoint of this confluence as well, simultaneously as the way the individual and the social structure each other, whether destructively or constructively. It is to this latter perception that we will now turn.

Chapter 6

Original Sin Known
in Its Ecclesial Overcoming

Homo Ecclesialis

In his work *Being as Communion,* the Orthodox theologian John Zizioulas has this to say:

> Patristic theology considers the person to be an "image and likeness of God." It is not satisfied with a humanistic interpretation of the person. From this standpoint patristic theology sees man in the light of two "modes of existence." One may be called the *hypostasis of biological existence,* the other the *hypostasis of ecclesial existence.*[1]

Zizioulas, whose theme here is not original sin but the creative patristic discovery of the notion of person, goes on show how the biological hypostasis is necessarily individual and, owing to the biological means of reproduction and eros's false promise of communion with the other, incapable of the ecstasy necessary to become a person. It is the ecclesial hypostasis, constituted by the new birth of baptism, which transforms both bodiliness and eros into an ontological reality which does not suffer from createdness.[2]

Here I do not wish to discuss Zizioulas's understanding of the term "biological hypostasis," which he derives from Maximus the Confessor.[3] What is important is the clear realization that it is from the eschatological notion of the ecclesial hypostasis — what we are becoming through ecclesial life — that what we were is to be understood. In a way that is slightly different from Zizioulas I shall hope to demonstrate that a eucharistic ecclesiology implies an understanding of original sin that is a development of the themes which we have been looking at up until now. Rather than juxtaposing biological and ecclesial hypostases, I shall juxtapose the ecclesial hypostasis (the foundational reality) and the

---

1. J. Zizioulas, *Being as Communion* (Crestwood, N.Y.: St. Vladimir's Seminary Press, 1985), 50.
2. Zizioulas, *Being as Communion,* 54.
3. Zizioulas, *Being as Communion,* 52 n. 46.

"an-ecclesial hypostasis" (my barbarism), suggesting that original sin is precisely being locked into the an-ecclesial hypostasis and that we know about the latter only from the vantage point of the former.

The first question we have to ask is whether the foundation of the Church is simply a theological reality, or whether, as a theological reality, it is not also descriptive of an anthropological reality. This is best approached through the Scriptures. One of the most vivid passages of the Old Testament (and perhaps also one of the most humorous) is the description in Exodus 7–10 of the competition between Aaron and the court magicians of the pharaoh with regard to the working of signs usually called the ten plagues of Egypt. After each of the plagues produced by Aaron, it is said that the magicians "did the same by their secret arts." We have, apparently, a mimetic competition between rival witch doctors. Then, at a crucial point, Aaron produces gnats, and this is too much for the magicians, who go to Pharaoh and say, "This is the finger of God." The humor of this passage lies in the absurdity of the sign which led to the magicians' recognition of the finger of God. For throughout what is at stake is not the petty show of miraculous one-upmanship, but the real sign that God is in fact working. This sign is on a completely different, and incomparable, level from the magic tricks worked before Pharaoh. It consists in the foundation of the people of Israel by taking them out of Egypt, giving them the law and making the covenant with them so that they can be the sign of God in the world.

That the humor involved has a real depth becomes apparent when we remember that we do not know of the plagues only from the Israelite point of view. There are other versions of the same events, those of the Egyptian writers Manetho and Apion, as recounted and refuted by Josephus in *Against Apion*. These accounts tell of a group of people suffering from dangerous diseases who were precipitating a crisis in Egypt because of the possibility of contagion. They were gathered together under a certain Moses and expelled from Egypt.[4] That is to say, the account of the plagues from the Egyptian point of view is a classic account of a crisis leading to expulsion as seen from the persecutors' viewpoint. The humor in the account is all the more remarkable for its demystification of the stereotypical accusations leading to an expulsion. We are dealing with two different perspectives on a foundational act: that of the victim people who see God as bringing them out of Egypt to form a people who will be a sign to the whole world, and that of the persecutors, who see only a threat to their social order.

---

4. For further details see J. G. Williams, *The Bible, Violence and the Sacred: Liberation from the Myth of Sanctioned Violence* (San Francisco: HarperSanFrancisco, 1991), 89–90.

It is Luke who brings out Jesus' own interpretation of this event most clearly in his reworking of the account of Jesus' facing up to his interlocutors' accusation that he cast out devils by Beelzebul (Luke 11:14–22). In the Lucan account, Jesus clearly puts his interlocutors into the position of the Egyptian magicians: the casting out of devils can be done by Jesus and by "your sons" — the question of the ultimate source of the casting out (whether God or Beelzebul) is as undecidable as it was in the competition between Aaron and the magicians. However, if it is by "the finger of God" that Jesus casts out demons (the same finger that the magicians recognized when confronted with the gnats),[5] then the kingdom of God has come upon them. That is to say, the real sign of God's presence for Jesus, as for Moses and Aaron, is the sign of the new people that is being founded, not the magic tricks: a sign that is on a completely different level of meaning and is in no way part of the world of competitive exorcisms.

This is to read the Lucan account in a theological light, making use of the (carefully provided) Old Testament allusions[6] for its interpretation. It might be left at that, as though what Jesus was saying were simply "you are like Egyptians and cannot recognize the real transcendence of God whose sign is his forming of a new Israel, since your Israel has become hard of heart like Pharaoh." That would be to interpret Jesus as merely engaged in an ad hominem polemic with his interlocutors, involved in a theological argument, about Israel, and casting himself as a new Moses leading forth a new people. At one level this is, of course, exactly what he is doing. However, as we have seen, in the Gospels there is no shift in theological understanding that does not imply a shift in anthropological understanding. Were we simply to leave this passage as though it were a (somewhat obscure) theological argument, we would miss the way in which Jesus was indicating something fundamental about humankind: there would be no recovery of a universal anthropology behind Jesus' act, and his "foundation" would not be revelatory of the sort of beings that humans are. What I would like to suggest is that the intervening lines in Luke's account (Luke 11:17–18), between the request for a sign and Jesus' casting of his interlocutors in the rôle of Egyptians, do indicate precisely Jesus' awareness of a universal anthropological principle at work in his foundation.

I have already shown the way in which the Gospels use the devil as a principle both of social cohesion and of division, and indeed as the

---

5. It is no accident, but very much part of Jesus' wit, that Beelzebul means "Lord of the flies."

6. A further indication that it is the Exodus account that is being alluded to is the request for a sign from heaven (Luke 11:16; see Exod. 7:3, 9; 10:1–3, etc.)

symbol for the whole social order. This is apparent here where the point of Jesus' ironic questioning of his interlocutors is exactly that Satan's kingdom is divided against itself and is on its way out of existence (see Luke 10:18). The structuring principle of Satan's kingdom is building up order by dividing and expelling (the familiar fruit of the mechanism of the emissary victim), and every kingdom and household shares in this structuring principle, seeking cohesion after the same model. Thus we have the structuring principle (Satan's kingdom), and the universal anthropological reality (every kingdom). Finally we also have a third use of the word "kingdom," the kingdom of God, which is presented as coming into being precisely as the transcendent overcoming of both the structuring principle and the universal anthropological reality.

The point is not merely an ad hominem argument about Egypt, which would leave the matter at the level of a squabble and would be revelatory of nothing at all, but the way Jesus uses Egypt to universalize the human condition and indicates the sort of foundation that he is making. The coming of the kingdom of God is the undoing of the whole social structure of the world, which is ultimately futile, because it is, to its very roots, self-destructive and based on self-destruction. The kingdom of God is coming about in the self-giving of Jesus himself, and it is this which is to permit a completely new social structure, not based on the Satan principle. In this light it is not surprising that both Luke and Matthew include very close to this passage what is effectively a summary of what Jesus has been saying: "He who is not with me is against me, and he who does not gather with me scatters" (Luke 11:23; Matt. 12:30). The point is clear: the kingdom of God is coming about in the person of Jesus and is the definitive overcoming of all other social structures. All other social structures tend to futility, scatter, do not unite, partake of the dispersion of what is divided against itself.

There seems little doubt, then, that in bringing about the kingdom of God Jesus sees himself not merely as reforming Judaism, but as making available a new universal foundation by universalizing Israel's experience. Egypt and its magi are no longer simply the historical taskmasters of Israel, but have become the universal principle of resistance to the sign which God is bringing about of an entirely new structure of social cohesion: from the victim rather than by exclusion of the victim.

Lest this be thought to be making one rather obscure passage bear too much weight, we can see the same understanding within quite different allusive frameworks in other places in the New Testament. In the Sermon on the Mount, Matthew shows Jesus as founding the new people of Israel, going further than Moses, teaching people to be deeper in their understanding of the victimary rôle of the new people than were the old, showing them how to break out of the stumbling blocks of desire, and so on. Finally, Jesus sums up the whole enterprise (Matt. 7:24–27) by comparing those who hear and do his words with those who build their house on the rock, while those who hear and do not do are like those who build their house upon the sand. The comparison of rock and sand seems to bring out exactly the same principle as in the passage on Beelzebul. God is the rock of Israel; Jesus is identifying himself with this rock; it is the only rock that is not overcome by any sort of vicissitudes. All other foundational principles are sand (a marvelous metaphor for the treacherous nature of the apparent solidity that mimetic rivalry and scapegoating produce), and their houses fall. Jesus' new foundation is not one rock against other (maybe lesser) rocks. In the light of the kind of foundation that Jesus is bringing about, all other foundations are simply futile and self-defeating.

Of course, for Matthew the image of the rock does not appear here alone. Simon becomes the rock on which Jesus builds his Church (once he has been converted from stumbling block into rock), and it is made quite clear that against the new gathering of the new Israel (the *ekklesía*) on this rock the gates of Hades will never prevail. The gates of Hades, rather than being an unfortunate lapse by Jesus or Matthew into mythology, stand for the cultural force of all social order flowing from and ordered toward death.[7] Hades, the house built on sand, kingdoms divided, and scattering as opposed to gathering refer to the same reality. Once again, the nature of the foundation that Jesus is bringing about reveals the nature of all other forms of social structure — and that means all other ways in which humans are locked into each other and lock each other in.

The same understanding can be seen in the Johannine working of the theme of Jesus as the true vine (John 15:1–17). This is not a piece of ecclesiastical moralizing, but the Johannine explanation of the way in which Jesus' foundation works. Where Israel had been God's vine or vineyard, Jesus turns out to be the true vine which God has been bringing into existence all along. The real construction of the people of God is to be found by building from and in Jesus. The alternative to being founded on this foundation is to be cut off, to wither and be gathered for burning. Withered branches gathered for burning is the Johannine equivalent of the Matthaean house built on sand or the synoptic scattering rather than gathering. John goes even further, in that he makes explicit the way in which this vine is founded: it is founded in the self-giving of Jesus for his friends (John 15:13), and it is their imitation of

---

7. See René Girard, *The Scapegoat* (London: Athlone, 1986), 147–48.

his self-giving ("you are my friends if you do what I command you") which is their abiding in him and their producing of fruit. In this way only their fruit will abide, because it is part of this new and definitive foundation: the true vine.[8]

In the light of these witnesses it becomes possible to read Luke's inter-pretation of Pentecost as the overcoming of Babel (Acts 2:1–13), not as a mere theologumenon unrelated to what Jesus himself thought he was doing, but as a very accurate interpretation of Jesus' own understand-ing of the nature of his foundation. In the first place, the simple phrase reproduced by Luke (11:23), "he who does not gather with me scat-ters," is shown to have considerably more depth than at first apparent. In the account of Babel (Gen. 11:1–9) the word "scatter" appears three times. The people build the tower lest they be scattered, and God thinks it is good to scatter them, for fear of what they will do. In this con-text God is still a continuation of the "envious" God of Genesis 3:22. In Jesus' phrase, however, the essential evangelical work of anthropo-logical demystification has been carried out: it is God who founds, and human beings who scatter. Thus the representation of Pentecost as the undoing of Babel is not only a fulfillment of the prophecies that God would gather his scattered people together (see Deut. 30:3; Jer. 31:10; Ezek. 11:17; 28:25). It is a decisive recasting in anthropological terms of human foundational order: the real foundation is God's foundation of the new people of Israel in Christ. It was not that God had scat-tered the people of Babel, but their foundational order, one grasped at avidly in order to avoid being scattered (Gen. 11:4), was in fact cast in the mode of human scattering. All human societal foundations are futile exercises in the production of a fragile order. The only real foundation is the one given in Christ's gathering. Behind the New Testament re-working of biblical images there is a quite specific understanding of the universal futility of human social order that is being overcome by the revelation of the true foundation.

This enables us to perceive a further New Testament "angle" onto the question of original sin. Previously we have seen an angle derived from an understanding of an original murder, that of Cain, as well as an angle derived from an understanding of an original distortion of desire, that of Adam. To this can be added the angle derived from an understanding of an original futility in the foundation of human societal order, that of

---

8. John, typically, gives much greater emphasis to the positive sign being brought about by Christ and very much less to the negative countersign to this same work. This is in line with his theological principle that the negative countersign is revealed as that which is minatory to Christ and is being overcome rather than as part of an independent dialectical reality toward which Christ himself is minatory (John 1:9–13; 3:16–21).

Babel. This nexus is bringing us closer to a perception of the authentic content of the doctrine of original sin.

The Content of Christ's Foundation

Having established *that* Jesus had a quite particular understanding of the universal nature of what it was that he was founding and thus of the possibility of a human ecclesial hypostasis as a particular way of being human, it then becomes possible to ask: what sort of foundation? The content of Christ's foundation then becomes a sure guide to what the an-ecclesial hypostasis might consist in: the sort of societal animal we are on our way out of being as we are incorporated (or grafted) into becoming ecclesial hypostases. This can be shown by the way in which the three "angles" on original sin are conflated in the foundation of the Church.

In the first place, and following the "Adam" angle on original sin as distorted desire, we can see that Jesus' moral teaching and his inducing his followers into discipleship was a practical founding of a group of contingent historical people who might learn the undistorting of desire. Jesus taught his disciples, and especially the twelve of the eschatological new Israel, not to stumble or be scandalized. Thus he prepared them to be his followers even through his death, so that after his death they might be foundational witnesses to him, as well as, in their imitative living toward martyrdom, being living signs of the foundational nature of his self-giving. The pacific imitation of Jesus beyond his death and through their own deaths is what forms the ecclesial hypostasis in their case. That is to say, they learn to receive their identities as human beings from an entirely nonrivalrous, nonenvious, nongrasping practice of life. They receive their identities as purely given from the one foundation, which is the self-giving victim, the stone rejected by the builders which became the head of the corner. As part of this, there is no need at all for any rivalry among themselves, any suggestion that it is they and not Christ who are foundational. The way the apostles are foundational is strictly derivative from the one foundation who is Christ.[9]

This enables us to glimpse the workings of the an-ecclesial hypostasis. Because it is shot through with distorted desire, it is unable to receive its identity gratuitously from another, but grasps at the other enviously and therefore is constantly engaged in shoring itself up over against the other by comparison and exclusion. The an-ecclesial hypostasis is thus permanently incapable of "gathering," because in order to gather it must

---

9. As Paul makes clear in 1 Corinthians 3:1–15.

scatter; in order to build it must expel. The an-ecclesial hypostasis is locked into the conflict between the one and the many, the individual and the social. Either one is part of a group which builds its unity at the expense of another, the rival, or one is an individual building up one's identity over against the group, turning oneself into a victim who is also a hero. In the an-ecclesial hypostasis there can be no overcoming the dialectical tension between group and individual, between uniformity and freedom, because the two are locked into each other as each other's negative counterparts.

When we say this, it means that there is no real fraternity possible in the an-ecclesial hypostasis, because the rôles being played out between people are always, perpetually, those of hero and victim, all of which depend on the "social" other as essentially something hostile, something from which identity must be grabbed as a prize, not received as a gift. It is the ecclesial hypostasis alone which, as discipleship produces the undistorting of desire, enables fraternity, because the social other is itself the bearer of gratuity. The identity of the group is enabled to flow without rivalry from a particular individual, the self-giving victim. So there is no longer the fatal dialectic between group and individual. It is this also that enables the overcoming of the tension between uniformity and freedom. If the group is seen as the concrete possibility of the gratuity flowing from the self-giving victim, then the group is also what gives the individual his or her identity and thus makes possible freedom. Freedom, instead of being freedom from the constraints of the group, becomes freedom brought into being by gratuitous dependence on the group. As the person concerned learns not to derive his or her identity over against the other, so the existential rôles of victim and hero collapse into the one unique rôle of brother. This is the depth of Jesus' remark in Matthew 23:8: "But you are not to be called rabbi, for you have one teacher and you are all brethren."

This dimension of the an-ecclesial hypostasis can be further understood from Paul's teaching on justification by grace through faith. As I have shown above, Paul's understanding of faith is the undoing of the distorted nature of desire by the making available of God as in no way an envious reality, but as a purely gratuitous self-giving. Faith in this reality is the beginnings of the undoing of desire formed in envy, starting from an envious perception of God. The ecclesial hypostasis therefore is one which receives its new identity (is made just) precisely by participation in the gratuitous ecclesial reception of identity from the forgiving victim. In this sense, ecclesial justification by faith is precisely the reception of a social belonging that is completely removed from any sense of self-justification. In one sense it is no justification at all, because it is an identity received as given. The an-ecclesial hypostasis is that which is permanently locked in the necessity for self-justification, which means a constant comparison of self with others, deriving identity over against the other. The self-justification of the an-ecclesial hypostasis consists in the acquisition of value, of worth, and of being in rivalry with others. The social form of this self-justification is the world of mutual scattering in order to found, rather than the reception of the foundation of being from the gratuitous other.

This understanding of the need for self-justification in the an-ecclesial hypostasis leads us directly into a further consequence in the self-understanding of the same an-ecclesial hypostasis. We might call this "the foundational mentality." The need to shore up identity, to justify oneself, is shown in the ordinary human way of seeking a fundamental (foundational) cause for things. If we can get back to a first cause, an answer to the question "why?" then we will be on solid ground, then we will be able to give an account of ourselves, who we are, where we are coming from, and where we are going. So the foundational mentality seeks to tell the story of origins in a way which justifies the present. The problem is that any such explanation is always a grabbing at a partial account of our identity, and the very notion of *cause*, with its forensic origin, involves us in an accusation (*ad causam*), an attempt to lay blame. There is all the difference in the world between this "foundational mentality," which is at its root an envious culpabilization of some other (even if in the very distant past), and the stunning lucidity of 1 John 3:2: "Beloved, we are God's children now; it does not yet appear what we shall be, but we know that when he appears we shall be like him, for we shall see him as he is." Here identity is something given as part of a becoming that cannot be grasped, but only received in patience. Identity is eschatological, not foundational.

It is perhaps the peak of perversity of the foundational mentality to have turned the very doctrine that teaches us its overcoming into the prime example of a foundational mentality. The foundational mentality has managed to turn original sin into a way of accounting for our present evil by blaming someone: Adam or, sometimes, the serpent. Thus original sin becomes a foundational excuse for not overcoming evil, a way of justifying the present state of affairs rather than being the understanding of what it is that is being overcome on our way out of it. It is (perhaps) the central aim of this essay to show that original sin, precisely as understood from the standpoint of the ecclesial hypostasis, is not foundational at all. It is the revelation of a failed, futile foundation. There is nothing solid about original sin, nothing on which anything can be based. The doctrine is above all not an exercise in culpabilization, not a seeking to attribute some foundational guilt, but a parting glance at the drastic nature and the futility of a condition out of which we are being empowered to move.

If I have insisted up till now on referring to the way in which Jesus *founded* a new people, this is because of the difficulty experienced in current ecclesiology in imagining the internal coherence between Jesus' teaching, life, death, and resurrection and the coming into being of the Church. However, at this stage it becomes possible to take a step back from the language of "foundation." The language is too dialectic, too involved in the human business of appropriating an identity over against some other, to reflect faithfully the reality of what Jesus was about. The sense in which Jesus was founding anything at all can be understood only as a subversion from within of any notion of foundation, because it was really an efficacious and constructive revelation of a purely gratuitous project that existed even before the human capacity for foundational distortion had come into being.

This gives us a way in to seeing how the second "angle" on original sin, the foundation of human order in murder symbolized by Cain's murder of Abel, is made available by the victimary self-giving of Jesus. The central moment of this is Jesus' own prior interpretation of his death in the Last Supper. It is at this point that the nature of the ecclesial and the an-ecclesial hypostases become apparent. The key word in this context is *dei*. All four Gospels show a clear understanding that Jesus *must* suffer.[10] We see two reasons behind this "must": so that the Scriptures be fulfilled (the "theological" reason), and because of the nature of the human order (the "anthropological" reason). Where it might be possible to read the necessity of fulfilling the Scriptures as suggesting that there is some divine plan to kill Jesus, the tendency of Jesus' own interpretations of this "must" is always toward the anthropological subversion of this understanding. The Gospels do not attempt to attribute this "necessity" to anything in God: when Jesus in his apocalyptic discourses indicates that "all these things must come about," he is referring to the cataclysmic convulsions of the human order which must not distract the disciples from their attention to the coming of the Son of man precisely as crucified and risen victim. The word *dei* in these contexts has a quite specific meaning: it refers to the necessity to which the human order, based on death, is in thrall. What enables Jesus to point this out is the willingness of divine gratuity to allow itself to suffer the consequences

---

10. Matthew 16:21; 26:54; Mark 8:31; Luke 9:22; 17:25; 22:37; 24:7; 26:44; John 3:14; 12:34.

of this human order precisely in order to free it from the realm of the necessity of death.

Jesus' Last Supper then is the way he acts out in mime the divine gratuity overcoming the human order of necessity, prior to the living out of that gratuity to its fullest consequences in his own death. He acts this out in terms of the bringing into being of the true people of God. Thus he reworks the language of the first Passover, the celebration by which the identity of the Jewish people as a victim people was given prior to their flight/expulsion from Egypt. He also reworks the language of the covenant of Exodus 24, by which God formed his alliance with Israel. Finally, he also brings to life the Isaian picture of the servant who ransoms a whole people through his suffering.

However, Jesus is not merely refounding Israel by using its sacred texts to give a new interpretation. That would be to substitute one sacrificial order for another. He is doing the inverse of that. God's original project for Israel was that it should be a people who would not be like the other nations, based on murder and sacrifice. For that reason he had taken them out of Egypt. It was their victimary self-understanding resulting from this which had permitted them the unique insight into the foundation of the human order to which the story of Cain and Abel bears witness: that human order is based on murder, but God does not justify that murder, and so all human order is ambiguous.

So where the human order tends to cover over the original murder, substituting animal victims for human victims and remaining ignorant of the murderous base of society, the people of Israel were already partially aware of this. Hence the ambiguity of the world of sacrifice in the Jewish Scriptures: both treated as vital and also decried by the prophetic insistence that it is peaceful human relationality and not sacrifice that is acceptable to God. Jesus takes the Jewish tendency to see the human relational order behind the world of sacrifice to its furthermost extreme. He interprets his own killing as undoing even the substitution of animals for humans, thus combining both the priestly and the prophetic dimensions of Jewish religion. In the Last Supper Jesus is clearly substituting a human for the animals and making of his own forthcoming death a revelation of the victimary basis of all societies, including even, sadly, Jewish society. It was Jewish society alone that might have had the possibility of grasping this and avoiding the murder of Jesus, but, as Caiaphas's prophetic and priestly remark (John 11:50) indicated,[11] even the Jewish people were under the thrall of the original necessity of

---

11. " 'You do not understand that it is expedient for you that one man should die for the people, and that the whole nation should not perish.' "

death and could be brought out of that thrall only by the revelatory self-giving into the realm of necessity of Jesus: hence the ironic exactness of Caiaphas's prophecy (John 11:51–52).[12]

Thus the Last Supper, as it brings into being the people who are to live from reception of the self-giving and forgiving victim and thus who are no longer part of the realm of necessity (that is, the ecclesial hypostasis), also reveals the foundational tragedy of the an-ecclesial hypostasis. This is that of a social order based on murder, in which all people are fatally tied into each other by the necessity of giving and receiving death under the illusion that death brings life. However, it does not reveal that suddenly, at a blow. It reveals that in complete dependence on, but in transcendent fulfillment of, the bringing into being of the ecclesial hypostasis which had its historical origins in the call of Abraham from out of Ur and the call of Israel from out of Egypt.

The depth of what is intended goes back even further: the bringing into being of the ecclesial hypostasis reaches further even than the call of Abel from out of death. The apostolic witness indicates a clear understanding that the creative self-giving of God is prior to the culture of death founded by Cain. The first letter of Peter (1:18–20) tells us that:

> You know that you were ransomed from the futile ways inherited from your fathers ... with the precious blood of Christ like that of a lamb without blemish or spot. He was destined before the foundation of the world but was made manifest at the end of the times for your sake.

That is to say, the bringing into existence of the ecclesial hypostasis is the original intention, and the original intention was made manifest in the midst of futility. The rescuing from futility is thus accidental to the original intention. The self-giving of God as creative of the ecclesial hypostasis is the original intention. Thanks to the reign of futility, this self-giving had to be made manifest in the self-giving to death of Jesus.

The same understanding is present in Revelation 13:8. The obvious reading of this verse suggests that the lamb was slain from the foundation of the world.[13] However, even if it is translated according to the *lectio facilior,* as referring to people whose names have (not) been inscribed, from the foundation of the world, in the book of life of the slaughtered lamb,[14] the nexus of ideas is the same. The calling into being of the ecclesial hypostasis by means of the self-giving of God is original

---

12. "He did not say this of his own accord, but being high priest that year he prophesied that Jesus should die for the nation, and not for the nation only, but to gather into one the children of God who are scattered abroad."

13. Thus Jerome in the Vulgate and the King James Bible.

14. Thus the RSV, Biblia Española, Biblia Latinoamericana.

and prior to the foundation of the world. The suggestion is that the nature of the foundation of the world[15] and the slaughtering of the lamb imply each other. The bringing into being of the ecclesial hypostasis by means of the gratuitous self-giving of God is original and anterior, and what being human is all about. The foundation of the cosmos is a tragic and futile distortion based on murder, which can only be undone by the original self-giving of God taking the form of a man substituting himself for the sacrificial lamb proper to the social order based on murder. In this way the original intention, the bringing into being of the ecclesial hypostasis, can be made manifest and brought into reality.

There is a further dimension to what I have called, with caution, Jesus' "foundation," or bringing into being of the ecclesial hypostasis. And it is a dimension which once again reveals the nonfoundational reality of that foundation. It is the element which brings together both Jesus' victimary self-understanding and the undistortion of desire which I have shown to be intrinsic aspects of the bringing into being of this hypostasis. This is the dimension of forgiveness, and it is not so much an additional dimension as the mode in which the other dimensions become present.

John brings this out by the way in which he has John the Baptist identify Jesus with the phrase "Behold the lamb of God who takes away the sin of the world" (John 1:29). The sin is a singular, global reality, and it is taken away by the self-giving of the victim risen as forgiveness. I suggest that this means that the only way that the self-giving of God can be made present in the world is by the unbinding of the way in which the world is locked (or bound) into the structure of futility based on murder. The gratuity is originally purely creative; there is nothing to forgive. The gratuity merely brings into being; being floats on gratuity. However, with the foundation of the order of the world, humans are locked into an identity that is much too small and constantly self-destructive. The way gratuity is experienced within such a world can only be as the unlocking, the unbinding, of the established order in order to be able to grow into what we shall gratuitously become.

Thus it is not only that Jesus by his teaching on the undistorting of desire and by his giving himself to be a human victim reveals both the ecclesial hypostasis and by extension its countersign, the an-ecclesial hypostasis. The mode of his presence is what permits the transformation of the latter into the former. The gratuitous self-giving makes it possible for being to float on gratuity by undoing the way in which it is locked into

---

15. *Katabolés kosmou* is the foundation of cultural order rather than the "creation of the universe."

grasping for foundations. In this sense the "foundation" of the Church is nothing other than the efficacious revealing of the forgiveness of sin, which is itself our only way back into God's original plan for us. It might be more correct to speak of the Church as an un-foundation, since what it is unbinding is precisely our being tied into foundations. J. Ratzinger points out that the early fathers

> expressed this fact with the bold image of the *casta meretrix:* by its own historical origin the Church is a prostitute, coming from the Babylon of this world; but Christ the Lord washed it and converted the prostitute into a wife. Urs von Balthasar has shown... that this is not only an historical affirmation, in the sense that once it was impure and now it is pure, but that it indicates the permanent existential tension of the Church. The Church lives perpetually from forgiveness, which transforms it from prostitute into wife; the Church of all generations is Church through grace, into which God is continually calling men from Babylon, where, of themselves, they live.[16]

It is in this that the new and definitive covenant made by Jesus consists: in the making present of a new way of being human that is the fulfillment of the original intention, access to which is made available by our being constantly unlocked from our insertion into the futility of the human foundation.

The Pauline Ecclesial Hypostasis

Were further evidence needed of the way in which the apostolic witness understands the bringing into being of the ecclesial hypostasis, then it is lavishly provided by Paul in his Corinthian correspondence. As R. Hamerton Kelly points out:

> The Corinthian correspondence, *prima facie,* shows the following signs which suggest that a Girardian interpretation would be appropriate:
>
> 1. A community split into factions by rivalry — 1 Cor 1:10ff.; 2 Cor 10–13.
>
> 2. Calls by the apostle to his readers to imitate him as he imitates Christ — 1 Cor 4:16; 11:1; combined with a lively concern with the nature of sacrifice and the proper attitude toward it — 1 Cor 10:14–22.
>
> 3. The self-understanding of the apostle as victim and scapegoat — 1 Cor 2:1–5; 4:9–13; 2 Cor 12:7–10.

16. From J. Ratzinger, "Franqueza y obediencia," in *El nuevo pueblo de Dios* (Barcelona: Herder, 1972), 284, with reference to H. U. von Balthasar, "Casta Meretrix," in *Sponsa Verbi* (Einsiedeln, 1961). The translation from Spanish is mine.

4. Exposition of the nature of Christian community as the body of the crucified victim — 1 Cor 12; see 1:18–2:5.

There are, therefore, in the Corinthian letters, four critical Girardian themes, which command our attention: rivalry, mimesis, community and victimage.[17]

In the first place, Paul understands the Corinthians as *koinônoi* — those who have been called into the fellowship of the sacrificial meal, the *koinônía* of Christ. This is clearly a subversive understanding of the notion of sacrifice since it is compared to those who partake in Israel's sacrificial meal and opposed to those who take part in idolatrous sacrificial meals or treat the Eucharist as if it were one such by cursing Jesus (1 Cor. 10:18–21; 12:3). The participation that is proper to Christians is that of those who have become participants in his victimary body. That it is "Christ crucified for you" who is the foundation of their new being is made clear by the ironic question in 1 Corinthians 1:13 — "Was Paul crucified for you?" — linked to Paul's clear understanding that there is only one foundation, Christ Jesus (1 Cor. 3:11). It is this that is foundational of the community, and the way into participation in it is by imitation of the self-giving that led to Jesus' being crucified. Hence the centrality of the Eucharist to Paul's discussion: it is the self-giving of the victimary body which enables the Corinthians to become one body in Christ. Hence also the necessity, for proper participation in the Eucharist, of a life that is an imitation of the self-giving of the victim.

Paul illustrates this by himself being an example of something despised, an offscouring, with victimary signs, even calling himself a scapegoat (1 Cor. 4:13), urging the Corinthians to become imitators of him (1 Cor. 4:16) even as he is of Christ (11:1). It is his free self-giving and willingness to subject himself to the condition of others for their own sakes that make Paul an imitator of Christ (1 Cor. 9:19–23). That is to say, there is a particular antidote to the world of rivalistic desires and factiousness which is destroying the community: the learning of a new sort of desire which is not in rivalry with any desire at all, because it is the pacific imitation of the one who is on his way into expulsion. Paul gives specific content to the notion of "flesh" here, out of which he urges his correspondents to grow. The flesh is precisely the world of rivalistic desire leading to futile foundationalism (1 Cor. 3:1–4). Paul could not, in fact, make it clearer than he does that the foundation that is Christ can be lived only from within a change of desires. He refers

---

17. R. Hamerton-Kelly, "A Girardian Interpretation of Paul: Rivalry, Mimesis and Victimage in the Corinthian Correspondence," *Semeia* 33 (1985): 67. This seminal essay is the first of which I have notice to apply Girard's hermeneutic systematically to Paul's thought.

to the rock which followed Israel in the desert (1 Cor. 10:4) and claims that this rock *was Christ*. The problem with the people of Israel was that they desired evil, and this is an example so that we should not desire likewise (1 Cor. 10:6).

Not only is the undistortion of desire the key way into insertion into the one foundation, the rock, that is Christ, but this immediately means that the person who is so inserted has no need to justify himself over against anybody at all. Those who live in the spirit, like Paul himself, do not derive their identity in any way at all from what others think, whether they praise or condemn, because the identity is purely given by the Lord (1 Cor. 4:1–7). Therefore there is no boasting, except in the Lord.

The theme of the overcoming of the *skandalon* also makes its appearance. Paul teaches quite specifically the way out of mimetic rivalry is to learn not to be a source of stumbling for the weak brother (1 Cor. 8; 10:23–30). The undoing of the *skandalon* is at the very heart of Paul's understanding of the edification of the Church. Paul's hymn to charity (1 Cor. 13) is entirely cast in terms of a form of desire that is peacefully mimetic — related to the other as model, and as self-giving, rather than in the mode of comparison with and tripping up of the other.

Thus we find clearly present in Paul's understanding of the ecclesial hypostasis the notion of the victimary foundation of the Church and the undistorting of desire as the way into belonging to that foundation, imitating the self-giving of Christ.[18] We also find a clear understanding that the whole enterprise of bringing into being the ecclesial hypostasis is understood within the terms of a creative forgiveness:

> Therefore if any one is in Christ, he is a new creation; the old has passed away, behold the new has come. All this is from God, who through Christ reconciled us to himself and gave us the ministry of reconciliation; that is, in Christ God was reconciling the world to himself, not counting their trespasses against them, and entrusting to us the message of reconciliation. (2 Cor. 5:17–19)

The unanimity of the apostolic witness regarding what is being brought into being, and what is the content of that out of which we are being brought, is absolutely apparent.

---

18. Hamerton-Kelly points out the importance of mimesis in the cult of Dionysus, the principal religious cult at Corinth ("A Girardian Interpretation," 72). By insisting on the mimesis of Christ even to the extent of becoming a victim, Paul is undoing the mimetic working of the Dionysiac cult, which was related to the ritualized *sparagmos,* or frenzied dismemberment (originally of Pentheus), associated with the god.

Excursus: The Particular Overcoming
of Particularity

Earlier I talked of the way in which Jesus universalized the experience of Israel coming out of Egypt as an explanation of the sort of kingdom that was being brought into being through him. This might be taken to mean that Jesus was aware of some universal principle (which we might call the overcoming of the realm of original sin) and that the Jewish tradition served him as a useful way of illustrating that principle. We would be able to strip away the particular cultural impedimenta to get to the universal principle that is really operative. Now I think that such an interpretation is a particularly subtle temptation to which much Western thought is especially vulnerable. What I would like to suggest is that universality is not something which lurks, disguised, beneath the make-up of particularity, but rather that it is only particularity which can bear universality.

Let me illustrate this temptation in a little more detail. It is easy to see the relationship between Jesus and Israel as one of a certain sort of prophetic critique. It is as though Jesus sees certain fundamental truths, proper to the Jewish tradition, and in their light he offers a critique of the Israel that he knows. At the root of Israel, as of all societies, is foundational murder, so Jesus reveals that fact by allowing himself to become a victim, and thus the critique of Israel is complete. There can now start up a new universal religion around and from the body of the forgiving victim. Such a religion can be universal because all human societies are really (and in ignorance) based on such murders, and so the religion which reveals the universal is alone capable of being universal.

This sounds rather like what I have been trying to say up till now, yet it is not. It seems to me that this way of talking gives adequate account of only one way in which Jesus was the "end" of the law — the sense in which he made it redundant. It does not give adequate account of the other, no less important sense in which Jesus was the "end" of the law: in the sense of its fulfillment. That is to say, Jesus, in revealing the victimary base of Jewish society (through his Last Supper and death), was not only engaged in a critique of Judaism, but was engaged in a creative act that was an innovative fulfillment of Judaism.[19] There is an unmistakable lack of passivity in Jesus' whole "path" to Jerusalem and living out of the passion, perhaps brought out particularly by John. Jesus

---

19. Here I part company with Hamerton-Kelly's application of the Girardian hermeneutic to Paul's thought in *Sacred Violence*. It seems to me that Hamerton-Kelly (despite his attempts to overcome his own dialectical thinking in his last chapter) does treat Paul as having discovered a universal principle beneath the trappings of Judaism, and consequently ditching the latter in favor of the new universal faith.

is creatively bringing something into being, and that bringing into being has to pass through his rejection, and he is in a hurry until it is done.

It was Jesus' innovative fulfillment *of Judaism* that made it possible for there to be born a universal approach to God. Jesus made use of a quite specific, contingent religious tradition, his own, in order to open up the possibility of something universal and available to all humans. That is to say, the quite specific, contingent particularity of Judaism is the particularity that made possible universality. There would have been no possibility of the making available of the universal victim except as part of the long and complex history of discovery by which Judaism became aware of God's noninvolvement in victimization and his partiality toward victims. It is not as though, once having made available the universal victim, the necessity for particularity was past, and so all that could fade away and we could live from universally applicable revealed principles flowing from the universal victim. Jesus actually brought into being a new particular people, a new, contingent, specific religious tradition. Or rather he offered Judaism the possibility of a new way of living its particularity: particularity as a way into universality rather than particularity as an obstacle to universality.

This bringing into being of a specific, contingent people is not merely something accidental, which just happened alongside the life, death, and resurrection of Jesus, events which were seen as making available certain universal truths. Rather it is only by our insertion into the specific contingent people that it becomes possible to make the story of Jesus' life and death universal. This is itself a creative effort, continuing the creative interpretative work of Jesus shown in his Last Supper. It is not as though Jesus brought into being a people which is able to hold on to some universal foundational truths, and so be saved. He brought into being a people that is called constantly to create, from the particularity in which we all start, an unheard-of universality. This involves a constant uncovering of the ways in which our particularities are inimical to universality.

Thus we are able to see another dimension of the ecclesial hypostasis. The ecclesial hypostasis is permanently engaged in creating universality by transforming a particularity which holds its being over against the other, into a particularity which is complementary to the other. The Church is the particular tradition whose relation to its own particularity is that it is this particularity that makes it capable of universality, because its particularity is not defined over against any other particularity. It is in fact a given particularity that loosens the grasped particularity of all other particular traditions into contact with which it comes. It is for this reason that it is simultaneously the most subversive of all cultural forces, constantly causing to crumble the barriers which protect group identity from the culturally other, and the most enriching of all cultural forces in that it enables whatever of cultural identity that is not held over against some other to flourish without distortion.

Where therefore the ecclesial hypostasis creates diverse universality out of the particular by empowering the particular to cherish that which is other, the an-ecclesial hypostasis produces universal sameness disguised as particular difference. By insisting on what makes one different (grasping identity, holding on to a particular foundation), one is constantly reducing oneself to the same as others who are doing the same. The more one thinks oneself different, the more the same one becomes (see any two people or groups or nations in a fight, each more and more convinced that they alone are right, unique, special, deserving, and so on). The universality that is produced in this way is always reductionist and never creative. What is universally present is the tedious nature of grasped particularism. The universal is made present precisely in the suppression of anything positive that the particular might have to offer.

This has certain consequences. We can talk of a certain sort of universalism which is a prescinding from the particular, and of which maybe Platonic ideas, and the Platonism never very far from the heart of Western culture, are a good example. The abstract universal notions or values which flow from this and which are held as if they were independent of the particular traditions which gave them birth are in fact more or less empty terms which mean entirely different things according to whether their universality derives from particularity or is suppressive of particularity. To give some crude examples: The notions of Liberty, Equality, and Fraternity do not exist independently of whether they are part of the ecclesial hypostasis that gave them birth or whether they are part of the an-ecclesial hypostasis. If they are part of the ecclesial hypostasis, then the content of Liberty has to do with the undistorting of desire by which I am locked into the other, so that I am able to relate to the other gratuitously, both in terms of receiving liberty from the other and being free to be gratuitous toward the other. If the notion is part of the an-ecclesial hypostasis, then liberty does not move beyond the notion of freedom from certain restraints or impositions brought about by the other (this is not to deny the immense importance that such freedom may have, but merely to indicate that the content of the notion is different). Equality is either the creative discovery of the complementary similarity of the other, or it is the envious reduction of the other to the same. Fraternity is either an abstract decree, or it is the arduous creative struggle to unbury Abel.

The suggestion that is at work here is that the concept of universality

is not and cannot be univocal. When we talk of the universality of saving grace and the corresponding universality of sin, we are not talking
about two things in strictly the same sense. In the case of the universality of saving grace, we are talking about the universality made present
by the saving and fulfilling of particularity: that is a quite concrete, visible, real notion of universality dwelling in the particularity of ecclesial
hypostases. In the case of the universality of sin ("all have sinned and
fall short," Rom. 3:23; "creation subjected to futility," Rom. 8:20) we
are talking of the universality that either prescinds from or suppresses
particularity, that is, a purely notional, abstract universality. The relationship of universality to particularity is determinative of the real
meaning of universality.

In this sense, the tragedy of original sin is not that it is universal, but
that it is the incapacity for universality that is revealed by the coming
into being of the ecclesial hypostasis in which alone particularity is made
capable of bearing universality. Original sin, the an-ecclesial hypostasis,
is simultaneously incapable of real particularity (and capable of only er-
satz particularity grasped at defensively over against others) and of real
universality (and capable of only abstract universality as the rhetoric of
rights or denunciations). The doctrine of original sin, rather than being
the abstract declaration of the universal equality in sin of all human beings, is the doctrine of the incapacity for equality outside the ecclesial
hypostasis. This can be seen even in the most basic existential terms. It
is life in the ecclesial communion that enables persons to discover, to
their relief, and relax into their similarity with others. It is the bringing
into being of the ecclesial hypostasis that consists in the recognition of
equality at the level of similarity in the distortion of desire and practice,
and the creation of equality at the level of dignity and the seeking the
good of the other. In the an-ecclesial hypostasis, equality can only be an
abstract, because the announcement of similarity is always a threat to
those who have all at stake in being "different."

What am I getting at with these rather subtle and apparently pointless
distinctions? It seems to me that they are vital if we are to recover the
sense in which the doctrine of original sin actually works as an ecclesial doctrine. As the discovery of that of which the ecclesial hypostasis
is no longer a part, is on the way out of, the doctrine is also part of
a movement from one sort of universality to another: from the universality that is really the omnipresent incapacity for universality to the
universality that is made possible by the bringing to life of a particular
life story. This means that the doctrine of original sin cannot simply be
"a universal truth" except insofar as it is discovered in particular life
stories as the "Egypt" out of which God is creatively bringing an "Is-

rael." The real ecclesial doctrine of original sin is believed in and lived out only by those who are no longer imprisoned in the reality to which it points.

All this, I'm afraid to say, has practical, political consequences. It enables us to look at two quite different universalizations with a critical eye. Let us look first at the conservative universalization. The conservative universalization is to treat original sin as a universal, that is, as a foundational reality. Because of this, politics consists in the clever management of people, all of whom are essentially self-interested. Neoliberal economics is based on the extraordinary notion of the "moral neutrality" of money,[20] and on the reception of Mandeville's famous perception that the private vice of envy is in fact a public virtue. That is to say, competition (rivalry) is an unambiguous good. This is, in fact, a deeply heretical misappropriation of the doctrine of original sin, in that it makes of the doctrine a foundational reality giving an account of and a basis for a present practice; it also misunderstands the sort of universality implied in the doctrine. This is because there is no real notion of an ecclesial hypostasis within the terms of reference of which *alone* can the doctrine be received and understood. The idea that the present reality is passing away owing to the coming into being in its midst of a completely different human order and that the doctrine of original sin is the view on that which is passing away from the rear deck of that which is coming into being is anathema to a way of thinking that seeks to master "present reality" and postpones "coming into being" into "the next life." The doctrine of original sin has been definitively sundered from the doctrine and presence of forgiveness, whose furthest stretching it is. We have a situation in which a doctrine revealing futility has been sequestered and put to work by the very futility to whose going out of being it points.

If the conservative distortion of the doctrine of original sin is the universalization and making foundational of what is only perceptible in its ecclesial overcoming, then the "progressive" distortion is in the universalization and attempting to make foundational of the ecclesial overcoming. So, at the political level, certain values are decreed to be universal (for instance, those of Liberty, Equality, and Fraternity), but rather than these values becoming universal by a creative overcoming of particular histories of oppression, inequality, and murder, a creative overcoming that always involves forgiveness, the creative roots of these universal values in particular histories of forgiveness are forgotten, or relegated, and the means of realizing these goods become independent

---

20. See, for example, the works of M. Novak.

of their end. The history of revolutions is only too eloquent in this regard. At a certain stage of recent Latin American history it was thought immensely important theologically to justify the participation of Christians with non-Christians (i.e., principally various Marxist groups) in certain sociopolitical projects. The way this was done was by the universalization of certain values to which both parties could be committed (like freedom, *vida,* etc.). Here I am discussing not the nature of the participation and its morality,[21] but the theological justification dependent on the possibility of universal human values. Does that justification question whether or not it can be really taken for granted that a Marxist and a Catholic mean the same thing by freedom or life? The richness of a notion is entirely dependent on the particular tradition which bears it, including the practice which makes it real. Yet there is no Christian notion of Freedom or *vida* that is not intrinsically part of a creative history of forgiveness.

This can be illustrated by differences in the rôle of denunciation of evil according to different traditions. Is denunciation of evil a good in itself, a necessary part of the struggle by which those in charge of, and manipulating, the current order are blamed, and the order therefore made less tenable, bringing closer the day when the order will crumble or be overthrown? Or is denunciation of evil the sad accidental consequence of the attempt to bring into being a concrete creative project for human beings? As that project is brought into being, so the forces of resistance to it are identified and denounced, not as a dialectical forging of identity in the struggle but as an invitation to be otherwise which includes an offer of the possibility of being otherwise. It is this that is the model of denunciation in the lives of the prophets, as they recalled Israel to fidelity to God's project in the covenant, or Jesus as he denounced the forces of resistance to his bringing about the new people of God. The former denunciation is intrinsic to the bringing down of the old and the bringing in of the new — and is part of the cycle of blaming and founding that characterizes the division against itself of futility. The latter is the way forgiveness brings to light what is on its way out of being. Put in another way: if what is original and omnipresent is conflict and the formation of a group depends on social conflict, then its being is always acquired and defined over against, and it can never be ecclesial. If what is original and anterior is gratuity, then ecclesiality can be called into being which is only accidentally (but no less strongly for that) critical of the surrounding reality. The former conflict-based model is au-

---

21. Often greatly to be preferred to the theology seen as vital for its underpinning!

tomatically incapable of communion. The latter, floating on forgiveness, is automatically constructive of communion.[22]

Conclusion

We started this section with the distinction between the ecclesial hypostasis and the an-ecclesial hypostasis. What I have tried to show is that in the apostolic witness the ecclesial hypostasis has a quite specific content and that this enables us to understand the nature of the an-ecclesial hypostasis in a way that goes beyond the somewhat abstract distinction made by Zizioulas that I quoted above. I would go further than this and suggest that it is in the light of this sort of understanding of the way the ecclesial hypostasis comes into being that we can begin to recover the sense of some very traditional understandings of the rites of initiation into the Church.

The catechumenate, whether before or after baptism (depending on whether the candidate is an adult or an infant), begins to introduce the candidate into the undistorting of desire and the teaching of the pacific imitation of Christ. That this is not a voluntaristic exercise is shown by the exorcisms, which unbind the candidate from belonging to the kingdom of Satan divided against itself and are properly celebrated as intrinsically related to the sense of baptism.[23] Baptism itself is then simultaneously the incorporation into the Church and the forgiveness of sin, because incorporation into the Church and forgiveness of sin are the same reality: induction into eternal life.

The very entry of a person into the beginnings of the ecclesial hypostasis is the unbinding of the an-ecclesial hypostasis. Hence the rite of baptism is also an anticipation of death, and thus the end of the an-ecclesial hypostasis based on and fated to death, and the beginning of the sharing in the risen life of Christ, the ecclesial hypostasis. All this leads directly to participation in the Eucharist. Here the making present of the self-giving and forgiving victim is the presence of the gratuity that

---

22. The theological justification of Christian base communities given by L. Boff in such works as *Eclesiogênese* (Petrópolis: Vozes 1977), chap. 3, "A comunidade eclesial de base é Igreja ou só possui elementos eclesiais?" 21–37, or, more recently, "CEBs: Que significa novo modo de toda a Igreja ser?" *Revista Eclesiástica Brasileira* 49, no. 195 (1989): 546–62, and his use of the model he has created as radically critical of the ecclesiastical "status quo" is not so much creative of a new way of being Church as perilously close to being simply destructive of the possibility of ecclesial hypostasis. Thank heavens the reality is bigger and better than the theory! For views of the ecclesiality of CEBs which avoid this trap see M. Azevedo, S.J., *Comunidades eclesiais de base e inculturação da fé* (São Paulo: Loyola, 1986), or A. Barreiro, S.J., "Raízes da consciência eclesial das CEBs," in *Convergência* 17, no. 158 (1982): 602–9.

23. See the comments on Luke 11 above, p. 159.

maintains, floating in being, the new hypostasis, enabling the neophyte to participate actively in the construction of the new creation.   ⁴

There is no need, then, to decry the traditional insistence that baptism removes original sin. If original sin is to be understood as being locked into the an-ecclesial hypostasis, then, by introducing a person into the ecclesial hypostasis — even as an infant who has yet to acquire active involvement in the overcoming of distorted desire (and must, above all, not be scandalized, or simply left to grow up in the world of desires distorted into *skandala*) — baptism does precisely remove original sin! The possibility of undistorted desire has begun to come about. It therefore makes perfect sense that there can be a baptism of desire: it is not only that a person may implicitly desire *baptism*. The baptism of desire consists in the first motions of grace-inspired overcoming of desire that is locked in scandal, whatever the explicit circumstances. That is already the beginning of the ecclesial hypostasis, already implicitly related to the self-giving of the one foundational victim whose creative desire overcomes all desire locked in futility. The universal christoformity of grace is never without its content: the bringing into being of the ecclesial hypostasis, the house on the rock!

Chapter 7

The Trinity, Creation, and Original Sin

I suggested in chapter 3 that the Christian understanding of creation was able to come into being to the degree in which Christ's death and resurrection removed the last traces of divine involvement in the maintenance of the order of this world.[1] While the perception of God was to some extent marked by hints of God's complicity in the mechanism by which humans maintain social order, then the notion of creation itself remained to some extent tied to a suppression of preexistent chaos. The perception of God as the self-giving human victim in the midst of violent human chaos permits the demythologization of God, the separation from involvement in violence and the creative self-manifestation of God as original gratuity.

I also suggested that the doctrine of the Trinity and the doctrine of original sin are mutually interrelated in exactly the same way. The New Testament bears witness to the way in which, as the understanding of God is separated from complicity in human violence, it becomes possible to understand the divine paternity of self-giving revealed in the life, death, and resurrection of the Son. Simultaneously there is understood the "other paternity" of those who do not know the Father because they are involved in casting out and killing. That is to say, there is an internal coherence of mutual implication in the coming into being of the two doctrines. The revealing of the Trinity is both the making clear who God really is, breaking through distorted notions of God, and the making clear the mechanisms which produce the distorted perception of God, thus making clear who humans are. It is the being locked in these latter mechanisms that is the content of original sin.

I would here like to suggest that the bringing into being of the ecclesial hypostasis, which we saw in the last section, the making manifest of the Father, and the discovery of the real sense of God as Creator

---

1. I would like to express my debt to J. Milbank's article "The Second Difference: For a Trinitarianism without Reserve," *Modern Theology* 2, no. 3 (1986): 213–34.

are essentially the same thing, and that the investigation of this essential identity will enable us to fill out the shape of what is meant by original sin by exploring the nature of the un-filial and the a-creatural dimensions of the an-ecclesial hypostasis.

A Johannine Witness[2]

The key passage here is Jesus' discourse in John's Gospel starting at chapter 14. I suggest here that in Jesus' discourse we have both Jesus' own awareness of his filiation from the beginning and his understanding that what he is about to do is to create the possibility of filiation for his disciples. The explanation of what Jesus is about in John 14 is not merely a revelation of eternal truths about the Father; it is Jesus' creative bringing into being of the possibility of the Paternity of the Father as something lived out by other humans than Jesus alone. So the disciples are told not to be troubled by the thought of Jesus' impending betrayal and death. Belief in the God who is without death and Jesus who is able to live toward death utterly unmoved by it should permit them to discover a new spaciousness in the Father. There is nothing in the Father that is determined by the monotony of necessity, the fruit of death, so there are many rooms in his house. John is letting us know that before his death Jesus was able to imagine creative diversity in God. That is, God is not something simply beyond death, a monotonous concept which is simply the inverse of the concept that it overcomes. Rather Jesus is able creatively to imagine God as in no way having anything to do with death, and hence as quite removed from monotony and univocity of concept.

Then we are told that Jesus goes to prepare a place for the disciples. A certain naïve reading sees this as Jesus going to open up heaven for the disciples after they die. I would suggest, however, that it is much more coherent to read this taking into account the special Johannine understanding of "I go," which is that Jesus' self-giving up to death is his going to the Father and is simultaneously what "prepares a place" for the disciples. That is to say, Jesus understands his self-giving up to death as the creative opening up of the possibility of divine paternity for the disciples. Thus, when Jesus goes to create the possibility of divine paternity, he will come again (through the Holy Spirit) and "take you to myself, that where I am you may be also" (John 14:3). That is to say, his presence after his self-giving works as bringing about the creation

---

2. I suggest the reader read these pages with John 14–16 at hand. See also chap. 3 of my *Raising Abel: The Recovery of the Eschatological Imagination* (New York: Crossroad, 1996).

of God's paternity in the disciples, which is the same as the bringing about their filiation: enabling the disciples to become children of God (see John 1:12).

To the request, then, of the way Jesus is going, he replies that he is the way, the truth, and the life, not in some abstract or mystical sense but in the sense that what he is bringing about (through the self-giving up to death which is about to take place) is the creative act of making possible the living out of God's paternity in the midst of human life: the way. Hence the reply to Philip's question "show us the Father." Jesus' reply that the Father is in him and he in the Father goes further than merely indicating that by watching him the disciples can see revealed, as by a reflection, who the Father is. It clearly does mean that, but to stay there is to ignore the creative element which Jesus is bringing about. This is indicated by Jesus' insistence on the works of his Father.

A certain traditional exegesis of these works sees them as the miracles or signs which Jesus produced validating his claims: these would be witnesses to his claim in a more or less straightforward apologetic sense. It would be more profitable, however, to interpret these within the context which John himself gives. This can be seen from Jesus' reply to those who objected to his working on the Sabbath in John 5:17: "But Jesus answered them, 'My Father is working still, and I am working.'" That is to say, the Father, in Jesus, is bringing about the continuation and fulfillment of creation itself. The sabbath for John is the symbol of interrupted creation which locks its observers in an inability to participate further in the works of the Father. Jesus' response to Philip in 14:9–11 then indicates that in him the Father is continuing and bringing about the definitive work of creation. Those who cannot believe Jesus about the complete mutual involvement of himself and the Father should look to see what sort of thing he is bringing about: only the Father could conceivably be at work in Jesus' opening up the possibility for creation to continue where it had been snarled up.

However, and this is the important element, it is not Jesus and the Father all by themselves who are bringing about the possibility of the fruition of creation, as it were by some sort of extrinsic divine fiat. What Jesus is creatively bringing into being is the human possibility of humans themselves becoming sharers in the bringing to fruition of creation. Thus, when Jesus says, "Truly, truly, I say to you, he who believes in me will also do the works that I do; and greater works than these will he do, because I go to the Father" (John 14:12), he is indicating that his going to the Father (i.e., his self-giving up to death) is creative of the possibility of those believing in him (and thus believing through him in the nondefinitive nature of death, and in the deathless nature of God) themselves becoming creative participants in creation. They will bring creation to fruition just as Jesus himself does, and they will be able to be more creative than he. The phrase "because I go to the Father" need not be interpreted in the negative sense of "because I will not be here myself to do greater works," a sense which is put into doubt by Jesus' claim that he will come back anyhow, taking the disciples to himself. Rather it must be interpreted in this sense: "*thanks* to the fact of my self-giving up to death *you* will be able to enter in ways as yet unheard of into the deathless creation which I and my Father are bringing about."

Jesus then indicates that when the disciples ask for something in his name, he will do it so that the Father may be glorified in the Son. That is to say, the disciples, as they come to dwell in the person of the Son, will be able actively to participate in the bringing into being in the world of the paternity of the Father. Jesus then goes on to explain how they are to come to dwell in his person and bring about the paternity of God in the world: by the loving obedience of his commandments. These commandments are shortly to be demonstrated as being brought together in one single commandment: the imitation of Jesus' self-giving love (John 15:12). By the Father sending the Holy Spirit, Jesus himself will come to the disciples, and they will see him. The world will not see him. From the world's point of view, his going to the Father is simply his death, and thus disappearance. The disciples will see him not owing to some ghostly, external appearances to them, but much more richly: because he lives, they will live also. That is to say, his life will be seen in their capacity to live beyond (rather than live toward, i.e., moved by) death. It is by their coming to live beyond death (which is the same as their learning to live lives of self-giving toward, but unmoved by, death) that they will know the complete mutual implication of the Son and the Father, because they will themselves be caught up in the making real and visible of that mutual implication.

This is the sense then in which Jesus will manifest himself to his disciples (John 14:21–22). It is important that *emphanizô* here is not "reveal," in the sense of draw open a veil on a previously hidden reality, but manifest in the sense of a creative making present. By the disciples' loving imitation of Jesus' self-giving, they will creatively make present Jesus' sonship, and thus the divine paternity, in the world which does not know it. Here John engages in an extraordinary repetition of the word *moné,* dwelling, which had appeared before in verse 2, in a way which is completely in line with the "de-celestialization" of this passage and its interpretation as opening up human creation of filiation, and thus of paternity, in the world. Where in 14:2 Jesus had announced that in his Father's house there are many *monai,* mansions, here we are told that it is by a person's loving imitation of Jesus' self-giving that the Father will turn this person into a *moné,* where it is the Father and Jesus who dwell in the person who is creating divine paternity and filiation, and not alone the man who moves to a divine dwelling. So the Father's house now appears clearly to consist in the creation of many dwellings among human beings.

This brings out the sense in which the *Paraklétos* who will come will be sent in Jesus' name (John 14:7). That is, he will bring into creative presence the person of Jesus through the loving imitation of his disciples. It is not that the Holy Spirit is simply a substitute presence, acting instead of Jesus, but rather it is by Jesus going to his death (and, by giving up his Spirit, bringing to completion his creative work: *tetelestai,* "it is accomplished," 19:30) that all Jesus' creative activity will be made alive in the creative activity of his disciples. The memory of Jesus here ("he will bring to your remembrance") is thus not in the first place the cure for the absence of the teacher, but the bringing to mind, and thus to the possibility of creative practice in dependence on Jesus, of Jesus' creative activity. This is the sense of the peace which Jesus leaves with his disciples: not the peace which is the result of the suppression of conflict or the resolution of conflict, such as is practiced by the mechanism of expulsion of the world, but the creative peace that brings into being: the primordial peace of the Creator from the beginning.

The sense then in which the disciples, if they loved Jesus, should rejoice that he goes to the Father, because the Father is greater than he, is not that if one loves someone one should be happy for that person if that person is going to something far bigger and better. Rather the sense is derived from 14:12, and the way in which because Jesus goes to the Father the disciples will be able to do greater works than he. Jesus' going to the Father (his creative self-giving, "foundational" of a new humanity) is a creative act of aggrandizement of the Father, conducted without any rivalry; and permitting the disciples themselves to become involved in just such creative aggrandizement. The synoptic hallowing of the Father's name or the Johannine glorification of the Father in the Son is precisely the nonrivalistic creation of humans making present God's paternity ever more widely. The phrase "for the Father is greater than I" (John 14:28), which was to cause so much trouble in the subordinationist controversies,[3] is much better understood as indicative of how

---

3. In the fourth century the Church was wracked by a series of controversies, which have become linked with the Alexandrian priest Arius, surrounding the relation between the Father and the Son. The so-called subordinationist position is one which is unable to accept the divine equality (consubstantiality) of the Father and the Son, seeking to maintain a monotheism unnuanced by a divine christology. To counter this the Councils of

undistorted mimetic desire both affirms the uniqueness of Jesus' Sonship and at the same time ensures that that uniqueness is not exclusive, but constantly and creatively brings about an ever wider process of creative filiation.

Jesus concludes by explaining to his disciples that he has told them all about the real sense of his going to the Father before it happens so that when it does take place, they may believe (John 14:29). At one level this can be read as merely saying: "I've told you this so that when my prophecy is fulfilled, you won't be caught by surprise, but will believe that what I was saying was true all along." However, that is seriously to underestimate the force of the words. For the purpose of the going to the Father (the self-giving "foundational" act) is precisely to create belief.

For John, Jesus' creative self-giving and bringing into being the ecclesial hypostasis is a making possible the manifestation of who the Father really is and the Son as the "foundational" possibility of participating in the deathless life of both of them. That is to say, belief is a gnoseological discovery which is simultaneously a participation in life. It is not such as a simple acquisition of truths, but as an expanding possession of the believer by the Father and the Son creating eternal life in the midst of this world through the creation of an imitative adhesion by the believer to the word and self-giving of Jesus. This can be seen from the importance John attributes to belief in other contexts. In John 6:40 and 47 Jesus solemnly assures those to whom he is talking that it is the will of the Father that "every one who sees the Son and believes in him should have eternal life" and that "he who believes has eternal life." In 11:25–26 he assures Martha that "I am the resurrection and the life; he who believes in me, though he die, yet shall he live, and whoever lives and believes in me shall never die." That this is absolutely central to John's whole understanding is restated when, in what exegetes take to be the last verse of the original Gospel (20:31), he explains that the reason for writing is "that you may believe that Jesus is the Christ, the Son of God, and that believing you may have life in his name."

In this we can see that belief plays a rôle for John that is ultimately identical with that of justifying faith in Paul. It is the access to the truth of God-beyond-death made manifest in the self-giving of Jesus, and this access it is which permits the reordering of the whole of a person's life so that it is no longer bound in by the parameters of death. So when Jesus says "now I have told you before it takes place, so that when it does take place, you may believe" (John 14:29), he is explaining the

---

Nicaea (325) and Constantinople (381) forged the classic expressions of the Christian faith in trinitarian monotheism, which is to be found in the Creeds they published.

whole purpose of his discourse: he has been outlining to his disciples the
creative sense which he is giving to his forthcoming death. The creative
sense is that he is bringing into being the possibility of a belief. This belief is in itself a creative, expansive thing, since, as the disciples believe
and are thus enabled to live without reference to death, by engaging in a
creative imitation of Jesus' self-giving, so the Father and the Son dwell in
them, turning them into manifestations of themselves (and their deathless nature) which are in turn (by the creative witness, or *marturia* of
the disciples) further creative bringings into being of belief. This is the
profound sense in which Jesus' going to the Father, his bringing into being the ecclesial hypostasis, is exactly the bringing into being of a belief.
The ecclesial hypostasis is what belief looks like as lived out in creative
imitation of Jesus' self-giving.

When Jesus then says that the ruler of the world is coming but has
no power over him, this is to repeat what we now know: that Jesus has
nothing to do with death. He goes through it so that the world may
know that there is a love which structures life and which is in no way
bound by or related to death. That is, once again, he goes in order to
create belief. Belief is the hypnotic draw into the security of imitation.
By it we are empowered ourselves to act as if death were not and so
to create life stories which have no end and which are not affected by
the judgment of this world with its story line etched in the monotony of
rivalry and death.

In John 15 and 16 we have the same reality explained further. I
indicated in chapter 6 the Johannine reading of the true vine as the explanation of the bringing into being of the ecclesial hypostasis. Jesus is
going to his death, which is to bring into being an ecclesial hypostasis
where alone growth is possible and always in dependence on the initial self-giving of the victim. There is in fact nothing static about the
image, for what it is designed to produce is exactly creative imitation
in the disciples, which is what obedience to the command to love one
another consists in. Having explained the creative bringing into being of
the ecclesial hypostasis as something which is to be continued, Jesus then
indicates (15:18–27) the sort of resistance that the world will oppose to
the ecclesial hypostasis which is coming into being. The problem with
the world is that it does not know the Father: that is to say, it is still
stuck within the parameters of a life which runs from death to death.
Those who are involved in pointing out and persecuting human victims
are by that very fact ignorant of the Father, knowing whom removes the
necessity of any involvement in being moved by and producing death.

So here we find set out with very great clarity the countersign to the
ecclesial hypostasis which Jesus is bringing into being: the involvement

in persecution and victimization by which the world maintains its order is the same as not knowing the Father. That is, it is the inverse of the bringing about of divine paternity in the world. The link between this passage and John 8:39–47 is clear: what is being described is the nature of those who are sons of the father of lies who was a murderer from the beginning. Jesus is also clear that his bringing into being the ecclesial hypostasis, and therefore the fulfillment of creation, is not merely something which happens in the midst of neutrality. The bringing into being of the ecclesial hypostasis by Jesus is precisely what identifies sin as sin and, identifying it, provokes resistance and hatred. There are only two possible modes of desire in John: hatred and love. Love, as we have seen, is the pacific imitative self-giving toward death which is creative of life. Hatred is the rivalistic distorted desire which ties a person ever more furiously into persecution, death, and murder "without cause." The one is the mode of desire proper to the Father; the other is the mode of desire proper to the world.

In John 15:24 Jesus says: "If I had not done among them the works which no one else did, they would not have sin; but now they have seen and hated both me and my Father." That is to say, Jesus has, by his works, unblocked the way in which creation was locked into being unfinished. It is the bringing into being of the ecclesial hypostasis as the fulfillment of creation which enables it to be possible to talk about sin. As the ecclesial hypostasis is brought into being, so sin is perceived in the aversion to the ecclesial hypostasis which is constitutive of the an-ecclesial hypostasis. Here we have a complicating factor in our understanding of original sin: ignorance of the Father is not merely overcome by correct information. The ignorance of the Father is inseparable from an aversion to the Father, an aversion whose content is that the bringing into being of the ecclesial hypostasis is an intolerable threat to the petty security held locked in place by death.[4] It is to this element of

---

4. The Johannine duality of desire corresponds exactly with the mimetic theory of desire put forward by Girard: for it is the revelation of the truth about desire that is the ultimate *skandalon* to desire itself. There is nothing "natural" in the movement from rivalistic desire to nonrivalistic desire, as though they were two comparatively equal possibilities. The nature of rivalistic desire is that it is constantly self-exacerbating toward death. The mere demonstration of another possibility of desire is taken not as a gratuitous offer to be different, but as a further obstacle to desire on the same level as itself. Thus it must be hated and expelled and hated and expelled even more than other obstacles, because of all obstacles this one reveals that its truth is death and that all its fury and exacerbation in trying to found and bring about identity are futility. This element of aversion as part of original sin is an unalienable part of the Church's teaching. For anyone who understands that there is no natural ability to pass from rivalistic to nonrivalistic desire because of the way rivalistic desire automatically locks itself into itself and interprets all alterity within terms of itself, there will never be the slightest danger of Pelagianism. It is all too clear that only a gratuitous irruption of something quite outside the world of

aversion that Jesus refers when he warns his disciples of the circumstances within which it will befall them to bring into being the ecclesial hypostasis (John 16:1–4).

It now becomes possible to look at the way Jesus talks of the Holy Spirit in a somewhat richer light. Jesus' going to the Father is what enables him to send the Spirit from the Father. Here, somewhat against the apologetic bad conscience fashionable among Catholic writers with relation to the Orthodox, it seems to me that Jesus is actively engaged in the bringing about of the reality of the Spirit in the midst of humankind. Just as his going to the Father involves the huge creative imagination of the possibility of bringing about a new mode of humanity which is the bringing into being of the fulfillment of creation, so it is in doing this that he brings into being from the Father the possibility of human practice being possessed by the Holy Spirit. Since this sounds like a bizarre heresy, I had better explain more fully. By making of his going to his victimary death a creative and deliberate act Jesus is bringing into being a certain visible and contingent practice which is a creation in the obvious human sense of a work of art, something never before imagined or brought into being by any human interpretative and imaginative conception. The creative fulfillment of the Father's creation is not the sudden bringing into being of some abstract and general universal which annuls the contingent telling of the human story. It is a creative bringing into being of a particular and contingent practice which is itself to be the constant possibility of the untelling of the human story and the making of the human story bear the weight of creatively reflecting the Father's creation.

In bringing into being, then, this contingent practice, Jesus was literally creating the possible historical terms of reference by which the Holy Spirit could become a historical reality, and it is thus he who sends the Holy Spirit from the Father. In his going to the Father he has brought about the historical possibility in contingent, linguistic, practical, institutional terms which make it possible for the Father to send the Holy Spirit. The ecclesial hypostasis is the creative living out of the historical practice inaugurated by Jesus' going to the Father: that is, the ecclesial hypostasis is the visibility of the Son's sending of the Holy Spirit. Thus

---

desires formed in rivalistic mimesis can begin to produce the change: the movement from rivalistic to pacific mimesis is miraculous in the strict sense. This is not to make of the incommensurability of the two modes of desire an insuperable dialectical opposition. From rivalistic mimetic desire there is no natural move to pacific mimetic desire: in this sense Nygren is right to show an absolute rupture between Eros and Agapé. However, where the dialectic imagination is wrong is in the inability to imagine that the gratuity of the gratuitous irruption is such that it unlocks rivalistic desire from within, turning it into the pacific desire that it could never be of itself: grace perfecting nature.

the Holy Spirit is the constant keeping alive of the practice inaugurated
by the Son. The Spirit is the Spirit of Truth bringing into being original
creation, whose presence in this world takes the form of an advocate un-
covering the lies of the world and defending the children of God who are
being brought into being from the persecutions of the Accuser, the liar
from the beginning. So the Spirit keeps alive the historical practice inaugurated by the Son, turning that practice into the paradigm by which sin,
righteousness, and judgment are to be understood. Sin is being locked
into aversion to the possibility of the belief which Jesus is bringing into
being: aversion to being drawn into a self-giving living out of desire
made possible by Jesus' having creatively forged a human living unaffected by death. Righteousness is the love which brings into being by
creative self-giving up to death because it is not moved by death. Judgment is the way in which this self-giving death reveals and thus brings to
an end the lie of the necessity of victimary death which is the governing
principle of this world.

The Spirit, then, will make it possible for this paradigm to become
creative of truth. It makes constantly visible and keeps in practice the
creative possibilities inaugurated by the Son's self-giving to death. It does
this in such a way that we are always able to find our way forward from
being children of the homicidal lie to being children of the Father. It
is important that this being guided into truth be understood not to be
an essentially negative thing, as though what is daring and creative is
our involvement in the world and what the Holy Spirit has come to
do is guide us back to our real origins and so permit us to be what we
really are — the model of the return to the womb.[5] The understanding at
work here is exactly the reverse: our being guided into truth is our being
opened into creative imitative use of the paradigm brought into being
by the Son: it is truth that is a daring dynamic reflection of God that
is being brought into being. Compared to this, all the apparent creative
darings of the world are so many stillbirths.

This, I suggest, enables us to understand something of the image of
the woman in travail which we find in John 16:20–24. Jesus' going to
his death of course produces sorrow for the disciples and joy for the
world. However, what Jesus is bringing about in his going to his death
is like a woman in travail. In fact his going to his death is the constitutive labor pain by which creation is able to bring forth the children of
God which had not been able to come to light while creation was under
the order of "this world." Jesus, the Son, is the human being who has

---

5. See Nicodemus's misunderstanding of being born *anôthen* and Jesus' correction,
"opening out" the understanding of the way the Spirit brings to birth (John 3:3–8).

always been coming into being, and now he really will come into being, through these labor pains, in the creative lives of the disciples who will manifest him. This is why they will ask nothing of him in that day, but will ask the Father in his name, because in that day they will *be* the son, the person of the son will have been brought to birth in them, and thus they can and will ask the Father directly. The joy which has been Jesus' from the beginning will be theirs, because it is the joy of being the son, and is an unalienable part of the sonship which has been brought to creative fruition in them.

It is not fanciful to suggest that here the Johannine understanding of the nature of the hypostasis brought into being by Jesus and the Pauline understanding evidenced in Romans 8:18–30 are identical. There too we have creation subjected to futility (v. 20). Paul understands it to have been bound to decay (that is, to death) by God (a reference to God's decree in Genesis that Adam and Eve, having done what they have done, must not be allowed to eat of the tree of life and so perpetuate their life in "fallen" mode forever).[6] However, this was done by God so that he could bring about, in time, a process by which the original promise of life could be brought about after all (v. 21). The sufferings of this present time (the persecutions and rejections to which Paul's audience is liable) are the groanings in travail of creation (v. 22) that, through them, will bring into being the authentic sons of creation: "the glorious liberty of the children of God." The first fruits of the Spirit lead us precisely into the active (and painful) living out of Jesus' self-giving practice (v. 23), by which practice "we wait for adoption as sons, the redemption of our bodies." Paul then goes on to indicate more fully the rôle of the Spirit, which is the power at work in the bringing to light the sons who are the culmination of creation. The Spirit's rôle as intercessor (v. 26) is exactly the same as John's understanding of it as defense counsel, or pleader for the defense, and the living out it makes possible is also the bringing into being of the many brethren of the firstborn Son (v. 29). The whole process is part of the original calling into being of sons predestined with and in the Son, and the whole process is indefectible (v. 30).

We have then two powerful sections of the apostolic witness to indicate the nature of the ecclesial hypostasis which is being brought into being. Both show that the bringing into being the of ecclesial hypostasis is identical with the bringing to fulfillment of creation: that is, the ecclesial hypostasis is the real sense of creation, which was ordered toward

---

6. The Catholic Doctors differ as to whether the one who subjected creation was God or Adam. In the light of my previous remarks on Pauline anthropology it would not seem to matter (and the ambiguity may well be deliberate). What does matter is the recognition of the temporary frustration of creation.

it. Both show that this process is trinitarian: the Father brings into being the life of sons through the Son by the spirit of the Son being made an active visible living out in the midst of the world.

The Structure of Jesus' Creative Imagination

At this stage of our analysis there seems no way of getting around a particular feature of the Johannine witness. This is John's sense of marvel at the extraordinary nature of Jesus' creative imagination. It is not merely that John puts into Jesus' mouth certain utterances of extraordinary boldness concerning his preexistence and so forth. What is more remarkable is that John depicts the structure of God's creative process as the human creative imagination of Jesus. In the three chapters of the Gospel on which I have just commented John paints out the humanly unimaginable: the creative content of an imagination that is in no way touched by death, how it is possible for a human imagination that is in no way marked by death to bring into being what amounts to the most prodigious human invention ever, the human structure by which what had appeared to be human nature is revealed, changed, and empowered to become something different.

Those who protest at the Johannine divine utterances concerning preexistence and unicity with the Father do not protest enough. Such phrases in themselves are positively innocuous compared to the grandeur of John's comprehension lying behind them. Those who protest are perhaps locked unwittingly into the sort of Docetism or Monophysitism[7] which they seek to denounce in these phrases, because they do not perceive that the real boldness of John's conception is that all this divinity was made present as a human creative imagination. John was convinced of nothing less than that the Son of God walked this earth with all the creative power and freedom of God as human creative power and freedom and made this creative power and freedom available through the human imagining into being of a way out of the systematic dead-end into which humans had locked the creative power and freedom which should have been ours.

---

7. Docetism is the name given to the view of some early Christians that Jesus was indeed God but only appeared to be human, so that his life, suffering, and death were only apparent and not real. This position is a recurrent temptation among some modern Christians who talk of Jesus as a sort of celestial magician. Monophysitism, or the doctrine that Jesus had only one nature, a divine one, and not two natures, a divine one and a human one which were in no sort of rivalry (the Church's teaching), is a subtler form of the same temptation as Docetism: that is, to say that "Jesus was human, but, above all, he was God." This suggests that the divinity needs to be saved or hedged off from the humanity as if there were some sort of rivalry between the two. The Catholic and Orthodox teaching is that Jesus is God *as* man.

The original man, then, with creative imagination intact because in no way shaded into futility by any sort of involvement with death, came among us and imagined into being the unleashing of the extraordinary possibility of our being allowed actively to share in that creative imagination and practice, bringing about our free creative movement into what we were originally to be. For John, however, the matter is not simply left at that: the depiction of the original man. John gives us a clear picture of the structure of the identity of that original man in his positive depiction of the workings of the trinitarian image. This depiction is the exact inverse of the understanding of rivalistic mimetic desire that we have seen Girard set out in his description of the way imitative rivalistic desire leads to victimization.

Thus we have, in John 5:17, the content of Jesus' equality with God: "My Father is working still, and I am working." Not only is God his Father, but God continues his creation on the Sabbath, and Jesus likewise. However, Jesus' identity as Son is in no way grasped or held independently of the Father (v. 19): "The Son can do nothing of his own accord, but only what he sees the Father doing; for whatever he does, that the Son does likewise." Jesus' identity is entirely dependent on that of the Father and is brought into being as a human in a quite specific way: the perfect imitation by the Son of the Father. In the original man, because there is no rivalry between Father and Son, the love between Father and Son is not worked out in blindness and shadow, but the Father is able to show clearly to the Son what the Father is doing. That is to say, the Father's creative expansion is able to flow directly into the Son's creative imagination such the Son can bring that expansion into being in the midst of humanity. Thus Jesus is able to understand how the completely deathless nature of the Father, who raises the dead and gives them life, will enable him himself to make available life to whom he will through his creative going to death to bring into being the visible living out of human life-beyond-death. Thus Jesus is working with complete creative freedom in bringing about life "to whom he will."

Jesus is perfectly clear that he is in absolute dependence on the Father: there could be no clearer indication of an interdividual psychology than this. The Other, the Father, is absolutely constitutive of who he is. Yet, because there is no appropriation of identity over against the Other who forms him, the complete dependence on the Other rather than being a limitation or a source of diminishment is exactly what enables the creative flow of life bringing about life to be made manifest and, being made manifest, to be made actual. Hence the completely mimetic understanding of testimony and reputation (or glory) in chapter 5. The testimony to Jesus is that the works he does are works that only the Father can do. He does not in any sense claim these as his own works, meaning that he gives testimony to himself. His own un-interrupted participation in the bringing into being of the fulfillment of creation, something only the Father can do of himself, is testimony that the Father is at work. Thus the Father, by doing the works through Jesus' active working, is bearing witness to Jesus. Only a nonrivalistic mimesis of creative dependence can account for the Johannine argument about testimony. If this were not proof enough, then its inverse is shown: Jesus' interlocutors are unable to believe because they receive glory from one another and do not seek the glory that comes from God. That is to say, because they are locked into the rivalistic mimetic bringing into be-ing of their identities they are unable to have their identities formed by peaceful mimesis of and from God. This is the equivalent of not having life and being stuck in the realm of death: they cannot "believe," that is, be drawn into the peaceful imitation of Jesus by which they would come to find themselves drawn into having their identities creatively given by God and thus accede to life.

In John 10 we have the same understanding at work: because of Jesus' perfect imitation of the Father, he is able to make present on earth as a real human practice the way in which the Father is the shepherd of Israel. He does this precisely by the creative going to his death which brings about one flock and one shepherd. What he is doing is bringing about the Father's shepherdliness by inaugurating a real human practice of shepherding a real human gathering into one. This is possible because there is no rivalry between him and the Father: they are an entirely interpenetrating reality. So "I and the Father are one" (John 10:30) is identical in content with "the Father is in me and I am in the Father" (John 10:38). The unicity is one of mutual possession, or "indwelling," to use the term untainted by association with rivalistic interpenetration. The psychological understanding that permits such statements is exactly that adumbrated by J. M. Oughourlian when he shows how, for the tri-angular mimetic theory of desire, "the Other is consubstantial with the self's consciousness."[8]

We can go further than this in the light of our reading of John 14–16. The triangular mimetic theory of desire in its rivalistic mode (the phe-nomenologically "normal" human mode) shows how desire is always desire according to the desire of the other. Thus the disciple comes to desire an object in imitation of the desire of the model, which eventually turns model and disciple into mutual rivals. The desire flowing between

---

8. "L'Autre est consubstantiel à la conscience du moi" (J.-M. Oughourlian, *Un mime nommé désir* [Paris: Grasset, 1982], 58).

the two people involved converts the object into an obstacle, and eventually annihilates the object, either physically, so that neither possesses it, or notionally, in that it loses all being for the two as they become destructively obsessed with each other. We can now see something of the inverse structuring of that same triangular mimetic desire in the way in which the love flowing between the Father and the Son, the Holy Spirit, actually brings the object into being.

Our word "desire" is automatically suspect under these circumstances, because it is redolent of some sort of lack, some sort of *envie* (as in the French, "j'ai envie de quelque chose"). As a word it cannot easily bear the weight of what flows between Father and Son. Even the word "love" is weak from its normal associations, because of the impression of the emotional spasms which it arouses. Neither of these can begin to bear the weight of the creative power bringing into being which is the love of the Father for the Son,[9] nor the equally creative participation in that bringing into being which is the Son's exact imaging and responding to that love in self-giving. Still less is it possible to imagine that this very creative nature of the self-giving between the two, which constitutes who they are in a constant dynamic creative growth, the constant creative diversity in self-giving forever glorifying each other, is in this unique case a further coequal creative "person." The purely beneficent imitation means that the self-giving love, identical with Father and Son, is their equal. The creative diversity that the beneficent imitation holds in being means that the Holy Spirit is distinct, and distinct precisely in its creative diversity.

To have recourse again to the inverse parallel: where two different people are locked into rivalistic mimesis, they are constantly reducing what was diverse to sameness, the tragic and monotonous sameness of the ever smaller spiral that is creative of nothing at all. Where two people need not fear their sameness but are able to enjoy it, then they can produce diversity among themselves in an ever wider spiral. The distinguishing factor is the nature of the interpersonal rapport, which in one case is "daimonic," locking them ever more fatally into each other and seeming to acquire a power over their lives that is independent of either of them. In the other case, the relationship itself takes off, independently of either of them to the point where both of them are aware that their relationship is other than either of them, and is a continuous beneficent force for growth. It is not merely that both possess each other (as the other two obsess each other), but that their interpenetration is

---

9. Here the word "engendering" rather than "creating" is traditionally used.

productive of a form of possession of each of them which is not merely identical with either of them.

Here it seems to me that we have a clear analogate for the Holy Trinity, and for the sense in which the Holy Spirit both is a "person" (hypostasis or holon) and is yet not "personal" in the same sense in which the Father and the Son are "persons." The further dimension we must bring out is that the creative love between Father and Son which is automatically engendering of identical diversity, of that which is both identical with, an exact image of, and yet constantly diverse, is what is capable of bringing into being. Such constant creative identity and diversity of love can have nothing at all to do with necessity; still less could it be necessary for them to create. Their constant interpenetrative enjoyment and aggrandizement of each other in a dynamic movement that is untrammeled by a "from" and a "toward" (implying lack and fulfillment) is itself much more creative than any conceivable "creation" which they might bring into being. However, purely gratuitously they might create something to share in all their dynamic diversity, and have.

The inverse parallel may be helpful once again: rivalistic mimetic desire tends constantly to reduce three realities to two and, finally, to one. So a model designates an object for the disciple (three realities); the disciple imitates the model with relation to the object, producing rivalry from the model. Model and disciple then gradually forget the object — the object becomes either unimportant or is destroyed so that neither "has" it — as they become obsessed with each other (reduction to two realities). The more obsessed with each other they become, the more like each other they become until they become one reality (strife). The inverse of this is that the creative love (the beneficent mimesis) between two is what calls into being an object that did not exist at all for both to enjoy and which they will enable to share in their enjoyment. The beneficent mimesis is not only creative of being, but it is creative of being that is able to participate in the beneficent mimesis by itself being creative. Because there is no envy at all in beneficent mimesis, it is a constant creation of ever more active ways of participation.

Here we have, it seems to me, the structure of Jesus' creative imagination in John 14–16. Jesus is aware of having been sent by the Father. That is, his condition as a human being is the creative making present of the eternal generation of the Son. His self-giving up to death is the exact image of the creative self-giving between Father and Son which eternally brings forth the Holy Spirit. So he is aware that his living out his life toward death in obedience to the Father is exactly his sending of the Holy Spirit: the making present in the conditions of humanity of the creative love between Father and Son in such a way that it can be participated in by human beings. It is therefore his whole life, going to his death, which brings about the concrete praxis by which humans will be enabled to participate in the Holy Spirit. This means our breaking out of the negative, destructive mimesis (in its violently structured forms) in which we live and our beginning to enter into the creative construction of diversity that is a dynamic reflection of God and that is the whole point of God's expansive creativity having bothered to bring this something out of nothing in the first place.

We can make some deductions then concerning basic anthropology from this trinitarian image of humanity. The constant creative diversity of love between Father and Son has brought into being an object out of nothing, which the Father brings into being in the image of the Son, who receives himself from the Father. Creation thus receives its being gratuitously from the Father through the Son and in the Holy Spirit as the endless dynamism of creative diversity-in-identity which forms an ever richer more participatory reflection of the creative love between the two. This calling, suggesting, into being from nothing at all culminates in a being able to share in the creative love of Father and Son as active participant on a level of equality with the Father and the Son — equality, of course, as something dependent and gratuitously received. For the active participation in the life of God to be real, gratuity risked ungratuity, and at a certain stage in the historical bringing into being of this human participation, in a concrete historical act,[10] humanity took its identity as appropriated rather than simply receiving it. The possibility of doing this was open to it as an unalienable concomitant of the bringing into being of gratuitous sharing in concrete historical terms. It was not necessary that this should happen: rather necessity was born the moment being became appropriated rather than lived as a becoming held floating on gratuity.

It is this historical act of the appropriation of being which was to have been given as given which we call "originating" original sin and which produced the whole structure of the human identity we now know: tied in and structured by rivalistic mimesis and victimage, the inverse of the creative mimesis which was to bring us to become sharers in divine life. We can say therefore that the bringing into being by Jesus of the understanding of the Holy Trinity was more than the act which finally permitted the separation of the perception of God from any involvement in the violent formation of perception (the *adokimos nous*) proper to the order of the "world." The bringing into being of the understanding of the Trinity was (and is) also the making accessible

---

10. In fact in the act which constituted the possibility of "history" as we know it.

of the original dynamic participation in God which is the fruit of the beneficent mimetic bringing into being of the creator Spirit, that is to say, the original image of God of which Genesis 1:26–27[11] gives us a distant inkling. Simultaneously there is made comprehensible the internal structure of the way in which that image is lived distortedly as part of the way that distortion is overcome. That is to say, simultaneously we can begin to perceive the structure of the trinitarian image of God in humans and the structure of the a-trinitarian hypostasis which is on its way out of being and which we describe as locked in original sin.

Creativity and Creatureliness

Traditionally, works of theological anthropology by Catholic theologians begin with an explanation of human creatureliness, then move on to look at humans under the influence of sin, and conclude with humans living the life of grace.[12] That is to say, these works follow what I have called the order of logic rather than the order of discovery. Here, faithful to the drift of the whole approach I have been setting out, a genetic approach to original sin, it is the order of discovery that is being followed.[13] This is, as I hope is apparent, for a deliberate theological reason: namely, that revelation and salvation are not separable realities, but that the discovery of who God is and who we are is itself an important part of salvation, not accessible in any depth except from within the process of salvation. This is in line with the basic thrust of the whole thesis that mimetic theory enables us to overcome the separation between objective and subjective (or existential) which threatens traditional approaches and permits us to rediscover that creatureliness is not a brute "fact" independent of existential awareness. It is rather the case that the process of revelatory salvation brings about creatureliness in us. To put this another way: there is a model of understanding according to which we were and are creatures but became proud, losing contact with our creatureliness, and so must become humble (*humilis* — in touch with

---

11. "And God said, 'Let us make man in our image, after our likeness,...' " etc.

12. Thus, for example, the structure of St. Thomas's anthropology in the *Summa Theologiae*. For more recent examples, see J. I González Faus, *Proyecto de hermano: Visión creyente del hombre* (Santander: Sal Terrae, 1987), and L. Ladaria, *Antropología teológica* (Madrid: UPCM, 1987; Rome: Univ. Gregoriana, 1987).

13. This is not supposed to be a dismissal of those whose approach is systematic rather than genetic. J. I. González Faus recognizes explicitly that in this field (as opposed to that of christology) a genetic approach is simply much more difficult to elaborate for a variety of reasons (*Proyecto de hermano,* 11). Because Girard's theory is a genetic theory, to put it to work in a way other than the genetic would be to distort the theory. Of course it is part of my claim that the fecundity for Catholic theology of mimetic theory is precisely that it makes possible, or at least easier, a genetic treatment of this subject.

humus) in order to recover that creatureliness. Rather than that model, I am proposing a model by which we managed to truncate our becoming creatures, but are nevertheless being inducted, as a joyful discovery, into becoming creatures. The joyful discovery is itself part of the becoming a creature.

I set out above the Johannine perception of Jesus as the original man, the trinitarian image of God, bringing into being a new creation. I stressed the extraordinary human creative imagination that was at work there precisely as part of being the original human (i.e., not as a divine "extra"). Because the trinitarian image was intact in Jesus' human living out of his divinity, Jesus was able creatively to imagine, and thus to bring into being, the possibility of humans becoming "children of God" by his bringing into being of the ecclesial hypostasis. I also indicated that the beneficent mimesis between Father and Son, made humanly available in Jesus' inauguration of a human practice which was his sending of the Holy Spirit from his Father, is by its nature expansive. When this expansion became, quite gratuitously, creative, part of its nature as gratuitously creative was to bring into being that which is able to share actively, and from dependent equality, in the expansive nature of divine life. In the case of created reality, this means humans bringing the whole of creation into creative participation in the life of God.

From this it is quite apparent that what we are now is a truncated form of creature, for sharing in the divine creativity is an inalienable part of what it means to be a creature. Yet our participation in God's creative process is something we can scarcely imagine, because our creativity and our creative imaginations are formed by exactly the same death-oriented parameters of distorted desire which cause us to regard putting to death as necessary for bringing forth or maintaining life. We are unable creatively to imagine, and thus bring into being, human participation in a deathless sociality. Jesus' creative imagining into being of a deathless creative sociality (the ecclesial hypostasis) revealed what we can become by ourselves being empowered, through our pacific, creative imitation of him (being the branches of the vine, bringing forth fruit). That is, it revealed that the true content of our discovery of our dependent creatureliness is our dependent (but utterly expansive) creativity. Jesus' creative imagining into being of the ecclesial hypostasis also, simultaneously, revealed our failure to be creatures in the failure of our creative imaginations and the failure of the things we do manage to create to be part of a deathless sociality.[14] That is, the revelation and

---

14. As well, of course, as our "destroying the earth" (Rev. 11:18).

making possible of our creative creatureliness also revealed the failure of creatureliness which we do in fact live out.

Seen in terms of mimetic desire this means that by the same act by which humans appropriate being, or identity, it is not so much that we become "creatures (objective) with distorted desire (subjective)," but that we settled for being un-creatures, incapable of participating in creativity which is the heart of human creatureliness. Either creatureliness is truncated by distorted desire's reduction of the object to a function of rivalry, or creatureliness is brought into being by the way beneficent mimesis brings into being "subject-objects" — interdividual hypostases — that which is capable of active sharing in divine glory.

This is not, of course, to dismiss all past and present human creativity as something intrinsically rotten. It is to suggest that all human creativity is shot through with vanity. This is the insight which J.-L. Marion brings out in his essay "The Reverse of Vanity."[15] Earlier in *God without Being* he analyzed the relationship between the idol and the icon in a way which is exactly compatible with the understanding of desire that I have set forth in my comparison between beneficent creative mimetic desire and rivalistic reductive mimetic desire. In this later essay he shows how the understanding of the vanity of things itself becomes possible only as a failed reaching-out for the true perspective on things. If there were no perception that what we can see could be seen differently (as imagined into being by God), then there would not be the sense of vanity. The sense of the vanity of things is itself testimony to a possibly different perception, but one which we can somehow never make. The moment of the perception of vanity is thus a negative bearing witness to another possibility, but the moment of the perception of vanity is itself a moment incapable of being sustained into the perception of things as created, because that moment collapses in vanity. It is this insight which enables Marion to interpret Paul's famous remarks about natural knowledge of creation in Romans 1 in a way which takes us right outside the rationalist and apologetic interpretation which culminated in Vatican I's *Dei Filius*:

> Vanity first becomes the vanity of the idol, and of the first of idols — that is thought, which refuses to glorify: the world, under certain conditions could glimpse its exterior (invisible distance to be traversed), but if it does not accomplish this excess where it is itself exceeded, its thoughts vanish immediately, because of their own vanity. Saint Paul formulates this precisely: "The invisible things of God, since [and by the fact of] the creation of the world, can, starting from on high, be seen in the mode

---

15. J.-L. Marion, *God without Being* (Chicago: University of Chicago Press, 1991), chap. 4, 108–38.

of spirit, in the works [as works done], and also the eternal power and divinity of God; such that they, men, cannot plead their cause, since having known God, they did not glorify him as God, nor did they render him thanks, on the contrary [and consequently] they went up in smoke by their thought, and their unintelligent heart was darkened. Pretending to be wise, they became fools — were distracted" (Rom. 1:20–22). What we translate by "went up in smoke," the Latin *evanuerunt* chosen by Saint Jerome, exactly renders *hebbel*: to fly off and dissipate like smoke or steam under an overly strong breath of spirit; the original Greek *emataiôthésan*, itself corresponds directly to the other equivalent of *hebbel* from the biblical Greek (in the Septuagint), *mataios;* therefore one could also translate, without contradiction, by "were struck with vanity, and with caduke insignificance." The distraction of men therefore comes from a situation that is as untenable as it is common: their thoughts are viewed by the invisible gaze of God, who sees them as creatures, and offers himself to be recognized as Creator — to be glorified as God. Instead of responding to this silent injunction by "making use of the world *as* not making use of it," men deny, by thoughts that are idolatrous and bent back upon themselves as invisible mirrors, the distance where the world is set in motion as creation. Creation not recognized as such, immediately finds itself struck with vanity, and thoughts, with distraction.[16]

To put this in another way: all human creative imagination and practice is capable of bearing creative witness to the glory of God, and this glory of God can even be perceived in the moment between the hint of givenness that is everywhere surrounding us and holding us up and our distortion of that givenness into appropriation, and thus futility. What we can perceive in and from creation (the world as we find it) is both subjected to futility (or vanity) and yet groaning in travail. There is present both God's dynamic creative gratuity bringing into being and the futile appropriative reduction into vanity, the order of this world. There is always, everywhere, possible, on the interface between these two desires, the perception of and the participation in, the glory of God. Yet the interface itself becomes, rather than a source of hope, a source of melancholy and boredom. Just as rivalistic desire is locked into aversion at the bringing into being of the ecclesial hypostasis, so it is locked into a resentful boredom at the possibility of creative bringing into being: both the aversion and the boredom give witness, a witness which can never be acted upon, to the presence of the other, the beneficent mimetic transcendence. The melancholy and boredom of vanity are part of the living out of the un-creaturely hypostasis, locked in original sin.

I will attempt to show in the next chapter why it is that this vision

---

16. Marion, *God without Being*, 129–30. I have reverted to the traditional spelling of God to avoid multiplying explanations.

must not be taken automatically as dismissing all human creativity as we know it. The world we know is a world where the truncated futility of human creativity is being made capable of producing signs that do reflect God, as well as still producing idols which reflect only our distorted desires. For the moment, it is to an examination of the ecclesial hypostasis as the bringing into being of creative creatureliness that I now turn.

Ecclesiality as Participation in Creation

In a penetrating essay entitled "Le mal, énigme du bien" Christian Duquoc raises a question never sufficiently grasped by traditional apologetic approaches to the question of evil.[17] These remain within a theodicy made inevitable by an understanding of salvation which sees evil as a (retributory) consequence of sin. The question raised by Duquoc is that of evil as being produced not by sin, but by "good." It is the bringing into being of *good* that is so often the cause of the worst evils. So, for instance, well-intentioned development agencies actually bring about, in exactly the degree to which they produce some partially successful projects, a series of evils as direct offspring of their success. In their attempts to establish the "new Jerusalem," or bring about a reform of morals, or whatever, the crusading good always manage to produce a direct backwash of rejected, destroyed people, outsiders and excluded. Duquoc is asking the question about the ambiguity of good. If doing and aiming at good itself is ambiguous, then this obliges us to detach God from any apologetic notion whereby God "permits" evil to bring about good. Duquoc follows his insight into the New Testament by examining what he describes in a memorable phrase as Jesus' *parcimonie du bien agir* — his parsimony in doing good.

Where Jesus is described as having "gone about doing good and healing all that were oppressed by the devil" (Acts 10:38), Duquoc points out that in fact Jesus' program of doing good was in one sense extremely limited: he didn't heal all the people who needed healing. On the other hand his program aimed at nothing less than a new creation, without which the doing of good could only be partial and partisan. In fact,

> The breadth of the program, in order to acquire validity within time and in order to be a demand for action with an eschatological aim that is not presently able to be realized, bore with it the disappearance, the absence, of its promoter, and his substitution by an element that is not bound by

17. Christian Duquoc, "Le mal, énigme du bien," *Le Supplément* 172 (March 1990): 65–78.

the human condition, the Spirit. The program is realized only outside the conditions of this world. It can be made present only by pointers.[18]

Here it seems to me that Duquoc's insight flows into the vision of original sin which I have been trying to set out. Jesus' self-giving up to death, inaugurating a practice which is the bringing into being of a certain sort of new, deathless sociality — the ecclesial hypostasis — gives quite a new sense to the bringing about of good.

It therefore becomes reasonable to ask what it might mean for those of us becoming inserted into this ecclesial practice to become active participants in the unlocking of creation. What counts as something which is not part of the vanity of human truncated creativity, which produces evil while seeking to produce good? By what sort of practice do we allow ourselves to be induced by the beneficent imitation of Jesus into bringing about the kingdom of God? The key phrase in the paragraph I have quoted above is, it seems to me, "it can be made present only by pointers." That is to say, the creative activity of God in the midst of the world is subjected to realizing itself as sign of something not available within the world as we know it. Were it available in "heavy" fashion, then it too would immediately be distorted by vanity and become another exercise in "righteousness" producing evil.

Here I seek to go further than Duquoc, whose principal aim is to show how any apologetic linked to an absolute notion of God as good which has not allowed that good to be redefined by the radical tolerance revealed by the Cross, is a Platonization of the Christian faith. I suggest that the creative activity of God made present in imitative dependence on the practice inaugurated by Jesus takes a very precise form: what we call the forgiveness of sin. I do not mean by this the particular occasions when we must, if we are to live in grace, forgive those who have done us some wrong and ask for forgiveness when we have done some wrong. I mean that the whole visible practice of the ecclesial hypostasis *is* the forgiveness of sin. The creative self-giving up to death (because unmoved by death) in the midst of human violence, forgiving that violence, *is* what divine creation looks like in the midst of the creation-shot-through-with-vanity in which we live.

This self-giving up to death in imitative dependence of the practice inaugurated by Jesus is just what "good" looks like in the midst of vanity — as something passing out of being. It is the visible and creative living out of this practice that is the creation of a sign that is also the living out of the beginnings of the new creation. The enormous effort required to turn our life into a sign of forgiveness going beyond death *is* the way in which,

18. Duquoc, "Le mal," 72.

in the midst of the parameters of vanity, we receive our participatory creatureliness as creativity. Furthermore, and here we have something deeply
disturbing: it is only the creation of a sign which breaks through the
tendency of vanity to reduce all to boredom. It is only the bringing into
being of the sign that enables the world to become for us creation, a reflection of the glory of God. For vanity, a sign is never enough; it is never
heavy enough, nor dense enough, and so is always emptied of sense and
presence. For the beneficent mimesis of God, the sign contains infinitely
more creative presence than all the apparent heavy presence of vanity.
It is not only a pointer to what is coming into being but is already the
creative presence of that coming into being, a coming into being which
the vanity of distorted desire can only see as a going out of being.

Here we have the sacramental principle behind both the creative li-
turgical celebrations of the ecclesial hypostasis[19] and the concrete living
out of the praxis inaugurated by Christ. The reality of the creative,
beneficent divine mimesis begins to be realized in the sign of forgiveness
created in the midst of the distorted mimesis of creative futility. In practical terms this means that our being inducted (and transformed) into the
ecclesial hypostasis always reaches us as the forgiveness of sins, and our
process of recovery of creatureliness always passes through our creating
signs of the forgiveness of sins for others.[20] This sign can never be created in the midst of the vortex of distorted desires which constitutes the
apparently "strong" social order of futility, because futility renders forgiveness an empty, pointless sign: a sign of weakness rather than creative
strength. Forgiveness can become a creative sign only among the rejects
of the order of futility, those cast out by its centrifugal force. Only they
are weak enough to become signs of creation precisely because in the
eyes of the world they are of no importance, on their way out of being,
making no contribution.

---

19. Here is not the place to elaborate a theology of the sacraments, but I hope that
enough has been said to see the possible fecundity of the principles at work here for
a theology of, for instance, eucharistic presence that would be quite outside scholastic
categories.

20. This is apparent even in strictly interpersonal terms. When I forgive someone who
has hurt me, I am not performing a juridical act. Before, I was a prisoner, locked (by
resentment) into the hurt which the other person inflicted on me, living in function of
that other person, and thus subjected to the receiving and giving out — perpetuation — of
violence. By forgiving that person I am actually participating in God's bringing me into
being as part of the new creation, not run in function of futility, but a sign of something
else. To the extent that the other person is enabled to see and participate in that sign (for
I may have to forgive the person without him or her knowing or asking for forgiveness),
then what I am creating is an efficacious sign of the reconciliation of all humanity with
God: the bringing into being of the new creation. It is this that is behind the Matthaean
insistence that we enter into the perfection of God by not allowing ourselves to be defined
by the violence of the other (Matt. 5:38–48).

We have, it seems to me, some insight then into why Jesus' practice of bringing into being the ecclesial hypostasis worked preferentially among the prostitutes and the tax collectors, as well as the importance St. Paul attributes to the unimportance of those called to be members of the Church in Corinth:

> For consider your call, brethren; not many of you were wise according to worldly standards, not many were powerful, not many were of noble birth; but God chose what is foolish in the world to shame the wise, God chose what is weak in the world to shame the strong, God chose what is low and despised in the world *even things that are not, to bring to nothing the things that are.* (1 Cor. 1:26–28; my emphasis)

People who are of no importance in the order of the world are especially suited to becoming signs of the new creation, because they have been emptied of being by the vanity of the old creation to such an extent that they can become signs of the new creation as they forgive and let go of the old which has cast them out.

Nor, alas, does this mean that the ecclesial pastoral task is to transform such outcasts into an army of "heavy" force that can then contest and overthrow the order of this world. To the extent that the marginalized, empty of "being," acquire force and come back into the world, to that extent they cease to be creative signs of forgiveness bringing into being the new creation, and become another part of the dialectic of power that is the order of the world, a sign of nothing at all. They become another example of the human attempt to realize "good" being immediately devoured by vanity, becoming part of the way in which we produce evil with the best intentions. The ecclesial pastoral task seems to be to stretch ever further toward those who are not, under constant threat of becoming part of the vain "good" of the world by stopping to look after "the ninety-nine sheep who never went astray." It is only the forgiving stretching toward those who are on their way out of being that is participative in the creative creatureliness of the new creation.

All this has merely been to try to unpack what is implicit in the starting point of this thesis: that God could come into the world to bring about the new creation only as forgiving victim, as that which was on its way out of being through expulsion. We can see then why we talk of original sin rather than an original condition or an original state. We talk of original sin because the only way that God can realize creation in our midst and involving us is as forgiveness. It is the creative *forgiveness,* which is the bringing into being of the ecclesial hypostasis through the self-giving victim on his way out of the world, that defines the state of the apparently "strong" world, in fact passing away, as one marked by original *sin.*

Chapter 8

Hope and Concupiscence

We have followed the way in which the presence to the disciples of the crucified and risen Lord was the presence to them of forgiveness. This has enabled us to see how the whole recasting of their world, for which the evidence lies in their apostolic witness, was made possible starting from the historical presence of redemption. In doing this we have been attempting, thanks to mimetic theory, to reproduce something of the coherent inner dynamic which structures that witness. There is, however, another dimension of the apostolic witness at which we must look if we are to grasp the shape of what we now call original sin, and that is a further eschatological depth of the presence of the risen Lord: that the resurrection was in the flesh. Girard has this to say at the end of his treatment of the scene from Shakespeare's *The Winter's Tale* where the (supposed) statue of Hermione comes to life, thus producing the conversion of her husband, whose heart had been hardened against her by jealousy:

> The more we examine the statue scene, the more we are reminded of what the resurrection is supposed to be, a resurrection *of the flesh*, in contradistinction to the vaporous world of spirits conjured up by mimetic idolatry. The delayed recognition of Jesus has nothing to do with a lesser visibility of his resurrected body due to the lesser reality of the shadowy afterlife to which he now would belong. The opposite is true. *This resurrection is too real for a perception dimmed by the false transfigurations of mimetic idolatry.*[1]

We have seen, in effect, how in the light of Christ's resurrection and as theology and anthropology were able to become distinct but related realities, two workings of mimetic desire could be detected: the purely pacific, creative mimesis at work in the Trinity; and the rivalistic mimesis which is a distortion of that, mimesis as grasped rather than received, which we have seen to underlie the psychology and anthropology of "fallen" sociality and which constitutes what we know as history.

---

1. René Girard, *A Theater of Envy — William Shakespeare* (New York: Oxford University Press, 1991), 342; my emphasis.

We have gone further than that, in fact, since we have seen the way in which the beneficent creative mimesis entered into history in a creative human project to enable us to leave our systematic dead-end and thus fulfil the original intention of the Creator that we should be active participants in the glory of God as creatures, as sons in the Son. Central to that possibility is the understanding that the man Jesus as he walked on earth should have had a creative imagination entirely formed by the pacific mimesis of love between the Father and himself. It is to this that John gave witness, as I set out in the previous chapter.

I attempted to characterize the content of Jesus' creative imagination by suggesting that it was an imagination unshaded by death: here I do not mean simply immortal (as though immortality were a simple concept), but that the cultural reality of death was not interior to it, enclosing it within its parameters, as is the case with "fallen" humans. It was not the debased mind of Romans 1:28 or the senseless heart of Romans 1:21. That is to say, it did not share in the shading into futility of minds that are unable to perceive created reality in the light of God. Jesus' creative imagination, being unshaded by death, had as the constant background to his action and project the real creative sense of God's creative reality. It was this which lay behind the project he inaugurated to enable humans to become active participants in this creative reality, a project which depended on his being able to treat death as if it were not. The creative alterity of God, and the reality (I am tempted to say tangible reality) of that creative alterity were perceived and talked about by Jesus during his life and ministry. I am going to refer to this creative imagination which rests on and derives energy from the creative alterity of God as the "eschatological imagination."[2]

The Eschatological Imagination

We are now able to look at a curious and apparently embarrassing aspect of the apostolic witness in a new light. It has long been noticed (since Weiss and Schweitzer) that the entire New Testament is soaked in eschatology. From 1 Thessalonians to the Apocalypse, including all the Gospels, the eschatological dimension is evidently present. One problem has been how to understand this dimension. Much of the discussion has been in terms of the so-called "expectation of the imminent end," which was held to have characterized the apostolic period and about which Paul, and probably Jesus, were held to have been simply mistaken. A

---

2. For a further look at several of the themes of this chapter see my *Raising Abel: The Recovery of the Eschatological Imagination* (New York: Crossroad, 1996).

further problem has been that of the language of the apostolic witness, which manifestly holds with extreme tenacity to the passing away of this world and the coming into being of the definitive world. Where this has been interpreted in terms of the apocalyptic currents which flourished in the Eastern Mediterranean during this period, it evidently creates an embarrassment for several generations of theologians and believers who have attempted, in the light of the thought of Hegel and Marx, to take seriously human history, and its possible salvific dimension.

The discussion has largely taken place in terms of a dilemma between what is often labeled as "Platonism" and "realism," or the suspicion that the language of the passing away of this world and the putting on of the incorruptibility, or imperishability, proper to the "next" world is a form of idealism which represents an escape from historical responsibility, and thus should be shunned out of faithfulness to the Gospels' demands of taking seriously the bringing about of the kingdom of God in the here and now. Part of the goad behind the discussion has been the famous jibe about religion being the opiate of the people and a certain *mauvaise conscience* about the accusation that Christian preaching has encouraged people to postpone hope of a better life to the hereafter and has thus failed to encourage practical participation in such changes as could reasonably ameliorate the present life.

I would suggest that mimetic theory enables us to break out of the horns of these two problems in a way totally coherent with the inner dynamic we have been pursuing thus far, and that it enables us to see the importance of a theology of original sin of the sort I have been attempting in letting us off the hooks, simultaneously, of the apparent problem of the delay of the *parousia* and that of the playing down of "this" world. This may offer a contribution toward the plea made recently by A. Gesché for the incorporation of *une eschatologique* in the theology of liberation:

> I know that a transhistorical, "celestial" eschatology can become an escape from history. But I'm not sure that it is necessarily so. And I wonder whether, in our world of today, the hiding away of a supernatural salvation, of an eschatological salvation in the strong sense, doesn't do harm to the historical salvation which we seek to bring about. Better still, it may be that it is a decisive task for us and one which awaits us all, for we have all fallen short in this domain, to demonstrate not only that the "supernatural" does indeed exist, but that it is ... historical. It is historical *because human history does indeed include within itself a "supernatural" and transhistorical dimension.*[3]

---

3. From "Les théologies de la libération et le mal," in A. Gesché, *Le mal* (Paris: Cerf, 1993), 154. The translation is my own, but the emphasis is proper to the author.

First, let us face the full force of the eschatological expression that we find in the New Testament. In the earliest texts Paul tells the Thessalonians that "you yourselves know well that the day of the Lord will come like a thief in the night" (1 Thess. 5:2) and that this day has as its content the Lord Jesus "revealed from heaven with his mighty angels in flaming fire, inflicting vengeance upon those who do not know God and upon those who do not obey the Gospel of our Lord Jesus" (2 Thess. 1:7–8). At the latest end of the apostolic witness, in 2 Peter 3:10, we also have the assurance that "the day of the Lord will come like a thief." It is at least plausible that the link of the Day with a thief in the night goes back to Jesus himself, and the sayings recorded in Matthew 24:42–44 and Luke 12:39–40.

In the time in between the text of Thessalonians and that of 2 Peter there has, however, been a change in the perception of how that "Day" is to be understood, a change that is evidenced even within the writings of Paul himself. In the first letter to the Corinthians Paul tells his audience:

> Now if any one builds on the foundation [which is Jesus Christ] with gold, silver, precious stones, wood, hay, straw — each man's work will become manifest; for the Day will disclose it, because it will be revealed with fire, and the fire will test what sort of work each one has done. If the work which any man has built on the foundation survives, he will receive a reward. If any man's work is burned up, he will suffer loss, though he himself will be saved, but only as through fire. (1 Cor. 3:12–15)

Rather than there being any emphasis on the Day as a certain moment, it has become a principle of revelation of a certain sort of continuity between this world and the next. The notion of "time" is also changing, since Paul tells his audience that "the appointed time has grown very short" (1 Cor. 7:29), and this is a reason for a certain sort of dealing with the world "as though they had no dealings with it. For the form of this world is passing away" (1 Cor. 7:31). Paul has also had time to think more clearly about the relationship between this world and the next and is able to explain about the different sorts of corporeality that correspond to each: the one perishable and mortal, and the other imperishable and immortal (1 Cor. 15:35–58).

By the time we get to 2 Peter, the relationship between time and the "Day" has changed to such an extent that it has become important to explain this to the audience by means of a piece of what one can only call "biblical metaphysics" — to the horror of those who see metaphysical thought as simply a betrayal of the evangelical message. The audience have to be told that with the Lord one day is as a thousand years, and a thousand years as one day. The Lord is not slow about his promise as some count slowness, but is forbearing toward you, not wishing that any should perish, but that all should reach repentance. (2 Pet. 3:8–9)

The notion of the Day has become detached from any ordinary understanding of time and has become the turning point of the dissolution of this world and the coming of new heavens and a new earth. Furthermore the changing understanding of the Day now embraces the possibility of salvation: time exists for repentance, not as a threat of a day of vengeance.

The corresponding process in the Gospels can be seen in the way in which even as early as Mark apocalyptic language has been subverted. Thus the coming of the Son of man, for which the disciples are told to watch — "for you do not know when the master of the house will come, in the evening, or at midnight, or at cockcrow, or in the morning" (Mark 13:35) — is then indicated as coming in the handing over[4] from the Last Supper in the evening, in the arrest at midnight, in Peter's betrayal and the trial before the priests at cockcrow, and then in the morning at the trial before Pilate. Jesus' prophecy of his coming before the chief priest appears to relate to his crucifixion.[5] This process of the concentration of eschatology in the key christological moments of the death and resurrection culminates in what is referred to (since Dodd) as the "realized eschatology" to be found in John's Gospel, where again it is in the exaltation of the Son of man (John 3:14–15) on the Cross that *to eschaton* irrupts into human history.

That there is a process of development within the New Testament with regard to the understanding of eschatology is denied by no one. Of course the interpretations of this process differ very widely. However, is it necessary to see this process as evidence of the primitive Christian community, and possibly Jesus himself, having been simply mistaken about the imminence of the end? According to this view, Jesus and the apostolic witnesses would have had their worldview formed entirely within the apocalyptic imagination and would thus have expected an imminent end. It would have been the weight of the reality of the end (the Day) not coming that gradually obliged the thought of the apostolic group to develop toward a realized eschatology and turned the "hope" that related so urgently to that end in the earlier epistles into the "patience" that comes to the fore in the later texts of the canon.

---

4. "Handing over" and "betrayal" are the same word in Greek.
5. For further details see T. J. Radcliffe, " 'The Coming of the Son of Man': Mark's Gospel and the Subversion of the 'Apocalyptic Imagination,' " in B. Davies, ed., *Language, Meaning and God* (London: Chapman, 1987), 176–89.

There is another, completely different possible interpretation, which is in line with the understanding of the development of the apostolic witness in the light of the resurrection that I have been attempting to set out: this is that the (unquestioned) development among the apostolic circle in the first century happened not because of the obligatory weight of "reality," but was part of the coherent internal development of the witness itself. We have seen how the presence to the apostolic witnesses of the crucified and risen Lord gradually produced a change in the understanding of who God was and what it is to be human. In this way there was gradually and simultaneously opened up the possibility of the perception of God as not only without any sort of violence, but indeed as gratuitous self-giving love; linked to this was the view of humankind as having been locked into a certain sort of reciprocal violence which disfigured the perception of God, but now being enabled to move out of that violence and that perception. In this way, I suggested, both theology and anthropology began to break out of a certain anthropomorphic language within which both had been insufficiently distinct.

It is at the very least plausible that what we have in the development of eschatological language from the "day of vengeance" to the Johannine realized eschatology is a different aspect of the same process: the process by which Jesus' own subversion of the apocalyptic owing to his own "eschatological imagination," of the sort I have outlined above, became able to be understood by people whose imaginations were thoroughly formed in the apocalyptic imagination of the surrounding ambience.

There are certain obvious ways in which Jesus' teaching, as attested by all the Gospels, was subversive of the three dualities that W. Meeks has shown to be characteristic of apocalyptic thought.[6] These three dualities are the cosmic (heaven / earth), the temporal (this age / the age to come), and the social (sons of light, elect, righteous / sons of dark, the "world," unrighteous). Jesus was manifestly subversive of the social duality, as evidenced by his fellowship with sinners and such parables as that of the Pharisee and the tax collector in the Temple. That he was subversive of the cosmic duality is shown in his preaching of the kingdom as coming about now: "today this Scripture has been fulfilled in your hearing" (Luke 4:21), "the time is fulfilled and the kingdom of God is at hand" (Mark 1:15), "but if it is by the Spirit of God that I cast out demons, then the kingdom of God has come upon you" (Matt. 12:28),

6. See W. Meeks, "Social Functions of Apocalyptic Language in Pauline Christianity," in D. Hellholm, ed., *Apocalypticism in the Mediterranean World and the Near East* (Tübingen, 1983), 689, mentioned in Radcliffe, " 'The Coming of the Son of Man.' "

and in the petition of the Lord's Prayer: "Thy kingdom come, thy will be done on earth as it is in heaven." That he was also subversive of the temporal duality is shown by his practice and recommendation of celibacy lived now for the kingdom, linked with his understanding that this is the condition of life lived in the resurrection (Matt. 19:10–12, linked to Matt. 22:23–33).

There is good prima facie reason, then, to think that the subversion of the apocalyptic imagination by what I have called Jesus' "eschatological" imagination is something proper to Jesus rather than something invented by a bewildered primitive community in the face of the indefinite postponement of the Day. The prima facie evidence deepens somewhat when we discover that at the root of Jesus' subversion of these dualities we always find what I have earlier called the intelligence of the victim. Jesus provides a prophetic criterion in terms of realizable ethical demands at the base of his subversion of these dualities: the social duality is recast in terms of the victim, so that the victim becomes the criterion for whether one is a sheep or a goat (Matt. 25) or for being a neighbor (the Good Samaritan, Luke 10); it is victims and the precariously placed who are to be at the center of the new victim people of whom is the kingdom of God that is coming into being (the Sermon on the Mount, Matt. 5–6). It can scarcely be surprising that this insistence, more in the line of the prophetic imagination than in that of the apocalyptic imagination, comes to be also subversive of the temporal and cosmic dualities. Thus the crucified and risen forgiving victim becomes himself the presence of the kingdom in the here and now. It is this that is being claimed in the "realized eschatology" of John: that the victim is the judge as victim and that passing into eternal life is related precisely to the criterion of the victim. The same is shown in the heavenly liturgy of the Apocalypse: the central criterion, around which the eternal liturgy revolves, and thus the principle of continuity between this life and the next, is the slaughtered lamb, the heavenly victim.

It is then at least plausible to suggest that the presence to the disciples of the crucified and risen victim is also the principle by which the duality of this age / the age to come is subverted, and a quite different understanding of time itself starts to come into being. This understanding might be characterized as that of time which is able to participate in eternity as opposed to time which is bent away from eternity. Where time is bent away from eternity, there can be only a dualism of opposition between this age and the age to come, and the irruption of God into human history must be a violent one, bringing to an end the present age and starting a new one. However, where the heavenly reality of the crucified and risen victim is already present to the apostolic group, permitting the beginnings of a life and human sociality that is not marked by death but whose members are free to lead lives of self-giving in imitation of Jesus because of their faith in the deathless nature of God, then there is a continuity already started between this age and the next. Human time itself, an inalienable dimension of physical human creatureliness, has begun to be able to participate in eternal life.

What I am proposing here is simply another aspect of what was already proposed with relation to the way the presence of the crucified and risen Lord to the apostolic group broke down the social duality between Jew and gentile, as evidenced in Acts. There is no doubt in Acts that the process by which the universality of the new people was brought into being by the risen victim was a difficult process: Peter had to be pushed by God into baptizing Cornelius; there were many conflicts over circumcision; Paul had to fight for years for it to be absolutely clear that there was no longer any social duality thanks to Christ. That is to say, the consequences of what was already present *in nuce* at Pentecost were not grasped immediately, and the apostolic witness gives evidence of the difficult process by which a truth inherent in the resurrection of the crucified victim became "received" or incarnated in the life of the Church. No one now suggests that it was the "weight of reality" (hordes of gentiles forcing themselves in) crushing against the Berlin Wall of an obstinate apostolic clinging to some misguided belief of Jesus that he was sent only to the lost sheep of the house of Israel that caused the development from Judaism to Catholicism. The inner coherence between the resurrection and the universality of the new faith is evident now, even if it wasn't at first.

What I am suggesting is that exactly the same slow and conflictual process is at work in the relationship between the apostolic group and "time."[7] It took considerable time before the full force of the consequences of Jesus' eschatological imagination, made available at the resurrection, was able to work the subversion of the prodigious inertia of cultural understanding (and the apocalyptic imagination proper to small, threatened groups of people) allowing that eschatological imagination to be possessed by the Church. Of course, as the apostolic witness testifies, there were Christians, probably many Christians, who did think in terms of an imminent coming of the end and for whom its delay was a matter of scandal (just as there were those who thought that all Chris-

---

7. It is no accident that it is in Luke/Acts, where the development from Israel to the new Israel through the body of the risen victim is clearest, that the effect this same process has on the understanding of time becomes clearest, with Jerusalem becoming abandoned by God (Luke 13:35) and then destroyed (Luke 21:20), thus leaving open a new time, the times of the gentiles (Luke 21:24).

tians ought to be circumcised). However, the apostolic teaching on this matter was not an "explaining away" of an embarrassment, but the slow outworking of a coherence internal to the presence of the crucified and risen victim, part of the irruption into the here and now of the definitive eschatological presence of God and the new human relationality which that makes possible.

We can begin to understand then something of the depth of Jesus' saying that not even the Son of man knows of the end (Mark 13:32), and why it is not important that he should know. The important thing is the beginning of the living out of the deathless time participating in eternity even now, something that already happens before this generation passes away. It is this new time that henceforth counts. The time that is passing away, the time of human history, is no longer a theological reality, and it will come to an end when it comes to an end — the Father knows when; this is not because of some future divine irruption in violence, but because it is abandoned to itself, no longer a theological reality. The theological reality is rather "redeeming the time, for the days are evil" (Eph. 5:16, see Col. 4:5). Any final "apocalypse" will be of purely human making, the outworking of the dynamism of death-related rivalistic desire. When finally history does work itself out to an end, there will be already present within it the criterion for its judgment: the coming of the victim in glory, whose presence had been hidden by the vain powers of this world for as long as they lasted.

What I have been attempting to describe is the coming into being of what I have called "the eschatological imagination." The important thing is that this be understood to be the slow working out of the same dynamic that we have seen with relation to the emergence of the theology that later became called trinitarian and the anthropology that later became characterized as one marked by original sin. As the deathlessness and nonviolence of the Father came to be appreciated, as well as the love that raised the creatively forgiving victim, so the continuity between this creation and the new creation was able to be understood, and a new sort of practical human involvement in eternal life starting now was made possible. This of course means that as the eschatological imagination emerged, so a certain sort of participation in time and history came to be seen as redundant or futile: the original sin from which we have been set free can be seen, on our way out of it, as being so deeply anterior to us that it involves us in living memory, time, and history in a radically distorted way.

Before I engage with the anthropological consequences of this understanding there is a further point to be brought out about the eschatological imagination as it emerged in the apostolic witness, and that is a point

linked to Girard's remark, quoted above, about the reality of Jesus' resurrection in the flesh being difficult to perceive because of the disciples'
perception formed in mimetic idolatry. There is no doubt that the apostolic group did possess a very firm hope in the reality of the world that
was coming, and in its physical and corporeal reality.[8] That is to say, as
they became possessed by the eschatological imagination, so their minds
were set free from the vanity discussed in the previous chapter: the futility of those not able to make the link between created reality and God.
The new perception of God enabled a completely new and refreshing relationship to God's dynamic creativity as a reality already coming into
being. Indeed it is the setting of the mind on this reality felt to be more
real than the surrounding reality-which-is-passing-away which was to
give the joy and peace necessary to be able to support the tribulations
of the present time, tribulations including the believer's own distorted
desires (Col. 3:1–5).

Of course, as the eschatological imagination emerged and the apocalyptic imagination waned, the structuring of this hope changed: it began
to be seen that this hope was internally structured by patience, or the
ability to put up with the vicissitudes of this world. Hence the emergence
of patience as an important virtue by the end of the canon: not patience
in the sense of "ceasing to be impatient" for the coming of the End, but
patience in the sense of being able to bear, or undergo, the troubles of
the sort of time that is on its way out of being because one is fixed on
a coming into being that is much more real and wholesome and nourishing to the imagination. The important thing to notice as this change
in the structure of hope took place is that what we are witnessing is *not
a diminution of eschatological urgency*. It is not as though the process
toward a realized eschatology was also the process toward a thoroughly
banal liberal unconcern about the next world. The urgency for the coming into being of the new world is just as strong and is an essential
part of the eschatological imagination as received in the Church from
Jesus. What has altered is the perception of the structuring of the alterity which gives grounds for that urgency, as the notion of time became
simultaneously redeemable (time as being made capable of participating
in eternity) and evil (time bent away from eternity and as abandoned
to its own futility). Now the urgency is fixed on the deathless creativity

---

8. I am much indebted in the following remarks to the work of A. Tornos, *Escatología*
1 (Madrid: UPCM, 1989). Tornos's magnificent analysis of the development of Christian
hope owes nothing to mimetic theory, so I am delighted to note the extreme similarity
of the conclusions he has reached to my own attempts to work out the implications of
mimetic theory for eschatology.

of God in which we will be able to participate fully as we persevere in doing good.

What I would like to suggest now is that it is insofar as we have an eschatological imagination urgently fixed on the deathless creativity of God that it becomes possible for us to do good. As our desires become retrained toward the promise of a reality that really is desirable and toward which we tend in urgent hope (for where our treasure is there also is our heart, Matt. 6:21), so we are enabled to become sufficiently untied from the world of our present desires to be able to work justice within this world. It is under this eschatological prism that it becomes possible for us to look at what might be meant by *concupiscentia*.

Hope and Concupiscence

When I refer to the coming into being of the eschatological imagination proper to the apostolic group and the early Church, I am talking about a real process of change of the very structure of consciousness by which faith in the newly revealed deathless nature of God and urgent hope in the newness of creation linked to this new perception of God, which newness is to include the believer, enable the believer to begin to undergo a radical restructuration of relationality. Here we are in the terrain which the Church has traditionally referred to as *concupiscentia*.

By *concupiscentia* the Church, speaking at Trent, understands the disordered state resulting from original sin such that even when a person has been set free from original sin (by baptism), that person is still heavily inclined to sin though this inclination can be successfully struggled against[9] (however almost certainly not without many falls into actual sin).[10] The Church is quite specific that concupiscence is not properly speaking sin, but is the result of sin, and inclines us to sin. This seems to be exactly the vision of concupiscence which arises from the understanding of original sin I have been attempting to set out. That is to say: original sin was discovered as it became possible to leave it. We were previously locked into a certain sort of aversion to the coming into being of the fulfillment of creation, such that we were unable to recognize even the possibility of such a thing. By our incorporation into the coming into being of that new creation, whether by baptism or desire, what has been removed has been our *being locked* into the aversion and the inability to recognize the alterity of God while formed by rivalistic mimetic desire. However, our being unlocked from that does not immediately prevent

---

9. Council of Trent, Decree on Original Sin, par. 5.
10. See Denzinger, 106–8; 471; 804; 832.

the fact that the whole of our actual, physical, psychological, historical, and cultural reality which has formed us completely continues to run our lives through the way in which our desire and our consciousness is cast.

This "being run by" the desires of this world is not a sin, but a condition, and one which we are called to collaborate in changing from within, so that we may "be run by" the beneficent creative mimesis of God which brings the new creation into being through and with us. Thus we may talk of the human being as pre-formed by the desires of this world and, simultaneously called into being re-formed, at the level of desire, into a creative creature who is a full participant in the creative mimesis of the Holy Trinity. The interface between these two modes of desire is exactly that described by St. Paul in the famous description of inner conflict in Romans 7:15–25.

Just in case the radicality of this understanding be passed by, let me underline the drastic nature of the understanding of concupiscence that is indicated. Every dimension of the human being — intelligence, sexuality, will power, affectivity, memory, way of being involved in history, sense of time, consciousness, and conscience — is radically distorted in all of us. And it is predistorted because the whole cultural reality of being human has not only formed us in some exterior manner, but it has formed the very parameters of our consciousness from within,[11] bringing us into being humans marked by the parameters of death. The depth of the distortion was able to become apparent only when the radical alterity of the new deathless creation began to become understood. In exactly the same way as it was the depth of forgiveness made present in the crucified and risen victim that revealed the depth of original sin tying us into death, so it is the reality of the hope made present in the eschatological imagination that reveals the cultural omnipresence of concupiscence; and this hope, of course, reveals this concupiscence as something that can be overcome.

The Anthropology of Time

In order to deepen this perception, let us have a look at just one dimension by which concupiscence can be understood as being human on the interface between the two desires, a dimension which will permit us to

---

11. Here I rejoin and am indebted to the interpretation of St. Thomas's understanding of concupiscence set out by J. B. Metz in his article "Concupiscencia," in H. Fries, ed., *Conceptos fundamentales de la teología* (Madrid: Cristiandad, 1966), 1:255–64. Metz compares the early Thomas's (and the Scotist-Suarezian) understanding with the more thoroughgoing anthropological vision of the later Thomas as evidenced in the *Summa Theologiae*. It is this latter vision that is compatible with what is being set out here.

see the radicality of the re-formation that is proposed by the eschatological imagination and will enable us to see how the understanding of
concupiscence makes available an understanding of human creativeness
as history. This dimension is the anthropological reality of time.

J.-M. Oughourlian has dedicated himself to the study of the way in
which hypnosis produces in the person under hypnosis a new "self of
desire" suggested into being by the hypnotizer. It is the hypnotist's suggestion which is the model for the desire that brings the new self into
being. Following the experimental observation of P. Janet, Oughourlian
illustrates the fact that the new "self of desire" produced under hypnosis is able to remember the life of the former "self of desire," while the
old "self of desire," once awakened, is quite unable to remember what
had gone on while the hypnotically induced "self of desire" was operational. Oughourlian draws the conclusion that this is further evidence
of the way in which it is mimetic desire which brings into being the
self, consciousness, and memory. However, he goes further: the same evidence demonstrates that "physical time" and "psychological time" are
quite different realities. For it is not that the original "self of desire"
when awakened has "forgotten" what went on when the hypnotically
induced "self of desire" was operational. It is rather the case that when
the hypnotically induced "self" was operational (physically in the past,
from the viewpoint of the now awakened original self), the original self
was simply not operational: the hypnotically induced self is *never* psychologically in the past for the original self; it is always in the future or
in some other psychological time inaccessible to the original self. This
leads Oughourlian to indicate that

> psychological time is, we must agree, the time of desire (just as the self is
> the self of desire, that is, formed by desire) and is not subjected to the laws
> of physical time. For movement constitutes time: the movement of univer-
> sal gravity constitutes physical time; the movement of universal mimesis
> constitutes psychological time, in other words, the memory, as well as
> sociological time, in other words, History.[12]

Oughourlian is then able to show that the objective reality of the formation of memory is that an anterior desire suggests into being a desire
which brings into being a self (as we have seen all along), but that this
has no psychological reality. Psychologically the same reality is seen the

---

12. J.-M. Oughourlian, *Un mime nommé désir* (Paris: Grasset, 1982), 298. My translation. Since the passage is very dense, I give the original French: "Le temps psychologique
qui est, il faut en convenir, le temps-du-désir, comme le moi est le moi-du désir, c'est-à-dire
formé par le désir, n'est pas soumis aux lois du temps physique. C'est le mouvement qui
constitue le temps. Le mouvement de la gravitation universelle constitue le temps physique.
Le mouvement de la mimésis universelle constitue le temps psychologique, la mémoire,
ainsi que le temps sociologique, l'Histoire."

other way around: the self appropriates the desire which in fact has formed it as its own and then claims anteriority or originality to the anterior desire which brought it into being. In this way, memory, structuring the whole of a human life story, is formed by what ranges from a "forgetfulness" to a denial of what in fact formed it. This of course renders the subject incapable of being pacifically formed and suggested into being by the desire that is anterior to it.[13]

From Oughourlian's point of view as a neuropsychiatrist and psychologist the interest lies in the different degrees of denial of the alterity of the desire forming the self. These can stretch from a simple "forgetfulness" (in comparatively "healthy" people) to a radical insistence on the originality of the self and "its" desire in comparatively psychotic or neurotic people. However, from a theological point of view the interest is other. It would follow from this model of understanding the structuring of the self and the memory that all actual configurations of memory are formed by desire as appropriated. Oughourlian attributes to Hegel having understood this:

> Physical time, as Hegel perceived, is passive annihilation. Psychological time is active annihilation. Produced by desire, by psychological movement, it advances by incorporating into itself the desire of the other. The memory within which the self of desire is inscribed is forgetfulness of that annihilation and remembrance of its result.[14]

In other words, all human memory and time *as we know them* are forged on the basis of a nonacceptance of the alterity of the other which forms them, and of grasping of that alterity as one's own.

That is to say, exactly the same configuration of desire which we have seen to be the structuring mechanism of original sin is also the structuring mechanism of the anthropological reality of time. However, if we, unlike Hegel, see this desire, the one known to us phenomenologically, not as essential to what it is to be human, but as a distortion of a pacific mimesis which is in fact anterior to it, it becomes possible to imagine a quite different structuring of the human memory, and thus of time, as one where human time and memory are able to be called (creatively suggested) into being by the anterior pacific mimesis. This

---

13. This is brought out in two extra pages which Oughourlian wrote for the English translation of *Un mime nommé désir* and which appear only there. See *The Puppet of Desire* (Stanford: Stanford University Press, 1991), 238–39.

14. Oughourlian, *Un mime,* 299. My translation. Again, owing to the density of the French I also offer the original text: "Le temps physique, Hegel l'avait pressenti, est néantisation passive. Le temps psychologique est néantisation active. Produit par le désir, par le mouvement psychologique, il avance en s'incorporant à mesure le désir de l'autre, en néantisant à mesure le désir de l'autre. La mémoire dans laquelle s'inscrit le moi-du-désir est oubli à mesure de cette néantisation elle même et souvenir de son résultat."

means that we can begin to imagine a human time which rests pacifically on that which calls it into being, and thus where the present is not formed by any sort of forgetfulness of the past, but where the memory is able pacifically to form an ever richer present. This suggests a way in which time (and thus the inextricably historical human being) is able to be participative of eternity rather than bent toward its own dissolution in futility, protecting itself from the future and distorting the past.[15] This becomes especially significant if we posit, with Girard, that properly human consciousness, culture, and signification came into being with the self-deception surrounding an act of victimization. It then begins to make sense that the revealing of the forgiving victim might make possible the reordering of human memory and thus of human temporality.

We have then a radically eschatological understanding of concupiscence: the human being formed in every dimension of his or her being by distorted desire, and consequently being pulled by that distorted desire even as that same human begins to be able to receive pacifically the suggesting into being of the pacific mimesis that is capable of turning his or her whole human life story into quite a different story. It is from the opening up of the human imagination to the deathless nature of God and God's gratuitously and urgently making available his true creative reality as something that each one can hope for as good *for me* that we begin to be able to set our minds on the things that are above (Col. 3:2), and so, nourished by the reality of real creation, begin to have our desire re-formed and so to overcome the different ways we are tied and drawn in by the desires that constitute "this world."

An Infantile Morality

If concupiscence is such a radically and universally distorted anthropological condition, then it becomes very clear why no amount of "law" is ever to be an appropriate base for a Christian morality. Law must, of its nature, share in the distorted anthropological state which it seeks to remedy, becoming, instead of the remedy, a particularly painful part of

---

15. In this I am rejoining an intuition of J. Ratzinger, as set out in his book *Eschatology: Death and Eternal Life* (Washington D.C.: Catholic University of America Press, 1988), 181–90), who seeks to make sense of the difference between an individual judgment at the time of death and the general judgment at the end of history in terms of St. Augustine's understanding of memory as set out in Book X of the *Confessions*. For Ratzinger as for Oughourlian, human temporality is constituted by relationality, and thus different types of relationality might produce different qualities of temporality. I would suggest that mimetic theory takes us at least one step further in grounding the eschatological imagination in a coherent theological anthropology.

the problem, as Paul clearly understood. I suggest that just as concupiscence can be properly understood only from within the "eschatological imagination" — as the anthropological condition "caught" between two different modes of desire — so Christian moral teaching can be properly understood only from within the perspective offered by the presence of two modes of desire.

It is frequently pointed out (for instance, by Tornos)[16] that the starting point for a Christian morality which follows Paul is an indicative "what you now are" (i.e., saved) followed by an imperative, i.e., "let not sin therefore reign in your mortal bodies." The understanding is that owing to our baptism we are now "ontologically" different, and so should behave differently. Behind this understanding is the familiar maxim: *agere sequitur esse.*[17] Of course this understanding is immensely difficult to put into practice for as long as it is apparent that our new ontological state is pretty notional and that our *esse* leads all too easily to various forms of *agere* which are in contradiction with Church teaching. There is nothing light about the burden or easy about the yoke of the morality which flows from this starting point. I would like to suggest that we are in a position to nuance this reading of the Pauline approach to morality from the perspective of mimetic theory and at the same time rediscover something of the infantility of the kingdom which is so emphasized by Jesus and so easily forgotten by moralists.

Let us take a passage which seems tailor-made for the "indicative leads to imperative" style of argument, Colossians 3:1–5:

> If then you have been raised with Christ, seek the things that are above, where Christ is, seated at the right hand of God. Set your minds on the things that are above, not on things that are on earth. For you have died, and your life is hid with Christ in God. When Christ who is our life appears, then you also will appear with him in glory. Put to death therefore what is earthly in you.

We have an indication of where we "really" are (hidden in Christ with God), and this is what leads to the imperative ("Put to death therefore... "). However, let us posit the eschatological imagination which I have attempted to set out above, and thus the reality of the creative beneficent mimesis of God toward which we are tending in hope as well as the presence of the distorted mimesis which has completely formed our anthropological state. We will see that the relationship between the indicative and the imperative is now subtly different.

---

16. Tornos, *Escatología,* 67.
17. "What one does flows from what one is."

As we have started to have our imagination re-formed by the deathless mimesis of God, and that means the promise of a new physicality and a new creation in which there is neither death nor its anthropological distortions, so there is being called into being within us a quite new mode of desire, a desire in pacific imitation of the divine mimesis, but a desire which is nevertheless a completely human desire. This desire is not merely some abstract force, but as a divinely initiated human desire is a desire *for* the promised creation, which is tended toward, as being so urgently and superabundantly good *for us*.

Thus, when we are called to "set your minds on things that are above, not on things that are on earth" (Col. 3:2), what we are being exhorted to is to allow our imagination to be centered on the good things that are in store for us and toward which we are tending in our urgent hope, *since it is this that begins to enable us to desire these things*. As we allow our imaginations to be nourished by what is good for us, so our desire becomes re-formed to tend toward these things. It is thus that the new creation begins to be formed in us, and it is thus that we are able to cease being driven by the force of distorted mimetic desire: that desire is undone from within. The important feature of this understanding of the roots of Christian morality is that it respects essentially the priority of grace over law: it is because we are being given something that we are able to do without other things. The inverse of this is, of course, the teaching that we must do without certain things *in order to* be given certain things, the catastrophic trap of a so-called Christian morality that is completely stuck within the "sado-masochism" of rivalistic desire, turning moral life into some sort of bargaining strategy for overcoming obstacles.

The approach to Christian morality that I am attempting to set out might justly be called "infantile," for it suggests that, rather than the child being dissuaded from participating in a noisy gang of children by the threat that, if the child does not cease to participate in the noisy gang, then the ice cream that the parent was going to give the child back at home will not be given after all, the parent comes to the scene of the noisy gang and starts to unwrap the ice cream in sight of the child. The child sees the ice cream beginning to be unwrapped. Desire is awakened in the child by the parent's suggestion. The desire for the ice cream recenters the child's behavior, and the child is able to leave the gang pretty painlessly.

Notice that what has happened, entirely in line with mimetic theory as set forth by both Girard and Oughourlian, is that an anterior desire, for the good of the child, has made use of an object, ice cream, to suggest into being a new desire in the child that effectively modifies its behavior.

Mutatis mutandis this model seems to be exactly what is at work in the way in which the New Testament appeals to the eschatological imagination as that which permits the modification of our behavior. It is worth stressing that it depends on an entirely positive view of desire: we can desire things that are good for us, and should, and these desires will not be frustrated — rather than having us engage in any purely voluntaristic struggle with our desires, which very struggle remains within the mode of the desire that is to be overcome.

In the light of this understanding of the reality of the closeness and urgency of the new creation that is made available by our imaginations being nourished by the deathless creativity of God, it then becomes possible to see the dynamic behind much of Jesus' teaching and practice with regard to the kingdom. Jesus' phrase about laying up for yourselves treasure in heaven, "for where your treasure is, there also is your heart" (Matt. 6:21), is manifestly not an exhortation to a self-denying asceticism whereby, if we were really adult, we would not be moved by treasures, whether here or anywhere else, but would, out of the very dignity of our adult sense of justice (or whatever), do the right thing. Jesus assumes that our need for treasure is not something which can be lobotomized by any amount of high-mindedness: we must have our desires re-formed around a more fulfilling treasure. If our eye (notoriously in Matthew's Gospel formed in mimetic rivalry, or not, as the case may be: Matt. 7:1–5; 20:15) is sound (rests on the goodness of one giving and is able to desire without frustration), then the whole body is sound; whereas if the eye is not sound (formed in mimetic rivalry) then the whole body (and thus all behavior) is full of darkness (Matt. 6:22–23).

That this understanding is not unique to Matthew can be shown by the way in which Jesus' pedagogy with his disciples in Mark's Gospel has recourse to children. First, to give the disciples a new model for desire in the wake of their dispute as to which of them is greatest, Jesus places a small child in their midst and takes the child in his arms (Mark 9:34–37). Shortly afterward Jesus has to rebuke the disciples for hindering the access of children to him: "whoever does not receive the kingdom of God like a child shall not enter it" (Mark 10:15).

Finally, James and John request places of honor, and the jealous indignation of the other disciples boils over (Mark 10:35–45). However, Jesus does not rebuke James and John for their desire — merely indicating to them the sort of tribulations they will have to go through before inheriting it. It is the other ten who are given a lecture presupposing the rivalistic nature of their own desire. James and John seem to have learned from the child. It is not of course that children are "innocent" in any way at all: it is just that they are less complicated about knowing what they want, running for it, and insisting on getting it. It is just such a pattern of desire that is able to receive the kingdom of God.

Did Jesus himself desire in this way? That is to say, was it the ability to imagine an urgent good for himself that enabled him to live as he did and give himself up to death? Apart from what we may deduce from the parables, there is at least one indication that the apostolic witness saw him as desiring in exactly this way and in this being the model for our desire:

> ...let us run with perseverance the race that is set before us, looking to Jesus the pioneer and perfecter of our faith, who *for the joy that was set before him* endured the Cross, despising the shame, and is seated at the right hand of God. (Heb. 12:1b–2, my emphasis)

We cannot, it seems, run away from the fact that the apostolic witness presents Jesus as having, in fact, taught in terms of heavenly rewards, a superabundance of heavenly rewards indeed, and expected these to be a motivating factor in the lives of those who were to follow him, and a motivating factor without any sense of shame that one is following him to get something, and something good for *me*. I hope I have shown that this does not depend on a crude "pie in the sky" theology, but is an essential part of the eschatological imagination that Jesus was opening up for the disciples, the beginnings of the possibility of a morality based on the calling into being and satisfaction of real desires, rather than the castration of or weird fencing matches with the desires that already drive us. This eschatological imagination is intrinsically related to the opening up of the vision of God. There remains the question of whether or not this vision is automatically hostile to any serious participation in human history.

Redeeming the Time

The letter to the Ephesians follows the same understanding of the eschatological imagination which I have been setting out in the light of mimetic theory. In the first place, the point of Christ's coming and of our redemption was the bringing into being of a new fulness, a uniting of heaven and earth, a fulness in which we should be sons in the Son (1:1–12). The revelation of this mystery includes the guarantee of an inheritance of which we shall take possession (1:13–14). The author is particularly keen that his hearers have their understanding of revelation widened: "having the eyes of your hearts enlightened, that you may know what is the hope to which he has called you, what are the riches of his glorious inheritance in the saints" (Eph. 1:18). That is to say, they are encouraged to center their imaginations on what is coming to them. They are also encouraged to know "what is the immeasurable greatness of his power in us who believe, according to the working of his great might" (Eph. 1:19). These two are not separable realities (they are the same sentence in Greek): the centering of the imagination on the inheritance is what permits the working of the great power in those who believe. The same idea is worked through again when the author tells his hearers that they were once dead through sins (full participants in the world of death-oriented desire), but have been made alive (participants in the beneficent mimesis of life) and raised up to the heavenly places, as awaiting the immeasurable riches of God's grace. It is because they are being given something through the opening up of their mind to the deathless creative generosity of God that they are saved, not because of any moral struggle of their own.[18]

There then follows an excursus about the overcoming of the separation between Jew and gentile and an apologia for Paul in his sufferings (2:11–3:21). The particular emphasis on the rôle of the apostle seems to be as one whose job it is to proclaim the hugeness of the mystery of God's generosity, so that people's minds may be broadened to be able to perceive and thus share in that generosity. With so much emphasis on God's glory and the "breadth and length and height and depth" (3:18) of it all, one would have thought that there would be no incentive at all for taking ordinary human history seriously. Yet that is not the direction that the author follows.

First we have Christ ascending to heaven, with his captives, and simultaneously pouring out gifts to human beings (4:8). The gifts are specifically ecclesial in order to make it possible for the children, who are still thoroughly prone to the winds and lies of this world, to grow into adulthood, thus reproducing as a body the humanity of Christ as a reality in the midst of this world (4:15). This is enormously significant: it means that the first fruits of the heavenly gifts for which we are to hope are already given us in the form of an ecclesial life that is a way of living and growing into the new age already.[19] It is not that we must hold on until we can escape "up" into the new, but the new is coming

---

18. Ephesians 2:8–9. This passage, so controversial at the time of the Reformation, sits perfectly within the mimetic understanding.

19. This seems to correspond exactly with the way in which Jesus' words about putting a faithful and wise servant over his household are to be found in the apocalyptic discourse in Matthew (24:45–51). Ecclesial ministry is specifically to be understood as forming people in watchfulness and hope for the Son of man: ecclesial ministry is completely invalidated where it is not conducted within this eschatological perspective ("But if that servant says to himself 'My Master is delayed...'").

"down" to form us even now. Given that that is what the Church is for, the author then draws very interesting conclusions about "the gentiles."

The gentiles, precisely in line with what we might expect, have futile minds and darkened understanding "alienated from the life of God because of the ignorance that is in them" (Eph. 4:18). Because of this it is not surprising that they are entirely run by the desires of the world and its old nature (4:19–22). However, those who have learned the things of Christ should be first "renewed in the spirit of your minds" and thus able to "put on the new man, the one created according to [after the likeness of] God in the righteousness and holiness of truth" (Eph. 4:23–24).[20]

The author then goes on to show what this putting on of a new man might mean, and there is nothing escapist about it: the putting on of a new nature is described as the redirection of the mimetically formed old nature. So instead of speaking falsehood to our neighbors (old man), or indeed not speaking to them at all — an escapism not even contemplated in the text — we must speak the truth to them, for we are members one of another: interdividuality is still the norm in the new nature as in the old. The thief must put the same desire that ran him in appropriation to its inverse, fecund effect: doing honest work with his hands that he may be able to give to those in need. Talk must be for edifying rather than destroying people, and all the anger and clamor and slander must be turned to forgiveness: a real mode of human presence introducing a different quality of interdividuality. The conclusion to this passage is almost embarrassingly apropos of the analysis that I have been trying to set out: "Therefore be imitators [*mimétai*] of God as beloved children, and walk in love as Christ loved us and gave himself up for us, a fragrant offering and sacrifice to God" (Eph. 5:1–2).

It is in the light of this that the following instructions about avoiding particular aspects of the world of desire proper to unreformed selves are to be read. These desires militate against the walking in love in such a way that one can offer oneself up as a sacrifice to God. By walking in the light, however, we are not expected simply to shun the darkness, but actively to show it up for what it is: "Take no part in the works of darkness, but instead expose them" (Eph. 5:11). There is no escapism here, but an awareness that by living the life of Christ we will show up the works of darkness. It was that living of the light, of course, which was what caused Christ to be turned into a sacrifice in the first place. The author draws from this the observation, not that we should flee to some heavenly place, but rather that we should learn to walk carefully. In the light of the foregoing, this can only mean that learning how to

---

20. I have altered the RSV translation, making it more literal.

live the eschatological imagination and the consequent reformation of
the self is a difficult process requiring wisdom, as we come to see by
which desires we are being drawn in any given situation: the heavenly
mimesis or the worldly. As we learn to walk carefully in this way, so we
will be redeeming the time, for the days are evil (Eph. 5:16).

We have, then, already within the apostolic witness a clear understanding that Jesus opened up an eschatological imagination, making
available a very strong hope, to be received in a childlike manner, which,
rather than encouraging a dissociation from history, encourages rather
the construction of a new way of living in time. The centerpiece of this
vision is the self-giving victim who himself makes possible the living out
of this new quality of history on earth. This new quality of history involves an active construction of light in the midst of the darkness of the
lies of this world. That is to say, it is the bringing into being of a counterhistory, which, unlike the history of this world, is centered already on its
continuation and fulfillment in the heavenly places.

The History of the Victim

It would be pure gnosticism to imagine Jesus as a heavenly messenger
come to give a specific mysterious knowledge forming the eschatological
imagination which enabled people to escape history. Such an interpretation was an obvious temptation from the earliest days of the Church,
and one against which the fathers fought. However, that is no part
of mimetic theory, as though it were a particular cosmological theory
which, once grasped, was of itself salvific. It is apparent from all that
has gone before that the understanding of God and the human being,
and thus the possibility of the eschatological imagination that I have
been setting out, was the fruit of a particular historical process of development, culminating in and radically reforged by the life and teaching
as well as the death and resurrection of Jesus of Nazareth. That is to
say, salvation is inherently historical.

It is of course inherently historical not only in how it came about, but
in how we are to be involved in it. This, of course, is where the vision
I have been setting out enters into conflict with any universalist vision
of history or progress. It suggests that there is no such thing as a universal secular history, but that there are only a multitude of histories,
constructed by people who by their work give sense to time. These histories are told from a multitude of starting points, all of which shade
off into futility except insofar as they are histories constructed around
the victim. The bringing into being of the ecclesial hypostasis, complete
with eschatological imagination, is the empowering of people to con-

struct history around those who are not, those who are going out of
being, those whom the vanity and power of the world have emptied of
sense and of meaning. This is not something merely accidental to the
salvation that is brought about by the crucified and risen victim: the
construction of the history of the victim is an imperative which is the
same as the bringing into being of the ecclesial hypostasis. The reality of
this history is, of course, not to be seen until the final judgment, when
it will be the risen victim coming in glory who is revealed as the real
criterion for the sense of all the life stories and constructions in which
we have been engaged. But the final judgment is not simply the collapse
of history and the beginning of "eternity." It is the manifestation of such
history as has been constructed that is able to share the life of God, and
does not shade off into the futility and meaninglessness of violence. The
assurance is that it is the forgiving victims of this order who will be the
judges, the principles of manifestation, of the reality of history. These
it will be who have made possible the continuity between this creation
and the new creation, who will have enabled God's original plan not to
be thwarted.

Where does this leave secular history? Is this process of the coming
into being of the history of the victim simply invisible except to the
somewhat suspect eye of "faith"? Does not the coming into being of
the history of the victim act in fact as a leaven within the history constructed through battles and newspapers, rape of bullion and deserts
created in lands once rich in grain? For Girard the answer is unquestionably yes. His essay "History and the Paraclete"[21] is an extended
meditation on the way in which the presence of the Gospel texts, making
visible the founding murder, has acted inexorably, and often against the
understanding of those who thought themselves faithful to those texts,
to reveal the mechanisms of persecution, the self-deception flowing from
murder that is the basis of the distorted desire of "this world." There is
then a process at work detectable even to secular historians whereby the
attempt to sacralize the order of this world is constantly being undone.
From this constant collapsing of sacralized reasoning, reasoning derived
from still mythical representations, it has become possible, and indeed
second nature, for anyone at all to detect representations of persecution. As these have been brushed aside — in each case requiring huge
courage on the part of those standing up to the prevailing sacralized
order — so a scientific and not a mythical understanding of causality
was able to be born. In the same way it became possible to understand
human capacity and human responsibility — the former becoming evi-

---

21. In René Girard, *The Scapegoat* (London: Athlone, 1986), 198–212.

dent rather before the latter and tending itself to be sacralized until the weight of the latter is borne in by experience. This is what history looks like under the shadow of the *pax nuclearis:* the full extent of human capacity becomes knowable, as does the responsibility for avoiding an entirely human apocalypse.

Maybe it is worthwhile to emphasize what is perhaps the negative, subversive aspect of the eschatological imagination that has been brought into being. It cannot guarantee that people will start to participate in constructing the history of the victim, but its presence in history, by shifting a real sacredness to the realm of an urgently imperative hope and to people on their way out of being, has produced, and continues to produce, a constant desacralization of history, against all the attempts to resacralize history whether of the right or of the left. The extent to which any notion of history as a universal process fatally involves its believers in massive human sacrifice is part of what became obvious, and thus collapsed, along with the Berlin Wall, in 1989. With it there collapsed a whole project of an attempt to give meaning to human life. To the extent that much theology, including much of what is best and most generous in theology, was wedded to an attempt to sacralize a certain understanding of human history, that theology also entered into crisis. History cannot be redeemed by any attempt to discover an immanent and supposedly universally knowable dynamic within it. That is an attempt to sacralize it by faith alone. History can be made sacred only by practical charity, by the painful construction of the story of the victim in the here and now. This painful construction is really possible only by those who have been set free from the fear of death by the knowledge of the risen victim,[22] and are thus able to install the justice of the kingdom of God in the place where it has no place.

Here we have, I hope, a task for a developing theology of liberation that is fuelled both by Gesché's plea for the development of an *eschatologique* that does not run away from the supernatural and by a desacralized view of history as something which is made sacred only by its construction around the victim. This is of course the sort of history that cannot be understood by the rulers of this age (1 Cor. 2:6–8) and has little place in the official tale told by "this world." It is not the least of the merits of mimetic theory to have offered us the possibility of making the most of the very best instincts and generosity of so much of what was sadly overshadowed by being wedded to an intrinsically conflictual understanding of sociology and history. Our future constructions of the history of the victim are set free to be both more locally

---

22. Whether implicit or explicit.

varied and more Catholic, without being any less drastic or calling forth any less for martyrial testimony.

Original Sin between Forgiveness and Creation

I have attempted to set out a theology whereby the crucified and risen victim is the centerpiece of the whole construct. It is the forgiveness that the risen victim brought that enabled the fruitful separation of anthropology and theology into a distinct dependence rather than a violent confusion. It is the risen victim also who proved to be what enabled the apostolic group to glimpse the true nature of God's creation as being the same self-giving that lay behind the self-giving of Christ on the Cross. It is therefore no surprise that it should prove to be the risen victim who is the point of continuity between this creation and the "new creation" which is bursting in on us through our being opened up into the creatures we were destined to be all along. The risen victim has proved to be the center point of time as well, enabling time to be participative of eternity.[23]

At every point, the understanding of original sin I have been setting out has been derivative from this understanding of Christ as risen victim, and at every point the derived understanding can find support in the apostolic witness. I think it worthwhile indicating the way in which this understanding emphasizes both the drastic difference between this world and the next, and the continuity. The difference arises because there the victim is glorious, whereas here the victim is annihilated. The continuity arises because it is the same victim who was annihilated whose forgiveness permits constructive participation in the new creation. The key point here is that the doctrine of original sin is inseparable from this difference and this continuity. If we have a very modest rather banal doctrine of original sin, then our eschatology must also be banal, and vice versa. If the continuity between this world and the next is other than in the risen victim, then it is, in the first place, a continuity unknown by the apostolic witness and, second, not a very exciting prospect. The drastic nature of the alterity of Christian eschatology implies the drastic nature of the sort of reductive homogeneity that we acquire for ourselves. This is, it seems to me, not the least of the reasons why it is worth pleading for a drastic vision of original sin: the banalization of original sin is the banalization of eschatology and simultaneously the allowing ourselves to be left to ourselves, possibly worse than any punishment.

---

23. See the rite for the Preparation of the Candle at the Easter Vigil: "Christ yesterday and today, the beginning and the end, Alpha and Omega, all time belongs to him, and all the ages, to him be glory and power, through every age forever."

With the strong doctrine of original sin that I have been trying to set out, it can become apparent how the presence of the forgiving victim enables us to break out of a particular mode of being human and gradually be transformed into transformers. When we have original sin forgiven, we are unlocked, unbound (to be exact). We cannot be forgiven our concupiscence in the same sense: indeed, concupiscence is not, properly speaking, sin, precisely because it cannot properly speaking be forgiven. However, the gradual process of the unlocking of our distorted desires and their recentering on "the things that are above" shares in the work of forgiveness: it is how we forge the forgiveness we have received into a real creative human presence for others, enabling them too to enter into the beneficent mimesis of the new creation. It is as we are unbound into the possibility of a creative imagination beyond death that we struggle in hope between forgiveness and the new creation in the time of liturgy and prayer.

Chapter 9

Reimagining the Symbol
of Original Sin

We are now close to the end of our tentative elaboration of a theology of original sin in the light of mimetic theory. Starting with the event of the resurrection and the presence to the apostolic group of the crucified and risen Jesus, we have been able to show a single, coherent process of development in which there emerged a new vision of God as deathless, creative relationality and, at the same time, a parting glance at a mode of humanity on its way out of being made available as it became possible to become a new sort of human. We have seen the way in which Jesus' bringing into being of the ecclesial hypostasis and his opening up of the eschatological imagination are the same reality, and it is this that has enabled us to look at humanity from the viewpoint of what is coming into being. Thus we have seen that there is a quite specific structure to the an-ecclesial hypostasis, that of death-related rivalistic mimetic desire. This structure is in resistance to the sort of alterity that has been opened up by the human forging of the new creation that was made possible by the coming, life, teaching, death, and resurrection of Jesus.

This has resulted in a view of original sin that is simultaneously eschatological and soteriological. We have been able to see the term "original sin" as a useful, and probably necessary, verbal instrument to characterize the human state of affairs that is opposed to the coming into being of the new creation. This perception has enabled us a view of concupiscence that is also eschatological: we might characterize it as the condition of humans who are being unlocked from the state of affairs in which they were formed in opposition to the form of alterity which characterizes the new creation. Concupiscence is thus the disposition, affecting the whole being even of such humans as have started to have their relationality reformed in the new mode of alterity, to resist being transformed into active constructors of the new creation. When the Church teaches us that Christ and the Virgin Mary were without

237

concupiscence, having been without original sin,[1] the content of what is being taught is that they were both (in different ways, of course) fully active constructors of the new creation and that the resistance that they suffered to their work of bringing about the new creation was exterior to them and not interior to them, as it is with us. They were not personally involved in the resistance to their own forging of the possibility of the new creation, whereas we are.

The whole vision thus far elaborated has placed great emphasis on the rôle of a historical event (the life, death, and resurrection of Jesus), seen as the subversive culmination of a whole interpretative tradition immersed in historical events (the history of the Jewish people). It is this unique historical event which made possible first the change of perception and thus the change of relationality, which we have seen to be the bringing into being of the ecclesial hypostasis and which we have also seen to be the human construction of a different history (which I have called, for short, the history of the victim). It is not, then, unreasonable to take a step further.

If the forging of the human possibility of bringing about the active construction of the new creation was set in being by a particular contingent event within a particular contingent history, then it obliges us to consider the state of affairs opposed to it as also a particular contingent history, that is to say, as something that need not have been the case. We must look into the question of the historicity of original sin.

The Historicity of Original Sin

Let it be quite clear that we are examining in the first place the sense in which the "state of affairs" revealed as on its way out of being by the coming into being of the ecclesial hypostasis is participative of history. We are not yet asking about an originary act. The quality of the historicity of original sin is a strict correlative of the quality of the historicity of salvation. This can be shown by comparison with a putative gnostic soteriology. Let us imagine that our salvation is the salvation of our souls, seen as beings which are not essentially related to corporeality and temporality. According to such a view, what Christ really came to do was conduct a secret deal with the Father, by dying to pay some diabolical or paternal ransom, thus enabling those souls touched by baptism to be whipped off to the Father on the dissolution of their corporeality. If such were the nature of our salvation, then it would be possible to

---

1. For Christ: Constantinople II (553), canon 12; for the Virgin: Trent, Decree on Original Sin, par. 6, and Pius IX, *Ineffabilis Deus* (1854).

imagine a doctrine of original sin which would have to do with some celestial crime of our spirits which condemned us to corporeality and temporality. The historicity of original sin would be irrelevant, because the historicity of salvation is irrelevant: it was the secret deal that took place under the cover of Christ's death that counted.

We can imagine a further, somewhat less gnostic account of original sin, which also has a different quality of historicity: Christ came down to pay in his flesh for the infinite offenses against God which humanity had piled up. He paid by suffering the infinite pains of the crucifixion, thus remitting the debt which the Father held against humanity. From then on, no debt is imputed to those who allow themselves to be covered by Christ's blood, and, on death, they may inherit heaven. In the light of this soteriology it would be possible to imagine a theology of original sin in which the first humans offended God, and God thus punished them by sentencing them to death and, in his rigor, imputed their sin to all their descendents, who therefore live under the mark of the punishment of the first humans and in some way inherit their guilt. Here, the historicity of original sin would be slight, because the offense and the sentence are related only extrinsically, as revealed by the fact that the salvation is also extrinsic. The only practical difference "before" and "after" the original offense would have been that humans now die as a punishment, and while they live, they are all guilty. Because humans can only be saved *from* history and not saved *in* history, history, after the first sin, is of no salvific relevance.

However, if salvation is, as I have attempted to set out, an essentially historical affair, by which essentially temporal, corporeal humans are enabled to shift from living out one sort of history into becoming active participants in another, a history which is able to be participative of the divine life, then it follows that in seeking to understand original sin we are looking at a state of affairs that is not only historical, but in fact coextensive with human culture. That is to say the "state of affairs" arose at the same time as human culture. When human historicity came into being as human culture, it came into being as the state of affairs we now know to be on its way out of being. This seems the inescapable conclusion of positing a single, unique event of salvation, prepared for by a long historical process, by which the new possible human historicity was brought into being. It is exactly this conclusion which underlies Paul's insistence that "all have sinned." Paul was not speaking as the result of extensive ethnological research in Australasia and the Olduvai Gorge. He was drawing the necessary conclusion from the uniqueness of what had occurred in Christ.

In the first place we have then a notion of the historicity of original sin corresponding to the notion of the historicity of salvation: a unique historical event revealing the coextensiveness of a certain futility with all human culture.

The second question about historicity concerns contingency and necessity. Given that salvation was the historical process by which a certain sort of alterity — the alterity of the deathless, creative nature of God — became discovered by or was revealed to human beings (the same reality is seen from both angles), and that the sort of salvation we are given is one by which we are empowered to construct a human history nourished by a different sort of human alterity, it is logical to conclude that the history not marked by this new alterity could, in fact, have been other. That it could have been other depends strictly on the fact that it is now being enabled to become other. This means that whatever it is that characterizes the futility that is coextensive with human culture is not a necessary, essential part of being this sort of animal, but is accidental to being this sort of animal. The fact of historical alterity reveals the fact of contingency. This precludes us from seeing the "state of affairs" as the result of biology, or nature, or God. This logical insight is available as early as the story of Cain and Abel, where it is made clear that Cain need not have killed his brother. The clearing out of either divine or natural causality in human murder that the Jewish understanding of salvation had already made available begins that process whereby it is understood that human futility is anchored in properly human contingent culture, that is, in history. This enables us to conclude from the historicity of salvation to the contingency and nonnecessity of original sin.

So far, let us remember, we have been examining the way that the "state of affairs" — what was traditionally called *peccatum originalis originatum* — is historical. We have concluded that it is historical in the sense that it is coextensive with human culture, which is a necessarily historical reality, and that it is historical in the sense that it is a contingent and not a necessary reality. We have concluded this entirely in the light of the salvation that has been offered and independently of any particular understanding of human origins, hominization, evolution, and so on. All that has been demonstrated is that any understanding of original sin that does not posit a futility that is coextensive with human culture and that does not posit the historical contingency of that futility is not compatible with the understanding of salvation which I have tried to develop and which I take, allowing for possible corrections from ecclesiastical authority, to be a fully Catholic understanding.

It is only at this point that it makes sense to raise the question of origins: of *peccatum originalis originans*, the originating *act*, the initial kick-start, of original sin. The question of the origin of original sin is strictly dependent on the coextensiveness of the state of affairs with human culture and the nonnecessary nature of that state of affairs. This was the way in which Paul brought Adam into his argument in Romans: not because he was attempting to found his understanding of Christ on his understanding of Adam, but because the universality of sin must have begun somewhere, and Adam was a more convenient way of talking about this than any other. It is the universality of sin which raises the question as to its origin, not some origin known about independently which explains the universality.

Continuing in our purely a posteriori deductive line of argument we can ask whether it is necessary to bother with the question of the origin of original sin at all. There is an obvious sense in which it is not necessary: the salvation of no one at all depends on their ability to deal with this question. On the other hand, given the nature of original sin as coextensive with human culture and as a nonnecessary reality, the conclusion that it had a historical beginning seems unavoidable. Once the conclusion has become unavoidable, the question cannot be unasked without a retreat into fideism. However, the sort of question that is being asked must first itself be examined.

When we ask about the origin of original sin are we asking about a cause in any ordinary sense? The search for a cause would be the search for a motor that was responsible for setting in motion a chain of other events. We would be seeking an explanation for something, as though we needed that explanation to make sense of something else. However, we don't strictly speaking need to know the origin of original sin to make sense of salvation. That it had an origin is enough. Even if we did, by some extraordinary revelation, discover exactly what happened, when and where and involving whom, it would add nothing at all to our understanding of salvation, because we could interpret nothing of that special revelation except in the light of the understanding of salvation that is already available to us. All that the special revelation could do would be to fill in the already available picture.

We need also ask about what we are doing in asking for a cause. It is often the case that the simple human activity of "the search for a cause" is not unrelated to the desire to accuse (*ad causam*) or blame someone for something. There is no shortage of ways of talking about Adam and Eve or the serpent that are ways of finding whom to blame for how things are. To follow that pattern of search for an origin would be to try to understand original sin within the framework of blaming someone for the present state of affairs and would be in contradiction with the whole approach I have been trying to set out, which is that original sin is to be understood only from the coming into being of forgiveness, as that which is being forgiven.

So instead of this approach to causality, can mimetic theory throw light on the business of searching for an origin? I rather think it can and will try to illustrate this with the help of a mimetic master text: Luke 6:39–42. This passage teaches about the blind leading the blind, the disciple not being more than the master, and the impossibility of removing the mote in the brother's eye while having a beam in one's own. It entirely presupposes a mimetic understanding of psychology. That is to say, all our knowledge of each other is projective and relational: our knowledge of someone else is inseparable from our relationality to that other person, and what we know of them depends on a real similarity between the other and ourselves such that we can properly project from our own experience and begin to understand the other. There is no question here of any possible neutral, objective vantage point onto the other. Relational, projective knowledge of the other is taken for granted by Jesus. The question which Jesus raises is as to the mode of projection. With the teaching concerning the mote and the beam, Jesus indicates that there are two ways of approaching a problem in someone else: the first is from the position of someone who is not aware of or maybe in denial of his own similarity to the other, in which case the result is an accusatory highlighting of the other's problem. It is obvious where this approach leads: the one challenged reacts by not accepting the accusation, will not be led by the one proffering such "objective" criticism, and will proffer criticism in return, and the two will enter into a process of mutual antagonism, which is the same as the two blind men falling into a pit: they have become a *skandalon* to each other.

The second mode of projection, which is the one which Jesus is recommending in insisting that the one proffering criticism first remove the beam from his own eye, starts from the acceptance of similarity. It is when someone recognizes that he is the same sort of beast as the person he wishes to correct and that he is driven by the same forces to do things which are at least analogous, when they are not identical, that he will be able to approach the other from a position of constructive complicity. That is to say, the whole direction of his approach to the other springs from the creation of a relation between the two that is a spreading of forgiveness. The modes of projection are always relational; the question is whether they are accusatory or forgiving; there is no other approach, or "third way," to the problem of another human being.

It therefore becomes evident that there is no theological approach to the question of an originating sin that is not projective in one or the other mode. I would suggest that the discourse which sees original sin as the foundational reality (Adam/Eve/the serpent is to blame, Jesus is the solution) is firmly stuck in the accusatory mode of projection, and ultimately does nothing but create stumbling blocks. If we are to be faithful to the whole approach to original sin thus far attempted, then our projection of an originating sin must be born from the mode of constructive complicity. In so doing we will be stretching the shape of forgiveness as far as there is anything to be forgiven.

So a first point about the sort of question we are asking when asking about an originating sin becomes clear: we are asking about the first people to be like us. We are doing so out of a grateful acceptance of their likeness to us and because of an awareness that we are able to accept that likeness on our way to becoming something else, and indeed that our learning to accept that likeness may actually help us construct a forgiveness that includes them. The question is not so much how "Adam's" sin affects us, as how Christ's forgiveness (which we are charged to make real) affects Adam. To put this another way: there is no properly theological approach to "our first parents" that is not a discourse of love concerning the first people to need the sort of constructive forgiveness that we first discovered ourselves to need. There is no independent anthropological starting point in the approach to original sin.[2]

When we face the question of the origin of original sin, then we are not attempting to find a cause. We are attempting a projection of a purely theological construct that will sit with the universality and contingency of the state of affairs which have come to light as a result of the bringing into being of the ecclesial hypostasis.

Having seen in what sense the question of the origin of original sin can be asked and seen that the postulation of a historical origin to a universal contingent state of affairs is unavoidable, we must then ask if by a historical origin we necessarily mean a fully human event. For instance, would it be acceptable to posit a genetic mutation in certain higher apes as the result of a radioactive release following a volcanic eruption or meteor shower and to say that the resulting animals, humans, emerged from a historical contingent happening of this sort? Would that be an acceptable theological projection? Manifestly not. We can all distinguish between something happening to someone, which is an event in a certain sense, an accident, and a properly human act which involves a participation which is either creative or destructive of who we are: we cannot

---

2. There is, of course, a comparatively independent anthropological starting point to the question of human origins — depending on paleoanthropological remains, archaeology, and so on. However, such research can never by itself yield information about an originating sin, since this is not an interpretation-free reality, but one which can be understood only from forgiveness, and thus theologically.

be forgiven for an accident. We can be forgiven only for doing something which makes us who we are and which we might not have done, and had we not done it, we would have been a different person. It is an event of this latter sort which must figure in our theological retrojection of the originating sin.

Finally we might ask whether it was necessary for our first parents already to have been fully human before this originating act took place, or whether it might have been in the doing of the originating act that they became human. The first projection, which is the one represented in Genesis, has as its necessary implication that none of the first humans died or had children or siblings who went away, before the originating sin was committed, since that would involve there being humans who are not in need of forgiveness, and the universality of the unique event of Christ would be denied. So the originating act must have happened in the first generation of humans, however they happened to be there. Of course we cannot know what it was to be a human before the originating sin, since our whole capacity for projection backward, which derives from Christ, is marked by forgiveness. We cannot say anything even about Christ as the Original Man except from within the prism of humans being forgiven and enabled to become cocreators as creatures. It is difficult to see[3] how this sort of projection is compatible with anything other than a belief in monogenesis of the sort described in Genesis.

However, it does seem possible to suggest that it was in the doing of the originating act that our first parents became human. In order for this to be the case, it must be shown that the act in which the proto-human became human was one which was both in continuity with certain sorts of proto-human acts, but yet not made necessary by those acts, and at the same time, that it was in rupture with them, in that the act that was done was able to affect the whole being of the new human in a way that no proto-human act had been able to. This sort of originating act would be compatible with a belief either in monogenesis or in "the monophyletism toward which contemporary evolutionism tends."[4] Constructing a theological retrojection of such an originating act is, of course, a considerably more complex affair than the sort of construct necessary for an originating act seen as posterior to an already achieved humanity. However, it is to just such a construction, while aware that it cannot be more than a possibly useful symbol, that I will now turn.

---

3. Or, in the phraseology of *Humani Generis*, "nequaquam appareat quomodo."
4. B. Pottier, *Le péché originel selon Hegel: Commentaire et synthèse* (Namur: Culture et Vérité, 1990), 227.

Reimagining the Symbol

Before proceeding, let me list the conditions which this symbol must satisfy:

(a) it must flow from the presence of the crucified and risen Christ;

(b) it must yield a human being who is recognizably similar to what we can now see ourselves as on our way out of being in the light of the forgiving presence of the crucified and risen Christ;

(c) it must describe the continuity and the rupture between this human being and a proto-human;

(d) it must describe a human event;

(e) it must describe the nonnecessity of the originating act;

(f) it must show the act to have been of the sort to have inaugurated the distinctively human culture which we find ourselves able to leave (to match the historical nature of salvation);

(g) it must show the act to have been of the sort to have shaped every aspect of that distinctively human culture (to match the completely pervasive nature of concupiscence).

Let us start then with the event which brought into being the new humanity: the self-giving up to death of Jesus in the hands of a more or less carefully structured collective murder, a self-giving which it was necessary to interpret beforehand by a sacrificial mime so that the positive effect of that death might be made available after it to those able to perceive its sense. We might posit therefore that the original act was a murder, after which the murderers began to keep alive the positive effects of their murder, as they understood it, by means of a series of sacrificial mimes. Would this "might" ("we might posit") be entirely arbitrary, or could we find support in the apostolic witness for such a move?

In order to understand the positive sense of the self-giving up to death of Jesus, the apostolic witness makes use, in different places, of four quite distinct stories from Genesis, all of which are interpreted in the light of the Cross and resurrection. To illustrate the sense of Christ's death, he is shown as moved by a self-giving which is the undoing of Adam's appropriation of divinity to himself (Paul's argument about Adam's desire in Romans 5–7, and the illustration of Christ's self-giving in Philippians 2). He is shown as undoing the order based on fratricidal murder from the beginning (John's reference to "Your Father..." in chapter 8, and the development of that in 1 John 3). Baptism into Christ's saving death is shown to be the real sense behind the story of Noah's Ark (1 Pet. 3:20–21). Finally Christ is shown as undoing the scattering of all humanity following on the attempt to appropriate human unity by human effort alone at Babel (Luke's presentation of Pentecost in Acts 2). That is to say, four quite distinct moments of Genesis, relating to desire, to murder, and to foundation of sociality, are shown to be capable of a strictly christological interpretation. Any symbol, then, of human origins that is capable of conflating these moments within a strictly christological interpretation has the advantage over other putative symbols of being exactly in line with the risen Christ's own hermeneutic of Scripture as explained on the road to Emmaus. It is precisely because it permits the construction of such a symbol that mimetic theory recommends itself in this context.

Let us attempt then a christological rereading of each one of these moments before attempting to discover their inner coherence. First, Genesis 3. The essence of the sin described in this passage is one of mimetic desire. An object (the fruit) became desirable when it became a way of appropriating something proper to someone else (the knowledge of good and evil proper to God). It was *only* when the object was seen as a way of appropriating what was proper to someone else that it became desirable. Hence the temptation was "to become like God." The temptation was not resisted: the object was appropriated, but more important than the object, desire thereafter functioned in the mode of appropriation, and relationality with the other became formed rivalistically. The other (whether human or divine) could be perceived only as a threat or rival. The immediate result of the appropriation was that good and evil became defined not according to God, but according to appropriation, which means that the self was not accepted as given, but had to be appropriated by forging itself over against some other considered as evil. The beginning of the forging of an identity "over against" is the self-expulsion from the paradise of receiving the self gratuitously.

For the story to work in Genesis there has to be an initial prohibition: the story could not have worked if God had not made available a way of entering into rivalry with himself by forbidding the eating of the fruit of the particular tree. The story could not have worked unless there were already an element of "imitate me / do not imitate me" built into the relationship between God and human beings *ab initio*. The possibility (though not the necessity) of double bind is thus already present, before the originating act, as emanating from God. However, this is entirely dependent on the story being a projection of an originating act that flows from a certain understanding of salvation: the Jewish understanding flowing from the covenant and the giving of the Torah. Yet Paul showed extensively that the problem with a salvation based on the law was that it locked one inextricably in a double bind. Salvation by Christ has come to replace salvation by the law. So in our christological projection we should do without the element of an explicit primal prohibition against eating from the tree. To be fully christological we need to understand there to have been no primal prohibition, but instead of the law, a person. This is fully in line with Jesus' culmination of the law in the linking of the love of God and the love of neighbor as oneself as the greatest of the commandments.

The "new commandment" can thus be seen as the commandment that we see each other as alike in the light of a nonappropriative mimesis, and this was what God wanted humans to be from the beginning. This need not have been explicit: the first human act might well have been, as it became possible to see the other as like me, to be tempted to appropriate that person for me, and then actually to appropriate that person. This would not have been contrary to an explicit divine command, but it would have in fact gone against the whole sort of human being that God was bringing into being, a being able to relate to the other in a pacific mimesis. The beauty of the christological rereading is that it enables us to forego an explicit sin against God that is independent of any sin against a fellow human being. The point of Christ's self-giving was precisely to bring out that sins against God are never directly against God, independent of any human mediation, but are always sins against a fellow human being.[5]

What does it mean for one human being to appropriate another? The obvious sense, given that we are constructing a symbol from the self-giving up to death of Christ, is that we appropriate another by taking his or her life, in short by killing. In this way it becomes perfectly plausible to combine all the key theological elements of the Genesis 3 story with a christological soteriology and come up with a symbol that involves a human putting to death. This putting to death is the result of the possibility of seeing another human being as like myself but being tempted to appropriate that other for myself, and doing so by putting the other to death. The result is an identity forged over against the dead other and thus the beginning of "life" acquiring a positive meaning over against "death": both these two become human cultural realities rather than

---

5. It seems curious that G. Martelet in his *Libre réponse à un scandale* (Paris: Cerf, 1986, 1992), 51–52, should be so keen to maintain a purely theological original sin prior to human fratricide, given that he is pleading for a christological starting point for understanding original sin; yet a christological starting point reveals precisely the simultaneity of a sin against God and a human being. The distortion of alterity affects my relation to both inseparably.

natural happenings. Human alterity, desire, and thus eventually human culture and interiority are forged from the corpse-which-gave-me-life.

This rereading of the Genesis story is strictly dependent on only one piece of "demythologization," and it is a piece of "demythologization" which the New Testament carries out anyhow in a slightly different context: the substitution of salvation by Christ crucified for salvation by the law. This leaves us with a person rather than a fruit and a positive divine creative design bringing into being people who might love each other rather than a prohibition. God is thus constantly calling us into a positive likeness of himself ("be like me, imitate me") without any double bind of the sort: "but do not be like me or imitate me in this one area."

The next "moment" of Genesis which is used by the apostolic witness to make sense of Christ's self-giving up to death is the story of Cain and Abel in Genesis 4. The essential elements of this story are as follows: we have the first humans whose identity is forged over against each other (that is, were born outside paradise). One kills the other in an act which he need not have done (Cain could have mastered his desire). The victim was innocent, and the rest of human society is founded from Cain. Culture comes into being and depends on God's threat of vengeance, should anyone retaliate against Cain, for its stability. But vengeance grows and multiplies, so that the seven-fold vengeance God threatens against anyone killing Cain becomes seventy-seven-fold by the time we reach Lamech. So here we have an unnecessary act of fratricide, founding human culture in violence. The peaceful continuity of human culture is guaranteed by God stepping in to maintain order by the threat of vengeance.

The christological rereading of this permits two pieces of "demythologization." The first is regarding the strictly fraternal one-to-one nature of the murder. Girard has shown, in his reading of the Romulus and Remus myth, that there is a tendency in the recounting of myths to hide the initially collective nature of the murder behind various stages of retelling.[6] So the version of the Romulus and Remus myth which most know is that in which Romulus kills his brother in one-to-one combat, and Rome is founded. However, behind this myth are other, older versions in which Remus is killed in a collective scuffle, *cecidit in turba,* as well of course as the hint, behind the story of Romulus's own disappearance into deification, that he was in fact murdered collectively later on himself. We can, then, read the story of Cain and Abel as a later crystallization of an earlier account of a collective murder, a crystallization that occurred as the collective nature of the murder, and thus the universal-

---

6. See René Girard, *The Scapegoat* (London: Athlone, 1986), 88–94.

ity of the responsibility, became obscured. The Genesis story would then be the partial recovery of the truth hidden behind the myth. That there were other people around beside Cain is shown even in the story as we have it by his fear of what other people will do to him, from which God protects him (Gen. 4:14–15).

This recovery of the collectivity of the original murder is a piece of "demythologization" which is entirely in accord with the christological rereading which we have been carrying out. Christ was not killed in a one-to-one combat,[7] but collectively put to death. Furthermore, the apostolic witness understands Cain's murder to be capable of a collective reading when Jesus addresses some Jews who had believed in him in John 8. They collectively seek to kill him because they are the sons of the devil who was a murderer from the beginning, that is, from the time of Cain: in John, Cain becomes the appropriate symbol for the collective murder of Christ. Exactly the same understanding can be seen in the Matthaean "Woes to the Pharisees." Jesus sees himself as making visible all the victims of murder from the beginning and sees those he is apostrophizing (a collectivity) as in solidarity with those murderers from the beginning. It is thus a perfectly legitimate christological rereading of the Cain and Abel story to reimagine the beginning as a collective murder: the "demythologization" of the individual murder is proper to the apostolic witness itself.

The second piece of christological rereading concerns the way in which it is God who guarantees the peace in the wake of the act of murder. Again, Girard shows that the prohibition against mimetic violence (vengeance) is something which flows from the experience of the founding murder itself. It was a frenzy of mimetic violence which led to the collective murder; the collective peace after the murder is such that it is attributed to the divinized victim. From this there are born prohibitions against the sort of mimetic behavior which led to the original violent crisis and simultaneously the ritual reenactment of that violence, sacrificing to the god (in imitation of the victim) in order to attempt to maintain alive the peace that resulted from the original murder. When, in Genesis 4, it is God who establishes the boundaries against vengeance, we have what is still a partial demythologization of the original birth of prohibitions against mimetic violence. This partial demythologization corresponds, once again, to the Jewish attitude toward the law, seen as a divine bulwark against multiplying violence. However, this very attitude comes in for a christological rereading in the apostolic witness. For Paul,

---

7. If one considers Christ's death as in one-to-one combat with the devil, then it is with the devil precisely considered as the governing principle of all collective murders.

the law, rather than being God's bulwark against human violence was a human way of sacralizing violence, as shown in the crucifixion of Christ and Paul's own zealous persecuting of Jesus in his followers. This is the same as the insistence in the Matthaean Sermon on the Mount that the law of itself does not reach us at the level of desire, but can be and is turned into an instrument of distorted desire.

In the light, then, of Christ's self-giving up to death bringing to an end the law and permitting a sociality which lives the deepest intention of the law without needing to be bound by the law, it becomes possible to engage in a rigorously christological demythologization of God's establishing the protective laws against violence. We have instead an original collective murder, from which there developed a series of prohibitions designed to ensure social order, attributed to a god or God. We have a partial demythologization of this in the Jewish law where we have a law whose deepest intention is to lead us away from fratricide altogether, and the final completion of this when Jesus' self-giving up to death reveals the complete absence of divine complicity in shoring up the human social order, but rather God's desire to bring into being a wholly different sociality which flows from, rather than being constructed over against, the victim. Our rigorously christological reading of Genesis 4 enables us to fill out the picture yielded by our reading of Genesis 3. We have a collective murder seen as inaugurating a culture, with all the key elements of prohibition against vengeance that produce sociality.

The story of Noah is less obviously a story of origins than either that of Adam and Eve or Cain and Abel, yet since it, too, is subjected to a christological rereading in the apostolic witness, I beg indulgence for a quick glimpse at this story too.[8] In the first letter of Peter it is pointed out that in the days of Noah "a few, that is eight persons, were saved through water. Baptism, which corresponds to this, now saves you" (1 Pet. 3:20–21). That is to say, the water of baptism corresponds to the water of the flood. Yet baptism, we know from Paul, is being immersed in the *death* of Christ, in order to be able to share in his resurrection, and it is he, and after him the Church, which the Ark prefigured. This implies a rather particular christological rereading of the Noah story: the implication is that the Ark actually went under the flood rather than escaping it miraculously! In this rereading, we would have all the violence abounding on the face of the earth and, at a time of particular mimetic crisis of indifferentiation symbolized by the Flood, the collective

---

8. See also René Girard, *Things Hidden from the Foundation of the World* (London: Athlone, 1987), 143, for a slightly different but entirely compatible vision of the Noah story.

putting to death of someone (Noah) or a group (Noah and his family). It was this putting to death which brought about peace, permitting the reestablishment of order, the categorization of animals, and the setting up of a new tribal system. There are of course many myths of this sort whereby a more or less hidden collective expulsion or murder is seen as producing a new social order where fruit or animals or foodstuffs start to abound as the result of a mysterious visitation in which it can either be the collectivity which perishes at the hand of a god or a god which perishes at the hand of a collectivity and, as a prize, leaves behind the basis for the new culture. The Noah story as we have it could very well be a Jewish demythologization of just such a story in the light of their experience of salvation from out of Egypt leading to the setting up of the covenant. Here Noah is saved from out of the flood, and God makes a covenant with him never more to destroy all flesh.

The Jewish rereading already shows the Jewish tendency to tell the story from the point of view of the victim, the tendency which we have already seen with relation to their flight from Egypt. The partial demythologization has God rescue Noah and his family from out of the hands of violent men, in order to establish a new peaceful sociality. The christological rereading merely takes this tendency one vital step further back, by revealing the founding murder and indicating that those who are prepared to share in the self-giving toward the founding death are those who will be brought to everlasting life. The new sociality is made possible because of the self-giving up to death, not a sociality derived from self-deceit following a collective murder, as in the myth behind the Noah story. Once again, the christological rereading, already implicit in the use of the Noah story in 1 Peter, points to an originating murder at the base of human sociality.

The final "moment" in the Genesis account of origins to receive a christological rereading in the apostolic witness is the account of the scattering of humanity at Babel. In the Lucan account of Pentecost we have an account of how the presence to the apostolic group of the crucified and risen Lord began the dynamic of forging a new unity of the whole of humanity from out of every race and tribe and nation and tongue. This, the beginnings of the catholicity of the new people of God, is strictly dependent on the self-giving up to death of Jesus: it is the risen dead one who makes possible this unity. The story of Babel is the inverse of this: human beings, who have only one tongue and few words (Gen. 11:1), seek to make a secure unity for themselves by building a tower. God, alarmed that if they succeed in building the tower nothing will be impossible for them, scatters them and confuses their language. We have the same pattern of mimetic desire as in Genesis 3 and a similar reaction from God. Human identity has to be grasped and appropriated in order as to make security; God scatters that identity lest humans, having achieved this identity, stop at nothing. This is similar to the way in which in the earlier story God expelled Adam and Eve from the garden lest they eat of the tree of life and eternalize their fallen state. Appropriative desire and a rivalistic God are the two similar elements.

Our christological rereading suggests that what we have originally is groups scattering from each other and forming separate languages which are in hostility to each other, as their respective sacrificial systems break down time after time and they fail to keep unity in the wake of successive attempts to grasp onto unity and security by sacrifices (at least initially human sacrifices). All sacrificial systems based on grasping security by victimizing tend to fail to produce unity, and groups forge language from their sacred victimary systems. This is the direct inverse of the self-giving up to death of Christ, which permits the forming of a sociality without any "over against" and in which all the scattered groups are able to find the real center of their language, their representational center. In the christological rereading, it is man who scatters himself, not God, because of the inherent futility of any building of social order at the expense of the victim. In between the original scattering and the christological gathering we have a Jewish rereading of the scattering derived from their understanding of being gathered together out of the Babylonian empire. The "confusion" of tongues (Heb.: *balal*) is an etymological joke at the expense of the arrogance of the imperial Babylonian attempt to dominate the earth, and the unfinished tower is a mocking look at one of the huge Ziqqurats which had the pretension in Babylonian religion of uniting heaven and earth. Once again we have an original tale of cultural scattering, a Jewish rereading of this, and a christological rereading of the Jewish partial demythologization. This christological rereading gives us back a plausible account of the theological elements proper to the original scattering seen in the light of the death that made possible the unscattering.

We have then a rigorously christological reading of each of the four major moments of the accounts of the origins in Genesis. In each case, the reading is legitimated by the use made of the respective story in the New Testament. In each case we have a "moment" that is compatible with a view on an originary scene as a founding murder. When the four "moments" are conflated, the combined effect is overwhelming. We have an understanding of desire which can easily be related to a murder, a murder related to a desire and to the founding of a culture and the establishment of prohibitions. We have the founding of a sociality from the excluded one, and we have the cultural tendency to be unable to maintain a grasped unity based on the same desire as the first two accounts, a cultural tendency overcome by a self-giving death. It is, then, with these elements that I propose to construct the christological rereading of an originary scene.

The Scene of Origin

Our scene of origin[9] is simultaneously the scene of the act whereby imitative patterns proper to anthropoids became the relatively distinct phenomenon of desire, and that whereby representation was born. That is to say, before this scene we have highly mimetic, but still instinctually controlled, anthropoids; after it we have humans, however dimly recognizable as such. To bring us to the threshold of this act we observe that the animal sociality of the higher apes is maintained by dominance patterns which function as a way of limiting the working of imitative rivalry away from the center of the group: the dominating member or members may be imitated, but there should be no *acquisitive* imitation of them. As the capacity for imitation grows,[10] more and more of a strain is put on this form of animal sociality and the instinctual patterns which prevent conflict from ending in bloodletting. Eventually we reach a "moment," if as such we may refer to it, in which we are at the absolute limit of the ability of instinctual controls to affect animal sociality and in which the capacity for imitation in every field has grown to such an extent that the structure of animal sociality has become impossible. There is no instinctual way of ordering the group any more, and this coincides with the collapse of the difference between a dominant member and any other: the more imitation grows, the more like each other the members become. With instinctual brakes at their weakest and imitative similarity at its height we have the optimal conditions for our scene of origin.

Acquisitive mimesis is no longer held in check by a dominant figure, and members have become similar. No member controls acquisitive mimesis, and so acquisitive mimesis flourishes among similar members. Simultaneously then with the flourishing of acquisitive mimesis there is born the possibility of perceiving the other as similar: it hasn't happened yet, but it is there as a possibility. There exists, at the same time

9. See Girard, *Things Hidden*, 84–104, 283–84; J.-M. Oughourlian, *Un mime nommé désir* (Paris: Grasset, 1982), 57–58; and E. Gans, *Science and Faith: The Anthropology of Revelation* (Lanham, Md.: Rowman & Littlefield, 1990), 1–17.

10. J. Monod observed that it is the powerful development of the mimetic function of the brain which characterizes the human. Given that this started in proto-humans, it is reasonable to suggest that it was the growth of this mimetic capacity which was a condition of possibility for hominization. See Girard, *Things Hidden*, 94–95.

as this, the possibility of *not* following undecidable acquisitive mimesis among similar members. Instinct has prepared animals for ways of ending conflict by one yielding to another without bloodletting. These of course depended on and built up the dominance pattern. The closer the members become to imitative equality, the less that instinct works. It would, however, be possible, at this point, when acquisitive mimesis and similarity are combined, for the first noninstinctual gesture to have been one of yielding to the other following previous patterns, but without previous constraints. This yielding could then have been imitated by the whole group. Such a primordial yielding would have involved establishing the beginnings of a noninstinctual sociality, a human sociality, based on a gratuitous mimetic recognition of the other and not on the appropriation of the other. We cannot begin to imagine where such a sociality would have taken us, and how it would have permitted the process of hominization which developed over a very long time after this initial act. It is enough for it to have been possible.[11] It was equally possible, however, for the mimetic rivalry to increase without any instinctual way of braking the conflict: as the mimetic frenzy escalated, so order became impossible. Acquisitive mimesis becomes antagonistic mimesis, the setting of all against all, and this eventually leads to the reconciliation of all against a member of the group, in his or her murder.

Here, then, we have the possibility of pacific or of appropriative mimesis, the "temptation" in the form of the growing group pressure, leading to an act. After the act we have an opening of the eyes, as in Genesis 3:7. Immediately after the paroxysm of violence which has culminated in the murder, there proceeds the miraculous peace which is perceived to be related to the common victim. A new type of attention has emerged:

> Beyond the purely instinctual object, the alimentary or sexual object or the dominant individual, there is the cadaver of the collective victim and this cadaver constitutes the first object for this new type of attention.[12]

From this attention we begin to acquire the beginnings of a "sacred center," the forging of which and the maintenance of which is the beginnings of a properly human culture. The process may have to be repeated thousands of times in the midst of thousands of crises over thousands

---

11. Here we have God calling into being the creature who is to become a sharer in his life without any sort of rupture: animal mimesis is able to move directly into sharing in the divine creative mimesis. This uninterrupted calling into being is the content of the "paradise" of Genesis.

12. Girard, *Things Hidden*, 99.

of years, but once the mechanism of the production of unity by the victim is in place, humanity as we know it is on its way. The gradually evolving ritual repetition of such scenes with the rhythmic cries that accompanied them could well be the origin of language. The gesture, once made, is irreversible, and the resulting culture is connatural with it.[13]

This scene of origin is a scene of the origin of human representation: we started with proto-human imitation, and we finished with the possibility of signs emerging from the collective awareness of the "miraculous" cadaver. The scene depends on a radical continuity and a rupture between animal and human. The continuity is in the working of imitation; the rupture is that that imitation has broken free from any instinctual constraint and become mediatized by a dead co-member. The way "I" am part of the sociality has to be defined as how "I" am driven not by instinctive drives or purely cerebral imitational patterns,[14] but by a group which has found a principle of order in the victim. Desire has been born as the way a new sort of alterity moves me, confirming me in appropriative patterns flowing from and leading to death.

The scene shows how the whole of nascent human culture is affected by the experience of the event. Such an event would have led to the establishment of ritual repetition, and then prohibitions; these it would have been which enabled sufficient periods of peace for the development of what we know as human culture. It is not improbable that it was increased mimetic capacity that led from periodic to permanent sexuality as it is found in humans. From this scene it becomes possible to understand why sexuality should, in the earliest extant representations we have (cave paintings, etc.), be linked to death and violence.[15] From the time of the break with instinct through aggravated imitation, there is no such thing as natural sexuality: all sexuality is shot through with the same tendency toward violence and death that structures the basis for human culture.

This entirely hypothetical scene satisfies all the conditions for an originating sin. The important thing about it is that none of the participants would have known what it was that they had done. The emerging consciousness would be something both new and exciting, and yet at the same time frightening and dangerous, because related to the victim. The emerging consciousness is also based on a misapprehension with regard

---

13. See Pottier, *Le péché originel selon Hegel*, 239: "But if Fessard allows us to think through the historicity of this gesture, Thomas, with his conception of the sin of nature, explains to us the irreversibility of this gesture owing to its consequences which are inscribed into us metaphysically" (my translation).

14. There is, of course, no "I" that is formed by instinct or biology alone.

15. For further details see G. Baudler, *God and Violence* (Springfield, Ill.: Templegate, 1992), 80–92.

to the magical efficacy of the victim rather than on the apprehension of the murderous unanimity of the survivors. There was a moment when our *humanandi* could have perceived their similarity to the victim and acted accordingly. Because of the violent act leading to the miraculous peace, they can now never see their similarity to the victim. Instead they are caught in forging an identity over against the victim, who thus becomes good and evil, worse than me and better than me, god and villain, but never the same as me. The whole of relationality developing from that is caught in the sort of alterity that is a denial of similarity rather than an acceptance of it. Human desire, memory, and time have been born in the mode of appropriation. *Homo necans* has appeared.

The scene manages to save the possibility of talking, as theologians have traditionally done, about the "prelapsarian" question. This is the counterfactual question about what would have been the case if there had been no fall. The theological necessity of being able to ask this question derives from the nonnecessary nature of the originating sin. If it was not necessary, then we must be able to ask what it would have been like if it had not happened — not that we have any clear idea of what an answer would look like. We could, however, say that there would have been no concupiscence, because all human appetites would have been run in the mode of pacific imitation. As to the question of death, we cannot imagine what it would have been like to be a human to whom death is not an interior reality, something that moves us from within, since we have no possible access to such a reality except for Christ. From Christ we can posit that the resurrected body was not simply continuous with the body before the crucifixion, as shown in the difficulty the disciples had in recognizing him. We can suggest therefore that the prelapsarian humans would have inherited incorruptible bodies that involved some sort of transformation of their corporeality. Whether this transformation is called death or not seems comparatively irrelevant: it would certainly not be the inextricably cultural reality which we know as death, nor the simple biological reality of death which we can perceive in other animals.[16]

---

16. The anathema which the Council of Carthage attached to the view that Adam would have died naturally whether he sinned or not (Denzinger, 101) was to refute the rationalism of the Pelagians. The danger of this rationalism lay in that it was trying to understand original sin and its consequences not from the view made available by the risen Christ, but from a straightforward glance on what we have around us, how things are. As we have seen, however, it was the resurrection of Christ that made available the understanding of death as a human cultural reality which need not be: there is no such thing as a simply natural human death, any more than there is a simply natural human birth, simply natural human sexuality, etc.

The Status of a Construction

When a theologian posits a scene of origins, certain warning bells go off. The bells are warnings about the dangers of *concordisme*. We have to look to the last century to see the origins of such fears. The problem arose as the theory of evolution was developed, with theologians devising more and more ingenious schemes for maintaining the literal truth of Scripture as they understood it, in agreement with such paleontological discoveries as they could assimilate.[17] The first phase of the "quarrel" between "theology" and "science" was the assertion that "theology" was right, and "science" wrong, even in the domain of science, about human origins: creationism was right because the Bible said so, and "proofs" which now seem farcical were adduced to back this up. However, the problem was not so much with the impossibility of reconciling "creation" and "evolution"; rather it was that a whole new intellectual perspective, that of development or evolution,[18] had opened up which was to affect every field of human knowledge. Once such a perspective has opened up, it cannot be closed by decree but has to be worked through to find out where it is helpful and where not. Gradually it became possible to understand that an evolutionary understanding of human origins was not necessarily incompatible with the Church maintaining its faith. What had to be avoided in the future was the linking of the Church's theological doctrine to any particular scientific understanding of human origins until such an understanding was absolutely proven (whatever that might mean). Thus we hope to avoid the scandal caused to the faithful by the Church's repeating its heavy-handed attempts to force scientific knowledge to fit orthodoxy.

Thus, if in a first phase the tendency of apologetics was to find "concordances" (agreements) between paleontological discoveries and Church teaching, the second phase may be characterized as a flight from any *concordisme*. The theologian must not, with a mixture of professional exegesis and amateur natural anthropology, present a scene which combines the two and say: that is how it must have been; see how theology and natural science agree. Thus, for instance, the entirely abstract hypothesis of G. Fessard, as elaborated and modified by B. Pottier.[19]

---

17. For a wry look at such efforts, see H. Rondet, *Le péché originel dans la tradition patristique et théologique* (Paris: Fayard [le signe], 1967), chap. 19: "Transformisme et Théologie," especially 278–81.

18. In this context it is worth remembering that Newman's notion of the "development of doctrine" preceded Darwin's *The Origin of Species* by several years. Both are the beginnings of the working out of the same new perceptual paradigm in their respective fields.

19. In Pottier, *Le péché originel selon Hegel*, 230–39. I am much indebted to this brilliant discussion.

Such a thesis is independent of any particular empirical understanding of human origins, and therefore compatible with many.

However, can we not move on a little from this fear of *concordisme?* There seems to be an analogy to this process in the attitude of the Church to social theory. At a first moment the Church wished to impose its understanding of how a society should be run; at a second moment theologians bend over backward to accept any and every "criticism" from the field of social sciences, treating theology as (effectively) a discipline which has no bite of its own on real life, exactly the liberal critique of it. In a third moment, thanks to such as Milbank, it becomes possible to recover the perception that theology *is* an entire social theory from a revealed perspective, a rival discourse to other social theories, whose internal problems it seeks to resolve more coherently.

Exactly the same seems to be the case with anthropology. This is able to be perceived the moment it becomes clear that no amount of empirical evidence, fascinating though it be, is going to make the key difference to any discussion about human origins. The key difference is fatally going to depend on our interpretation of such evidence as we have. That is to say, no assessment of human origins is ever going to be anything other than an a posteriori elaboration depending entirely on a current view of what it is to be human. A dialectical materialist need have no difficulty with a view leaving human origins in the hands of evolution without any particular moment of rupture; a Cartesian will seek a moment of rupture at which the human mind appeared; and so on. Traditional evolutionary descriptions of hominization are unable to describe the element of specificity in humans: they are able to describe the continuity with what went before, but not the rupture. The need to be able to describe both continuity and rupture in something like an originary scene, all of whose conditions of possibility are purely prehuman and yet whose outcome is human, is held in common by any modern questioner who is not satisfied with the notion that what structures human consciousness, or language, is simply an unconscious process. Given this, it would be a failure of responsibility on the part of Christian theology not to attempt a reconstruction of origins to fit the anthropology which is a necessary part of its revealed vision.

This means taking certain quite particular stands in the field of anthropology, stands that are relatively independent of the theological vision being illustrated. As E. Gans has pointed out:

> The real debate ... is not between science and religion, but between generative anthropology, which takes as its basis the punctual origin of man, and positive anthropology, which conscientiously studies the various as-

pects of proto-human evolution but cannot formulate a hypothesis to explain how man the user of language emerged from it.[20]

It is by no means apparent that Christian theology could construct a christological symbol of original sin corresponding to a historical working of salvation that does *not* formulate a hypothesis explaining how man the user of language emerged from proto-human evolution. However, in this Christian theology is not some weird, outlandish fossil sticking its head in the sand and hoping that the inexorable tide of unruptured evolution will simply go away. The inexorable tide of unruptured evolution is a problem from many other points of view beside that of Christian theology and corresponds to a particular current view of what it is to be human that has no authority but its own internal coherence.

In the light of this we can see the importance of the following observation of Gans: "That there exists a scene of origin for human representation, that is a scene of the origin of language, is a fundamental thesis independent of the specifics of any particular reconstruction of this scene."[21] The option for a scene of origin or not is not a question of empirical evidence, but a consequence of the view of humanity whose origins are being searched for. The particular reconstruction will depend entirely on what elements are regarded as constitutive of humanity. In this field, then, as a radically alternative anthropological vision, Christian theology has every right to posit its version of an original scene. It has a particularly rich series of factors that such a scene must take into account: the nonnecessity of the particular outcome of the scene, the involvement in death at the level of human desire that the scene must illustrate, and so on. These flow from the christology which reveals a different sort of humanity as on its way into being.

To engage in such a reconstruction is not part of a feared *concordisme* but part of the proper intellectual responsibility of the Christian theologian. No thoroughgoing anthropological viewpoint can do without some approach to the question of where the human it sets out to describe came from in the first place. Christian theology is, among other things, just such a thoroughgoing anthropological vision. All such viewpoints are obliged to pay attention to such empirical evidence as emerges and helps fill out their picture without ever imagining that such empirical evidence can ever be decisive in an area which can only be examined interpretatively, since it is dealing with the emergence of the possibility

20. Gans, *Science and Faith*, 2
21. Gans, *Science and Faith*, 3.

of interpretation. In making such a reconstruction we are not proving anything at all. We are merely trying the better to tell our story.

Mysterium Caecitatis

Why do we bother to tell this story at all? Why not content ourselves with the kerygma of salvation, with announcing the Good News of the self-giving to death and the resurrection of Jesus? Why should the Church bother with a doctrine of original sin? Is it not a fond speculation, a subtle curiosity, that some ecclesiastical intellectuals feel the need to satisfy rather than something to do with our salvation? Often it is treated as though it were just that: a doctrine which must be kept alive out of loyalty to the magisterium, but whose practical sense is of little value. Just as Karl Rahner pointed out that it would make little difference to the lives of most Christians if the Church were suddenly to backpedal on the doctrine of the Trinity and preach instead an unnuanced monotheism,[22] so it might be said that the average Christian would not be affected by the suspension or abandonment of the doctrine of original sin. Some treatments of the doctrine clearly regard it as a *skandalon* that must ingeniously be got around rather than a properly edifying part of the Christian faith.[23]

This seems to me entirely wrongheaded. Rahner's response to what he perceived to be a problem was not to seek to jettison the doctrine, but to begin to recover the sense of the Church doctrine. This is what I too have tried to do with original sin. What I have attempted to set out is the way that the development of a properly Christian anthropology is not an additional extra that one may or may not work at in addition to the more important matters of salvation, but rather that the coming into being of a Christian anthropological vision is a development simultaneous to and rigorously dependent on the coming into being of the Christian understanding of God. In this sense I would see the road to Chalcedon not as the invasion by supposedly static Greek thought processes of the original freshness of a Semitic understanding of the Christ, nor even as the necessary consequence of maintaining fidelity to the original Semitic freshness of the Gospel in the midst of a cultural world formed and dominated by Hellenistic thinking. I would rather suggest that the road to Chalcedon is the necessary outworking of the mutual implication of the understanding of God and of human beings that became available at the resurrection, and that such an outworking would

---

22. Karl Rahner, *The Trinity* (London: Burns & Oates, 1970).

23. For instance, the presupposition of G. Martelet's *Libre réponse à un scandale,* or the drift and conclusion of Villalmonte's numerous studies.

have had to (and has to) forge something similar to Chalcedon in whatever cultural circumstances exist: wherever human idolatry confuses and mixes the deathlessness of God and the deathfulness of man.

The doctrine of original sin, then, is not, I suggest, merely a matter of words. Words are part of the way in which the Holy Spirit keeps alive the possibility of the divine regard in the midst of and as the Church, and thus keeps salt salty in the midst of humanity. Let me refer once again to the mimetic master text Luke 6:39–42. We have seen the importance of the understanding behind this text. It goes straight to the heart of a blind perception tending to accusation and offers instead a forgiving, creative perception, based on complicity. The function of the Church's doctrine of original sin, whether its symbol be the straightforward fruit and tree of Adam and Eve or the somewhat more complex version I have set out, is to keep alive the beam in my eye. We can go even further: God keeps alive the beam in my eye by making that beam a living Cross, a beam on which there hangs a murdered victim.

Does this keeping alive the murderous beam mean that God is involved in a noncomplicit accusation against us, denying his similarity and thus being part of an endless divine double bind? Rather the reverse: it means that God was fully prepared to become completely similar to us, but in order to construct a forgiving sociality with us. The doctrine of original sin is not an accusation against humanity, and by keeping it alive the Church is not engaged in an accusation against humanity. What the Church is keeping alive is the possibility that even those who bear the tremendous burden of being "right" may recognize their complicity with those who are not, and so construct a sociality that is not cruciform.

If, in the light of this, I may be permitted an untypically polemical excursus, it will help me draw out some of the implications of what I am calling the *mysterium caecitatis*. There are a number of pits into which any treatment of sin, let alone original sin, can fall. One of these is the notion that from the viewpoint of the Catholic faith we are obliged, or even able, to give an explanation of evil, and thus of sin as part of that explanation. Along with an explanation of evil, we might be asked to explain human misery, the suffering of children, the continuous presence of war and exploitation. All these have served in times past as starting points for attempts to explain original sin: Augustine, for example, dealt with the question of original sin, among other approaches, as part of his answer to the question "Whence does evil come?"[24] The same Au-

---

24. See A. Villalmonte, "El problema del mal y el pecado original en san Agustín," *Naturaleza y Gracia* 38 (1991): 235–63.

gustine came back time and again to the question of suffering children: how can their suffering be explained unless as the *poenae*, "penalties," of a transmitted original sin?[25] At Trent, the bishop of the Canaries, Baltasar de Heredia, reckoned that we know about original sin from our experience of *bellum*, conflict, among ourselves.[26] Others have suggested (and maybe this is the most typical "believing" reaction to any question about original sin) that we know about original sin because of the account of the fall of Adam in the book of Genesis and that this permits us to understand the presence of evil in the world. That is to say, from a biblical text in which appear sin, death, and a serpent we are thought to be authorized to expatiate about the nature of evil as it is found in our universe. We are endowed with insight into what Paul, more cautiously, calls the *mysterium iniquitatis* (2 Thess. 2:7). Evil, in this light, would be one of the things that "is," about which we can "know" as part of our understanding of God and human nature.

What has gone before is an implicit challenge to the above point of view, even considering the grandeur of some of its proponents, ancient and modern. My starting point has been rather limited. It is that in the Catholic faith we have no available explanation for evil or sin as such, not because we may not have many insights into such things, but because we don't have an explanation of anything at all. We have a salvific revelation: what is revealed as something now operative is the mystery of God's plan of salvation for us. This plan of salvation enables us to know the Father and share in his life by sharing in the life and death of his Son. Any Catholic understanding of evil cannot be part of a general human understanding of evil, and this for two reasons. In the first place there is no such thing as a general human understanding of evil any more than there is a general human understanding of good. It is contingent and competing human traditions that give shape and form to differing notions of good and evil, and such traditions all carry with them, either explicitly or implicitly, a theology that undergirds them.[27] Secondly, the Catholic faith considers itself radically subversive of all forms of human knowledge (1 Cor. 1:18–25) because of a very peculiar epistemological starting point: the resurrection within historical circumstances of a murdered man as the beginnings of a new creation.

What we have then is not a general "philosophical" explanation

25. See A. Villalmonte, " 'Miseria' humana y pecado original: un gran tema agustiniano," *Revista Agustiniana* 33, no. 100 (1990): 111–52.

26. Quoted in J. I. González Faus, *Proyecto de hermano: Visión creyente del hombre* (Santander: Sal Terrae, 1987), 301, 305.

27. See J. Milbank, *Theology and Social Theory: Beyond Secular Reason* (Oxford: Blackwell, 1990).

which can be extended to an explanation of such things as evil, nor
even a description of how things are that are, from which we might
deduce a description of evil, even a description in terms of privation
of being or privation of good.[28] We have a contingent human transmission of a form, a shape, of salvation. This I have shown to mean
that our only approach to the question of evil or of sin (and thus of
what original sin might be) is when we look at "that which we are on
our way out of." This is a particularly difficult epistemological starting
point, and we might do well to remember what happened to Lot's wife
when she turned around to see that which she was on her way out of.
Much treatment of sin, and original sin, is the theological equivalent
of a pillar of salt: something that is no longer on its way out of anything. Something that just is. And if sin is something that just is, then
it is a stumbling block over which we just have to stumble and perhaps conclude that we haven't really been offered any salvation at all.
My attempt has been rigorously to maintain the dynamic of salvation
throughout, from which alone a certain limited insight can be gained
into sin and into original sin.

My plea therefore is in favor of respecting what I have called the *mysterium caecitatis*. We have only one way into an understanding of what
sin, including original sin, might be, and that is starting from the resurrection. That is to say, there is a certain radical blindness as to both
good and evil that began to be unveiled only as a result of the resurrection. The forgiveness of sins, which became part of both the preaching
and the power that flowed from the resurrection and is its central meaning, is what enables us to approach the question of sin. It therefore
behooves us to proceed somewhat gingerly in deciding what sin might
be, because the permission we have been given to look back is a healing
and forgiving permission, and any claim to understand sin that is not an
understanding of how it is forgiven is automatically suspect. We must
be careful not to know too much. If, in the Genesis story which Catholics customarily associate with original sin, one of the first fruits of the
fall was the knowledge of good and evil, does it not suggest that that
knowledge, at least in its current form, is inappropriate to us?

I am laboring this point, which might be called a challenge to epistemological promiscuity, not only with regard to such approaches to
original sin and sin in general as have started from a metaphysical question about evil, concern at human misery, or a sad reflection on the

---

28. This is not to minimize the importance of such metaphysical distinctions as have
permitted Catholic thinkers to deprive evil of "being"; it is merely to indicate that the
overall theological framework of thought within which such distinctions are possible is
not that of a description or explanation, but a dynamic creative momentum of salvation.

omnipresence of violence. That would suggest a certain bias against "ancient" approaches. However, I also have in mind a no less epistemologically promiscuous set of modern thinkers. A reading of some of the liberation theologians suggests a curious suspension of critique before the question "how do you *know*" that such and such an action or structure is evil? To take two examples: Leonardo Boff in a celebrated article entitled "¿Qué es hacer teología desde América Latina?" appears to regard faith as a horizon, so with no real content of its own. Faith "enters in the determination of the type of analysis of reality" which is chosen, but "respects the rationality proper to (human) science" and finally will "opt for that sort of analysis which is most compatible with its direction...and whose categories...most vigorously decipher the mechanisms which, for faith, form structural sin."[29] The content of faith is in fact given, as Boff goes on to indicate, by a suitably modified form of dependency theory. Good and evil are thus defined in terms of that theory, and it is in the light of that theory that Boff, and those who follow the same pattern of thought, are able to wax lyrical about evil, injustice, structures of sin, and so on.

Another example is Pablo Richard's article "Teología en la teología de la liberación." His starting point is "the radical experience of death and of life,"[30] especially among the poor and oppressed, the majority of the population of Latin America. It is within this mystery of death that God is revealed. Richard goes on to assess how this experience affects the understanding of theology in liberation theology and ends with the now traditional plea that base communities be treated as the criterion for the ecclesiality of the Church. At no stage does he indicate how he *knows* in what the evil he describes consists, or what is the epistemological starting point for his confident critique of theology, of ideology, his reading of the Bible, his criteria for ecclesiality. Now lest it be thought that this is simply another conservative attack on liberation theology, let me indicate that, in the case of Boff's article as well as Richard's, I am largely in sympathy with the direction of their social (but not their ecclesial) critique. My question is, "Yes, but how do you *know?*" It seems too easy to know good and evil as these authors do. What enables such a massively clear vision of the evil in the world? Is personal blindness merely a result of the sort of social belonging of the subject, a blindness from which they are exempt owing to their theology? Does not the very dialectical nature of their vision of what is good and evil suggest that the

29. Leonardo Boff, "¿Qué es hacer teología desde América Latina?" in *Liberación y cautiverio,* Encuentro Latinoamericano de Teología (Mexico City, 1975), 136.

30. Pablo Richard, "Teología en la teología de la liberación," in *Mysterium Liberationis* (Madrid: Trotta, 1990), 1:201.

vision does not flow from grace but is itself part of the problem, part of the blindness?

There is an important point that is worth making here lest it be thought that I am simply insisting that there is no way of knowing that something is evil outside the Christian faith. Such a suggestion would obviously be nonsense. Most people know, irrespective of creed or culture, for instance, that it is wrong to boil babies or to rape anyone. Such people can say that it is not as part of their being forgiven that they know this. They just do know it and trust that any normal decent human being also knows it. I hope so. My point is this: any understanding of good and evil that exists is not merely a piece of information about an act, but a part of a human social order, as part of the maintenance of that social order. There is no knowledge of good and evil that is not also part of a socially constructed relationality which is either inclusive or exclusive, but never neutral. So the question legitimately arises whether knowing that something is good or evil is known within the framework of accusation (whether of self or others), or within the framework of forgiveness (of others or self). It is, as the Lucan text suggests, part of the particularly Christian understanding of sin that any accusatory knowledge of sin has a particular propensity to blindness about complicity and that only forgiveness enables us to see. I hope to have shown that there is a specifically Catholic understanding of sin that is part of a quite specific understanding of a construction of a real human framework of forgiveness, and that the awareness of original sin is at the same time one of the most elusive and one of the most important building blocks in that construction.

If the great "masters of suspicion" sought constantly beneath the varied patterns of human behavior a reduction to "what is *really* at work" in this behavior, class struggle, will to power, oedipal libido, it may not be an entirely unfortunate metaphor to see God himself as the ultimate master of suspicion. His suspicion is not, however, a reductive accusation, but is itself the beginnings of a creative forgiveness, letting us off the hook of our pretensions by suggesting to us that we are all actively involved in blindly creating victims, and need not be. The ecclesial function of the doctrine of original sin is to participate in the Holy Spirit's keeping alive among us of the creative suspicion of God. This essay has no other ambition (but no less an ambition) than to be a contribution to that function.

Part 3

Is This What
the Church Believes?

Chapter 10

Is This What the Church Believes?

Stories and Their Limits

While I am aware that much of what has gone before appears somewhat different from traditional accounts of original sin, it is my hope that a certain flair for orthodoxy will have been sniffed out. However, it would be wrong simply to rely on that and not to attempt to find out whether the traditional teaching of the Church on original sin is — in its key points, the points from which no Catholic understanding can prescind — compatible with what I have set out.

This, of course, notoriously, raises problems of method. The hermeneutics of magisterial documents is a highly complex matter, touching on questions of different cultural horizons, attempts to isolate exactly what a document is insisting on, or anathematizing, from such explanation as seemed logical or necessary at the time, but does not in fact form part of what is being insisted on, and so forth. In the area of original sin, there is no shortage of such treatment of magisterial texts, and particularly of the text of Trent's decree on original sin, which is the most recent definitive pronouncement on the matter.[1] To repeat such investigative feats would be a quite different theological exercise from the one I have been attempting.

My exercise has been one in storytelling: an attempt to tell the story of salvation in such a way as to draw out the necessary implications for that story in the area which has traditionally been called "original sin." When it comes to attempting to assess whether my story is Catholic there are two quite different angles of assessment which come into view: one which I can make some headway toward satisfying in the text, and another which is entirely out of my hands. The second is the more important: the sense in which the catholicity of a text or a theology can never be determined by an individual, but always depends on the appre-

---

1. E.g., A. Villalmonte, "Qué enseña Trento sobre el pecado original," *Naturaleza y Gracia* 26 (1979): 167–248; J. M. Rovira Belloso, "El pecado original según el concilio de Trento: Estudio de interpretación del dogma," in *Revista Catalana de Teología* 1 (1976): 183–230.

ciation of and reception by the Church. In the case of an essay like this, that would mean whether or not such Catholics as read it find that it leads to a deeper understanding and practice of the faith, an enriched participation in the sacramental and ecclesial life, a renewed ability to perceive the Gospel as Good News and thus preach it, the overcoming of certain stumbling blocks in their theological understanding or their approach to ecclesial life, or, on the other hand, if those reading it find it reductive of their life of faith, of prayer, belittling of their sacramental participation, introducing or sharpening stumbling blocks in their ecclesial life and perception. The assessment of catholicity in this sense, of whether this essay is a *praedicatio gratiae,* is of necessity out of the author's hands.

This leaves the first angle of assessment of the catholicity of my story, the one toward which I can make some headway in satisfying. This is a comparison of such texts of the magisterium as bear upon the matter with what I have been trying to set out. A certain understanding of the function of those texts is implied by this and so had better be set out. The understanding is this: that Catholics in every age are called to announce the Gospel of Grace to the whole world. In order that they do this, the Holy Spirit keeps alive the inner coherence of the Old and New Testaments revealed in the life, death, and resurrection of Jesus. This keeping alive of the inner coherence, which is the presence of the crucified and risen Lord, impels Catholics constantly toward the task of reinterpretation of the scriptural texts, in the midst of whatever cultural circumstance they find themselves, precisely in order to be faithful to them. Mere repetition of received words or phrases can be as deep a betrayal of the sense of Scripture as reinterpretations convenient to the interpreter.

The keeping alive by the Holy Spirit of the inner coherence of Scripture is achieved not only in the active production of preachers and teachers, but also in the vigilance over those preachers and teachers that is carried out by their pastors. It is they who have to ask the question: "Is what you have been teaching in symphony with the Catholic faith?" To them has been entrusted the task of determining where a certain telling of the story might not in fact be marked by elements of self-delusion, of insufficient critical digestion of the forces of contemporary cultural life. Thus it has always been part of their gift to be able to posit the borderline for the story in certain directions: "With whatever joy and dynamism you are telling the story, if you are not able, because of your own internal logic, to avoid this or that conclusion, then you are not telling the Catholic story, yours is not a *praedicatio gratiae:* such as hearken to your words will not, through them, find Life."

This does appear to be the way the magisterium has worked over the centuries: comparatively rarely does it, as magisterium, try to tell the story; comparatively frequently it intervenes in the development of the stories of others (which may include its own members wearing different hats) to indicate that certain paths are dead-ends. What a Catholic theologian can responsibly do is to attempt to listen to such interventions as have pointed out dead-ends in the matter under examination and, listening, ask whether he or she has avoided such turnings. This is, of course, yet another exercise that is not free from the risk of self-delusion. It is as possible to "make the magisterium agree with me" as it is to use Scripture to justify oneself, rather than let it chivvy one into being justified by grace. The emotional chastity needed to allow baptized ears to hear the deepest intention of the Holy Spirit speaking through the mutable words of the magisterium will always be a spiritual discipline and never ultimately a matter of technical accomplishment. It is for this reason that the second angle of assessment of my own story, or any story that purports to be a *praedicatio gratiae,* its reception in the Church, is so much more important than the first.

Having indicated, then, something of the direction and the limits of what is proposed in this chapter, we may turn to an attempt to listen to the dead-ends that the magisterium has pointed out in the area of original sin.

Listening to the Church

It would be possible to go through all the magisterial pronouncements concerning original sin from the provincial Council of Carthage in 418 to the present day. This would in fact be repetitious since several of the most important documents take up and repeat earlier documents more or less verbatim. The repetition at least has the merit of determining the degree of authority enjoyed by a particular text in the cases where its original authority is dubious. Thus Trent's assumption of certain texts of Carthage and Orange makes redundant the question of whether such teaching was binding, a question that might have arisen owing to the nonecumenical nature of the earlier councils. I will therefore look first at such texts as are not repeated and look at such as are principally in their most authoritative context.

(a) The provincial Council of Carthage (418) met to discuss the problems raised by Pelagius's telling of the Christian story in such a way as to promote moral renewal. One of the dead-ends that the council indicated was as follows:

Whosoever should say that the first man, Adam, was created mortal, in
such a way that whether he sinned or not he would have undergone bodily
death, that is to say leaving the body would not be a punishment for sin,
but a necessity of nature, let him be anathema.[2]

Here the weight of the intention of the teaching is expressly concerned with the idea that human mortality is a necessity of nature. I
have already indicated in a different context my interpretation of this
canon.[3] Here therefore it is enough to set out that it was not part of the
subject matter before the council to define whether Adam really existed
or not, nor in what sense one should understand death as a punishment
for sin. The key point was the insistence that human death, as we know
it now, is not something willed by God and is not properly speaking
natural. If it had been something natural then Christ's death would not
have redeemed death, because human death would not be a fallen reality and would thus be in no need of redeeming. The teaching is a quite
simple piece of Christian anthropology in the light of Christ's vanquish-
ing of death: human death is always and everywhere a reality capable of
and in need of redemption.

The second canon of Carthage, concerning infant baptism, was later
adopted with small alterations by Trent and will be examined when we
get there. The next important magisterial text to deal with original sin is
the first chapter of the *Indiculus* of Pope St. Celestine I.[4] This reads:

In Adam's transgression [*praevaricatio*] all men lost "their natural possibility" and innocence, and no one would have been able to lift himself,
by means of his own free will, out of the abyss of that ruin were he not
lifted up by the grace of the merciful God, as is proclaimed and taught by
Pope Innocent of blessed memory in his letter to the Council of Carthage:[5]
"He [Adam] acted of his own free will when he used his gifts imprudently;
he fell into the depth of his transgression and remained submerged, finding no means by which he could rise from there; entrapped forever by his
freedom he would have remained prostrated by the oppression of his ruin,
had he not been raised up later by the coming of Christ, who, by means
of the purification of the new regeneration, cleansed through the washing
of baptism all previous vice."

Here the teaching is quite clear and simple: the salvation which Christ
brought for us has as its direct corollary that no one can save him-

---

2. The canons of the Council of Carthage are to be found at Denzinger, 101–8. This is
canon 1, Denzinger, 101.

3. Chapter 9, p. 256, n. 16.

4. The *Indiculus* appears as Denzinger, 129–42; the chapter here in question is at Denzinger, 130. The whole is of uncertain date, probably late in the pontificate of Celestine,
who died in 432.

5. In fact the synod of Carthage of 416, not the council of 418.

self. Anyone who tells a story in which we can save ourselves is not telling the Catholic story. In anthropological terms this means that for a Christian anthropology it is necessary that the human be described as other-dependent. The interdividual anthropology which I have used is completely compatible with this view, relating the way in which the human is in any case formed through alterity to the way in which God made available a complete transformation of the human by introducing a completely new "other" into human alterity, the "other" of the Father himself, revealed through the presence of the forgiving victim.

(b) The next important magisterial moment came a century later, with the Second Council of Orange in 529.[6] Orange's canons on original sin were largely assumed into the text of Trent's decree with some alterations; however, owing to the difference of context of the two councils, it is worth attempting to understand the intention of Orange. The first canon says:

> If anyone denies that through the offense of Adam's transgression the whole man, body and soul, was changed for the worse, but believes that only the body was subjected to corruption, while the soul remained unharmed, that person is deceived by the error of Pelagius and goes against Scripture which says: "the soul that sins shall die" (Ezek. 18:20) and: "do you not know that if you yield yourselves to anyone as obedient slaves you are slaves of the one whom you obey" (Rom. 6:16) and again "whatever overcomes a man, to that he is enslaved" (2 Pet. 2:19).

Here the intention is the insistence that the whole human being is personally involved in the state of sin which characterizes the human race. One is not merely affected by original sin, as one might be by a contagious disease, but it forms one from within. The frame of reference in which this is set out is of course that which presupposes the primacy of the historical Adam. However, the central insistence of the text is entirely compatible with a christological reinterpretation of Adam's sin. In this view the important thing is that owing to Christ's salvation and the coming into being of a state where the whole human can be changed for the better, it becomes possible to see the way in which such humanity as has not been touched by that change for the better is living in a state of subjection to corruption. Anthropologically the insistence of the text is on our complete dependence on grace in every aspect of our life for our being brought to human fulfillment: to a mimetic description of sin (such as that at work in the quotes from Romans and 2 Peter) corresponds a mimetic description of grace (such as I have tried to set out in this essay).

---

6. For the complete texts, see Denzinger, 173b–200; for the canons on original sin see Denzinger, 174–75.

The second canon of Orange on original sin reads as follows:

If anyone maintains that Adam's transgression harmed himself alone, and
not his descendants, or that there was indeed passed to the whole human
race by one man death, which is the penalty for sin, but not also sin itself,
which is the death of the soul, that person attributes injustice to God and
contradicts what is said by the Apostle: "Sin came into the world through
one man and death through sin and so death spread to all men as all
sinned in him." (Rom. 5:12. Vulgate)

This canon is extremely interesting from the point of view of the perspective I have been trying to propound, since it suggests that a real
problem with Pelagianism, or semi-Pelagianism, in its search for a scriptural self-justification was its attempt in some way to detach Adam's sin
from ours. That is to say, the Pelagian reading of the Adam story was
prepared to concede its literal truth, in this sense being in agreement
with the Catholics, who assumed the same. The difference lay in the fact
that the Pelagian reading was not prepared to allow that our state be
rigorously the same as that of Adam after his sin. It might even be said
that what is condemned here is the attempt at a reading that starts from
Adam, treating him as a foundational reality, and yet not allowing for
Adam to be reached by the retro-projective vision coming from Christ
(which is what Paul's quote here is about). What is forbidden is making
of Adam a "special case": he must be able to be read both as the ini-
tiator of fallen humanity and as the content of that fallen humanity in
all of us. Of course this entire problem is obviated the moment a christological rereading becomes the interpretative key: the content of the
universal sinfulness is made known to us by Christ, and the extension of
that sinfulness, in order to be universal, necessarily goes back to our first
father. The key insistence of this intervention of the magisterium is on
the rigorous identity of the sinful condition to be found in all humans,
whether this is read as from Adam to us, or from us to Adam.

(c) The next major magisterial treatment of the matter is also the
most important of such interventions: that of the Council of Trent. Here
we have it on the authority of the papal legates that what was being
sought was not a general definition of original sin.[7] What was wanted
was a response to the problems of the "winds of doctrine" by which

---

7. In a letter to Cardinal Farnesi of May 28, 1546 they say "non consentiremmo che
s'entrasse a disputar dell'essentia e della diffinitione quiditativa del peccato originale, es-
sendo in ciò li dottori cattolici molto varii e non facendo a proposito." "We will not allow
[them] to get into disputes about the essence or the quidditative definition of original sin,
since in this matter the Catholic Doctors have very varied opinions, and it is not relevant
to the matter at hand" (from the *Concilium Tridentinum . . . nova collectio,* Görres Gesell-
schaft, 10:503; quoted by J. I. González Faus, *Proyecto de hermano: Visión creyente del
hombre* [Santander: Sal Terrae, 1987], 345, n. 85).

the Christian people were being carried about.[8] Hence the decree is brief and written in pastoral rather than erudite terms. It serves as the preamble to the decree on justification which was to be the centerpiece of Trent's teaching and which begins with a reference back to it.[9] Trent has the honor of having accepted on behalf of the Church much of the criticism of the reformers against the Church, and thus, rather than merely attacking the reformers and defending the status quo (which might have raised real questions about the presence of the Holy Spirit at the Council), it first aimed its attention at the semi-Pelagianism inherent in the optimism of Renaissance humanism, making sure that no one would think that the Catholic Church had, by the sixteenth century, come to teach Pelagianism. In this way it laid the way for it to be understood that in its rejection of Lutheranism it was not simply accepting Pelagianism. Rather it was rejecting the too narrow dialectic which was able to conceive only of either Lutheranism or Pelagianism: the Catholic faith is not on the same plane of argument as either.

With this in mind we can look at each of the five canons of Trent.[10] Canon 1 reads as follows:

> If anyone does not acknowledge that the first man, Adam, when he acted against God's command in paradise, immediately lost that holiness and justice in which he had been created and, because of the sin of such a transgression, incurred the anger and displeasure of God and consequently death, with which God had previously threatened him, and with death a captivity under the power of him "who" henceforth, "had the power of death, that is, the devil" (Heb. 2:14); and that the whole Adam, because of that sinful disobedience, was changed in body and soul for the worse: let him be anathema.[11]

Trent here is taking up the first canon of the Council of Orange (see above), and is making some additions in the light of theological arguments which had occurred in the interim. It had been possible to understand St. Anselm's view that original sin incurred the loss of original holiness and justice in such a way that this loss had no real effect on the resulting human nature. Thus Trent indicates that the loss of original holiness and justice is not something which had no effect on the resulting human nature. Rather it must be said that the change for the worse of the whole Adam and the loss of original holiness and justice are two

---

8. Proemium to the Decree on Original Sin, Denzinger, 787.
9. Denzinger, 793.
10. I reproduce the English translation of each decree from N. Tanner, ed., *Decrees of the Ecumenical Councils* (London: Sheed & Ward, Washington: Georgetown University Press), 2:666–67, except where I indicate otherwise.
11. Denzinger, 788.

different ways of referring to the same thing. This is St. Thomas's position when he teaches that original sin is formally the loss of original justice and materially *concupiscentia* (Ia-IIae, q. 82, a. 3 resp.). The burden of the teaching seems to be that the whole of humanity from Adam onward is in a state, of its own making, ruled by the power of death which is contrary to the state willed for humanity by God.

Here there may be raised a number of questions. The first concerns whether or not Trent meant to canonize a particular interpretation of Genesis 3 in this text. Such an interpretation would make belief in a formal sin of disobedience by a particular person against a particular commandment to be the essence of original sin and oblige Catholics to maintain this against any other reading of Genesis 3. Yet we know that the council was not asked to deliberate on the essence of original sin,[12] but was attempting to deal with errors in theological anthropology of a Pelagian and a Lutheran variety. There is no attempt, for instance, to condemn St. Thomas's view that pride, not disobedience, was the first sin (IIa-IIae, q. 163, a. 1).

More important from the point of view of the present study is the question of whether it obliges Catholics to hold that Adam's death was an extrinsic punishment (i.e., not intrinsically related to the nature of the offense) by an angry God. If such a position were obligatory, then the theology of original sin presented in this study could not be considered Catholic. However, it is most unlikely that this was the intention of the council, since neither the language of God's anger nor the internal relationship between the offense and its consequence was under scrutiny. A further piece of evidence that an interpretation of "the anger of God" as a way of talking about an intrinsic anthropological relationship between a human act and the resulting rule of death would not contradict Trent can be found in Trent's doctrine and canons on the Mass.[13] Whereas in the first draft of this text (1552) mention was made of the Mass placating God's anger, in the promulgated document this was dropped.[14] If it is possible for the effects of the central sacrament of salvation to be understood without reference to God's anger, then it is also possible to understand what that saving sacrament puts right without reference to God's anger. It seems to be permissible, then, to read the first canon on original sin as referring to the relationship between sin and the human state ruled by death as an intrinsic one which is not according to the will of God. Such a reading does, I would suggest, maintain alive better

12. See the quote of the papal legates above.
13. Denzinger, 937–56.
14. See D. N. Power, *The Sacrifice We Offer: The Tridentine Dogma and Its Reinterpretation* (Edinburgh: T. & T. Clark, 1987), 103–4.

than the extrinsicist reading the central teaching of this canon, which is the reality of the death-related change for the worse affecting the whole human being.

The second canon of Trent is almost identical with the second canon of Orange and reads as follows:

> If anyone declares that the sin of Adam damaged him alone and not his descendants, and that the holiness and justice received from God, which he lost, he lost for himself alone and not for us; or that, while he was stained by the sin of disobedience, he transmitted only death and bodily pains to the whole human race, but not that sin which is the death of the soul: let him be anathema, for he contradicts the Apostle saying, "Sin came into the world through one man, and death through sin, and so death spread through the whole human race because everyone has sinned" (Rom. 5:12).[15]

The addition to Orange is the phrase "the holiness and justice received from God, which he lost, he lost for himself alone and not for us." This takes into account the understanding of original sin as formally a loss of original justice and materially concupiscence which we have seen above. The point is that the whole Adam is in a parlous state (canon 1) and so are we all (canon 2). The movement is an anthropological one from the first human to all humans. Adam is internally involved in death, and so are we all. The point of "death of the soul" is that we are talking about something that does not admit of a cure, a slow getting better that is made possible by a human struggle, but only of a resurrection, a miracle of grace given to someone who is totally helpless as regards salvation.

The question arises as to whether Trent meant to canonize the movement from Adam to all of us in such a way as to make obligatory a reading of original sin that uses Adam as foundational. If that were the case, it would rule out the theology of original sin which I have elaborated, proceeding from the resurrection of Christ to Adam. If one follows the path I have taken, the order of discovery rather than the order of logic, then canon 2 precedes canon 1: Christ's resurrection reveals (inter alia) that we are all in a parlous state of spiritual death and subject to a bodily death not willed by God (canon 2), and this universality of the fallen state has to be applied back to the very origins of humanity so as to include our first father (canon 1). However, it does not appear that Trent, by following the order it did, meant to canonize the foundational view of original sin as a reality independent of and epistemologically prior to our salvation. It is merely the case that the

---

15. Denzinger, 789.

understanding of history which Trent followed was the unquestioned
pacific possession of its cultural horizons and was common to a Renaissance humanist such as Erasmus, the reformers, and the fathers of the
council.

This leads us into Trent's third canon:

> If anyone asserts that this sin of Adam which, one by origin and passed on
> to all by propagation and not by imitation, inheres in everyone as some-
> thing proper to each, is removed by human or natural powers, or by any
> remedy other than the merit of the one mediator, our Lord Jesus Christ,
> who has reconciled us to God in his own blood, being "made our right-
> eousness and sanctification and redemption" (1 Cor. 1:30); or if anyone
> denies that the actual merit of Christ Jesus is applied to both adults and
> infants through the sacrament of baptism duly administered in the form
> of the Church: let him be anathema; for "there is no other name under
> heaven given among people by which we must be saved" (Acts 4:12).
> Hence that saying: "Behold the Lamb of God, behold him who takes away
> the sins of the world" (John 1:29). And that other: "For as many of you
> as were baptized, have put on Christ" (Gal. 3:27).[16]

Trent follows on with its description set within the framework "We
are all sinners; Christ is the solution." Here it begins to set out the solution. The central intention of the canon is that there is no way out
of the parlous state described before except by the gratuitous gift of
Christ, and that the normal form of this gratuitous gift of salvation is
incorporation into the Church by baptism. In this it is a standard teaching against Pelagianism. However, before it gets to its point, it has two
further anthropological addenda concerning the ironclad nature of the
parlous reality of sin binding us to Adam: that original sin is one in its
origin, and that the link is "by propagation and not by imitation." Each
of these is designed to avoid certain possible misunderstandings. The
first addendum (*origine unum est*) goes against the interpretation there
was only one original sin, Adam's, and that in the rest of us this original sin is imputed rather than a real anthropological reality.[17] Against
this view the council insists that original sin is one in its origin (that
is, that there was a real concrete historical act), but is in each of us as
something proper to each of us. Original sin cannot be understood as
simply an original act, which has had deleterious effects on all of us,
making us the victims of someone else's enormity. Rather we are all con-
stitutively participants in the enormity that had its origin in a concrete
historical act. This nuance is very much easier to render within the theo-

---

16. Denzinger, 790.
17. On this, and the possible interlocutors envisaged, see González Faus, *Proyecto de
hermano*, 348.

logy of original sin that I have tried to set out, whereby our collective participation in the reign of death revealed by the resurrection must have had a historical origin, than in the framework within which Trent had to work.

The second addendum, that the reign of death by which we are linked with Adam flows *propagatione non imitatione,* is an equally important anthropological insistence. The phrase has its origin in Augustine's argument against Pelagius. The latter seems to have wanted a neutral moral "moment" in each person's life, whereby that person could sin or not sin, following human bad examples or the good example of Christ. Augustine saw that this meant that it was at least theoretically possible that someone might not need the grace of Christ to be saved. He sought therefore to exclude the possibility of any neutral moral "moment" without thereby declaring human nature as such to be intrinsically evil, the Manichaean position[18] from which he had freed himself with such difficulty. His solution, marked by his personal awareness of the strength of disordered libido, was to see the historical biological act of procreation as sinful in such a way that it was this which guaranteed that each historical human was sinful from conception. Trent was not seeking to canonize Augustine's moral biology, but was seeking to exclude any morally neutral moment in any human's life: from the beginning of our lives and without being intrinsically evil by nature we are preinvolved in sin.[19]

In the light of the understanding of original sin that I have attempted to set out, it becomes possible to read Trent's point as simply claiming that there is no such thing as a purely "natural" human being; it is not as though we are first a biological or natural reality and then, later, become a cultural reality. All human beings are, from conception, always a completely cultural reality. This goes back to the very beginning of

---

18. Mani was a third-century Persian who taught a gnostic religion of absolute dualism between light and darkness. Some light having been imprisoned in matter, itself a thing of darkness, the life struggle is to liberate light from darkness by ascetic means. Augustine was for a while an adept of this religion, whose basic structure recurs in almost all human religious discourse, before becoming an ardent opponent of it. The word "Manichaean" is commonly applied to almost any sort of absolute dualism between good and evil, spirit and matter, and so on.

19. By this stage it should be unnecessary to point out that Girard's mimetic interdividual psychology is not touched by Trent's *non imitatione.* Mimetic psychology does not admit of any morally neutral "moment"; rather it describes the way in which entirely other-dependent humans inescapably have their very interiority and consciousness structured by mimesis. It is therefore completely in agreement with the notion that all humans living within a culture brought into being by a rivalistic mimesis are by the fact of their coming into being structured from within by that rivalistic mimesis, from which the only salvation is the coming into being of a human culture inaugurated by and producing a pacific mimesis.

human culture: part of what it means to be human is to be intrinsically and inseparably cultural including even the mode and moment of human generation. This cultural reality has been revealed, by the coming into being of the new human cultural reality inaugurated by the death and resurrection of Christ, to be one that is utterly shot through with death-related desire to such an extent that death-related desire *appears* to be entirely natural. Once again it would seem that Trent's intention is less awkwardly maintained within the christological rereading of original sin than within the "foundational Adam" reading. It is of course manifest that the christological rereading depends entirely on there being only one savior, who is universal, of whom all have need, and whose form of salvation is ecclesial: this is clearly in line with the major intention of canon 3.

Where canon 3 had brought into play the absolute necessity of Christ's salvation and its ecclesial form, by referring to baptism, canon 4 goes on to deal with the specific question of infant baptism:

> If anyone says that recently born babies should not be baptized even if they have been born to baptized parents; or says that they are indeed baptized for the remission of sins, but incur no trace of the original sin of Adam needing to be cleansed by the water of rebirth for them to inherit eternal life, with the necessary consequence that in their case there is being understood a form of baptism for the remission of sins which is not true, but false: let him be anathema. For the saying of the Apostle, "Sin came into the world through one man and death through sin, and so death spread through the whole human race because everyone has sinned" (Rom. 5:12), must be understood not otherwise than as the Catholic Church in its entire extent has always understood it. For, according to the rule of faith transmitted from the apostles, even small children, who could not yet of themselves have committed any kind of sin, are truly baptized for the remission of sins in order that what they contracted by generation may be cleansed in them by regeneration. For "unless one is born again of water and of the holy Spirit, he cannot enter the kingdom of God" (John 3:5).[20]

This canon, with minimal alterations, is a reproduction of the second canon of the provincial Council of Carthage.[21] It is not strictly concerned with original sin but with defending the licitude of the pastoral practice of infant baptism. Whereas at Carthage it was the practice of infant baptism which was seen as an important "proof" of the existence of original sin in infants ("why else does the Church baptize them if they don't have original sin? The fact of washing implies the existence of dirt"), at Trent the logic is, more correctly, inverted: because

---

20. Denzinger, 791.
21. Denzinger, 102.

they have original sin in exactly the same way as an unbaptized adult, it is therefore at least admissible that they be baptized, and when they are baptized, they are baptized every bit as efficaciously as if they were adults.

The place of this canon in the decree of Trent suggests that it can be read as a test of whether the anthropological understanding set out in the previous canons has been properly grasped. It is as if it were to say: "If you have followed our teaching in the first three canons, then it will not occur to you that infants should not be baptized, because you will understand that the coming into being of the new cultural anthropological reality inaugurated by Christ makes it evident that there is no human being who is, of him or herself, part of that new cultural anthropological reality: every human being who comes into the world is by that very fact part of the cultural anthropological reality formed by the reign of death, and therefore depends for his or her eternal life on being born again into the new cultural anthropological reality. If you balk at infant baptism on principle, then the chances are that you have not understood our teaching in the first three canons."

The fifth canon of Trent requires considerable care in the interpretation: the other four canons are standard anti-Pelagian stuff, whether borrowed (canons 1, 2, and 4) or made to measure (canon 3). In canon 5, having shown that the Catholic faith is not Pelagian, Trent turns to distinguishing its story from the newly born Lutheran story:

> If anyone says that the guilt of original sin is not remitted through the grace of our Lord Jesus Christ which is given in baptism, or even asserts that all which pertains to the true essence of sin is not removed, but declares it is only erased and not attributed: let him be anathema. For God hates nothing in the reborn, because there is no condemnation for those who are truly buried with Christ by baptism into death, "who do not walk according to the flesh" (Rom. 8:1) but, putting off the old person and putting on the new person created according to God, become innocent, stainless, pure, blameless and beloved children of God, "heirs indeed of God and fellow heirs with Christ" (Rom. 8:17), so that nothing at all impedes their entrance into heaven. The holy council confesses and perceives that in the baptized, concupiscence or a tendency to sin remains; since this is left for the struggle [ad agonem],[22] it cannot harm those who do not give consent but, by the grace of Christ, offer strong resistance; indeed, "that person will be crowned who competes according to the rules" (2 Tim. 2:5). This concupiscence the Apostle sometimes calls sin (Rom. 7:14, 17, 20), but the holy council declares that the Catholic Church has

---

22. Here I depart from the translation in Tanner, which reads "as a form of testing" and which would contradict James 1:12–13.

never understood it to be called sin in the sense of being truly and properly such in those who have been regenerated, but in the sense that it is a result of sin and inclines to sin. If anyone holds a contrary view: let him be anathema.[23]

Here again we have Trent making a necessary anthropological distinction so that a real human salvation is possible. If the Pelagian heresy had been to render a real salvation unnecessary, since humans could themselves transform themselves into people worthy of heaven, the problem raised by the Lutheran position was that it made a real human salvation impossible. Such is the degradation of human nature, in this view, that it can never be made worthy of heaven, but a counterfactual worthiness can be imputed to it. Put in other terms, the Pelagian emphasis had so emphasized human merit as to risk making grace redundant, while the Lutheran emphasis had so emphasized grace as to make merit impossible. Trent had to come up with the anthropological distinctions necessary to maintain the traditional teaching of the Church that a real transformation of the whole person is possible or, in other terms, that the form which grace takes in human lives is merit. That is to say, God, in giving us heaven, is giving us something entirely gratuitous, but does this by crowning the real human life histories of each of us; these real human life histories have entirely been made possible by grace but are nevertheless really and authentically *our* life histories which we have forged. Either alternative to this point of view effectively posits a necessary rivalry between humans and God.

Thus Trent's first point in this canon is that the incorporation of a person into the ecclesial hypostasis is the same thing as the beginning of that person's being really transformed, having his or her whole person reconstituted from within. A person's being unlocked from the mode of being human constituted by distorted desire is such that it is the same thing as that person ceasing to be a "child of wrath." Lest anyone think that this means that salvation is only a nominal or superficial change, compatible with a completely unchanged life, Trent goes on to make the vital anthropological point that it is completely normal for this real change to be lived while facing resistance from the way in which all our human faculties have been formed. To put it another way: once we have been enabled to start rewriting our stories as ones where we have become receivers of our new identity as children and heirs of God, then that story we have started to write is our real story. However, that story is always and everywhere forged as the story of how we overcome the

---

23. Denzinger, 792.

resistance to the new hypostasis that is coming into being, a resistance which is interior to us as well as exterior.

Thus it becomes necessary for Trent to make its vital distinction about *concupiscentia:* that it is not sin in the true sense of the word. If it were sin in the true sense of the word, that would mean that there were two contradictory life stories going on simultaneously: a story of "how I am saved" and a story of "how I am lost." By denying that *concupiscentia* is sin in the true sense of the word, Trent is indicating that there is only one life story being forged, one of how I am empowered to become a co-constructor in salvation. This does mean adopting the view that in the human being, "being-run-by-another" is not in itself a bad thing. The important thing is by which "other" we are run. Our having been constituted in and run by the other of distorted desire is such that it will take a long time and much effort for the effects of that alterity to be undone by our being reconstituted and run by the other of pacific desire. Angels are wholly and instantly transformed according to by which "other" they are run. In humans the transformation is no less real and complete, but occurs over time and as a flowering of a new sort of personal involvement with the new "other." All of this is merely to say that in humans, the dynamic of forgiveness enabling participation in the new creation, as made present in the death and resurrection of Christ, is given us as a process.

It must I suppose be evident that the distinction which the council makes about concupiscence (for which the biblical Greek word is, of course, *epithumía*) is in fact the linchpin on which the whole of my essay depends. As against an interpretation of Girard which regards him as suggesting that desire as such is always intrinsically evil (i.e., is *hamartía* in the proper sense of the word), I have attempted to show that desire for Girard has a double valency: transcendent and deviated, and that it is this latter which corresponds to sin, not desire *tout court.* Were this not the case, then Girard would be a Lutheran thinker and his thought would not be compatible with the Catholic faith. However, as it is, it seems to me that he has given us a fecund way of making sense in dynamic terms of the "ambi-valence" of concupiscence. That is, he has provided an interdividual psychology which shows that "being-constituted-by-another" is simply part of being human, the key question being what sort of relationship to which other. It therefore makes sense that the effects of our being run by the old other, deviated desire, will be coterminous with the human cultural reality to be overcome — that is to say, until death, the last part of each human's cultural reality to need redemption — while at the same time saying that from the moment when we become "slaves to righteousness," the whole of our selves-formed-by-alterity, however slowly and invisibly, is being transformed.

Trent has a sixth canon, indicating that it does not want what has been said to be taken as seeking to decide the debate as to whether the Virgin Mary was or was not immaculately conceived. This issue was, of course, resolved independently in 1854. It is no part of this essay to seek to include Mary in original sin. Indeed, the doctrine of her redemption *praevisis meritis Christi* fits much more easily within the christological interpretation of original sin that I have been setting out than in the "forward from Adam" view, which requires something like divine leapfrogging. In lieu of a much longer treatment of this theme, it might be said that where the traditional view might hold that *because* the Virgin was immaculately conceived, *so* she must have been bodily assumed into heaven (because she was without the corruption of sin), the view resulting from what I have been setting out would say that *because* she was assumed bodily into heaven (i.e., was and is fully personally involved with the bringing into being of the new creation), *so* she must have been immaculately conceived (i.e., she was never at any stage personally involved in that resistance to the coming into being of the new creation which characterizes the rest of us).

(d) With that we can leave Trent, the most recent definitive magisterial *prise de position* on our subject matter, and jump four hundred years to the middle of the twentieth century. The two remaining magisterial texts which I shall look at are of a quite different nature from those that went before. The first, *Humani Generis* (1950), is an encyclical of Pope Pius XII concerning "certain false opinions which threaten the foundations of Catholic doctrine."[24] The second is the address of Paul VI to theologians at a symposium on original sin held at his request in 1966.[25] Neither of these texts represents an attempt to propose anything new about original sin. Both are part of the office of vigilance exercised by the pastoral authority of the Church indicating, in the first case, the incompatibility of certain opinions with the maintenance of the Catholic understanding of salvation and, in the second, certain minimal points which must be maintained in any reinterpretation of the doctrine of original sin in the changed theological atmosphere following the Second Vatican Council. In this sense, the second text, only sixteen years after the first, represents an authoritative interpretation of what was important in the earlier text.

---

24. Denzinger, 2305–30. Eng. trans.: *False Trends in Modern Teaching* (London: Catholic Truth Society, 1950).

25. For the introductory allocution see *Acta apostolicae sedis* 58 (1966): 654.

We need spend, therefore, little time examining *Humani Generis*. It must be read in the context of the colossal conflict between the Church and "modernity," the movement (born in hostility to the Church and not until recently aware of how much it was parasitical on the vision of the world made possible by the Christian faith) to set reason free from the shackles of tradition and authority. Because the encyclical was written within the terms of reference of that conflict, it would appear to be an attempt to settle by authority issues concerning human origins that modernity would rather settle by reason and empirical investigation. In the light of the continuing collapse of modernity's confidence in the possibility of delivering a vision of anything that is objective and not "perspectival," however, it becomes possible to read *Humani Generis,* stuck as it is within a neoscholastic framework and a ghetto-like approach to developments in thought outside the Church, as an important assertion of the Church's right and duty to continue telling its own story in the midst of the conflicting voices emerging around it. It is as though it were saying "the Church can and should not have its story, how it keeps alive Christ's bringing into being of salvation, rewritten by those for whom the keeping alive of such a creative imagination could and should be subjected to the apparently empirical data of a positivist approach. This latter approach radically misconstrues what it is to tell the sort of story which the Church is trying to tell."

The key points of *Humani Generis* that relate to our subject matter are the warning to tell no story of the origins of the human race which compromises the following belief:

> That souls are immediately created by God is a view which the Catholic faith imposes on us[26]

and the insistence that no opinion can be allowed which suggests the existence of other humans who were not descended from Adam,

> or else supposes that Adam was the name given to some group of our primordial ancestors. *It does not appear how* such views can be reconciled with the doctrine of original sin, as this is guaranteed to us by Scripture and tradition, and proposed to us by the Church: which is that it proceeds from a true sin committed by a single Adam, which is transmitted by generation to all, and is in each of us as proper to each.[27]

"It does not appear" deliberately leaves open the possibility that it may become possible to describe an original historical act affecting its participants and the whole subsequent human race in such a way that

---

26. *Humani Generis,* par. 36, Denzinger, 2327.
27. Par. 37; Denzinger, 2328; I have altered part of Ronald Knox's English translation, which is more emphatic than exact.

the sin is in each as proper and which does not flow rigorously *ab uno Adamo*. Pius XII is here *not* trying to interpret Genesis (in which case he would have had to mention Eve as co-initiator of original sin). He is interpreting Romans 5:12–19 and the Council of Trent (which are cited in a note in the text of the encyclical). That is to say, his primary concern is, as it had to be, the strict maintenance of the Pauline doctrine of the universality of human sinfulness which became known as the consequence of the uniqueness of Christ's salvation.

These points seem well brought out by Paul VI in his allocution to theologians working on original sin.

> It is evident that you will not consider as reconcilable with the authentic Catholic doctrine those explanations of original sin, given by some modern authors, which start from the presupposition of polygenism which is not proved, and deny more or less clearly that the sin which has been such an abundant source of evils for humankind has consisted above all in the disobedience which Adam, the first man and the figure of the future Adam, committed at the beginning of history. Consequently, these explanations do not agree either with the teachings of Holy Scripture, sacred Tradition and the Church's magisterium, which says that the sin of the first man is transmitted to all his descendents by way of propagation, not of imitation, that it is "proper to each" and is "death of the soul," i.e., the privation and not merely the absence of holiness and justice, even in newborn infants.
>
> As to the theory of evolutionism, you will not consider it acceptable if it is not clearly in agreement with the immediate creation of human souls by God and does not regard the disobedience of Adam, the first universal parent, as of decisive importance for the destiny of humankind. This disobedience should not be understood as though it had not caused in Adam the loss of the holiness and justice in which he was constituted.[28]

The main points can be summarized as follows: (1) avoid any theory of origins which is not compatible with a unique historical sin of the first Adam (who is to be understood in the light of the new Adam); (2) avoid any theory of origins which is not compatible with the immediate creation of human souls by God and which does not allow for Adam's sin to have made a decisive difference to the human condition. The remainder of the text is evidently allusive to Trent. A particular question is raised by Paul VI's repeated use of the word "disobedience" to describe Adam's sin. I understand this to be a way of talking about the sin and not a definitive pontifical intervention to define the nature of Adam's sin. I have already indicated St. Thomas's (never censored) opinion that

---

28. *The Christian Faith in the Doctrinal Documents of the Catholic Church*, ed. Neuner and Dupuis (London: Collins, 1983), 141.

the original sin was one of pride, a position which is evidently more compatible with a mimetic anthropology than a sin of disobedience.

However, if, as is probable, Paul VI was referring with his use of the word "disobedience" to Romans 5:19 ("For as by one man's disobedience many were made sinners, so by one man's obedience many will be made righteous"), then the context of the language changes. Christ's obedience becomes the paradigm by which Adam's disobedience is to be judged. Christ's obedience was manifestly not of the positive, voluntarist sort: "I will obey such and such a command." Rather it is a way of referring to the whole pattern of a life lived in responsive listening to the will of his Father, a pattern of life that, as John brings out, was an uninterrupted pacific mimesis of the Father. In the light of this, we should interpret Adam's disobedience not in terms of his refusal to obey the single explicit prohibition in Genesis 3:3, but instead in terms of his failure to live in responsive listening to (or pacific mimesis of) the Father who was calling him into (human) being. It is the obedience of Christ which defines the content of the disobedience of Adam, not vice versa.

With regard to the two substantive points of the papal allocution, I hope it is apparent that the Girardian "construct" of an original sin uses a monophyletic model of origins in such a way that an original historical act is committed by the first Adam of just such a nature as to illustrate the salvation wrought by the new Adam. Where the Pauline model in Romans has one man's obedience highlighting one man's disobedience, this model brings alive the way in which the obedience of the individual new Adam in the midst of a collective violence undoes a human situation brought about by a unanimous collective act against an individual at the beginning of history. This certainly keeps alive the way in which the original "disobedience" was of decisive importance for the destiny of humankind, structuring indeed the whole of human culture. Once again what is important here is the fidelity of the model to the Pauline teaching in Romans rather than the particular question of whether it was "one individual" called "Adam" who started off the culture structured by original sin. Again, the absence of Eve in the papal text suggests that it is fidelity to Romans 5, and not fidelity to the letter of Genesis 3, which is the key factor.

This leaves the question of "the immediate creation of human souls by God." I take it that the term "soul" is, in the words of the Congregation for the Doctrine of the Faith, "a verbal instrument which is simply unavoidable for the retaining of the Church's faith."[29] By means of this verbal instrument the Church describes the human as a being who is

---

29. "Letter on Certain Questions in Eschatology" of May 17, 1979.

relationally dependent on God for being brought into being and maintained in existence in such a way as is not circumscribed by mortality.[30] That is to say, the notion of human soul as used within the Catholic faith can have no meaning except as something brought into being by God. Nor could there be a mediate cause for the creation of a soul, since the immediate relationship to God of what is distinct in its createdness to the body is part of what the word "soul" means. We can talk of God's mediated creation of our body: in bringing a body into being, God can and does use secondary causes, like parental intercourse. However, there can by definition be no intermediate causes between God's creative bringing into being of this "becoming active" participant in God's life, and the "becoming active" participant in God's life. God's love for someone (which is what we are talking about) may have to be *shown* to that person (if that person is a human) mediately, through bodily signs, gestures, abundance of fruit, fine weather, and so on, but the love itself is always an immediate relation direct to the person. Indeed the gift of the body, which is created mediately, is a sign of the love for the person, which is by definition immediate: love *for* the person. Any theory of original sin which did not permit it to be said that God immediately creates human souls would be making a mistake not about immediacy, but about what a human soul is.

Having said this, mimetic theory offers a fine anthropological perspective on exactly this question. The understanding of creation is rigorously christological. That is to say, it was the gratuitous self-giving of Jesus up to death and his resurrection as forgiving victim which enabled the purely gratuitous *von unten* nature of creation to begin to be understood: we are offered coming into being out of a humility deep beyond imagination. In the case of every one of us since our first father(s), we are offered coming into being as a personal relationship, called by another into a participation in that other. Creation, properly speaking, is not complete in the case of each of us until we have been made fully alive in our participation in the life of that other. Yet we are all, since our first father(s), caught in the inverse of participation in this fecund mimesis: we are caught in the appropriation of our coming into being for ourselves, which is the ultimate frustration.

So in our description of the creation of the human soul, first there is creative beneficent mimesis, which has never been withdrawn; God has never repented of his plan to call such an unlikely a thing as matter into

---

30. See J. Ratzinger, *Eschatology: Death and Eternal Life* (Washington, D.C.: Catholic University of America Press, 1988), chap. 5, "The Immortality of the Soul," and especially 150–53, "The Dialogical Character of Immortality."

active participation in his life. Everywhere this creative beneficent mimesis is lived by us in rivalry and distortion. This we discovered when God
revealed to us the original splendor of his mimetic creative plan, by his
Son's subverting our distorted mimetic culture from within and creating
a way out of that into the beneficent creative mimesis of God. There is
no human, from the day we were first called beyond being anthropoids
into becoming humans and when we settled for something less, who is
not called to be part of that beneficent creative mimesis, even where, in
our present state, that creative call has to take the form of forgiveness
producing that cracking open of the human heart which we call repentance.[31] That, I trust, indicates that mimetic theory is rather apt as a way
of describing the immediate creation of every human soul by God.

We have now been through the principal texts of the magisterium of
the Church dealing with original sin. It is not my claim that they have
really been saying all along what I have been trying to say in this essay.
My claim is marginally more modest! It is that there is at least latent
in these texts the possibility of talking of original sin in the way I have
been, and that to do so obscures none of the key points of the Church's
teaching. I would hope that it might be possible to go further and say
that by telling the story as I have, it becomes possible to see the internal
coherence and unity of the Church's definitive points in this area in a
clearer and more fruitful way. However, that is for others to judge.

The Witness of Augustine

A further way in which an interpretation of a particular doctrine can
be verified is by placing it alongside the views of other interpreters of
the doctrine, particularly of those who, while their teaching is not to be
confused with the magisterium of the Church, nevertheless have been
recognized by the magisterium as being particularly reliable guides in
their exposition of the Catholic faith. The two giants of the Western
Church in this area are St. Augustine and St. Thomas Aquinas. So I will
attempt very briefly to put what I have been trying to set out alongside
the thought of these two in the area of original sin with a view to trying
to see if such differences as can be perceived are legitimate, or whether
they tend to destroy the Catholic story.

Augustine's views on original sin open up a huge minefield of different interpretations, as well as a bibliography so massive as to render
comments such as my own pretty much otiose. However, remembering
that this essay is a speculative attempt to set out a doctrine of original

---

31. See Trent on contrition, chapter 6 of the decree on Penance (Denzinger, 987).

sin in the light of Girard's mimetic theory, an attempt that recognizes the magisterium as referee and Augustine and Thomas as linesmen, even an Augustinian ignoramus can cast a brief glance at the Doctor of Hippo's flag in this area, so long as he pretends to no originality.

It seems important to start with a basic minimum of what Augustine (who appears to have coined the term "original sin," which he uses indiscriminately — and thus, in the light of Trent, properly — to apply to originated and originating original sin) regarded as central to the doctrine. Augustine's doctrine was forged on two fronts: against the Manichaeans and against the Pelagians. Their labels are comparatively unimportant; they represent two abiding temptations for anthropology which must be avoided if the Catholic story is to be told. A. Villalmonte summarizes Augustine's concern to maintain the Catholic faith as follows:

> The Catholics say that man, created good, fell into sin, and thus can be redeemed and is in need of redemption; the Pelagians say that, since man is born healthy, he needs no doctor; the Manichaeans say that, being substantially evil, man cannot be redeemed.[32]

Augustine also arrived at the conclusion — tired out by the difficulty of attempting to explain the origin of the soul (a weak point in his argument of which Julian of Eclanum tried to make much), as well as fatigued by the arguments with the Pelagians — that the question of our origin was not ultimately important: of ultimate importance is the question of our end. So long as we confess our absolute need for Christ's salvation there is no danger.[33] Thus Augustine was prepared to relativize his own anthropology just so long as our incapacity for salvation and necessity for Christ is preserved. In the light of this understanding I cannot see Augustine raising his linesman's flag against the vision of original sin which I have set out, which derives entirely from Christ's salvation, and whose understanding of desire specifically saves the goodness of being human while recognizing the distorted living out of that which we are helpless to overcome except through gratuitous alterity.

There are quite specific points of difference between Augustine's vision and the one which I have been setting out, even prescinding from

---

32. A. Villalmonte, "El problema del mal y el pecado original en San Agustín," *Naturaleza y Gracia* (1991): 235–63. I have translated note 47 on 261. Villalmonte gives the following references: *De nupt. et concup.*, II, 3, 9: PL 44, 441; *C. duas epist. pelag.*, II, 2: PL 44, 572; *C. Felix man.*, II, 8: PL 42, 837.

33. "Whence, if the origin of the soul is unclear, as long as the redemption is clear, there is no danger. For we do not believe ourselves to be born in Christ, but rather to be born again in him, howsoever we may have been born" (*Epist* 190, 1:3; PL 33, 857; quoted by Villalmonte, "Miseria humana y pecado original: un gran tema agustiniano," *Revista Agustiniana* 33, no. 100 [1990]: 151, n. 66; see also *Epist* 167, 1:2; PL 33, 720).

the obvious ones of the literal reading of Genesis and the consequent hamartiological vision in which sin is epistemologically prior to salvation.[34] The first is Augustine's recourse to theodicy. Two recurrent questions in Augustine's thought on original sin are those of the origin of evil and a search for the explanation for human (and particularly infantile) suffering.[35] Both of these starting points are related to Augustine's prime concern: avoiding Manichaeism (which had a standard answer to the question of the origin of evil), while maintaining the absolute need for salvation for all including infants, whose suffering therefore must have something to do with an original sin. The need to deal with these two areas pushed Augustine into taking rather literally the notion of God actively punishing people, a step which produced the (just) horror of Julian of Eclanum. Augustine claims that if even newborn babes are miserable, it must be because they have somehow been involved in some wrongdoing, that is, original sin. When Julian retorts that this is to accuse God of torturing children because of someone else's sin, which is a grotesque blasphemy against God, Augustine replies that it is far worse an accusation against God to have them suffering without being involved in original sin, for that would be to make God completely unjust, causing them misery without them even deserving it.

It is sadly easy to see how from the starting point of Augustine's theodicy, a conclusion like this would have to be reached. However, the moment we put the starting point itself into a christological framework, we see that it would make of Christ a sinner in a real, personal sense. Since he suffered on the Cross, he must have been a sinner. Blaming the victim for what befalls him is an argument from within the circle of victimary mimesis and means that gratuity can never really be perceived. It can never be perceived that the victim is, in fact, innocent: "there's no smoke without fire" really is as old a lie as "dulce et decorum est pro patria mori," and both are rigorously sacrificial in the same sense. Augustine of course did *not* want to interpret literally the verse "For our sake God made him to be sin who knew no sin" (2 Cor. 5:21); that fateful step toward gnosticism was taken by Luther.[36] Augustine reads

---

34. Here is a good example of Augustine's vision, inscribed within the "we are all sinners, Christ is the solution" model: "Hence, from the misuse of free will there started a chain of disasters: humankind is led from that original perversion, a kind of corruption at the root, right up to the disaster of the second death, which has no end. Only those who are set free through God's grace escape from this calamitous sequence" (*City of God,* Bk. XIII, chap. 14, trans. Bettenson [London: Penguin, 1972], 523).

35. See the articles by Villalmonte mentioned in notes above for a specific treatment of each of these areas.

36. For details of Luther's dabblings in the occultistic teachings of Hermes Trismegistus, their effects in his doctrine, and Melanchthon's horrified appreciation of these as "Mani-

this verse metaphorically. But if Christ who suffered was only "made sin" metaphorically, why should suffering in infants be the result of sin in any more real sense? It would seem that Augustine does in fact mix arguments derived from salvation with arguments derived from what we might call "unsaved reason" (what González Faus splendidly calls Augustine's *lógica atroz*). The latter arguments may have seemed strong at the time: in the end they serve to create scandals for faith. If Julian was ultimately trapped in a version of God who was ultimately more "decent" (in an educated Roman way) than effervescently gratuitous, he was at least right to want to protect the God revealed by Jesus from Augustine's attributions of violence.

It seems to me that we have a much richer understanding of original sin if we leave the question of the origin of evil and the cause of human misery to a different discussion. There is only one theodicy really admissible in Christian theology, and that is the theodicy worked by Christ and commented on by Paul in Romans 1:17 (the revelation of the justness of God); or available in 1 John 1:5 (the revelation that God has nothing to do with darkness). In the light of this, original sin is no less linked with punishment than before, but punishment is understood as our involvement in self-punishment, from which, precisely, the revelation of God's justice has come to set us free. Where Marcion was so moved by the discovery of the absolute nonviolence of God that he felt obliged to jettison the Old Testament, Augustine, unparalleled interpreter as he was, was capable of the inverse error, that is, of a fundamentalist reading of Scripture. So he would often produce Exodus 20:5 or Deuteronomy 5:9 as proof that God punishes the sins of the fathers in the children and wave this against Julian's production of Ezekiel 18 to counter it.[37] It is anachronistic however to criticize him for not reading the Old Testament as a development in understanding which culminated in Christ when we consider what a recent conquest is *Dei Verbum* 15! R. Schwager has pointed out how slow has been the process in Christian history of reinterpreting God's anger and violence, and thus the possibility of finding a hermeneutic, such as the Girardian, which permits us to avoid either the Marcionite separation

---

chaean deliria," see the interview given by Luther scholar T. Beer in *30 Dias* (the Brazilian edition of *30 Giorni*), February 1992, 54–59.

37. Augustine could, when he wanted to, interpret verbs predicated of God metaphorically. Take this example from *The City of God* XIV, 11: "It is true that God is said to alter his decisions; and so we are told in Scripture, by a metaphorical way of speaking, that God even 'repented.' But such assertions are made from the standpoint of human expectation" (trans. Bettenson, 568). Now substitute the word "temper" for "decisions" and "punishes" for "repented"!

of Old and New Testaments, or the fundamentalist yoking of them into too indiscriminate a unity.[38]

Much more interesting than the obvious differences between the vision of original sin I have been setting out and Augustine's are their similarities: Augustine scholar A. Wohlmann has made a very interesting comparison between the thought of Girard and Augustine.[39] Her study misreads Girard at some key points, for instance, when she claims that the development of Girard's understanding of desire does not include in any way the existence of God.[40] She also seems keen to create some unnecessary oppositions between Girard's thought and that of her hero, oppositions which can always be strengthened by treating Girard as a theologian manqué rather than a literary critic who has developed a theorization of an insight into human relationships. However, having said that, she does bring out quite how much the two thinkers have in common, and particularly in the two key areas of Girard's thought: the victimary structure of society and the structuring effect of desire.

In the first place, Augustine's vision of human history and culture is set out from a parallel that is also to be found in Girard: the comparison between Cain and Abel and Romulus and Remus.[41] Book XV of *The City of God* deals with this specifically. Augustine regards Cain as the founder of the earthly city,[42] by which he means all of human culture. Abel, by contrast, a shepherd who was slain, prefigures the slain shepherd of the human flock. We have human culture founded on a murder and the ecclesial hypostasis founded on a victim. This vision provides the undergirding criterion for Augustine's criticism of all pagan society, including Rome, founded on Romulus's murder of Remus; it enables Augustine, like Girard, to criticize the need for the earthly city to found its unity over against some enemy, thus effectively making peace dependent on war; it enables him to criticize pagan sacrificial practice, which derives from lies; it enables him to show the involvement of pagan gods in exacerbating violence. In all this Augustine sounds remarkably like Girard (and, of course, vice versa).

Another point of contact is the duality of desire which runs through the thought of both authors and which in fact structures both of their

---

38. R. Schwager, "The Theology of the Wrath of God," in P. Dumouchel, ed., *Violence and Truth: On the Work of René Girard* (London: Athlone, 1988), 44–52.

39. "René Girard et saint Augustin: Anthropologie et théologie," in *Recherches Augustiniennes* 20 (1985): 257–303.

40. Wohlmann, "René Girard et saint Augustin," 275.

41. Girard reported to me in conversation (Piracicaba, Brazil, June 1990) that he had not known of this coincidence, but that it was pointed out to him sometime after the publication of *Des choses cachées*.

42. "Conditor terrenae civitatis" (*City of God*, XV, 7 end, trans. Bettenson, 606).

visions. There can be no Christian thought which does not admit of a duality somewhere in its vision, since eschatology, transformation, alterity, without which no telling of the Christian story can do, cannot be conceived within a monistic framework. Augustine and Girard agree that this duality is best maintained by treating desire as capable of two valencies: in Girard's terms we have pacific or rivalistic mimesis; in Augustine's we have "amor Dei usque ad contemptum sui" and "amor sui usque ad contemptum Dei." I quote Augustine's most famous reference to this duality, so that the reader may see how clear Augustine is on this point and also how his understanding of each of these "loves" is mimetic:

> We see then that the two cities were created by two kinds of love: the earthly city was created by self-love reaching the point of contempt for God, the heavenly city by the love of God carried as far as contempt of self. In fact, the earthly city glories in itself, the heavenly city glories in the Lord. The former looks for glory from men, the latter finds its highest glory in God, the witness of a good conscience. The earthly lifts up its head in its own glory, the heavenly city says to its God: "My Glory; you lift up my head." In the former the lust for domination lords it over its princes as over the nations it subjugates; in the other both those put in authority and those subject to them serve one another in love, the rulers by their counsel, the subjects by obedience. The one city loves its own strength shown in its powerful leaders; the other says to its God, "I will love you, my Lord, my strength."[43]

The mimetic nature of these loves is shown by Augustine's understanding of glory, which is acquiring one's identity through the eye of the other, whether God in the case of *amor Dei,* or by providing bread and circuses for the masses, and so achieving reputation and glory, the social cement of the cities of antiquity, in the case of *amor sui.*

It is not only here that Augustine's understanding of desire is mimetic. His whole doctrine of creation depends on humans becoming dynamic images (imitations) of God: Girard's (much less fully developed) transcendent imitation. It is only natural then that sin is the realm of the *perversa imitatio Dei*[44] inaugurated by the devil. Wohlmann shows, furthermore, that for Augustine, desire is not only mimetic, but triangular, as it is for Girard: "I classify the human race into two branches: the one consists of those who live according to man, the other of those who live according to God."[45] Where desire is "according to" rather

---

43. *City of God,* XIV, 28, trans. Bettenson, 593.
44. *De Gen. ad litt.* VIII 14, 31, quoted by Wohlmann, "René Girard et saint Augustin," 269, n. 38.
45. *City of God,* XV, 1, Bettenson's translation (595) altered to bring out Wohlmann's point in "René Girard et saint Augustin," 271.

than directly "for" we are obviously in the terrain of mediated triangular desire. Wohlmann even uses Girard's distinction between "internal" and "external" mediation of desire to highlight some of Augustine's experiences which he comments on in the *Confessions*.[46] It would appear, despite Wohlmann's attempts to show how Augustine is one-up on Girard at every point, that Girard's much more rigorous theoretization of a simple insight goes straight to the heart of Augustine's thought and permits us to develop certain theological insights rather more systematically than the more instinctive genius of the African doctor.

An important question results from this: given the abundant clarity of Augustine's understanding of the mimetic nature of desire, the centrality of desire in his anthropology, and his understanding of how the *imitatio perversa* leads to murder and the mendacious foundation of the human city, why did he not move to an interdividual rather than an individual understanding of psychology (what a difference it would have made to Western thought if he had!)? If it is possible to offer an answer to such a question at all, it can be only extremely tentatively. I will make two rash suggestions: one related to Augustine's description of the "soul" and the other to his Manichaean past. Neither of these pretends to offer an explanation of why Augustine did not follow his mimetic understanding of desire; but they both reveal key moments at which he did not.

Augustine expounds his understanding of the soul in Book X of *De Trinitate*, in a text both difficult and important, not least because of the way it seems to have paved the way that led to Descartes.[47] Augustine starts with the notion that knowledge comes about from hearsay: it is because someone tells us about something that we begin to burn to want to know it. Here we have desire very much formed by another: we would not love that which we did not know, and in order to know it we have to be suggested into knowing it by others:

> Just as the human loves what he knows only in a general way and seeks to know it better, so also when some particular thing, or things, which he does not yet know are highly praised, he creates in his mind imaginary forms by which he is excited to love them. (X.2, 4)

However, Augustine then turns (in X.3, 5) to the soul's knowledge of itself: he explicitly asks whether the soul loves itself, and if that is the result of it having heard from others of its own beauty, which is how it comes to know and thus love absent things. Augustine even goes as far

---

46. Wohlmann, "René Girard et saint Augustin," 280–81.
47. C. Taylor, *Sources of the Self: The Making of the Modern Identity* (Cambridge: Harvard University Press, 1989), shows both the road from Augustine to Descartes and, perhaps more importantly, the vital differences which separate them (127–42).

as suggesting that maybe it is when it loves one like it that it loves itself before knowing itself:

> It knew therefore other souls from which it could make an idea of itself, and thus knew itself to be of the same genus.

This would be a fully projective understanding of self-knowledge and demand an interdividual understanding of the constitution of the self.

It is here, in the third paragraph of X.3, 5, that Augustine leaves this path. He notes that eyes know other eyes better than themselves, because they can see other eyes, but need a mirror to see themselves: eyes work by projection, but, according to Augustine, souls don't:

> For the eyes can never see themselves except in a mirror: however, in no way must it be thought that when it comes to contemplating incorporeal things something is also brought in, as if the soul were to know *itself* as in a mirror.[48]

A reason is not given: it is just asserted that incorporeal things don't work in the same way. With this, and without a backward glance to criticize Our Lord for his misunderstanding of the soul in Luke 6:39–42, Augustine leaves his mimetic understanding and moves into demonstrating the direct self-knowledge of the soul, which is to be his path to demonstrating the inherence in each other of memory, will, and understanding, and thus to his psychological analogate for the Trinity, one derived from within an individual and not from relationality between persons.

The second place where Augustine does not follow through his own mimetic insights is in his radical insistence on the free will as being the place from which sin, and thus all evil, proceeds. This radical insistence seems to have been because of the opposite, Manichaean doctrine which he had held earlier:

> It still seemed to me then that it was not we ourselves who sinned, but I know not what strange nature which sinned within us, because of which my pride took delight in considering myself exempt from guilt, and not having to confess, when I had done some evil, my sin, so that You might heal my soul, for it was against You that I sinned. But, in truth, I was all that, and my impiety had divided me against myself.[49]

When Augustine came to confront the Pelagians on the subject of the sinful will, he found himself with the difficulty that both he and they held a very strong belief in the free will as the origin of sin. He had to

---

48. "Nunquam enim se oculi praeter specula videbunt: nec ullo modo putandum est etiam rebus incorporeis contemplandis tale aliquid adhiberi, ut mens tanquam in speculo se noverit."
49. *Confessions,* V, 10, 18.

find a way in which the free will in all of us is always automatically distorted from our conception. He found it in his doctrine of Adam's sin passed on by propagation. I have suggested that we can describe our free will being automatically distorted from our conception in terms of the fact that humans are constitutionally mimetically interdividual and that the moment a human culture of distorted desire is formed, this will automatically mean that every human brought into being is formed from within, from the moment of conception, by distorted desire.

I wonder whether the text I have quoted above from the *Confessions* doesn't indicate why Augustine would not arrive at such a view himself. It sounds, in this one particular point, too like the Manichaeism he had rejected: it suggests that human beings are such that we are moved by another. Augustine had no difficulty with that when it comes to being moved by God. But the experience of recognizing himself to be moved by another had become associated in his mind with an abandonment of moral responsibility brought about by a complacent belief in the force of evil powers which moved one. Part of his conversion from Manichaeism was his grabbing of his soul as something that was truly his and entirely his responsibility: "But, in truth, *I was all that*, and *my impiety had divided me against myself.*"[50] The most influential story of the soul in Western Christendom begins with a radical act of appropriation of the self and a negation of the self's intrinsic alterity. It was this memory of Manichaeism, I suggest, which meant that Augustine could not extend his mimetic insights more rigorously into his anthropology.

I hope enough has been said to back my hope that while Augustine might have been surprised by some of the developments I have advanced from premises shared by himself and Girard, he would recognize that since none of these imperils the central need for Christ's salvation, and none of them involves us in Pelagianism or Manichaeism, he need not raise his linesman's flag and put my attempt off the Catholic playing field.

The Witness of Thomas

We can be more succinct in our treatment of Thomas's views on original sin, in part owing to the scattered references to his thought earlier in my essay and in part owing to Trent's use of his thought, as represented by Cajetan and other fruits of the Thomistic revival of the late fifteenth and early sixteenth centuries. Thomas was faithful to the Augustinian

---

50. "Verum autem *totum ego eram*, et *adversus me impietas mea me diviserat*" (*Confessions*, V, 10, 18, emphasis mine).

school in taking Genesis literally, even to the point of discussing the sort of immortality that might have been given by the fruit of the tree of life. He concludes that a fruit, being itself perishable, properly speaking could not give incorruptibility to anything else, but might for a certain time, after which Adam would either have had to be transferred to a spiritual life elsewhere or else have had to eat another fruit (Ia, q. 97, a. 4). And this is the same thinker who, when asked if the names of the saved are literally written in a scroll in heaven (a claim made in a book no less canonical than Genesis), was able to reply that probably not, but that it did no harm to think so![51]

Thomas's treatment of Genesis in the *Summa* shows, however, an emphasis somewhat different from Augustine's: he expounds the state before the fall as part of his exposition of creation. The richness of his account is owing to the splendid opportunity given him by the "pre-lapsarian" question to engage in counterfactual anthropology, that is, to come to a closer understanding of what we really are by asking questions about what might have been. It is not original to suggest that his angelology has a somewhat similar function, serving as a check that human anthropology remains authentically human. He first expounds the prelapsarian question as part of his exposition of creation (Ia, qq. 90–102), and it is his realism about creation which is to make his approach to fallen human nature so very carefully balanced when he gets to it (Ia-IIae, qq. 80–89, and IIa-IIae, qq. 162–65).

Thus, when Thomas asks whether the sin of the first father was transmitted by generation to his descendants (Ia-IIae, q. 81, a. 1), he replies that this is what is taught by the Catholic faith and then explains this in terms of what he calls a sin of nature: original sin is only a sin of this person insofar as this person receives the nature of the first person. What he means by this is further elucidated by his view that

> Original sin worked in this way: that first a person infected nature, and thereafter nature infected the person. Christ, however, in the reverse order first repairs that which is of the person, and afterward will simultaneously repair in all people that which is of nature. (III, q. 69, a. 3 ad 6)

This wonderful quote came as a surprise to me as I came to ask whether St. Thomas could have been persuaded to accept the thesis I have developed. I have my answer: for this is exactly the view of original sin that I have suggested to arise from Girard's account of mimetic interdividuality, where I have but started from the way in which Christ first repairs the person, suggesting that it was thus that it became possible to

---

51. Quoted without reference in G. K. Chesterton, *St. Thomas Aquinas* (London: Hodder & Stoughton, 1947), 102.

acquire an anthropological vision of the sort of nature that was on its way out of being, that is, being repaired. I then looked at what sort of original act by what sort of original person would have been necessary to produce that sort of nature.

This is, I suspect, the interesting point of Thomas's vision from the point of view that I have been studying: since he is more interested in creation and anthropology than in history, the actual flow of events matters much less for him than for St. Augustine: Thomas is not bothered by chains of catastrophes spreading out from the first sin, but calmly suggests that many things (like the need for sexual procreation[52] and for education[53]) are the same after the fall as they would have been before. (H. Rondet, in his classic work on original sin, is simply wrong to say that Thomas thought that there would have been masters and servants even without the fall.[54]) It is this anthropological centering of his vision in creation which enables his understanding to be read both in the (hamartiocentric) order of logic, and in the (soteriological) order of discovery.

Let me give another example: when Thomas is discussing the penalty for the first sin, in an aside on paradise, he says:

> that place of earthly paradise, even though it no longer serves mankind for his use, does however serve him as a document: for he knows himself to have been deprived of such a place on account of sin; and since he is instructed by those things which are corporally in that paradise about those things pertaining to the celestial paradise, whose entry for man was prepared by Christ. (IIa-IIae, q. 164, a. 2 ad 4)

It is clearly no great intellectual leap to move from this position, which regards paradise as a counterfactual document, to one deriving the whole vision of original sin from "those things pertaining to the celestial paradise, whose entry for man was prepared by Christ," regarding paradise as a necessary possibility to safeguard the contingency of the first sin. Nothing of essence is lost in this change of perspective.

---

52. St. Thomas is particularly true to St. Dominic's longing to save the Catholic faith from the pessimism of the Albigensians when he insists that sexual pleasure would have been greater in the state of innocence *and* would have been within the regency of reason (Ia, q. 98, a. 2 and Ia-IIae, q. 82, a. 3 ad 1).

53. There being a lack of knowledge proper to the condition of a growing creature as well as the ignorance resulting from original sin (Ia, q. 101).

54. H. Rondet, *Le péché originel dans la tradition patristique et théologique* (Paris: Fayard [le signe], 1967), 191, refers in note 12 to Ia, q. 98, a. 1 ad 3, which corresponds to the harmonious way in which people could have taken from the common wealth what was necessary; in Ia, q. 96, a. 4 it is specifically denied that there would have been servitude in the state of innocence, this being distinguished from the need for leadership proper to a social animal like the human being even in the state of innocence.

One might go even further: Thomas had a very clear and simple definition of original sin. Formally it is a privation of original justice, and
materially it is concupiscence (Ia-IIae, q. 82, a. 3). Now when it comes
to defining something as a privation of something else, it is clear that we
are dealing with an ancillary concept rather than a foundational one. Is
an essential difference made to the content of the definition if the "foundational" concept is "original justice" understood as "what Christ is
bringing into being" rather than "what we lost through Adam"? I would
suggest that Paul would certainly have opted for the former. Thomas
(in this making Anselm more rigorous) seems to have understood that
"original sin" must be understood as an ancillary concept, thus at least
leaving the way open for the more christocentric view. In the moderately
evolutionary view of what led up to and made possible the originating
sin which I have set out, the Thomistic definition of that sin can perfectly well be upheld: concupiscence was brought into being when the
first human act forged humanity along the lines of rivalistic mimesis. If
the first human act had been one of pacific mimesis, then human sensu-
ality and the nascent capacity for representation would have been forged
within that creative harmonious order.

Permit me one final indication of the compatibility of Thomas's
thought with what I have being trying to set out. It is one which can
only rejoice the heart of anyone seeking to recover the subtlety of the
Pauline imagination, as well as the irony and ambiguity of its language
about God's anger and wrath. In Ia-IIae, q. 87, a. 7 Thomas addresses
the question (which I put to Augustine above) about whether every pain
is the result of some fault. Thomas answers positively, with very careful
nuances obviously designed to make Christ's sufferings less of a magic
exception to this rule.[55] In the course of his reply he has this to say:

> Principally the penalty of original sin consists in that human nature be left
> to itself, destitute of the help of original justice, from which follow on all
> the penalties which come upon humans through their flawed nature.

Here Thomas has manifestly recaptured the language and theological
sense of Romans 1. He and Paul agree that God's anger, or punish-

---

55. Although Thomas gradually dropped the Anselmian argument about Christ's death
being a vicarious satisfaction, he never completely eliminated its traces from his thought.
On this see the careful exposition of P. Grelot in *Péché originel et rédemption à partir de
l'épître aux romains* (Paris: Desclée, 1973), 220–23. See also H. McCabe, *God Matters*
(London: Chapman, 1987), 90–92. It must be in the nature of the Girardian thesis that
Christ should not be a magic exception to the rule "no victim without fault," since that
would make his death not really revelatory of anything. Christ's death should rather be
read in the much more active sense of the single definitive explosion of the whole cultural lie which finds words in phrases like "no victim without fault," "no smoke without
fire," etc.

ment, is best imagined as the leaving of human nature to itself, which is identical with the privation of original justice.

So we have a fine point: "the privation of original justice" is exactly equivalent to "leaving human nature to itself." Thomas, like Augustine, is certainly convinced that the first sin was in fact mimetic: he explains this at length in his answer to the question of whether or not the pride of the first man consisted in desiring to be like God (IIa-IIae, q. 163, a. 2). No, it did not, since it is in our nature to desire to be like God (pacific mimesis), but both man and the devil wanted to be like God on their own account (rivalistic mimesis):

> Indeed both sought to become equal with God, in as far as both wanted to be their own norm in contempt of the order of divine law.

Now if the first sin was this mimetic appropriation, then it means that this mimetic appropriation of self is the equivalent of both the privation of original justice and of leaving human nature to itself. So relinquishing nature to itself (on the part of the human being) is the same as appropriating it (on the part of man). If we are rigorous in our mimetic analysis, this means that *there was no active privation of original justice on the part of God.* It is rather the case that the appropriation of what can be received only gratuitously is by definition a self-privation of gratuity. Thomas is here on the very threshold of moving out of the sphere of any language of God punishing at all or any conception of original sin in terms of an active punishment by God: all the elements are present in his thought to enable us to take the step we have.[56]

If then we take that Girardian step, of course it becomes important to say that not only was there no active privation of original justice by God, but indeed God "immediately" set in action the work of restoring the possibility of gratuity being received gratuitously by preparing and sending his Son to bring into being a human, visible acting out of that gratuity such that we might learn to participate in it. The next step in this vision is to see that it is only from the viewpoint of the visible acting out of the new gratuity that we can understand what had gone wrong in the first place: we are able to imagine an account of salvation and original sin where the element of divine anger and punishment has taken its proper place as part of a history of increasingly ironic juxtapositions of words and concepts which impel the Christian imagination into a deeper understanding of the love and gratuity of the God revealed in Christ. That is all that I could have wished to demonstrate in this essay.

---

56. For a further indication of Thomas's tendency in this direction, see IIa-IIae, q. 24, a. 10 (resp.). "For God only turns himself from a human to the degree that a human turns from him or herself."

Some Questions Posed by Other Doctrines

Up until now I have attempted to verify the compatibility of my essay with the magisterium of the Church and with two major monuments to the tradition of the Church in texts which are specifically related to the matter in hand: the theology of original sin. Some might say that this is enough, and we could leave the matter at that. I am not sure that it is enough, for two reasons. In the first place, the Catholic faith is a living, developing organic whole, and what was a true expression of the faith in a certain period might no longer be sufficient to maintain that faith in a later period. In this sense it might be possible to produce an archaizing account of original sin which would not fall foul of the words of the councils and would yet represent a step backward in the intellection of the faith insofar as it would have no real bite on the living of that faith in the present day. Secondly, there is no part of Catholic doctrine which is an island unto itself: all the different areas depend upon each other for mutual illumination. Thus it becomes possible to ask whether certain elements of Catholic understanding, which in themselves do not specifically have to do with original sin, might not be rendered impossible to maintain because of a particular interpretation of that doctrine.

For these two reasons I have chosen three interlinked areas of Catholic understanding, not in themselves part of the doctrine of original sin, as questions to pose to my interpretation. They act as controls with regard to whether my understanding really is compatible with the Catholic faith as it has developed over the centuries. Each of these questions opens up vistas worthy of far more attention than they will receive here; nevertheless it seems incumbent upon an attempt to demonstrate the catholicity of an interpretation of original sin that it show something of the direction that an interpretation of these questions might take. The three interlinked areas are (1) the Catholic view of "reason," (2) the Catholic maintenance of the possibility of talking about a "natural law," and (3) the traditional Catholic insistence on the pursuit by Catholics of a rational ethical politics in the midst of human imperfection and fragility.

Let me suggest first why the doctrine of original sin needs to be checked against its possible effects in these areas. I will do so with recourse to the traditional triad made evident at Trent: the Lutheran position, the Pelagian position, and the Catholic position. I am well aware of course that each of these labels embraces a spread of positions rather than just one. Briefly, if one takes a Lutheran, or purely supernaturalist, position, with a corresponding essential corruption of all human faculties, there can be no real room for a positive appreciation of the rôle of reason in the human perception of God: only revelation can help; likewise, we can have no access to natural law, for our natures are too corrupt to be able to yield any reflection of the Creator's goodness or intention for us; furthermore, human politics are part of an essentially perverse kingdom, best constrained by the necessary evil of harsh authority, and the sociality of the kingdom of heaven has no incidence until the hereafter. The Pelagian position would invert this approach: human reason is highly trustworthy and can easily know about God if we make the effort; the natural law is easily discoverable, is autonomous from the point of view of revelation, and is not so radically different from the human status quo; and with sufficient moral fervor we can indeed build the kingdom of God here on earth. It is not surprising, in the light of this, that political conservatives have tended to find support in a Christianity shading toward (when not fully advocating) the Lutheran position, with its simultaneous suppression and postponement of hope for change, while political progressives have tended toward a Christianity imbued with differing degrees of Pelagianism, with its tendency to identify theological hope with the effort for real changes now, thus sanctifying the current struggle as of God.

The Catholic position has been worked out against the threats posed by both these tendencies present in different guises over the centuries. In the first place it insists that, in the abstract, human reason has a natural capacity to know the truth about God and about the good to be done, though in fact that capacity has been so damaged by original sin that we could attain to knowledge of the truth and the good only with immense difficulty were it not for divine revelation.[57] Secondly, and coherent with this, it insists on the no doubt difficult possibility of discovering and communicating a natural law of human behavior inherent in the human heart which is a certain fully human and reasonable participation in the divine law. Among the tasks of Catholic teachers is to insist that in our being, and never having ceased to be, this sort of creature, there is an indelible directedness toward the Creator.[58] Finally, and more difficult to describe exactly because we enter into the sphere of practical history, the Catholic instinct seems to be to insist both on the urgent necessity of Catholics taking an active, reasoned, ethical part in the political sphere to bring about signs of the kingdom of heaven, and yet on the fact that such realizations will always be fragmentary within

---

57. For a classic statement of this position, see *Humani Generis*, pars. 2–3; Denzinger, 2305.

58. See the very recent magisterial exposition of this position in *Veritatis Splendor*, pars. 42–45.

a social and political world that will always be imperfect this side of the general resurrection.[59]

The question thus raised is whether the consequences of the understanding of original sin I have sought to present fall within the scope of the Catholic understanding. Here it is worth saying that we are dealing with very fine issues: even within the frame of reference of undoubtedly Catholic thinkers it is possible to interpret Augustine in such a way as so to remove the remains of the Creator's goodness in his creatures that we end up with a simply diabolical earthly order, and perhaps (if we have a strong ecclesiology) a theocratic, caesaro-papist subordination of the state to the Church; likewise it has been possible to interpret Thomas's "creating space" for different realms of natural reality in such a way as to remove their necessary relatedness to a publicly knowable supernatural end, and thus reduce the Church to the sphere of an optional private extra in the midst of an autonomous natural social life.

I would like to suggest that what I have sought to present falls foul of neither of these traps. I will comment very briefly on how one might begin to develop an understanding of each of the three interlinked areas in the light of mimetic theory.

What rôle is left for human reason within mimetic theory? Let us start by conceding that the understanding of original sin I have developed is radical. It posits that human culture was born from and tends to maintain its order by means of a lie — the *méconnaissance* of its victimary foundations. Furthermore, this lie was only really completely revealed for what it is by the death and resurrection of Christ. So far we seem to have a highly "supernaturalist" position. In biblical terms, we have no difficulty in understanding Paul's radical dismissal of the wisdom of this age, which, unable to perceive God's wisdom, crucified the Lord of glory (see 1 Cor. 2:6–8). Are we able to make equal sense of the same Apostle's insistence on humans being able to know God and being without excuse if they do not (see Rom. 1:19–20)? I would suggest that we do: mimetic theory might tentatively be called a metaphysics of mimetic alterity. Humans constituted by and living in the world of rivalistic mimetic desire are no less mimetically constituted in alterity than the revealer of the divine beneficent mimesis: his human nature is the same as ours. This means that humans do not need to cease to be the sort of animal that they are in order to see the lie which has constituted us. Put in other words: we are capable of recognizing that we are wrong.

---

59. For what I take to be an "instinctively Catholic" elaboration of position on this point, see J. Ratzinger's 1984 essay "A Christian Orientation in a Pluralistic Democracy," in *Church, Ecumenism and Politics: New Essays in Ecclesiology* (Slough: St. Paul, 1988), 204–20.

Another way of saying this is that, having been able to see, thanks to the coming of Christ, what we were and what we are to become, we can also see that it has always been within the abstract possibility of all (adult) humans everywhere to have come, no doubt through an arduous and incomplete process, to the perception of the victim and to have sided with her or him. It may have been the case that this has indeed happened historically in myriad occasions unknown to us in the petty hells of tribal life, in satrap-ridden city-states, and so on. Girard has, notoriously, shown that just such insight did occur from time to time in certain great works of theater and literature. It is one of the abiding wonders of *Violence and the Sacred* that one of its first reviewers declared it to be not only a great book, but a unique one "because it gives us at last the first authentically atheistic theory of religion and of the sacred."[60] I consider this to be a just remark: there is no *deus ex machina* in Girard's work. His thought is able to be entertained within rational discourse by nonbelievers, because its anthropology and the embryonic theology which emerged in later works (to the annoyance of some who then accused Girard of crude apologetics) form a seamless robe.

Since mimetic theory posits the ineluctably mimetic nature of human relationality, it is able to make place both for humans being very wrong, and yet for humans to be able to find the truth and do it even where an explicit revelation is not available. The — at least abstract — possibility of humans coming to the truth is the vital maintenance of the possibility of humans being wrong. If humans could not come to the truth without a change of essential nature, it would mean that humans could not properly speaking be wrong. They could only have been duped by someone else or enclosed in a dark space. Real conversion would be impossible; only extrinsic change would be possible. For humans to be able to be wrong and for humans to have the possibility, related to being the sort of animal we are, of coming to knowledge of the truth, is the same thing. I have sought, in the light of mimetic theory, to describe the doctrine of original sin entirely within the framework of the joy of being wrong. It is, I suggest, and despite the apparent (and real) radicality of the distortion it posits in our nature, a rather strong version of the maintenance of the possibilities of human reason.

A similar point is clearly at stake in the question of whether or not mimetic theory can contemplate the existence of something like a natural law. Can it include the possibility that when those without the revelation of the forgiving victim "do by nature what the law requires, they are a law to themselves, even though they do not have the law.

---

60. G.-H. De Radkowski, in *Le Monde*, October 27, 1972.

They show that what the law requires is written on their hearts" (Rom. 2:14–15)? I would suggest that it would be difficult to reconcile mimetic theory with an understanding of natural law that sees that law in static terms. However, it would seem that such a static view of natural law would be a misunderstanding of the Church's concept.[61] The concept depends on a dynamic vision of God's creation. We might say that the point of "natural law" is grasped at an experiential level when, for instance, the person who seeks to reform her life according to the divine law discovers not that she has become an entirely different sort of creature, but that she has become more fully what she was always meant to be. Seen in more abstract terms, the suggestion is that by our active participation in the divine life we do not create an entirely new and arbitrary creation, but we share in the bringing into being of God's creation, and we share in this by the use of our practical reason: our knowledge of good and evil is capable of being true because it is being given to us as our own as we use it in dynamic conformity with what God is bringing into being.

The eschatological vision of God's creation which I have attempted to set out is helpful in showing how mimetic theory relates to this. The fulness of the divine law, that is, what we are meant to be, becomes available as a result of Christ's resurrection. From the viewpoint of the resurrection it becomes possible to see God as having always called us into being gratuitously, longing for us to become his imitators, and thus taking an active part in constructing his image in us. The divine law is ultimately that we become perfect imitators of God, so that our whole personal and social bodiliness can become a real reflection of God's nature. From this we can see that just by the fact of being bodily mimetic human interdividuals, the possibility of the construction of who we really are, personally, corporally, and socially, is already inscribed in us. It really is we, our reason, our bodies, our relationality, who can take an active part in the construction of the beneficent imitation: these things are not done despite us, even if we always have to *learn* to create ourselves according to the divine imitation. It therefore becomes possible to say that certain acts can never be properly human acts, because they are never properly creative of participation according to the beneficent mimesis of God. Furthermore, it becomes possible to talk of these acts in a relatively autonomous way. For instance, it is against natural law to take an active part in a lynching (and one wonders, pace traditional Church teaching, if there really are circumstances in which a human execution is anything other than that — arguments about "necessary for

---

61. To judge by *Veritatis Splendor.*

the good of society" reproduce the wisdom of Caiaphas, not the divine Wisdom), for that is always to appropriate social identity by rivalistic mimesis. Likewise it may be against natural law under certain circumstances to avoid being lynched, because to do so would be to fail to participate in beneficent mimesis. Paul's dictum that it is forbidden to do evil that good may come seems to be enriched by a mimetic understanding of natural law: that means are inseparable from ends is at the very heart of mimetic theory, where the act and the desire creating it are inseparable. What is particularly brought out by mimetic theory in the circumstances of human society is that the living of natural law will always tend to be martyrial.

The final question put to mimetic theory is about whether it can contemplate the possibility of a rational ethical politics in an imperfect world. As I understand it, the question of the religious attitude to politics will always depend on a more or less implicit eschatology. As we are able to receive the eschatological imagination that was in Christ, an imagination centered on the deathless mimetic beneficence of God, so this deathless mimetic beneficence enables our creative imagination to be re-formed in such a way that we are able to take an active part in the construction of the kingdom here and now. Thus the eschatological imagination is neither a way of postponing active construction until the hereafter, nor a clear utopian blueprint for what must be done now. Rather it is the way in which the risen victim rains down his gifts to us in the particular circumstances in which we find ourselves, enabling us to construct the new human sociality that is centered around, rather than built over against, the victim. What the eschatological imagination permits is the "redeeming of the time": small but real, reasoned, human historical acts which bring at least that part of human history into participation in the beneficent mimesis of God.

This, I would suggest, is very specifically the patient working out of rational ethical politics in the midst of an imperfect and fragile sociality. In the first place, it is structured by hope lived in patience: what is brought into being will not necessarily be either highly visible or apparently effective or successful and depends for its realization on the ability of those doing it to resist adversity. There is no grand master plan for what is being brought into being, or rather there is, but it is unknowable to us. We are charged with building small and often apparently unfinished, maybe mysterious and disappointing, stories, whose place in an overall scheme we cannot detect. That might sound like a blueprint for religious irrationality; however, what I have been referring to as "the master plan" is the story of the victim, and all our small stories are stories of the victim.

The particular point that I would like to bring out is that the construction, by means of reasoned dialogue and careful coherent action, of an earthly city which does not create victims is something in which every adult human on the face of the planet is in principle able to understand. It is a project which starts wherever one happens to be and with whomsoever one happens to be and needs no special language of revelation: the moment its point is seen, including one's complicity in its contrary, it becomes an imperative for action. It is a political project that must be worked on at every level of human social existence: it can be realized by small groups in base communities and by cabinet ministers in palaces of government. It is, I suspect, very much more difficult for the latter than for the former, because the distorted mimetic gravity of centers of power is so much stronger than among the weak and powerless. However, in principle, such people can work out ways of avoiding causing victims, of succoring such as have become victims, of creating new projects to prevent the marginalization of whole swathes of their own or other nations' populations.

Because we are dealing with the ungovernable world of human desire, no grand schemes which fail to take account of desire will ever work, hence the need for politics to be above all the art of small, ethically consistent moves, talked about and discussed, adapting the actions taken to ever changing circumstance. There are two considerations here: the intelligence of the victim is kept alive and nurtured by the eschatological imagination. That is, the sort of politics which I am hinting at is not in the first place a matter of morals, but of imaginative creation. The Catholic becoming involved in politics at whatever level can and should seek to have a constant re-creation of the possibilities of what he or she might construct, how she or he might serve, in the light of nutrition provided by the eschatological imagination, the mind centered on "the things that are above." This can scarcely ever mean taking certain steps "because the Lord told me to" — a simple supernaturalism, which must always be the exception rather than the rule: obedience to God's voice being essentially ecclesial rather than individual.[62] It must usually mean finding ways of working out reasonably with other people what is the best thing to do to create a victim-free society. That will always involve having to find ways of acting in which means and ends are part of the same act and structured by the same beneficent mimesis. That in turn means that involvement in a rational and ethical small-step politics will always also tend to the martyrial.

---

62. St. Thomas More rather than St. Joan of Arc, though maybe this is an Englishman's prejudice. However, their construction of the kingdom was crowned in both cases in the same way.

The eschatological imagination is precisely what gives people the creative capacity to make truth the center of social life rather than merely power, or interest, or fame. And to make truth the center of social life is not something that can be established and then relaxed from, but involves a constant uncovering of lies and the constant risk of expulsion and becoming the focus of the wrong sort of unity. However primitive or complex a social group, the essential dynamic is the same and can always be talked about. New formations of the old lie can continually be perceived and subverted. The way in which good projects suddenly turn into traps can be noticed, changed, through an imagination always alive to the victim. Justice is never simply established in the earthly city; it is always forged as sign by witnesses to a different city. But it really is forged, continually, by small acts creative of justice in the midst of fragility, and these acts can be discussed and re-projected, and altered, and mistakes made and new perceptions brought into being. The politics I am talking about does not consist in the pursuit of power, but in the slow, dogged pursuit of emptying power of its terrifying futility: we are obliged by our belief that Christ's death has redeemed death itself to believe that even politics can be redeemed.

It has not been my brief here to attempt an essay in political theory, a task for which I am not qualified. I merely wish to show that the mimetic theory I have been expounding, with its radical view of original sin, is not simply inimical to a politics of small steps, nor simply a demonization of any possible human political state, and need lead to neither resignation nor utopian fanaticism. Its emphasis on the supernatural is not to the detriment of, but to the empowering of, real, reasonable, discussable, mutable human action. That is not to say that I think such action anything other than extremely arduous. I hope it is not rare. I am aware that mine is manifestly an understanding that is more congenial to small comparatively powerless groups than to the webs of power which enmesh themselves in the conceits of planning, the victimary mimetic lies of economic theory, and all the theater of "who's in, who's out."[63] We have to believe indeed that that can be redeemed, but more important, I suspect, in a meditation on original sin at the end of the twentieth century, after the collapse of both the colonial order and the projected Marxist utopias, is to try creatively to imagine catholicity out of diversely harmonious fragments, a communion of half-known bloodstained stories turned into signs of forgiveness.

Enough has been said, I hope, to indicate that in the face of each of the three interlinked spheres of reason, natural law, and rational politi-

63. Shakespeare, *King Lear*, Act V.3, l.15.

cal ethics, the understanding of original sin that I have been developing does not have to be ruled out of court. It is neither supernaturalist to the detriment of the natural, nor naturalist with some appropriated autonomy from the supernatural. It describes an anthropology where the natural enjoys a relational (rather than relative) autonomy within the supernatural, and thus requests right of abode within the Catholic theological city, among the scribes of the New Jerusalem coming down from heaven.

Bibliography

Principal Works by René Girard

Mensonge romantique et vérité romanesque. Paris: Grasset, 1961. Eng. trans.: *Deceit, Desire and the Novel: Self and Other in Literary Structure.* Trans. Yvonne Freccero. Baltimore: Johns Hopkins University Press, 1965.
Dostoievski: du double à l'unité. Paris: Plon, 1963. In English see *Resurrection from the Underground: Feodor Dostoevsky.* Trans. James G. Williams. New York: Crossroad, 1997.
La violence et le sacré. Paris: Grasset, 1972. Eng. trans.: *Violence and the Sacred.* Baltimore: Johns Hopkins University Press, 1977.
Critiques dans un souterrain. Lausanne: L'Age d'Homme, 1976; Paris: Grasset, 1983.
"To Double Business Bound." Baltimore: Johns Hopkins University Press, 1978.
Des choses cachées depuis la fondation du monde. Paris: Grasset, 1978. Eng. trans.: *Things Hidden from the Foundation of the World.* London: Athlone, 1987.
Le bouc émissaire. Paris: Grasset, 1982. Eng. trans.: *The Scapegoat.* London: Athlone, 1986.
La route antique des hommes pervers. Paris: Grasset, 1985.
A Theater of Envy — William Shakespeare. New York: Oxford University Press, 1991. French trans.: *Shakespeare — les feux de l'envie.* Paris: Grasset, 1990.
Quand ces choses commenceront...Entretiens avec Michel Treguer. Paris: Arléa, 1994.
The Girard Reader. Ed. J. G. Williams. New York: Crossroad, 1996.

Other Works

Adams, R. (interviewer). "Violence, Difference, Sacrifice: A Conversation with René Girard," *Religion and Literature* 25, no. 2 (Summer 1992): 9–33.
Alison, J. "AIDS como lugar de revelação: Girard e uma teologia pastoral," in H. Assmann, ed. *René Girard com teólogos da libertação* (q.v.).
———. "Justification and the Constitution of Consciousness: A New Look at Romans and Galatians," *New Blackfriars* 71, no. 834 (January 1990): 17–27.
———. *Knowing Jesus.* London: SPCK, 1993.
———. *Raising Abel: The Recovery of the Eschatological Imagination.* New York: Crossroad, 1996.
Assmann, H., ed. *René Girard com teólogos da libertação: Um diálogo sobre ídolos e sacrifícios.* Petrópolis: Vozes, 1991.

Assmann, H., and F. J. Hinkelammert. *A idolatria do mercado: Ensaio sobre Economia e Teologia.* Petrópolis: Vozes, 1989.

Baudler, G. *God and Violence: The Christian Experience of God in Dialogue with Myths and Other Religions.* Springfield, Ill.: Templegate, 1992. Orig.: *Erlösung vom Stiergott.* Munich: Kösel Verlag, 1989.

Bertonneau, T. F. "The Logic of the Undecidable: An Interview with René Girard," in *Paroles Gelées.* UCLA French Studies 5 (1987): 1–23.

Davies, B., ed. *Language, Meaning and God: Essays in Honour of Herbert McCabe, O.P.* London: Chapman, 1987.

Davies, W. D. *Paul and Rabbinic Judaism.* New York: Harper & Row, 1967. Rev. ed. of 1948 original.

Deguy, M., and J.-M. Dupuy. *René Girard et le problème du Mal.* Paris: Grasset, 1982.

Derrett, J. D. M. *Law in the New Testament.* London: Darton, Longman and Todd, 1972.

———. *The Making of Mark.* 2 vols. Shipston on Stour: Drinkwater, 1985.

———. *The Victim: The Johannine Passion Narrative Reexamined.* Shipston on Stour: Drinkwater, 1993.

Dreyfus, F. *Jésus savait-il qu'il était Dieu?* Paris: Cerf, 1984.

Dubarle, A.-M. *The Biblical Doctrine of Original Sin.* New York: Herder and Herder, 1964. Orig.: *Le péché originel dans l'Écriture.* Paris: Cerf, 1958.

Dumont, L. *Essays on Individualism: Modern Ideology in Anthropological Perspective.* Chicago: University of Chicago Press, 1986.

Dumouchel, P., ed. *Violence et Vérité: autour de René Girard.* Paris: Grasset, 1985. Eng. trans.: *Violence and Truth: On the Work of René Girard.* London: Athlone, 1988.

Dumouchel, P., and J.-P. Dupuy. *L'enfer des choses: René Girard et la logique de l'économie.* Paris: Seuil, 1979.

Dupuy, J.-P. *Ordres et désordres: Enquête sur un nouveau paradigme.* Paris: Seuil, 1982.

Duquoc, C. *Messianisme de Jésus et discrétion de Dieu.* Geneva: Labor et Fides, 1984.

———. "Pecado original y transformaciones teológicas," *Selecciones de Teología* 18, no. 72 (1979): 275–84.

———. "Le mal énigme du bien," *Le Supplément* 172 (1990): 65–78.

Flick, M., and Z. Alszeghy. *El hombre bajo el signo del pecado: Teología del pecado original.* Salamanca: Sígueme, 1972.

Galvin, J. P. "Jesus as Scapegoat? *Violence and the Sacred* in the Theology of Raymund Schwager," *The Thomist* (April 2, 1982): 173–94.

Gans, Eric. "Christian Morality and the Pauline Revelation," *Semeia* 33 (1985): 97–108.

———. "Pour une esthétique triangulaire," *Esprit* (November 1973): 564–81.

———. *Science and Faith: The Anthropology of Revelation.* Lanham, Md.: Rowman and Littlefield, 1990.

Gesché, A. *Le mal.* Dieu pour penser 1. Paris: Cerf, 1993.

———. "Pecado original y culpabilidad cristiana," *Selecciones de Teología* 21, no. 81 (1982): 57–66.

González Faus, J. I. *Proyecto de hermano: Visión creyente del hombre*. Santander: Sal Terrae, 1987.

———. "Violencia, religión, sociedad y cristología: Introducción a la obra de René Girard," *Actualidad Bibliográfica* 18 (1981): 7–37.

Grelot, P. *Péché originel et rédemption à partir de l'épître aux romains*. Paris: Desclée, 1973.

Hamerton-Kelly, R. "A Girardian Interpretation of Paul: Rivalry, Mimesis and Victimage in the Corinthian Correspondence," *Semeia* 33 (1985): 65–81.

———. "Sacred Violence and Sinful Desire: Paul's Interpretation of Adam's Sin in the Letter to the Romans," in *The Conversation Continues: Studies in Paul and John in Honor of J. Louis Martyn*. Ed. R. Fortna and B. Gaventa. Nashville: Abingdon, 1990, 35–54.

———. *Sacred Violence: Paul's Hermeneutic of the Cross*. Minneapolis: Fortress, 1992.

———, ed. *Violent Origins: Walter Burkert, René Girard, and Jonathan Z. Smith on Ritual Killing and Cultural Formation*. Stanford: Stanford University Press, 1987.

John Paul II. *Veritatis Splendor*. Vatican City, 1993.

Kasper, W. *The God of Jesus Christ*. London: SCM, 1984.

Kerr, F. "Rescuing Girard's Argument?" *Modern Theology* 8, no. 4 (October 1992): 385–99.

———. "Revealing the Scapegoat Mechanism: Christianity after Girard," in M. McGhee, ed. *Philosophy, Religion and the Spiritual Life*. Cambridge: Cambridge University Press, 1992.

———. *Theology after Wittgenstein*. Oxford: Blackwell, 1986.

Ladaria, Luis F. *Antropología teológica*. Madrid: UPCM, 1987; Rome: Univ. Gregoriana, 1987.

Lohfink, N. "Antiguo Testamento: El desenmascaramiento de la violencia," *Selecciones de Teología* 18, no. 72 (1979): 285–93.

———. *Violencia y pacifismo en El Antiguo Testamento*. Bilbao: Desclée de Brouwer, 1990. Orig.: *Gewalt und Gewaltlosigkeit im Alten Testament*. Freiburg: Herder, 1983.

———. "Il dio violento nel Antico Testamento e la ricerca d'una società nonviolenta," *Civiltà Cattolica* (1984): 30–48.

McCabe, H. *God Matters*. London: Chapman, 1987.

MacIntyre, A. *After Virtue*. London: Duckworth, 1982.

———. *Whose Justice? Which Rationality?* London: Duckworth, 1988.

———. *Three Rival Versions of Moral Enquiry*. London: Duckworth, 1990.

McKenna, Andrew J. "Biblical Structuralism: Testing the Victimary Hypothesis," *Helios* 17, no. 1 (1990): 71–87.

———. *Violence and Difference: Girard, Derrida, and Deconstruction*. Chicago: University of Chicago Press, 1992.

———, ed. *René Girard and Biblical Studies*. *Semeia* 33 (1985).

Marion, J.-L. *God without Being*. Chicago: University of Chicago Press, 1991. Orig.: *Dieu sans être: hors texte*. Paris: Fayard, 1982.

Martelet, G. *Libre réponse à un scandale: La faute originelle, la souffrance et la mort*. Paris: Cerf, 1986; 5th ed., 1992.

Mathews, A. C. "Knowledge of Good and Evil: The Work of René Girard," pp. 17–28 in *To Honor René Girard*. Saratoga, Calif.: Anma Libri, 1986.

Metz, J. B. "Concupiscência," in *Dicionário de Teologia*. São Paulo: Loyola, 1975, 1:251–60.

Milbank, J. "The Second Difference: For a Trinitarianism without Reserve," *Modern Theology* 2, no. 3 (1986): 213–34.

——. *Theology and Social Theory: Beyond Secular Reason*. Oxford: Blackwell, 1990.

——. "Postmodern Critical Augustinianism: A Short Summa in Forty-Two Responses to Unasked Questions," *Modern Theology* 7, no. 3 (April 1991): 225–37.

——. "The Name of Jesus: Incarnation, Atonement, Ecclesiology," *Modern Theology* 7, no. 4 (July 1991): 311–33.

——. "Enclaves, or Where Is the Church?" in *New Blackfriars* (July 1992): 341–52.

Morin, L. "Le désir mimétique chez l'enfant: René Girard et Jean Piaget," in *Violence et Vérité*. Ed. P. Dumouchel, 299–317.

North, R. "Violence and the Bible: The Girard Connection," in *Catholic Biblical Quarterly* 47 (1985): 1–27.

Oughourlian, J.-M. *Un mime nommé désir*. Paris: Grasset, 1982. Eng. trans.: *The Puppet of Desire: The Psychology of Hysteria, Possession, and Hypnosis*. Trans. Eugene Webb. Stanford, Calif.: Stanford University Press, 1991.

Pieper, Josef. *El concepto de pecado*. Barcelona: Herder, 1979. German orig.: *Über den Begriff der Sünde*. Munich: Kösel-Verlag, 1977.

Pikaza, X. *Dios como Espíritu y Persona*. Salamanca: Secretariado Trinitario, 1989.

——. *El evangelio: Vida y pascua de Jesús*. Salamanca: Sígueme, 1990.

——. *La Madre de Jesús: Introducción a la mariología*. Salamanca: Sígueme, 1990.

——. "El hombre bíblico y la ruptura de fronteras," *Sal Terrae* (December 1990): 815–32.

Pinkaers, S. "La violence, le sacré et le christianisme," *Nova et Vetera* (Fribourg) 54 (1979): 292–305.

Pius XII. *Humani Generis*. Eng. trans.: London: Catholic Truth Society, 1950.

Pottier, B. *Le péché originel selon Hegel: Commentaire et synthèse*. Namur: Culture et Vérité, 1990.

Radcliffe, T. J. " 'The Coming of the Son of Man': Mark's Gospel and the Subversion of the 'Apocalyptic Imagination,' " in B. Davies, ed., *Language, Meaning and God*, 176–89.

Ratzinger, J. *Introduction to Christianity*. San Francisco: Ignatius Press, 1990. Orig.: *Einführung in das Christentum*. Munich: Kösel-Verlag, 1968.

——. *Eschatology: Death and Eternal Life*. Washington: Catholic University of America Press, 1988. Orig.: *Eschatologie — Tod und ewiges Leben*. Regensburg: Friedrich Pustet Verlag, 1977.

——. *Teoría de los principios teológicos*. Barcelona: Herder, 1985. Orig.: *Theologische Prinzipienlehre*. Munich: Erich Wewel Verlag, 1982.

————. *Church, Ecumenism and Politics: New Essays in Ecclesiology.* Slough: St. Paul, 1988. Orig.: *Kirche, Ökumene und Politik.* Cinisello Balsamo: Paoline, 1987.

————. "Retrieving the Tradition: Concerning the Notion of Person in Theology," *Communio* 17 (Fall 1990): 439–54.

Rondet, Henri. *Le péché originel dans la tradition patristique et théologique.* Paris: Fayard (le signe), 1967.

Sanders, E. P. *Paul and Palestinian Judaism.* London: SCM, 1977.

Schwager, Raymund. *Must There Be Scapegoats? Violence and Redemption in the Bible.* San Francisco: Harper & Row, 1987. Orig.: *Brauchen Wir Einen Sündenbock?* Munich: Kösel-Verlag, 1978.

————. "Pour une théologie de la colère de Dieu," in *Violence et Vérité: Autour de René Girard.* P. Dumouchel, ed. 59–68.

————. "Christ's Death and the Prophetic Critique of Sacrifice," *Semeia* 33 (1985): 109–23.

————. "La mort de Jésus," in *Recherches de Science Religieuse* 73, no. 4 (1985): 481–502.

————. "Imiter et suivre," *Christus* 133 (January 1987): 5–18.

Segundo, J.-L. *La historia perdida y recuperada de Jesús de Nazaret.* Santander: Sal Terrae, 1991.

————. *Evolución y culpa.* Teología abierta para el laico adulto 5. Buenos Aires: Carlos Lohlé, 1972; in English see *Jesus of Nazareth, Yesterday and Today,* 5 vols. (Maryknoll, N.Y.: Orbis Books, 1984–88).

Taborda, F. "Batismo e Crisma" (manuscript). CES-SJ: Belo Horizonte, 1992.

Tanner, N., ed. *Decrees of the Ecumenical Councils.* 2 vols. London: Sheed & Ward; Washington, D.C.: Georgetown University Press, 1990. Orig.: G. Alberigo, ed. *Conciliorum Oecumenicorum Decreta.* Bologna: Istituto per le Scienze Religiose, 1973.

Tena, P., and D. Borobio. "Sacramentos de iniciación cristiana: Bautismo y Confirmación," pp. 27–180 in D. Borobio, ed., *La celebración en la Iglesia.* Salamanca: Sígueme, 1988.

Torres Queiruga, A. "Culpa, pecado y perdón," *Selecciones de Teología* 115 (1990): 175–82.

Tustin, F. *The Protective Shell in Children and Adults.* London: Karnac, 1990.

Valadier, P. "Bouc émissaire et révélation chrétienne," *Études* 357 (1982): 251–60.

Vandervelde, G. *Original Sin: Two Major Trends in Contemporary Roman Catholic Reinterpretation.* Amsterdam: Rodopi N.V., 1975.

Varone, F. *El dios "sádico": ¿Ama Dios el sufrimiento?* Santander: Sal Terrae, 1988. Orig.: *Ce Dieu censé aimer la souffrance.* Paris: Cerf, 1985.

Vaz, H. C. de Lima. "Além da modernidade," in *Síntese* 18, no. 53 (1991): 241–54.

Vázquez, Ulpiano. *El discurso sobre Dios en la obra de E. Lévinas.* Madrid: UP Comillas, 1982.

Villalmonte, Alejandro. *El pecado original: Veinticinco años de controversia, 1950–1975.* Salamanca, 1978.

———. "¿Qué enseña Trento sobre el pecado original?" in *Naturaleza y Gracia* 26 (1979): 167–248.

———. "'Miseria" humana y pecado original: Un gran tema agustiniano," *Revista Agustiniana* 33, no. 100 (1990): 111–52.

———. "El problema del mal y el pecado original en San Agustín," *Naturaleza y Gracia* 38 (1991): 235–63.

Williams, James G. *The Bible, Violence and the Sacred: Liberation from the Myth of Sanctioned Violence.* San Francisco: HarperSanFrancisco, 1991.

Wohlmann, A. "René Girard et saint Augustin: Anthropologie et théologie," *Recherches Augustiniennes* 20 (1985): 257–303.

Index

acquisitive mimesis: defined, 12–13
Adam and Eve
  assigning blame to, 241–44
  a christological reading of the story
    of, 246–47
  the Council of Carthage on, 272
  the Council of Trent on, 275–78
  the devil and, 157
  Humani Generis on, 285
  the *Indiculus* on, 272
  Jesus' moral teaching and, 168
  Paul on, 147–56
  Pelagianism on, 274
  Pius VI on, 286, 287
  the Second Council of Orange on,
    273, 274
  the universality of sin and, 241
AIDS, 107
an-ecclesial hypostasis, the, 168–70,
  180–81, 184–85
animals, 14, 33–34, 253–54
anonymous Christians, 91
Anselm, St., 275, 300
antagonistic mimesis. *See* conflictual
  mimesis
anthropology
  christology and mimetic, 53–55
  conversion and mimetic, 62
  elements of a comprehensive
    theological, 27–33
  faith and mimetic, 55–62
  and the foundation of the church,
    162–63
  interdividual, 273
  interdividual psychology and, 31
  mimetic theory's consequences for,
    37–47
  on the originary scene, 258–59
  the originating sin and, 243n.2
  overview of mimetic, 22–27
  prehuman evolution and mimetic,
    33–37
  relation of positive and generative,
    65–66

  role and status of theological, 47–48
  of time, 222–25
  trinitarian theology and mimetic,
    49–53
  the Trinity and, 202
apostles. *See* disciples, the
Arius, 190n.3
Assmann, H., 38n.31
Augustine
  on Adam, 279
  blame leveled against, 1
  on desire, 148
  on grace, 43n.39
  Manichaeanism and, 279n.18
  metaphorical reading by, 292n.37
  model of the Trinity of, 49
  on original sin, 261–62, 289–97,
    291n.34
  Pelagianism and, 12, 12n.2

Babel, 167–68, 251–52
baptism, 184, 185, 250, 280–81
Barth, K., 40, 50–51
base communities. *See* Christian base
  communities
Baudler, G., 255n.15
Berlin Wall, the, 234
Bertolucci, B., 92
Boff, L., 184n.22, 264
Brown, R., 120
Burkert, W., 43n.40

Cain and Abel
  Augustine and Girard on, 293
  a christological rereading of the story
    of, 248–50
  the devil and, 156–57
  justice and, 134
  original sin and, 171–72
  story of, as the foundational
    assassination, 96–97
Cajetan, 297
Cartesianism, 56

317